Lecture Notes in Artificial Intelligence   1624

Subseries of Lecture Notes in Computer Science
Edited by J. G. Carbonell and J. Siekmann

Lecture Notes in Computer Science

Edited by G. Goos, J. Hartmanis and J. van Leeuwen

Springer
Berlin
Heidelberg
New York
Barcelona
Hong Kong
London
Milan
Paris
Singapore
Tokyo

Julian A. Padget (Ed.)

Collaboration between Human and Artificial Societies

Coordination and Agent-Based Distributed Computing

 Springer

Series Editors

Jaime G. Carbonell, Carnegie Mellon University, Pittsburgh, PA, USA
Jörg Siekmann, University of Saarland, Saarbrücken, Germany

Volume Editor

Julian A. Padget
Department of Mathematical Sciences
University of Bath
Claverton Down
Bath BA2 7AY, United Kingdom
E-mail: jap@maths.bath.ac.uk

Cataloging-in-Publication data applied for

Die Deutsche Bibliothek - CIP-Einheitsaufnahme

Collaboration between human and artificial societies : coordination and agent
based distributed computing / Julian A. Padget (ed.). - Berlin ; Heidelberg ;
New York ; Barcelona ; Hong Kong ; London ; Milan ; Paris ; Singapore ; Tokyo :
Springer, 1999
  (Lecture notes in computer science ; 1624 (Lecture notes in artificial intelligence)
  ISBN 3-540-66930-2

CR Subject Classification (1998): I.2.11, D.1.3, C.2, D.3

ISBN 3-540-66930-2 Springer-Verlag Berlin Heidelberg New York

Typesetting: Camera-ready by author
SPIN 10703260   06/3142 – 5 4 3 2 1 0   Printed on acid-free paper

Preface

The full title of the HCM network project behind this volume is *VIM: A virtual multicomputer for symbolic applications*. The three strands which bound the network together were parallel systems, advanced compilation techniques and artificial intelligence with a common substrate in the programming language Lisp. The initial aim of the project was to demonstrate how the combination of these three technologies could be used to build a virtual multicomputer — an ephemeral, persistent machine of available heterogeneous computing resources — for large scale symbolic applications . The system would support a virtual processor abstraction to distribute data and tasks across the multicomputer, the actual physical composition of which may change dynamically. Our practical objective was to assist in the prototyping of dynamic distributed symbolic applications in artificial intelligence using whatever resources are available (probably networked workstations), so that the developed program could also be run on more exotic hardware without reprogramming.

What we had not foreseen at the outset of the project was how agents would unify the strands at the application level, as distinct from the system level outlined above. It was as a result of the agent influence that we held two workshops in May and December 1997 with the title "Collaboration between human and artificial societies".

The papers collected in this volume are a selection from presentations made at those two workshops. In each case the format consisted of a number of invited speakers plus presentations from the network partners. The speakers submitted draft manuscripts or abstracts which were distributed as preliminary proceedings at the meetings. The presentations frequently stimulated plenty of discussion — wreaking havoc with the schedule! Following the two meetings, revised versions of the full papers were refereed by the programme committee and on occasion by external referees (acknowledged below). These comments were forwarded to the authors to guide them in improving their papers. It is the final results of these endeavours that appear here.

April 1999   Julian Padget
                                                      VIM Network Coordinator

Organization

Program Committee

Ulises Cortés   Universitat Politécnica de Catalunya
Julian Padget   University of Bath
Christian Queinnec   Laboratoire d'Informatique de Paris 6
Hans Voss   GMD – German National Research Center for Information Technology
Carles Sierra   Institut de Investigació en Intel.ligència Artificial, CSIC

Referees

Russell Bradford   John Fitch   Josep Puyol
Harry Bretthauer   Enric Plaza   Viçenc Torra
Emmanuel Chailloux

Acknowledgements

We are particularly grateful to Ulises Cortés, Miquel Sànchez-Marré, Javier Béjar and other members of the Departament de Llenguatges I Sistemes Informàtics (LSI) at Universitat Politécnica de Catalunya (UPC) for the organization of the first workshop in Lanjarón and to Vincenzo Loia and other members of the Dipartimento di Informaticà ed Applicazioni at Università degli Studi di Salerno and staff of the Centro Universitario Europeo per i Beni Culturali for the organization of the second workshop at Villa Rufolo in Ravello.

Our thanks are due to the program committee and especially the other referees for helping to bring this volume to fruition. We also wish to record our appreciation for the support received from Alfred Hofmann of Springer Verlag in realizing the publication of this volume.

Finally, we express our thanks to the European Commission for funding the project through their Human Capital and Mobility programme under contract CHRX-CT93-0401, 1994-97 inclusive.

Table of Contents

III Coordination and Collaboration

Introduction

The objective of this introduction is to outline the origins and development of the VIM project in order to give a background to the papers which follow. Then, for each paper, we give a brief synopsis and relate it to the larger picture.

The network brought together 15 partners researching the areas of parallel and distributed systems, compilation for parallel execution and artificial intelligence. Our original goal was to demonstrate AI applications running on distributed architectures and across local and wide-area networks. The VIM partners were:

- AI Lab Vrije Universiteit Brussel (BE)
- Christian Albrechts Universität zu Kiel (DE)
- GMD FIT.KI St.Augustin (DE)
- GMD FIRST Berlin (DE)
- Universitat Politécnica de Catalunya, Barcelona (ES)
- Institut de Investigació en Intel.ligència Artificial (CSIC), Bellaterra (ES)
- Universitat Rovira i Virgili, Tarragona (ES)
- ILOG s.a., Paris (FR)
- INRIA, Rocquencourt (FR)
- University of Bath (GB)
- University of Southampton (GB)
- University of Warwick (GB)
- CNR Napoli (IT)
- Università di Pisa (IT)
- Università di Salerno (IT)

What the network had not foreseen was how the original goal of distributed AI applications was going to be satisfied in quite different ways from those originally envisaged, through the topic of agents. This emerged as a strong collaboratory theme in the second half of the project, largely inspired by the modelling of the Spanish fish market (la lonja) as a multi-agent system. The first version of this was developed between CNR Naples and IIIA Bellaterra in 1995 and several complete rewrites followed, as understanding of the architecture of agents and the architecture of platforms for electronic commerce increased.

In Part I, we have grouped together the papers on languages and systems, laying out some of the technology that was researched and developed in the framework of the project in order to support multi-agent systems. In Part II, we present material focussing on the internal architecture of agents and how various classical AI techniques are being adapted for an agent context. Finally, in Part III, we explore architectures within which agents interact, looking at both general problems, such as negotiation, coordination and decision-making and application-derived problems in information finding through the web.

I Languages and Systems

Briot and Guerraoui: A Classification of Various Approaches for Object-Based Parallel Distributed Programming Jean-Pierre Briot gave this invited presentation at the first workshop, surveying the vast range of object-oriented languages, focussing in particular on those aiming to support parallel and distributed programming. The authors identify three novel categories by which to classify systems: *applicative,* where distribution and concurrency are provided through libraries (see for example work done in EuLisp as part of this project [10]), *integrative,* where these facilities are merged with object behaviour (see for example the Meroon system [11], also related to the VIM project and other work in EuLisp [9]) and *reflective,* where they are intimately bound up with the protocols of the language (see also the next paper [5]).

Kind and Padget: Towards Meta-Agent Protocols Since the first papers on ObjVlisp and later the Common Lisp Object System, those involved in object-oriented language design have looked to meta-object protocols to provide an extra dimension of flexibility in applications development. The idea put forward in this paper is an exploration of a similar notion for agent-oriented programming. One of the most difficult requirements to satisfy in agent construction is the need to adapt: not only is change intrinsic to the kinds of problems to which agent-oriented approaches are applied, it is also a necessary consequence of agent mobility [2]. Although change can be avoided or at least minimized, it is a fundamental property of the potentially most fruitful agent application areas. The intention set forth in this paper is to separate out the concerns of the application from the meta-level while maintaining a unified framework in the reflective style identified in the preceding paper.

Sodan: Examples of Fuzziness in Compilers and Runtime Systems Although the title refers to compilers and runtime systems, the thesis behind the paper is of the wider applicability of fuzziness to complex problems and, linking it to this project, how fuzziness could be applied to distributed systems and hence agents. Specifically, the approach has been used in the configuration of distributed programs for multiple heterogeneous target environments, where fuzzification permits the combination of qualitative and quantitative attributes and just plain incomplete knowledge, to make a reasonable choice in a high-dimension decision space.

Goerigk and Simon: Towards Rigorous Compiler Implementation Verification The matter of security — in its many forms — is a critical factor in the development of web-based programs and even more so when the application is electronic commerce. One aspect of security is to decide whether the results of a compiler can be trusted and the technologies presented in this paper outline how a completely verified compiler has been developed for a subset of Common Lisp. Hence, it provides a blueprint for the development of verified compilers and a foundation for secure distributed computing where correctness certificates

— that the generated code is a correct compilation of the source — could accompany mobile code. In this way, it complements Java-style security violation checking and the higher level algorithmic certification of proof-carrying code [7].

Cerri: Shifting the focus from control to communication: The STReams OBjects Environments model of communicating agents Stefano Cerri gave this invited presentation at the second workshop. The domain of the agent programming language is an active research area, impinging on and extending primarily the object languages. But while the classical focus in programming languages has, not unnaturally, been on computation, communication is a complementary issue with equal weighting in the agent arena, as evidenced by the desire to reach agreement [8,6] on a language framework for inter-agent communication. In this paper, we are presented with an integrative approach (to use Briot and Guerraouis' terminology) to the provision of communication and coordination based on first class streams, objects and environments in the Scheme language.

Cruickshank and Glaser: Direct manipulation, scalability and the internet The link between the physical and the virtual world can often be a clumsy one and the demands imposed by interactions between humans and agents are stressing this link further. The metaphor demonstrated in this paper shows how graphical specifications of interactions can be constructed and subsequently animated, working in the domains of the Macintosh, Windows and the Unix shell.

II Agents and capabilities

Cerri, Loia and Gisolfi: Towards the Abstraction and Generalization of Actor-based Architectures in Diagnostic Reasoning Diagnosis in manufacturing, medicine and science has long been a popular computer application area from the early days of expert systems. Distributed agents have been taken up as a means to structure such diagnosis engines better and, in particular, to support the independent exploration of different analyses and their subsequent assessment. Here, the authors report experience with constructing a user model in an intelligent tutoring system and diagnosing faults in a physical system. Abstracting from these application-specific systems, they outline a common architecture for agent-based diagnosis to operate in a distributed environment.

Craig: Converting Declarative into Procedural (And Vice Versa) Reflection is widely seen as a necessary means to adaptation in agent behaviour. The ELEK-TRA production rule system, outlined here, demonstrates how reflection can be used to move between declarative and procedural interpretations of knowledge, and so form a viable core for agent behaviour specification.

Sànchez-Marré, Cortés, Béjar, R.-Roda and Poch: Reflective reasoning in a Case-Based Reasoning Agent In this third paper looking at classical AI in agent architectures, attention turns to case-based reasoning (to which we return in the Broadway web-browsing application [4] of the penultimate paper). In this work, the application pull derives from waste-water treatment plant control. Once again, the pattern that emerges is one of agent-oriented thinking helping the structure of the system. Specific contributions to the utilisation of CBR are a new similarity measure for comparing the current situation with past cases, a utility measure for deciding when to forget cases and a suggestion for pruning the case library which are drawn together in an extended CBR agent cycle. The preliminary experimental evidence indicates these measures are effective in reducing the size of the case library over time without reducing its effectiveness.

Moreno, Cortés and Sales: Modelling rational inquiry in non-ideal agents The fourth paper in this group is more abstract, not being directly influenced by a particular application area. Rather, the goal is to build rational agents which are systems permanently engaged in the process of rational inquiry. The authors propose modelling the process of rational inquiry using conceivable situations, which are in place of the possible worlds in a Kripke semantics, and so, the paper explains, enable logical omniscience and perfect reasoning to be avoided.

Riaño: On the process of making descriptive rules While in some domains, the construction of the rules for a system is a person-to-person knowledge elicitation exercise, in areas amenable to classification, it has been recognized that the data collected about the qualitative and quantitative attributes of the samples can be used to synthesize production rules. This paper comes in two parts: (i) a survey of the field (ii) introduction of several novel techniques, first presented in the author's thesis, combined with several examples of use, including the waste-water treatment plant already discussed in the third paper of this group.

III Coordination and Collaboration

Sierra, Faratin and Jennings: A Service-Oriented Negotiation Model between Autonomous Agents Nick Jennings made this invited presentation at the first workshop and the paper itself is a reprint from MAAMAW'97 [1]. It describes a formal model of how agents may reach agreement starting from the generation of an initial offer by one party, evaluation of that offer by the other party, generation of a counter offer and so on, until the process terminates as a result of an evaluation satisfying one party's acceptance criteria. Various conditions on the criteria and counter offers are identified in order to guarantee convergence.

Geldof and van de Velde: Competing software agents support human agents The Ecran Total film festival takes place in Brussels each summer, offering several movies every day in different locations around the city. The work reported here describes a process of web-browsing supported by agents, each tasked with satisfying different user-supplied criteria (programming, production, content) while others make recommendations, maintain the user's diary and advertise future movies. The output from these agents is combined by a template-based text generation system to present a stylised discourse to the user, including hyper-text links to the actual Ecran Total pages containing the complete (static) information.

de Jong: Coordination Developed by Learning from Evaluations Many multi-agent systems are founded on the assumption that each agent knows of the existence of all its acquaintances and so communication and coordination patterns are programmed in, subconsciously or otherwise. A more challenging, but more realistic situation is one of *emergent* communication (the language/ontology problem) and coordination. The experiments reported here seek to demonstrate the emergence of coordination. The chosen scenario is one where at least four agents are required to capture a randomly moving prey. The results suggest that a simple learning agent working with three fixed agents can rapidly acquire high competence for the given problem.

Prakken and Gordon: Rules of Order for Electronic Group Decision Making - A Formalization Methodology While the negotiation of the first paper in this section emphasizes the commercial interest and aspect of agent research, it can also be viewed as a bilateral form of decision-making. The move to a multi-lateral scenario, and one in which the attributes over which there is dispute are less easily quantified, leads to consideration of more sophisticated decision-making frameworks. The idea presented in this paper is to formalize in first order logic the widely known "Robert's Rules of Order" for use in a virtual setting, specifically, the ZENO [3] shared workspace and mediation system.

Jaczynski and Trousse: Broadway: A case-based system for cooperative information browsing on the world-wide-web The second paper about agent-supported web browsing uses case-based reasoning to provide generic assistance in the form of links which are potentially relevant to the search in which the user is engaged. The browsing advisor observes the user searching through a series of documents, attempts to infer the goal and subsequently recommends documents that may be of use. Aspects that make Broadway different from other web advisors are that as well as looking at sequences of documents – rather than just the current one – it is also capable of learning from a group of users and is browser software independent.

Rodríguez-Aguilar, Martín, Garcia, Noriega and Sierra: Towards a Formal Specification of Complex Social Structures in Multi-agent Systems The final paper of this volume concerns the Fishmarket project [12], which itself was one of the major collaborative forces in the VIM network. Since the first work on Fishmarket in 1995, much has been learnt as the model and the implementations have been refined (or discarded and rewritten!). The potentially contentious thesis of this paper is that formalized models of electronic institutions, such as the Spanish fish market, are the most appropriate social structure for many multi-agent systems.

The thesis is explored via a detailed case study of the fish market by establishing a dialogue framework, a performative structure and rules of behaviour.

References

1. Magnus Boman and Walter van de Velde, editors. *Multi-agent rationality: 8th European Workshop on Modelling Autonomous Agents in a Multi-Agent World, MAAMAW'97, Ronneby, Sweden, May 13–16, 1997: proceedings*, volume 1237 of *Lecture Notes in Computer Science and Lecture Notes in Artificial Intelligence*, New York, NY, USA, 1997. Springer-Verlag Inc.
2. P.M. Charlton. *Self-configurable software agents.* PhD thesis, University of Bath, 1999.
3. Thomas F. Gordon, Nikos Karacapilidis, and Hans Voss. Zeno – a mediation system for spatial planning. In U. Busbach, D. Kerr, and K. Sikkel, editors, *CSCW and the Web - Proceedings of the 5th ERCIM/W4G Workshop*, number 984 in GMD Technical Reports, pages 55–61, Sankt Augustin, 1996. GMD.
4. M. Jaczynski and B. Trousse. Broadway: A case-based system for cooperative information browsing on the world-wide web. In *Proceedings of the Workshop on Collaboration between Human and Artificial Societies*, volume 1624 of *LNAI*, pages 267–287. Springer Verlag, 1999.
5. A. Kind and J.A. Padget. Towards meta-agent protocols. In *Proceedings of the Workshop on Collaboration between Human and Artificial Societies*, volume 1624 of *LNAI*, pages 30–42. Springer Verlag, 1999.
6. Yannis Labrou and Tim Finin. A proposal for a new kqml specification. http://www.csee.umbc.edu/~jklabrou/publications/tr9703.ps, 1997. Also available as a UMBC technical report.
7. G. Necula. Proof-carrying code. In *POPL'97: The 24th ACM SIGPLAN-SIGACT Symposium on Principles of Programming Languages*, pages 106–119, New York, 1997. ACM, ACM.
8. FIPA ACL. Foundation of Intelligent Physical Agents. Agent communication language. http://drogo.cselt.stet.it/fipa/spec/fipa97.htm, 1997.
9. J.A. Padget. Foundations for a virtual multicomputer. In *Parallel Symbolic Languages and Systems – PSLS'95*, volume 1068 of *LNCS*, pages 336–343. Springer Verlag, 1995.
10. J.A. Padget, G. Nuyens, and H. Bretthauer. An overview of EuLisp. *Lisp and Symbolic Computation*, 6(1/2):9–98, 1993.
11. C. Queinnec. Dmeroon overview of a distributed class-based causally-coherent data model. In *Parallel Symbolic Langages and Systems – PSLS'95*, volume 1068 of *LNCS*, pages 297–309. Springer Verlag, 1995.
12. J.A. Rodríguez, P. Noriega, C. Sierra, and J.A. Padget. FM96.5 A Java-based Electronic Auction House. In *Second International Conference on The Practical Application of Intelligent Agents and Multi-Agent Technology: PAAM'97*, 1997.

Part I

Languages and Systems

A Classification of Various Approaches for Object-Based Parallel and Distributed Programming

Jean-Pierre Briot[1] and Rachid Guerraoui[2]

[1] Laboratoire d'Informatique de Paris 6 (LIP6)
Université Paris 6 - CNRS
Case 169, 4 place Jussieu, 75252 Paris Cedex 05, France
Jean-Pierre.Briot@lip6.fr
[2] Département d'Informatique
École Polytechnique Fédérale de Lausanne
CH-1015, Lausanne, Suisse
guerraoui@di.epfl.ch

Abstract. This paper aims at classifying and discussing the various ways along which the object paradigm is used in concurrent and distributed contexts. We distinguish the *applicative* approach, the *integrative* approach, and the *reflective* approach. The applicative approach applies object-oriented concepts, as they are, to structure concurrent and distributed systems through libraries. The integrative approach consists in merging concepts such as: object and activity, message passing and transaction, etc. The reflective approach integrates protocol libraries intimately within an object-based programming language. We discuss and illustrate each of these approaches and we point out their complementary levels and goals.

Mr. President and fellow citizens of New York: The facts with which I shall deal this evening are mainly old and familiar; nor is there anything new in the general use I shall make of them. If there shall be any novelty, it will be in the mode of presenting the facts, and the inferences and observations following that presentation. Abraham Lincoln[1]

1 Introduction

It is now well accepted that the object paradigm provides good foundations for the new challenges of concurrent, distributed and open computing. Object notions, and their underlying *message passing* metaphor, are strong enough to structure and encapsulate modules of computation, whereas the notions are flexible enough to match various granularities of software and hardware architectures.

---

[1] Address at the Cooper Institute, New York, February 27, 1860.

J.A. Padget (Ed.): Human and Artificial Societies, LNAI 1624, pp. 3–29, 1999.

Most of object-based[2] programming languages do have some concurrent or distributed extension(s), and almost every new architectural development in the distributed system community is, to some extent, object-based. For instance both the Open Distributed Processing (ODP) and the Object Management Group (OMG) recent standardization initiatives for heterogeneous distributed computing, are based on object concepts [53].

As a result, a lot of object-based concurrent or distributed models, languages, or system architectures, have been proposed and described in the literature. Towards a better understanding and evaluation of these proposals, this paper discusses how object concepts are articulated (applied, customized, integrated, expanded...) with concurrency and distribution challenges and current technology. Rather than an exhaustive study of various object-based concurrent and distributed programming systems, this paper aims at classifying and discussing the various ways along which the object paradigm is used in concurrent and distributed contexts.

By analyzing current experience and trends (as for instance reported in [50,28]), we have distinguished three main approaches to in object-based concurrent and distributed programming: the *applicative* approach, the *integrative* approach and the *reflective* approach. This paper discusses and illustrates successively these three approaches.

The *applicative* approach applies object-based, and most often object-oriented concepts[3], as they are, to structure concurrent and distributed systems through libraries. The *integrative* approach consists in unifying concurrent and distributed system concepts with object-based concepts. The *reflective* approach integrates protocol libraries within an object-based programming language.

Although these approaches may at first glance appear concurrent, in fact they are not. More precisely, the research directed along these approaches have complementary goals. The *applicative* approach is oriented towards system-builders and aims at identifying basic concurrent and distributed abstractions. The *integrative* approach is oriented towards application-builders, and aims at defining a high level programming language with few unified concepts. The *reflective* approach is oriented towards both application-builders and system-builders. The main goal is to provide the basic infrastructure to enable (dynamic) system customization with minimal impact on the application programs. The success of a reflective system relies both on a high level programming language, and on a rich library of concurrent and distributed abstractions.

---

[2] Peter Wegner [59] proposed a layered terminology: *object-based* is used for languages and systems based on the notion of *object* (and *message*), *class-based* adds the concept of *class*, and *object-oriented* adds further the *inheritance* mechanism. Object-oriented languages and systems are by far the most common.

[3] This is because class and inheritance concepts help at structuring and reusing libraries.

2   Overview

The first approach is *applicative* (Sect. 3). This approach applies object concepts, as they are, to structure concurrent and distributed systems through class libraries. Various components, such as processes, files, and name servers, are represented by various object classes. This provides genericity of the software architectures. Programming remains mostly standard (sequential) object-oriented programming. Roughly speaking, the basic idea is to extend the library, rather than the language.

The second approach is *integrative* (Sect. 4). It aims at identifying and merging object concepts with concurrency and distribution concepts and mechanisms. Languages and systems among the integrative approach often integrate/unify object with activity (the concept of *active object*), and message passing with various synchronization protocols, such as sender/receiver synchronization and transactions. However, integrations are not always that smooth and some concepts may conflict with others, notably inheritance with synchronization, and replication with communication (see Sect. 4.6).

The third approach is *reflective* (Sect. 5). The idea lies in the separation of the application program with the various aspects of its implementation and computation contexts (models of computation, communication, distribution...), themselves described in terms of *meta*-program(s). Reflection may also abstract resources management, such as load balancing and time-dependency, and describe it with the full power of a programming language. The *reflective approach* may be considered as a bridge between the two previous approaches as it helps at transparently integrating various computing protocol libraries within a programming language/system. Moreover, it helps at *combining* the two other approaches, by making explicit the separation, and the *interface*, between their respective levels (roughly speaking: the integrative approach for the end user, and the applicative approach for developing and customizing the system).

3   The Applicative Approach

3.1   Modularity and Structuring Needs

The basic idea of the *applicative* approach is to apply encapsulation and abstraction, and possibly also class and inheritance mechanisms, as a structuring tool to design and build concurrent and distributed computing systems. In other words, the issue is in building and programming a concurrent or distributed system, with an object-oriented methodology and programming language. The main motivation is to increase modularity, by decomposing systems in various components with clear interfaces. This improves structuring of concurrent and distributed systems, as opposed to Unix-style systems in which the different levels of abstraction are difficult to distinguish and thus to understand.

Applied to distributed operating systems, the *applicative* approach has led to a new generation of systems, such as Chorus [57] and Choices [20], based on the concept of *micro-kernel*, and whose different services are performed by various specialized servers. Such systems are easier to understand, maintain and extend, and should also ultimately be more efficient as only the required modules have to be used for a given computation.

We illustrate the applicative approach through: (1) abstractions for concurrent programming, in particular through examples in Smalltalk, where a basic and simple object concept is uniformly applied to model and structure the whole system through class libraries, and (2) abstractions for distributed programming, such as in the Choices operating system, which organizes the architecture of a generic distributed operating system along abstract notions of class components, which may then be specialized for a given instantiation/porting of the (virtual) system.

3.2   Abstractions for Concurrent Programming

Concurrent programming in Smalltalk. Smalltalk is often considered as one of the purest examples of object-oriented languages. This is because its motto is to have only a few concepts (object, message passing, class, inheritance) and to *apply* them *uniformly* to any aspect of the language and environment. One consequence is that the language is actually very *simple*. The richness of Smalltalk comes from its set of class *libraries*. They describe and implement various programming constructs (control structures, data structures. . .), internal resources (messages, processes, compiler. . .), and a sophisticated programming environment with integrated tools (browser, inspector, debugger. . .).

Actually, even basic control structures, such as loop and conditional, are not primitive language constructs, but just standard methods of standard classes, which make use of the generic invocation of message passing. They are based on booleans and execution closures (*blocks*). Blocks, represented as instances of class BlockClosure, are essential for building various control structures that the user may extend at his wish. They are also the basis for multi-threaded concurrency through *processes*. Standard class Process describes their representation and its associated methods implement process management (suspend, resume, adjust priority. . .). The behavior of the process scheduler is itself described by a class, named ProcessorScheduler. The basic synchronization primitive is the semaphore, represented by class Semaphore. Standard libraries also include higher abstractions: class SharedQueue to manage communication between processes, and class Promise for representing the eager evaluation of a value computed by a concurrently executing process.

Thanks to this uniform approach, concurrency concepts and mechanisms are well encapsulated and organized in a class hierarchy. Thus, they are much more understandable and extensible than if they were just simple primitives of a programming language. Furthermore, it is relatively easy to build up on the basic standard library of concurrency classes to construct more sophisticated concurrency and synchronization abstractions [18]. Examples are in the Simtalk [8] or Actalk [16,17] frameworks. Figure 1 shows a sample of the hierarchy of activity/synchronization classes provided by Actalk libraries. They implement various synchronization schemes, such as guards, abstract states, synchronization counters... (see in Sect. 6). Within the Actalk project, Loïc Lescaudron also extended the Smalltalk standard scheduler into a generic scheduler to parametrize and classify various scheduling policies [38].

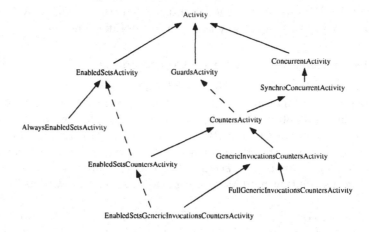

Fig. 1. Hierarchy of activity/synchronization classes in Actalk

EuLisp. EuLisp [55], a Lisp dialect including its object system, also follows the applicative approach for concurrency. Basic abstractions for concurrency and for synchronization (respectively, threads and locks) are defined by classes (respectively, class **thread** and class **lock**).

Eiffel (Variations on). Although the Eiffel programming language has been initially designed for sequential computation, several works have been conducted afterwards to address concurrency concerns. Some of them are described in [50].

The approach proposed by Bertrand Meyer [51] is applicative, in that it is an application of object concepts, and *minimalistic*, in that the idea is to expand the scope of existing standard Eiffel concepts and mechanisms (thus to increase their genericity) without introducing new ones, or rather the minimum. Notably, semantics of Eiffel assertions, by pre- and post-conditions, is redefined, when in a concurrent context, as waiting until conditions are satisfied (along the principles of behavioral synchronization, later detailed in Sect. 4.4).

Additional constructions and mechanisms being often necessary, they may be described and implemented through libraries, by applying the object methodology to organize them. For instance, class **Concurrency** [34] encapsulates an activity (associated to an object) and remote asynchronous message passing.

Alternatively, but following the same applicative approach, concurrency has been introduced in the ÉPÉE environment [33] at the level of complex data structures (e.g., a matrix). ÉPÉE follows a data-concurrency (SPMD) model of concurrency, as opposed to an activation/control-concurrency (MIMD) model, as for class Concurrency (and, more generally speaking, for integrative languages based on the concept of *active objet*, as we will later see in Sect. 4.3). Indeed, objects represent duality (and unification) between data and procedures (potential activation). ÉPÉE provides libraries of abstract structures which may be placed on several processors, without any addition to the Eiffel language.

3.3   Abstractions for Distributed Programming

Smalltalk libraries. The HP Distributed Smalltalk product provides a set of distributed services following the OMG (CORBA) standard, themselves implemented as Smalltalk-80 class libraries. Smalltalk offers libraries for remote communication, such as Sockets and RPC, as well as standard libraries for storage and exchange of object structures for persistence, transactions, and marshaling. The *Binary Object Streaming Service (BOSS)* library provides a basic support for building distribution mechanisms, e.g., persistence, transactions, and marshaling.

Projects like GARF [23,24] and BAST [25,26] go a step further in providing abstractions for fault-tolerant distributed programming. In GARF, two complementary class hierarchies have been developed for various communication models (point-to-point, multicast, atomic multicast...) and object models (monitor, persistent, replicated...). For instance, class Mailer implements remote message passing. Class Abcast (a subclass of Mailer) broadcasts an invocation to a set of replicated objects, and ensures that the messages are totally ordered (ensure the consistency of the replicas). These classes constitute the adequate support for the development of fault-tolerant applications where critical components are replicated on several nodes of a network [32].

The BAST project aims at building abstractions at a lower level. Roughly speaking, BAST provides distributed protocols, such as total order multicast and atomic commitment, that are used in the implementation of GARF classes. For instance, BAST supports classes UMPObject for unreliable message passing, and subclassses RMPObject, RMPObject, and RMPObject respectively for reliable, best effort and fifo (first in first out) message passing.

Choices. Choices [20] is a *generic* operating system, of which objective is not only to be easily ported onto various machines, but also to be able to adjust various characteristics of both hardware, resources, and application interfaces such as: file format, communication network, and memory model (shared or distributed). An object-oriented methodology is presented together with the system, both for the design of distributed applications, and for the design of new extensions to the Choices kernel.

A specific C++ class library has been developed. For instance, class Object-Proxy implements remote communications between objects, classes Memory-Object and FileStream represent memory management, and class ObjectStar provides some generalized notion of pointer. Class ObjectStar provides transparency for remote communications without need for a pre-compilation step.

This class is also useful for the automatic garbage collector. Class `Disk` abstracts and encapsulates a physical storage device which may be instantiated, e.g., in class `SPARCstationDisk` when porting Choices onto a SPARC station.

The experience of the Choices projects shows that a distributed operating system, developed with an object-oriented methodology and programming language (C++ in this case), helps at achieving better genericity and extensibility.

Beta. In a similar approach, a library of classes (named patterns in Beta) for distributed programming has been developed with and for the Beta programming language [14]. For instance, class `NameServer` represents a name server which maps textual object names to physical references. Class `ErrorHandler` manages partial errors/faults of a distributed system. The point in this work is to be able to add distributed features to a given sequential/centralized program, without changing the program logic, i.e., only through additions, as opposed to changes [14, page 199].

3.4   Evaluation of the Applicative Approach

In summary, the applicative approach aims at increasing the flexibility, yet reducing the complexity, of concurrent and distributed computing systems by structuring them as libraries of classes. Each aspect or service is represented by an object. Such modularity and abstraction objectives are very important because concurrent and distributed computing systems are complex systems, which ultimately use very low-level mechanisms, e.g., network communication. Furthermore, such systems are often developed by teams of programmers, and in such context, having separate modules with well defined interfaces is of primary importance. Finally, the difficulty with maintaining and extending Unix-like systems comes mainly from their low modularity and insufficient level of abstraction.

Although progress is made towards that direction, as noted above, it is still too early to exhibit a standard class library for concurrent and distributed programming. We need, both a good knowledge of the minimal mechanisms required, and also a consensus on a set of such mechanisms, involving different technical communities, notably: programming languages, operating systems, distributed systems, and data-bases. The fact that the semaphore abstraction became a standard primitive for synchronization, leads us to think that other abstractions for concurrent and distributed programming could also be identified and adopted. Indeed, through a well defined interface (`wait` and `signal` operations), and a known behavior (metaphor of the train semaphores), the semaphore represents one standard of synchronization for concurrent programming. Such a basic abstraction may then be used as a foundation to build various higher-level synchronization mechanisms. Classification and specialization mechanisms, as offered by object-oriented programming, are then appropriate to organize such a library/hierarchy of abstractions.

Andrew Black has proposed a similar study of abstractions for distributed programming [11]. He suggested, as a first exercise, to decompose the concept of transaction into a set of abstractions. The goal is to represent concepts such as *lock*, *recovery*, and *persistence*, through a set of objects that must be provided by a system in order to support transactions. The modularity of this approach would help defining various transaction models, adapted to specific kinds of applications. For instance, a computer supported cooperative application does not need strong concurrency control constraints as for a banking application[4]. Both Venari [61] and Phoenix [29] projects aim at defining various transactional models from a set of minimal abstractions.

4   The Integrative Approach

4.1   Unification Needs

The amount of issues and concepts required represents one of the major difficulties of concurrent and distributed programming. In addition to classical constructs of sequential programming, concurrent and distributed computation introduces concepts such as *process*, *semaphore*, *monitor* and *transaction*. The applicative approach helps at structuring concurrency and distribution concepts and mechanisms, but it keeps them disjoint from the objects structuring the application programs. In other words, the programmer still faces at least two major different issues: programming with objects, *and* managing concurrency and distribution of the program, also with objects, but *not the same objects !* To give an example, let's consider an application for trafic simulation. It will define domain objects such as cars, roads, traffic lights, etc. If made concurrent or/and distributed, this application will also include other kinds of objects to control concurrency and distribution, such as threads, semaphores, transactions, etc. They are completely distinct and of different nature from application domain objects.

Furthermore, when using libraries, the programming style may become a little cumbersome, as the distribution aspects (and more specifically the manipulation of the objects implementing them) add up to the standard programming style. For instance, the introduction of asynchronous and remote communication model in Eiffel class `Concurrency` (see Sect 3.2), forces to some amount of explicit message manipulation (e.g., see [34, pages 109–11]), as opposed to standard implicit message passing. One may then choose to *integrate* such a construct directly into the programming language as a language extension, such as Eiffel// [22], or a brand new language.

In summary, rather than leaving both the object programs and the management of concurrency and distribution orthogonal, the *integrative* approach aims at merging them by integrating concepts, and offering a unified object model for the programmer.

---

[4] The second kind of application requires a strict serialization of transactions through a locking mechanism, whereas the first kind does not need it.

4.2 Dimensions of Integration

There are various possible dimensions of integration between object-based programming concepts and concurrency and distribution concepts. We will consider
three main different dimensions. Note that they are relatively independent of
each other. Thus, as we will see, a given language or system may follow one
dimension of integration but not another one.

A first integration between the concept of an object and the concept of a
process (more generally speaking the concept of an autonomous activity) leads
to the concept of an *active object*. Indeed, an object and a process may both
be considered as communicating encapsulated units[5]. Actor languages [40,1] are
a typical example of programming languages based on the notion of an active
object.

A second dimension of integration associates synchronization to object activation, leading to the notion of a *synchronized object*. Message passing is then
considered as an implicit synchronization between the sender and the receiver.
Furthermore one often associates mechanisms for controlling the activation of
invocations at the level of an object, e.g., by attaching a guard to each method.
Note that the concept of an active object already implies some form of synchronized object, as the existence of a (single) activity private to the object actually
enforces the serialization of invocations. However, some languages or systems,
e.g., Guide [5] or Arjuna [56], associate synchronization to objects although they
distinguish the notions of object and activity. Another more recent example is
Java [37], where a new private lock is implicitly associated to each newly created
object.

A third dimension of integration considers the object as the unit of distribution, leading to the notion of a *distributed object*. Objects are seen as entities
which may be distributed and replicated on several processors. The message
passing metaphor is seen as a transparent way of invoking either local or remote
objects. The Emerald distributed programming language [10] is an example of
distributed programming language based on the notion of distributed object.
One can also further integrate message passing with the transaction concept as
to support inter-object synchronization and fault-tolerance [41,27].

As noted above, these dimensions are rather independent. For instance, Java
is partially integrated in that it follows a model of synchronised objects, but
not a model of active object (object and thread are kept separate). Java does
not follow a model of distributed object either – actually it does not unless
one uses the remote method invocation (RMI) facility which then makes remote
invocation become transparent.

4.3 Active Objects

The basic idea leading to the concept of an *active object* is to consider an object
having its own computing resource, i.e., its own private activity. This approach,

---

[5] This similarity has been for instance noted in [51].

simple and natural, is quite influent [63], following the way traced by actor-languages [40,1]. The concept of an active object is also a natural foundation for building higher-level autonomous *agents*, for distributed knowledge-based systems.

The independence of object activities provides what is usually called *inter-object* concurrency. When, for each active object, requests are usually processed one at a time: this is called a *serialized object*. In other computation models (e.g., Actors [1]) an active object is allowed to process several requests simultaneously, thus owning more than one internal activity: this is called *intra-object* concurrency. This increases the expressive power as well as the overall concurrency. But this requires a further concurrency control in order to ensure object state consistency (as we will see below).

4.4   Synchronized Objects

The presence of concurrent activities requires some degree of synchronization, i.e., constraints, in order to ensure a correct execution of programs. Synchronization may be associated to objects and to their communication means, i.e., message passing, through various levels of identification.

Synchronization at Message Passing Level. A straightforward transposition of the message passing mechanism, from a sequential computing context to a concurrent one, leads to the implicit synchronization of the sender (caller) to the receiver (callee). This is called *synchronous* transmission: to resume its own execution, the sender object waits for (1) completion by the receiver of the invoked method execution and then (2) the return of the reply.

In case of active objects, the sender and the receiver own independent activities. It is therefore useful to introduce some *asynchronous* type of transmission, where the sender may resume its execution immediately after sending the message, i.e., without waiting for completion of the invoked method by the receiver. This type of transmission introduces further concurrency through communication. It is well suited for a distributed architecture, because if the receiver (the server) is located on a distant processor, the addition of the communication latency to the processing time may be significant. Finally, some languages (e.g., see in [63]) introduce some mixed kind of transmission, which immediately returns an eager promise for (handle to) a (future) reply, without waiting for the actual completion of the invocation.

Synchronization at Object(s) Level. The identification of synchronization with message passing, that is with requests invocation, has the advantage of transparently ensuring some significant part of the synchronization concerns. Indeed synchronization of requests is transparent to the client object, being managed by the object serving requests.

In case of serialized active objects, requests are processed one at a time, according to their order of arrival. Some finer grain or rather more global concurrency control may however be necessary for objects. We will then consider three different levels of synchronization at the object(s) level. They respectively correspond to: the internal processing of an object, its interface, and the coordination between several objects.

Intra-Object Synchronization. In case of *intra-object* concurrency (i.e., an object computing simultaneously several requests), it is necessary to include some concurrency control in order to ensure the consistency of the object state. Usually, the control is expressed in terms of exclusions between operations[6]. The typical example is the readers and writers problem, where several readers are free to access simultaneously to a shared book. However, the presence of one writer excludes all others (writers and readers).

Behavioral Synchronization. It is possible that an object may temporarily not be able to process a certain kind of request which is nevertheless part of its interface. The typical example is the bounded buffer example, which may not accept some insertion request while it is full. Rather than signaling an error, it may delay the acceptance of that request until it is no more full. This makes synchronization of services between objects being fully transparent.

Inter-Objects Synchronization. Finally, it may be necessary to ensure some consistency, not just individual, but also global (coordination) between mutually interacting objects. Consider the example of a money transfer between two bank accounts. The issue is in ensuring the invisibility of possible transient and inconsistent global states, while the transfer takes place. Intra-object or behavioral synchronization are not sufficient. We must introduce a notion such as an atomic transaction [7], to coordinate the different invocations.

Synchronization Schemes. Various *synchronization schemes* have been proposed to address these various levels of concurrency control. Many of them are actual derivations from general concurrent programming and have been more and less integrated within the object-based concurrent programming framework.

Centralized schemes, as for instance *path expressions*, specify in an abstract way the possible interleavings of invocations, and may be associated in a natural way to a class. The Procol language [13] is based on that idea. Another example of centralized scheme is the concept of *body*. That is, some distinguished centralized operation (the *body*), explicitly describes the types and sequence of requests that the object will accept during its activity[7]. Languages like POOL [4] and Eiffel// [22] are based on this concept.

---

[6] Note that the case of a mutual exclusion between all methods subsumes the case of a serialized object (as defined in Sect. 4.3).

[7] This concept is actually a direct offspring of Simula-67 [9] concept of *body*, which actually included support for coroutines. Note that this initial potential of objects for concurrency was then abandoned, both for technological and cultural reasons, by most of Simula-67 followers. This potentiality started being rediscovered from the late 70's, actor-languages appearing as new pioneers [40].

Decentralized schemes, such as *guards*, are based on boolean activation conditions, that may be associated to each method. Synchronization counters are counters recording the invocation status for each method, i.e., the number of received, started and completed invocations. Associated to guards, they provide a very fine grained control of intra-object synchronization. An example is the distributed programming language Guide [5].

Finally, a higher level formalism is based on the notion of *abstract behaviors*. This scheme is quite appropriate for behavioral synchronization (introduced in the previous section). The idea[8] is as following: an object conforms to some abstract behavior representing a set of *enabled methods*. In the example of the bounded buffer, three abstract behaviors are needed: `empty`, `full`, and `partial`. The abstract behavior `partial` is expressed as the union of `empty` and `full`, and consequently is the only one to enable both insertion and extraction methods. After completing the processing of an invocation, next abstract state is computed to possibly update the state and services availability of the object.

Note that, although integration of synchronization schemes with object model is usually straightforward, this integration impacts on the reuse of synchronization specifications (see Sect. 4.6).

4.5 Distributed Objects

An object represents an independent unit of execution, encapsulating data, procedures, and possibly private resources (activity) for processing the requests. Therefore a natural option is to consider an object as the unit of distribution, and possible replication. Furthermore, self-containedness of objects (data plus procedures, plus possible internal activity) eases the issue of moving and migrating them around. Also, note that message passing not only ensures the separation between services offered by an object and its internal representation, but also provides the independence of its physical location. Thus, message passing may subsume both local and remote invocation (whether sender and receiver are on the same or distinct processors is transparent to the programmer) as well as possible unaccessibility of an object/service.

Accessibility and Fault-Recovery. In order to handle unaccessibility of objects, in the Argus distributed operating system [41], the programmer may associate an exception to an invocation. If an object is located on a processor which is unaccessible, because of a network or processor fault, an exception is raised, e.g., to invoke another object. A transaction is implicitly associated to each invocation (synchronous invocation in Argus), to ensure atomicity properties. For instance, if the invocation fails (e.g., if the server object becomes unaccessible), the effects of the invocation are canceled. The Karos distributed programming language [27] extends the Argus approach by allowing the association of transactions also to asynchronous invocations.

---

[8] See e.g., [46] for a more detailed description.

Migration. In order to improve the accessibility of objects, some languages or systems support mechanisms for object migration. In the Emerald distributed programming language [10], and the COOL generic run-time layer [39], the programmer may decide to migrate an object from one processor to another. He may control (in terms of *attachements* in Emerald) which other related objects should also migrate together.

Replication. As for migration, a first motivation of replication is in increasing the accessibility of an object, by replicating it onto the processors of its (remote) clients. A second motivation is fault-tolerance. By replicating an object on several processors, its services become robust against possible processor failure. In both cases, a fundamental issue is to maintain the consistency of the replicas, i.e., to ensure that all replicas hold the same values. In the Electra [44] distributed system, the concept of remote invocation has been extended in the following fashion: invoking an object leads to the invocation of all its replicas while ensuring that concurrent invocations are ordered along the same (total) order for all replicas. Andrew Black also introduced a general mechanism for group invocation well suited for replicated objects [12].

4.6   Limitations

The integrative approach attempts at unifying object mechanisms with concurrency and distribution mechanisms. Meanwhile, some conflicts may arise between them, as we will see below.

Inheritance Anomaly. Inheritance mechanism is one of the key mechanisms for achieving good reuse of object-oriented programs. It is therefore natural to use inheritance to specialize synchronization specifications associated to a class of objects. Unfortunately, experience shows that: (1) synchronization is difficult to specify and moreover to reuse, because of the high interdependency between the synchronization conditions for different methods, (2) various uses of inheritance (to inherit variables, methods, and synchronizations), may conflict with each other, as noted in [49]. In some cases, defining a new subclass, even only with one additional method, may force the redefinition of all synchronization specifications. This limitation has been named the *inheritance anomaly phenomenon* [46].

Specifications along centralized schemes (see Sect. 6) turn out to be very difficult to reuse, and often must be completely redefined. Decentralized schemes, being modular by essence, are better suited for selective specialization. However, this fine-grained decomposition, down at the level of each method, partially backfires. This is because synchronization specifications, even if decomposed for each method, still remain more or less interdependent. As for instance in the case of intra-object synchronization with synchronization counters, adding a new write method in a subclass may force redefinition of other methods guards, in order to account for the new mutual exclusion constraint. (See [46] for a detailed analysis and classification of the possible problems.)

Among the recent directions proposed for minimizing the problem, we may cite: (1) specifying and specializing independently behavioral and intra-object synchronizations [58], (2) allowing the programmer to select among several schemes [46], and (3) genericity, by instantiating abstract specifications, as an alternative to inheritance for reusing synchronization specifications [49].

Compatibility of Transaction Protocols. It is tempting to integrate transaction concurrency control protocols into objects. Thus one may locally define, for a given object, the optimal concurrency control or recovery protocol. For instance, commutativity of operations enables the interleaving (without blocking) of transactions on a given object. Unfortunately, the gain in modularity and specialization may lead to incompatibility problems [60]. Broadly speaking, if objects use different transaction serialization protocols (i.e., serialize the transactions along different orders), global executions of transactions may become inconsistent, i.e, non serializable. A proposed approach to handle that problem is in defining local conditions, to be verified by objects, in order to ensure their compatibility [60,30].

Replication of Objects and Communications. The communication protocols which have been designed for fault-tolerant distributed computing (see Sect. 4.5) consider a standard client/server model. The straightforward transposition of such protocols to the object model leads to the problem of unexpected duplication of invocations. Indeed, an object usually acts conversely as a client and as a server. Thus an object which has been replicated as a server may itself in turn invoke other objects (as a client). As a result all replicas of the object will invoke these other objects several times. This unexpected duplication of invocations may lead, in the best case, to inefficiency, and in the worst case, to inconsistencies (by invoking several times the same operation). A solution, proposed in [47], is based on *pre-filtering* and *post-filtering*. Pre-filtering consists in coordinating processing by the replicas (when considered as a client) in order to generate a single invocation. Post-filtering is the dual operation for the replicas (when considered as a server) in order to discard redundant invocations.

Factorization vs Distribution. Last, a more general limitation (i.e., less specific to the integrative approach) comes from standard implementation frameworks for object factorization mechanisms, which usually rely on strong assumptions about centralized (single memory) architectures.

The concept of class variables[9], supported by several object-oriented programming languages, is difficult and expensive to implement for a distributed system. Unless introducing complex and costly transaction mechanisms, their

---

[9] As supported by Smalltalk.

consistency is hard to maintain, once instances of a same class may be distributed among processors. Note that this problem is general for any kind of shared variable. Standard object-oriented methodology tends to forbid the use of shared variables, but may advocate using class variables instead.

In a related problem, implementing inheritance on a distributed system leads to the problem of accessing remote code for superclasses, unless all class code is replicated to all processors, which has obvious scalability limitations. A semi-automatic approach consists in grouping classes into autonomous modules as to help at partitioning the class code among processors.

Some radical approach replaces the inheritance mechanism between classes, by the concept/mechanism of *delegation* between objects. This mechanism has actually been introduced in the Actor concurrent programming language Act 1 [40]. Intuitively, an object which may not understand a message will then delegate it (i.e., forward it[10]) to another object, called its *proxy*. The proxy will process the message in place of the initial receiver, or it can also itself delegate it further to its own designated proxy. This alternative to inheritance is very appealing as it only relies on message passing, thus is fits well with a distributed implementation. Meanwhile, the delegation mechanism needs some non trivial synchronization mechanism to ensure the proper handling (ordering) of recursive messages, prior to other incoming messages. Thus, it may not offer a general and complete alternative solution [15].

4.7   Evaluation of the Integrative Approach

In summary, the integrative approach is very appealing by the merging it achieves between concepts, from object-based programming, and those from concurrent and distributed programming. It thus provides a minimal number of concepts and a single conceptual framework to the programmer. Nevertheless, as we discussed in Sect. 4.6, this approach unfortunately suffers from limitations in some aspects of the integration.

Another potential weakness is that some too systematic unification/integration may lead to some too restrictive model (too much uniformity kills variety !) and may lead to inefficiencies. For instance, stating that every object is active, and/or every message transmission is a transaction, may be inappropriate for some applications not necessarily requiring such protocols, and their associated computational load. A last important limitation is a *legacy* problem, that is the possible difficulty with reusing standard sequential program. Some straightforward way is the encapsulation of sequential programs into active objects. But, note that a cohabitation between active objects and standard ones, called *passive objects*, is non homogeneous, which requires methodological rules for distinction between active objects and passive objects [22].

---

[10]   Note that, in order to handle recursion properly, the delegated message will include the initial receiver.

5   The Reflective Approach

As we earlier discussed, the applicative approach (library-based approach) helps at structuring concurrent and distributed programming concepts and mechanisms, thanks to encapsulation, genericity, class, and inheritance concepts. The integrative approach minimizes the amount of concepts to be mastered by the programmer and makes mechanisms more transparent, but at the cost of possibly reducing the flexibility and the efficiency of mechanisms offered. Indeed programming languages or systems built from libraries are often more extensible than languages designed along the integrative approach. Libraries help at structuring and simulating various solutions, and thus usually bring good flexibility, whereas brand new languages may freeze too early their computation and communication models. In other words it would be interesting to keep the unification and simplification advantages of the integrative approach, while retaining the flexibility of the applicative/library approach.

One important observation is that the applicative approach and the integrative approach actually address *different* levels of concerns and use: the integrated approach is for the application programmer, and the applicative approach is for the system programmer. In other words, the end user programs its applications, with an integrative (simple and unified) approach in mind. The system programmer, or the more expert user, builds or customizes the system, through the design of libraries of protocol components, along an *applicative* approach.

Therefore, and as opposed to what one may think at first, the *applicative* approach and the *integrative* approach are *not* in competition, but rather *complementary*. The issue is then: How can we actually combine these two levels of programming ?, and to be more precise: How do we *interface them* ? It turns out that a general methodology for adapting the behavior of computing systems, named *reflection*, offers such kind of a glue.

5.1   Reflection

Reflection is a general methodology to describe, control, and adapt the behavior of a computational system. The basic idea is to provide a representation of the important characteristics/parameters of the system in terms of the system itself. In other words, (static) representation characteristics, as well as (dynamic) execution characteristics, of application programs are made concrete into one (or more) program(s), which represents the default computational behavior (interpreter, compiler, execution monitor...). Such a description/control program is called a *meta-program*. Specializing such programs enables to customize the execution of the application program, by possibly changing data representation, execution strategies, mechanisms and protocols. Note that the *same* language is used, both for writing application programs, *and* for meta-programs controlling their execution. However, the complete separation between the application program and the corresponding meta-programs is strictly enforced.

Reflection helps at decorrelating libraries specifying implementation and execution models (execution strategies, concurrency control, object distribution) from the application program. This increases modularity, readability and reusability of programs. Last, reflection provides a methodology to open up and make adaptable, through a *meta-interface*[11], implementation decisions and resources management, which are often hard-wired and fixed, or delegated by the programming language to the underlying operating system.

In summary, reflection helps at integrating protocol libraries intimately within a programming language or system, thus providing the interfacing framework (the glue) between the applicative and the integrative approaches/levels.

5.2   Reflection and Objects

Reflection fits specially well with object concepts, which enforce a good encapsulation of levels and a modularity of effects. It is therefore natural to organize the control of the behavior of an object-based computational system (its meta-interface) through a set of objects. This organization is named a *Meta-Object Protocol (MOP)* [35], and its components are called *meta-objects* [43], as meta-programs are represented by objects. They may represent various characteristics of the execution context such as: representation, implementation, execution, communication and location. Specializing meta-objects may extend and modify, locally, the execution context of some specific objects of the application program.

Reflection may also help at expressing and controlling resources management, not only at the level of an individual object, but also at a broader level such as: scheduler, processor, name space, object group..., such resources being also represented by meta-objects. This helps at a very fine-grained control (e.g., for scheduling and load balancing) with the whole expressive power of a full programming language [54], as opposed to some global and fixed algorithm (which is usually optimized for a specific kind of application or an average case).

5.3   Examples of Meta Object Protocols (MOPs)

The CodA architecture [48] is a representative example of a general object-based reflective architecture (i.e., a MOP) based on *meta-components*[12]. CodA considers by default seven (7) meta-components, associated to each object (see Fig. 2), corresponding to: *message sending, receiving, buffering, selection, method lookup, execution,* and *state accessing*. An object with default meta-components behaves as a standard (sequential and passive) object[13]. Attaching specific (specialized)

---

[11] This *meta-interface* enables the client programmer to adapt and tune the *behavior* of a software module, independently of its *functionalities*, which are accessed through the standard (*base*) interface. This has been named by Gregor Kiczales the concept of *open implementation* [36].

[12] Note that meta-components are indeed meta-objects. In the following, we will rather use the term *meta-component* in order to emphasize the pluggability aspects of a reflective architecture (MOP) such as CodA. Also, for simplification, we will often use the term *component* in place of *meta-component*.

[13] to be more precised, as a standard Smalltalk object, as CodA is currently implemented in Smalltalk.

meta-components allows to selectively changing a specific aspect of the representation or execution model for a single object. A standard interface between meta-components helps at composing meta-components from different origins.

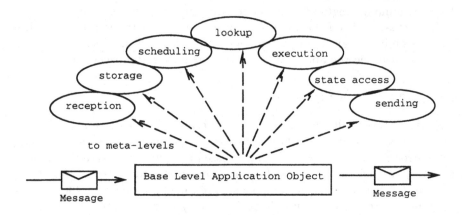

Fig. 2. Meta-components in CodA

Note that some other reflective architectures may be more specialized and may offer a more reduced (and abstract) set of meta-components. Examples are the Actalk and GARF platforms, where a smaller amount of meta-components may be in practice sufficient to express a large variety of schemes and application problems.

The Actalk platform [16,17] helps at experimenting with various synchronization and communication models for a given program, by changing and specializing various models/components of: (1) *activity* (implicit or explicit acceptance of requests, intra-objet concurrency. . .) and *synchronization* (abstract behaviors, guards. . .), (2) *communication* (synchronous, asynchronous. . .), and (3) *invocation* (time stamp, priority. . .). The GARF platform [23], for distributed and fault-tolerant programming, offers a variety of mechanisms along two dimensions/components: (1) object control (persistence, replication. . .) and (2) communication (multicast, atomic. . .).

More generally speaking, depending on the actual goals and the balance expected between flexibility, generality, simplicity and efficiency, design decisions will dictate the amount and the scope of the mechanisms which will be opened-up to the meta-level. Therefore, some mechanisms may be represented as *reflective methods*, but which belong to *standard* object classes, that is, without explicit and complete meta-objects.

Smalltalk is a representative example of that latter category. In addition to the (meta-)representation of the program structures and mechanisms, as first class objects (see Sect. 3.2), a few very powerful reflective mechanisms offer some control over program execution. Examples are: redefinition of error handling message, reference to current context, references swap, changing the class of an object... Such facilities actually help at easily building and integrating various platforms for concurrent, concurrent and distributed programming, such as Simtalk, Actalk, GARF, and CodA itself [18].

5.4 Examples of Applications

To illustrate how reflection may help at mapping various computation models and protocols onto user programs, we will quickly survey some examples of experiments with a specific reflective architecture. (We chose CodA. See [48] for a more detailed description of its architecture and libraries of components.)

Note that, in the case of the CodA system, as well as for almost all other examples of reflective systems further described, the basic programming model is *integrative*, while reflection enables the customization of concurrency and distribution aspects and protocols, by specializing *libraries* of meta-components.

Concurrency Models. In order to introduce concurrency for a given object (by making it into an *active* object, along an integrated approach), two meta-components are specialized. The specialized *message buffering* component[14] is a queue which will buffer incoming messages. The specialized *execution* component associates an independent activity (thread) to the object. This thread processes an endless loop for selecting and performing next message from the *buffering* component.

Distribution Models. In order to introduce distribution, a new meta-component is *added*, for *marshaling* messages to be remotely sent. In addition, two new specific objects are introduced, which represent the notion of a *remote reference* (to a remote object) and the notion of a (memory/name) *space*. The remote reference object has a specialized *message receiving* component, which marshals the message into a stream of bytes and sends it through the network to the actual remote object. This latter one has another specialized *message receiving* component which reconstructs and actually receives the message. Marshaling decisions, e.g., which argument should be passed by reference, by value (i.e., a copy), up to which level..., may be specialized by a *marshaling descriptor* supplied by the *marshaling* component.

Migration and Replication Models. Migration is introduced by a new meta-component which describes the form and the policies (i.e., when it should occur) for migration. Replication is managed by adding two new dual meta-components. The first one is in charge of controlling access to the state of the original object. The second one controls the access to each of its replicas. Again, marshaling decisions, such as: which argument should be passed by reference, by value, by move (i.e., migrated, as in Emerald [10]), with attachments..., may be specialized

---

[14] The default *buffering* component is actually directly passing incoming messages on to the *execution* component.

through the *marshaling descriptors* supplied by the corresponding component. Also one may specialize aspects such as which parts of the object should be replicated, and various management policies for enforcing the consistency between the original object and its replicas.

5.5   Other Examples of Reflective Architectures

Other examples of representative reflective architectures and their applications are quickly mentioned in the following. Note that this is by no means an exhaustive study.

Dynamic Installation and Composition of Protocols. The general MAUD methodology [2] focuses on fault tolerance protocols, such as: server replication, check point... Its specificity is in offering a framework for *dynamic installation* and *composition* of specialized meta-components. The dynamic installation of meta-components enables the installation of a given protocol only when needed, and without stopping the program execution. The possibility to associate meta-components, not only to objects, but also to other meta-components (which are first-class objects), enables the layered composition of protocols.

Control of Migration. The autonomy and self-containedness of objects, further reinforced in the case of active objects, makes them easier to migrate as a single piece. Nevertheless, the decision to migrate an object is an important issue which often remains with the programmer responsibility (e.g., in Emerald [10]). It may be interesting to semi-automate such a decision, along various considerations such as: processor load, ratio of remote communications... Reflection helps at integrating such statistical data (residing for physical and shared resources), and at using them by various migration algorithms described at the meta-level [54].

Customizing System Policies. The Apertos distributed operating system [62], represents a significant and innovative example of a distributed operating system, completely designed along an object-based reflective architecture (MOP). In supplement to the modularity and the genericity of the architecture gained by using an applicative (object-oriented) approach (as for Choices, already discussed in Sect. 3.3), reflection brings the (possibly dynamic) customization of the system towards application requirements. As for instance one may easily specialize the scheduling policy in order to support various kinds of schedulers, e.g., a real-time scheduler. Another gain is in the size of the micro-kernel obtained, which is particularly small, as it is reduced to supporting the basic reflective operations and the basic resources abstractions. This helps at both the understanding and the porting of the system.

Reflective Extension of an Existing Commercial System. A reflective methodology has recently been used in order to incorporate extended[15] transaction models into an *existing* commercial transaction processing system. It extends a standard transaction processing monitor, in a minimal and disciplined way (based on upcalls), to expose features such as: lock delegation, dependency tracking between transactions, and definition of conflicts, and to represent them as reflective operations [6]. These reflective primitives are then used to implement various extended transaction model, such as: split/join, cooperative groups...

5.6   Related Frameworks for Interfacing Customizations.

We finally mention two examples of frameworks for customizing computational behaviors, which are closely related to reflection.

The Composition-Filters Model. The SINA language is based on the notion of a *filter*, a way to specify arbitrary manipulation and actions for messages sent to (or from) an object [3]. In other words, filters represent some reification of the communication and interpretation mechanism between objects. By combining various filters for a given object, one may construct complex interaction mechanisms in a composable way.

Generic Run-Time as a Dual Approach. The frontier between programming languages and operating systems is getting thinner. Reflective programming languages have some high-level representation of the underlying execution model. Conversely, and dual to reflection, several distributed operating systems provide a generic run time layer, as for instance the COOL layer for the Chorus operating system [39]. These generic run time layers are designed as to be used by various programming languages, thanks to some upcalls which delegate specific representation decisions to the programming language.

5.7   Evaluation of the Reflective Approach

Reflection provides a general framework for the customization of concurrency and distribution aspects and protocols, by specializing and *integrating* (meta)-*libraries* intimately within a language or system, while *separating* them from the application program.

Many reflective architectures are currently proposed and getting evaluated. It is too early yet to find and validate some general and optimal reflective architecture for concurrent and distributed programming (although we believe that CodA [48] is a promising step in that direction). Meanwhile, we now need more experience in the practical use of reflection, to be able to find good tradeoffs between the flexibility required, the architecture complexity, and the resulting efficiency. One possible (and currently justified) complain is about the actual

---

[15]   That is, relaxing some of the standard (ACID) transaction properties.

relative complexity of reflective architectures. Nevertheless, and independently of the required cultural change, we believe that this is the price to pay for the increased, albeit disciplined, flexibility that they offer. Another significant current limitation concerns efficiency, consequence of extra indirections and interpretations. Partial evaluation (also called program specialization) is currently proposed as a promising technique to minimize such overheads [45].

6   Integrating the Approaches

As already pointed out in the introduction, the *applicative, integrative* and *reflective* approaches are not in conflict, but are instead complementary. The complementary nature of these approaches extends to their relationship to language: the applicative approach does not change the underlying language; the library approach either defines a new language or adds new concepts to the language; and the reflective approach requires the use of a specific type of language.

Among the examples of languages and systems given in the paper, some have been built following more than one approach. This is the case for instance for the ÉPÉE [33] parallel system (see Sect. 3.2), which on one hand is based on the integration of object with distribution, and on the other hand is implemented with libraries. Other examples are Actalk [16] and GARF [23] (see Sect. 3.2), which offer libraries of abstractions for concurrent and distributed programming, that may be transparently applied, and thus integrated to programs, thanks to the reflective facilities of Smalltalk.

We believe that future developments of object-based concurrent and distributed systems will integrate aspects of the three approaches. A very good example is the current development around the Common Object Request Broker Architecture (CORBA) of the OMG [52]. CORBA *integrates* object and distribution concepts through an object request broker, which makes remote communication partially transparent. In that sense, CORBA follows the *integrative* approach. CORBA also specifies a set of services to support more advanced distributed features such as transactions. For instance, the CORBA object transaction service (named *OTS*) is specified and implemented in the form of a class library of distributed protocols, such as *locking* and *atomic commitment*. In that sense, CORBA follows the *applicative* approach. Finally, most of CORBA implementations provide facilities for message reification (messages can be considered as first class entities – e.g., smart proxies in IONA Orbix), and hence supports customisation of concurrency and distribution protocols. In that sense, CORBA implementations follow (to some extent) the *reflective* approach.

Conclusion

Towards a better understanding and evaluation of various object-based concurrent and distributed developments, we have proposed a classification of the different ways along which the object paradigm is used in concurrent and distributed contexts. We have identified three different approaches which convey different, yet complementary, research streams in the object-based concurrent and distributed system community.

The *applicative* approach (library-based approach) helps at structuring concurrent and distributed programming concepts and mechanisms, through encapsulation, genericity, class, and inheritance concepts. The principal limitation of the approach is that the programming of the application, and of the concurrent and distribution architecture, are represented by unrelated sets of concepts and objects. The applicative approach can be viewed as a bottom-up approach and is directed towards system-builders.

The *integrative* approach minimizes the amount of concepts to be mastered by the programmer and makes mechanisms more transparent, by providing some unified concurrent and distributed high level object model. However, this is at the cost of possibly reducing the flexibility and efficiency of the mechanisms. The integrative approach can be viewed as a top-down approach and is directed towards application-builders.

Finally, by providing a framework for integrating protocol libraries intimately within a programming language or system, the *reflective* approach provides the interfacing framework (the glue) between the applicative and the integrative approaches/levels. Meanwhile, it enforces the separation of their respective levels. In other words, reflection provides the *meta-interface* through which the system designer may install system customizations and thus change the execution context (concurrent, distributed, fault tolerant, real time, adaptive...) with minimal changes on the application programs.

The reflective approach also contributes in blurring the distinction between programming language, operating system, and data base, and at easing the development, adaptation and optimization of a minimal computing system dynamically extensible. Nevertheless, we should strongly remind that this does not free us from the necessity of a good basic design and finding a good set of foundational abstractions.

Acknowledgements

We would like to thank the anonymous reviewers for their suggestions in revising this paper.

Note that this paper is a revised version of a technical report, published as: No 96-01, Dept. of Information Science, the University of Tokyo, January 1996, and also as: No 96/190, Département d'Informatique, École Polytechnique Fédérale de Lausanne, May 1996. Another paper [19], to appear in late 1998. has been based on this analysis, but includes many more examples, notably with numerous addings from the parallel computing field.

References

1. G. AGHA, *Actors: A Model of Concurrent Computation in Distributed Systems*, Series in Artificial Intelligence, MIT Press, 1986.
2. G. AGHA, S. FRØLUND, R. PANWAR, and D. STURMAN, A Linguistic Framework for Dynamic Composition of Dependability Protocols, *Dependable Computing for Critical Applications III (DCCA-3)*, IFIP Transactions, Elsevier, 1993, pages 197–207.
3. M. AKSIT, K. WAKITA, J. BOSCH, L. BERGMANS, and A. YONEZAWA, Abstracting Object Interactions Using Composition Filters, [28], pages 152–184.
4. P. AMERICA, POOL-T: A Parallel Object-Oriented Language, [63], pages 199–220.
5. R. BALTER, S. LACOURTE, and M. RIVEILL, The Guide Language, *The Computer Journal*, Special Issue on Distributed Operating Systems, Vol. 37, n° 6, CEPIS - Oxford University Press, 1994, pages 519–530.
6. R. BARGA and C. PU, A Practical and Modular Implementation of Extended Transaction Models, Technical Report, n° 95-004, CSE, Oregon Graduate Institute of Science & Technology, Portland OR, USA, 1995.
7. P. BERNSTEIN, V. HADZILACOS, and N. GOODMAN, *Concurrency Control and Recovery in Database Systems*, Addison Wesley, 1987.
8. J. BÉZIVIN, Some Experiments in Object-Oriented Simulation, *ACM Conference on Object-Oriented Programming Systems, Languages and Applications (OOPSLA'87)*, Vol. 22, n° 12, December 1987, pages 394–405.
9. G.M. BIRTWISTLE, O.-J. DAHL, B. MYHRHAUG, and K. NYGAARD, *Simula Begin*, Petrocelli Charter, 1973.
10. A. BLACK, N. HUTCHINSON, E. JUL, H. LEVY and L. CARTER, Distribution and abstract types in Emerald, *IEEE Transactions on Software Engineering*, Vol. 12, n° 12, December 1986.
11. A. BLACK, Understanding Transactions in the Operating System Context, *Operating Systems Review*, Vol. 25, n° 28, January 1991, pages 73–77.
12. A. BLACK and M.P. IMMEL, Encapsulating Plurality, *European Conference on Object Oriented Programming (ECOOP'93)*, edited by O. Nierstrasz, LNCS, n° 707, Springer-Verlag, July 1993, pages 57–79.
13. J. VAN DEN BOS and C. LAFFRA, Procol: A Concurrent Object-Language with Protocols, Delegation and Persistence, *Acta Informatica*, n° 28, September 1991, pages 511–538.
14. S. BRANDT and O.L. MADSEN, Object-Oriented Distributed Programming in BETA, [28], pages 185–212.
15. J.-P. BRIOT and A. YONEZAWA, Inheritance and Synchronization in Concurrent OOP, *European Conference on Object Oriented Programming (ECOOP'87)*, edited by J. Bézivin, J.-M. Hullot, P. Cointe and H. Lieberman, LNCS, n° 276, Springer-Verlag, June 1987, pages 32–40.
16. J.-P. BRIOT, Actalk: a Testbed for Classifying and Designing Actor Languages in the Smalltalk-80 Environment, *European Conference on Object Oriented Programming (ECOOP'89)*, edited by S. Cook, Cambridge University Press, July 1989, pages 109–129.
17. J.-P. BRIOT, An Experiment in Classification and Specialization of Synchronization Schemes, to appear in *2nd International Symposium on Object Technologies for Advanced Software (ISOTAS'96)*, edited by K. Futatsugi and S. Matsuoka, LNCS, Springer-Verlag, March 1996.

18. J.-P. BRIOT and R. GUERRAOUI, Smalltalk for Concurrent and Distributed Programming, In Special Issue on: Smalltalk, edited by Rachid Guerraoui, *Informatik/Informatique, Swiss Informaticians Society, Switzerland*, (1):16–19, February 1996.

19. J.-P. BRIOT, R. GUERRAOUI, and K.-P. LÖHR, Concurrency and Distribution in Object-Oriented Programming, *ACM Computing Surveys*, to appear in late 1998.

20. R. CAMPBELL, N. ISLAM, D. RAILA, and P. MADANY, Designing and Implementing Choices: An Object-Oriented System in C++, [50], pages 117–126.

21. R. CAPOBIANCHI, R. GUERRAOUI, A. LANUSSE, and P. ROUX, Lessons from Implementing Active Objects on a Parallel Machine, *Usenix Symposium on Experiences with Distributed and Multiprocessor Systems*, 1992, pages 13–27.

22. D. CAROMEL, Towards a Method of Object-Oriented Concurrent Programming, [50], pages 90–102.

23. B. GARBINATO, R. GUERRAOUI, and K.R. MAZOUNI, Distributed Programming in GARF, [28], pages 225–239.

24. B. GARBINATO, R. GUERRAOUI, and K.R. MAZOUNI, Implementation of the GARF Replicated Objects Platform, *Distributed Systems Engineering Journal*, February 1995, pages 14–27.

25. B. GARBINATO, P. FELBER, and R. GUERRAOUI, Protocol classes for designing reliable designing reliable distributed environments, *European Conference on Object Oriented Programming (ECOOP'96)*, edited by P. Cointe, LNCS, n° 1098, Springer-Verlag, June 1996, pages 316–343.

26. B. GARBINATO and R. GUERRAOUI, Using the strategy design pattern to compose reliable distributed protocols, *Usenix Conference on Object-Oriented Technologies and Systems (COOTS'97)*, edited by S.Vinoski, Usenix, June 1997.

27. R. GUERRAOUI, R. CAPOBIANCHI, A. LANUSSE, and P. ROUX, Nesting Actions Through Asynchronous Message Passing: the ACS Protocol, *European Conference on Object Oriented Programming (ECOOP'92)*, edited by O. Lehrmann Madsen, LNCS, n° 615, Springer-Verlag, June 1992, pages 170–184.

28. R. GUERRAOUI, O. NIERSTRASZ, and M. RIVEILL (editors), *Object-Based Distributed Programming*, LNCS, n° 791, Springer-Verlag, 1994.

29. R. GUERRAOUI and A. SCHIPER, The Transaction Model vs Virtual Synchrony Model: Bridging the Gap, *Distributed Systems: From Theory to Practice*, edited by K. Birman, F. Cristian, F. Mattern and A. Schiper, LNCS, n° 938, Springer-Verlag, 1995.

30. R. GUERRAOUI, Modular Atomic Objects, *Theory and Practice of Object Systems (TAPOS)*, Vol. 1, n° 2, John Wiley & Sons, November 1995, pages 89–99.

31. R. GUERRAOUI ET AL., Strategic Directions in Object-Oriented Programming, *ACM Computing Surveys*, Vol. 28, n° 4, December 1996, pages 691–700.

32. R. GUERRAOUI and A. SCHIPER, Software based replication for fault-tolerance, *IEEE Computer*, Vol. 30, n° 4, April 1997, pages 68–74.

33. J.-M. JÉZÉQUEL, Transparent Parallelization Through Reuse: Between a Compiler and a Library Approach, *European Conference on Object Oriented Programming (ECOOP'93)*, edited by O. Nierstrasz, LNCS, n° 707, Springer-Verlag, July 1993, pages 384–405.

34. M. KARAORMAN and J. BRUNO, Introducing Concurrency to a Sequential Language, [50], pages 103–116.

35. G. KICZALES, J. DES RIVIÈRES and D. BOBROW, *The Art of The Meta-Object Protocol*, MIT Press, 1991.

36. G. KICZALES (editor), Foil For The Workshop On Open Implementation, http://www.parc.xerox.com/PARC/spl/eca/oi/workshop-94/foil/main.html, October 1994.

37. R. LEA, *Concurrent Programming in Java*, Addison-Wesley, 1997.

38. L. LESCAUDRON, Prototypage d'Environnements de Programmation pour les Langages à Objets Concurrents : une Réalisation en Smalltalk-80 pour Actalk, PhD Thesis, LITP, Université Paris VI - CNRS, France, TH93.11, May 1992.

39. R. LEA, C. JACQUEMOT, and E. PILLEVESSE, COOL: System Support for Distributed Programming, [50], pages 37–47.

40. H. LIEBERMAN, Concurrent Object-Oriented Programming in Act 1, [63], pages 9–36.

41. B. LISKOV and R. SHEIFLER, Guardians and Actions: Linguistic Support for Robust, Distributed Programs, *ACM Transactions on Programming Languages and Systems*, Vol. 5, n° 3, 1983.

42. C.V. LOPES and K.J. LIEBERHERR, Abstracting Process-to-Function Relations in Concurrent Object-Oriented Applications, *European Conference on Object Oriented Programming (ECOOP'94)*, edited by M. Tokoro and R. Pareschi, LNCS, n° 821, Springer-Verlag, July 1994, pages 81–99.

43. P. MAES, Concepts and Experiments in Computational Reflection, *ACM Conference on Object-Oriented Programming Systems, Languages and Applications (OOPSLA'87), Special Issue of Sigplan Notices*, Vol. 22, n° 12, December 1987, pages 147–155.

44. S. MAFFEIS, Run-Time Support for Object-Oriented Distributed Programming, *PhD Dissertation*, University of Zurich, Switzerland, February 1995.

45. H. MASUHARA, S. MATSUOKA, K. ASAI,, and A. YONEZAWA, Compiling Away the Meta-Level in Object-Oriented Concurrent Reflective Languages Using Partial Evaluation, *ACM Conference on Object-Oriented Programming Systems, Languages and Applications (OOPSLA'95), Special Issue of Sigplan Notices*, Vol. 30, n° 10, October 1995, pages 300–315.

46. S. MATSUOKA and A. YONEZAWA, Analysis of Inheritance Anomaly in Object-Oriented Concurrent Programming Languages, *Research Directions in Concurrent Object-Oriented Programming*, edited by G. Agha, P. Wegner and A. Yonezawa, MIT Press, 1993, pages 107–150.

47. K. MAZOUNI, B. GARBINATO, and R. GUERRAOUI, Building Reliable Client-Server Software Using Actively Replicated Objects, *Technology of Object-Oriented Languages and Systems (TOOLS-Europe'95)*, edited by I. Graham, B. Magnusson, B. Meyer and J.-M Nerson, Prentice Hall, March 1995, pages 37–53.

48. J. MCAFFER, Meta-Level Programming with CodA, *European Conference on Object Oriented Programming (ECOOP'95)*, edited by W. Olthoff, LNCS, n° 952, Springer-Verlag, August 1995, pages 190–214.

49. C. MCHALE, Synchronization in Concurrent, Object-oriented Languages: Expressive Power, Genericity and Inheritance, *PhD Thesis*, Dept. of Computer Science, Trinity College, Dublin, Ireland, October 1994. (ftp://ftp.dsg.cs.tcd.ie/pub/doc/dsg-86b.ps.gz).

50. B. MEYER (editor), Concurrent Object-Oriented Programming, Special Issue, *Communications of the ACM (CACM)*, Vol. 36, n° 9, September 1993.

51. B. MEYER, Systematic Concurrent Object-Oriented Programming, [50], pages 56–80.

52. T.J. MOWBRAY and R. ZAHAVI, *The Essential CORBA: System Integration Using Distributed Objects*, John Wiley & Sons and The Object Management Group, 1995.
53. J. NICOL, T. WILKES, and F. MANOLA, Object-Orientation in Heterogeneous Distributed Computing Systems, *IEEE Computer*, Vol. 26, n° 6, June 1993, pages 57–67.
54. H. OKAMURA and Y. ISHIKAWA, Object Location Control Using Meta-Level Programming, *European Conference on Object Oriented Programming*, edited by M. Tokoro and R. Pareschi, LNCS, n° 821, Springer-Verlag, July 1994, pages 299–319.
55. J. PADGET, G. NUYENS, and H. BRETTHAUER, An Overview of EuLisp, Journal of Lisp and Symbolic Computation, Vol. 6(1/2), pages 9–98, 1993.
56. G.D. PARRINGTON and S.K. SHRIVASTAVA, Implementing Concurrency Control in Reliable Distributed Object-Oriented Systems, *European Conference on Object Oriented Programming (ECOOP'88)*, edited by S. Gjessing and K. Nygaard, LNCS, n° 322, Springer-Verlag, 1988, pages 234–249.
57. M. ROZIER, Chorus, *Usenix International Conference on Micro-Kernels and Other Kernel Architectures*, 1992, pages 27–28.
58. L. THOMAS, Extensibility and Reuse of Object-Oriented Synchronization Components, *International Conference on Parallel Languages and Environments (PARLE'92)*, LNCS, n° 605, Springer-Verlag, June 1992, pages 261–275.
59. P. WEGNER, Dimensions of Object-Based Language Design, *ACM Conference on Object-Oriented Programming Systems, Languages and Applications (OOPSLA'87)*, *Special Issue of Sigplan Notices*, Vol. 22, n° 12, December 1987, pages 168–182.
60. W. WEIHL, Local Atomicity Properties: Modular Concurrency Control for Abstract Data Types, *ACM Transactions on Programming Languages and Systems*, Vol. 11, n° 2, 1989.
61. J. WING, Decomposing and Recomposing Transaction Concepts, [28], pages 111–122.
62. Y. YOKOTE, The Apertos Reflective Operating System: The Concept and its Implementation, *ACM Conference on Object-Oriented Programming Systems, Languages and Applications (OOPSLA'92)*, *Special Issue of Sigplan Notices*, Vol. 27, n° 10, October 1992, pages 414–434.
63. A. YONEZAWA and M. TOKORO (editors), *Object-Oriented Concurrent Programming*, Computer Systems Series, MIT Press, 1987.

Towards Meta-Agent Protocols

Andreas Kind and Julian Padget*

School of Mathematical Sciences
University of Bath
Bath BA2 7AY, UK
ak1@maths.bath.ac.uk
jap@maths.bath.ac.uk

Abstract. Software agents "live" in changing environments. Perception and actions of agents need to adapt dynamically to new situations. This paper is concerned with meta-agent protocols, an approach to support the modular and portable implementation of various kinds of agent systems. Meta-agent protocols are derived from object-based reflective systems that allow access to the state and structure of a program during its execution. A meta level interface to the internal representation of agents can provide support for introspection and adjustment of agents. Meta-agent protocols result in a clear separation between application level and meta level (e.g. dynamic communication protocols, dynamic modification of behaviour, fault tolerance, monitoring, dynamic performance optimization) in agent systems which leads to modular as well as portable application components.

1 Introduction

The Internet is a dynamic and distributed system. It is constructed from open services built around a standard communication framework. Due to computer mobility, varying network latency, bandwidth and connectivity there is an increasing demand for off-line computation. The idea is that program modules are sent off to run on remote machines and later return to report to the user. In order to fulfill a task without user interaction, agents need to have some degree of mobility, autonomy and determination. Furthermore it can be envisaged that particular problems require cooperation with other agents.

Before agent-based systems became *en vogue* recently, related work has been done in the field of object-based concurrent systems. Typically, object-based concurrent applications rely significantly on flexible control of computation during run-time. Reflective capabilities can provide such flexibility by means of *meta-objects* that model structural and behavioural aspects of objects. From the modeling aspect, the combination of object-oriented programming and reflection is therefore a natural one [8]. Encapsulation, data abstraction and incremental extension provide a suitable "hook" for computational reflection. But there is

---

* This work was supported by the Commission of the European Communities within the HCM programme (project VIM, contract #CHRX-CT93-0401).

J.A. Padget (Ed.): Human and Artificial Societies, LNAI 1624, pp. 30–42, 1999.

another reason to combine reflection and specifically dynamic object technology (i.e. dynamic typing, garbage collection, dynamic linking). Reflection aggravates data/control flow prediction and subsequent compiling optimizations. It is therefore obvious to add reflection to an object-oriented dynamic language, like Common Lisp or Smalltalk, which already trades flexibility against performance.

Computational reflection is the ability of a program to access its structure and state during execution [14]. Reading access—in the sense that a program observes and therefore reasons about its structure and execution state—is referred to as *introspection*. Modification of a program's structure and execution state by a program itself is called *intercession*. Both aspects of computational reflection, introspection and intercession, are based on *reification*, the encoding of program and execution state as data.

Reflection in computational systems is driven by demand for extended flexibility. Perhaps the simplest introspective operator is `type-of` which is typically provided in dynamically typed programming languages. The operator returns a value that represents the type of its argument and therefore reveals already a little insight into the representation of data during run-time. A bit more introspective information is necessary to write a generic walker to "walk" over arbitrary data structures including primitive and (possibly user defined) compound data structures. A print function could use such a generic walker to visualize arbitrary data structures in a nested way. In this case, introspection can help to find out about the length, type, structure and access of data objects.

Intercession can be useful to handle evolving models. Some problem domains are intrinsically dynamic and cannot be correctly represented by a static model in a computational system. Supposed, we have a network of classified nodes. Unpredictably, within the real world new nodes appear, which require to be added as well to the model. With regard to a specific feature which these new nodes incorporate (but no other node before), it may desirable to extend the hierarchy of node classes with a new class. Dynamic class creation is however only possible by modifying existing classes, i.e. by intercession.

The two most popular object-oriented dynamic languages, Smalltalk [5] and CLOS (Common Lisp Object System) [3,4], provide classes and methods as first-class objects so that partly, the object system itself can be implemented in terms of objects, classes and methods (reification). Since classes and methods are first-class values in the language, the structure and behaviour of the object system can be observed (inspection) and modified (intercession). The interface for inspection and intercession is generally known as meta-object protocol [7]. The essential idea of a meta-object protocol is to enable language users to adapt the semantics of the language to the particular needs of their applications.

In a similar vein, we investigate the combination of reflection and mobile software agents. Tools and languages for the development of mobile agents provide a primitive to let an agent move from one place to another. Typically the destination place is on a different machine so that the agent is suspended, serialized, transmitted, deserialized and finally resumed at the new location. The underlying hardware topology and the communication protocols as well as other aspects, like dynamic communication protocols, dynamic modification of behaviour, fault tolerance, monitoring, dynamic performance optimization etc., are generally inter-mangled with the application itself. Consequently, the complete application has to be rewritten when for instance the interprocess communication protocol has changed. Hence, applications are not portable.

By using *meta-agents* to handle all aspects of a multi-agent system which are not directly related to the application level, a clear separation can be achieved between the implementation and its environment as well as implementation details. In fact, it should be possible to switch between different kinds of interprocess communication (e.g. directly socket-based, MPI, http) without the need to change the multi-agent application. In general, development, maintenance and portability of multi-agent systems could be significantly enhanced by combining computational reflection with multi-agent systems.

The paper presents in Section 2 a mobile agent model that is combined in Section 3 with a meta-agent protocol. The protocol is driven by a need to have a facility to switch between different communication and migration protocols in a simple and flexible way. To be specific, we wanted to experiment with different architectures in the development of a multi-agent system modeling the Spanish Fishmarket [13]. Sections 4 and 5 present two examples how the agent model and its reflective facility can be used. Related work is discussed in Section 6. Finally, the appendix gives the detailed specification of the proposed meta-agent protocol.

2   The Agent Model

Our agent model is based on two different run-time concepts: agents and places. *Agents* are regarded as computational entities in a technical sense. An agent is always (with regard to its locus of execution) hosted by a *place*. The place where an agent starts execution for the first time is called *home*. Typically, several agents visit the same place at the same time, perform computations and possibly exchange *messages*. An agent can send messages only to agents at the same place. A place may be linked with other places so that agents can *migrate* from one place to another.

Our model is derived from actors [6,1,2] and the Telescript language [16]. Computation in actor systems is entirely based on concurrent message-passing between computational entities, called *actors*. In the original actor model, each actor has an address, a behaviour defined by a script, a list of addresses of acquainted actors to which messages can be passed and a link to an actor which deals with messages that cannot be understood. The basic operations on actors are send (sending messages), let (lexical scoping), cond (control flow branching) and become (state handling).

In contrast to computation in actor systems, we put less emphasize on the exchange of messages but focus on function calling. Most computation in our model is conceived as being performed by an extensible set of agent operations rather than exclusively by message-passing. We imagine operations as being defined within a full fledged programming language. However, the only way to communicate with other agents is by sending messages. The receipt of a message has no default impact on the computation of an agent, i.e. the agent application determines how the agent behaves when a particular message has arrived. In this sense, agents have no default behaviour.

The user is able to add and remove agent behaviour dynamically in the form of functions. On receipt of a message, all added functions which constitute the overall behaviour of an agent are subsequently applied with three arguments: (i) the receiving agent, (ii) the sending agent and (iii) the message itself. Within each function it has to be checked individually if a received message is considered (i.e. understood). If a message is not understood the function is simply aborted.

By sending a message to an agent, an optional function can be specified which is automatically invoked iff the agent receives a reply to the message being send. In fact, the reply function is added as behaviour which is removed again after a reply is handled[1]. In order to provide this functionality, messages are divided into requests and replies where reply/request pairs have identical identification numbers.

Places are mainly responsible for scheduling the visiting agents as well as adding and removing agents.

So far we have described in an abstract way the basic run-time concepts of an agent model which we take as a basis for a meta-agent protocol. The agent model is general enough to host features of higher-level agents, e.g. cooperation, autonomy, mobility and adaptability. Many aspects, like the grade of concurrency, the structure of messages and the semantics of behaviour, are deliberately excluded from the agent model. No particular notion of agent-hood is favourized as there is a broad dissension about the defining features of an agent [10].

3   A Meta-Agent Protocol

The main idea behind the meta-agent protocol as described in this paper is to handle the key functionality, i.e. message-passing and agent migration, not by agents themselves but by another computational entity called *meta-agent*. The meta-agent of an agent has operations to deal with tasks that can intuitively be described as being above the main task of an agent (i.e. in the meta-level). We do not specify whether meta-agents are agents by themselves. Hence, it depends on a specific implementation if meta-agents can send/receive messages and have a meta-agent assigned in the same way as they are meta-agents for other agent.

Figure 1 shows the level of indirection through the meta-level. Each agent is connected to an individual meta-agent, which contains information about the corresponding agent and provides an interface to handle messages and migration.

A portable agent application (with regard to different meta-agent implementations) is allowed to specialize structures and interfaces for places, agents and messages. As long as the required interfaces are provided, any meta-agent object

---

[1] Of course, part of the reply function could be to re-install the reply behaviour to handle further replies after a multi- or broadcast.

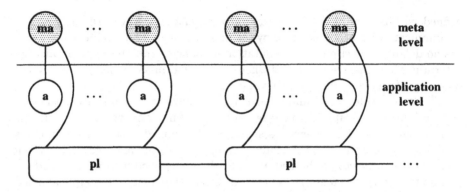

Fig. 1. Meta level and application level. Each agent a is linked to a meta-agent ma and vice versa. Communication between agents and migration of agents between places (pl) is controlled by meta-agents.

should be suitable to accompany an agent. The agent/meta-agent relationship is dynamic in the sense that a meta-agent object can be linked to an agent during its execution.

The protocol between agents, meta-agents and places is specified in Tables 3, 4 and 2. An agent is created with make-agent. The provided initial keyword list is used to create an agent object with a home place and a name. The accessor functions agent-name, agent-meta, home, place and behaviour are used to access the agent name, the associated meta-agent, the place of creation and the list of functions describing the agent behaviour. add-behaviour and remove-behaviour are used to modify agent behaviour. The function send is used to send messages between agents. If the message is a request and a function is supplied, a reply behaviour is added to the agent. The reply behaviour is automatically removed after the first matching reply for the request message. The actual sending is performed by the meta-agent object. Similarly, the migrate function uses the meta-agent to perform the actual migration of the agent object.

4   Example: Even/Odd Factorial

This section presents a small example on how the agent model can be used to implement a pair of agents (named even-factorial and odd-factorial) which exchange messages to compute the factorial function. As their names suggest, the first agent can only compute the factorial of even numbers, whereas the second agent's capability is limited to odd numbers.

The following function[2] is used to implement the behaviour of even-factorial:

```
(defun even-fact-behaviour (self from msg)
  (let ((x (message-body msg)))
    (cond
     ((or (replyp msg)
          (not (eq (message-subject msg) 'factorial))
          (oddp x))
      ;; ignore message
      ())
     ((< x 2)
      (let ((reply (make-reply to: msg reply: 1)))
        (send self from reply)))
     (t
      (let ((a (find-agent (place self) 'odd-factorial))
            (request (make-request subject: 'factorial body: (- x 1)))
            (reply-bhv (lambda (reply-to reply-from reply-msg)
                         (let* ((res (message-reply reply-msg))
                                (r (make-reply to: msg
                                               reply: (* res x))))
                           (send reply-to from r)))))
        (send self a request reply-bhv))))))
```

If the received message msg is a reply, the message subject not factorial or the body of msg is odd, the message is ignored. Otherwise, the cond-statement further distinguishes between values less than 2 and all other values. The former case results in a reply message with reply value 1. In the latter case, a corresponding agent to compute odd factorial numbers is looked up, a request message for (- x 1) is created and a reply behaviour is defined in order to break down the computation into multiplication. The reply behaviour reply-bhv specifies that the reply to the request to compute the factorial (- x 1) is multiplied with the current even value and finally returned to initial sender from.

5 Example: Socket Meta-Agent

The second example shows the actual benefit of the meta-agent protocol. By redefining the meta-agent function meta-migrate a multi-agent system can be used in a distributed fashion based on socket connections.

We assume two specialized kinds of places, namely local and remote socket places which are used for convenience reasons to store the relevant host name and port number. The meta-migrate function uses host and port information to establish a connection to a remote place daemon. Furthermore, an object stream os is connected to the socket connection to handle marshalling the agent/meta-agent couple. The function setter is used in the expression (setter

---

[2] The function is written in EuLisp [12,11] which is in the way it is used here very similar to the Scheme programming language.

meta-place) to to retrieve the funtion for re-setting the meta-place slot at the meta-agent ma.

```
(defun meta-migrate (ma pl)
  (let ((c (make <connection> host: (place-host pl)
                             port: (place-port pl)))
        (os (make <object-stream> mode: 'w)))
    (connect os c)
    (unwind-protect
        (progn
          (write ma os)
          (remove-agent (meta-place ma) (agent ma))
          ((setter meta-place) ma ()))
      (disconnect os))))
```

Local socket places are created with an initial function placed which runs a place daemon. If a connection is established to the daemon, an agent can be read from the object-stream os and added to the list of visiting agents using add-agent.

```
(defun placed (pl)
  (let (c)
    (unwind-protect
        (while (setq c (make <connection> socket: (place-socket pl)))
          (let ((os (make <object-stream> mode: 'r)))
            (connect os c)
            (let ((ma (read os () ())))
              (add-agent pl (agent ma))
              ((setter meta-place) ma pl))
            (disconnect c)))
      (disconnect c))))
```

6   Related Work

Dynamic modification of the semantics of message delivery in actor-based architectures was one of the objectives to have reflection in ABCL/R [15]. In this approach, each agent can reason about and act upon the agent itself by using a meta-object, which represents the structural/behavioural aspects of an agent. Later, the reflective facility was extended into group-wide reflection [9]. This work is focused on group communication and message delivery. However, in this paper we tried to address agent communication *and* migration in one protocol.

Meta-*object* protocols have been discussed in depth in the context of Lisp, particularly Common Lisp [7]. Here, the protocol is used to provide access to the semantics of the Common Lisp Object System (CLOS). Message sending (apart from method invocation) and object migration is not addressed with the reflective capabilities of CLOS. Furthermore, meta-object protocols are designed for object-oriented languages and their particular features, like dynamic method lookup, class instantiation, etc. With meta agent protocols, as presented here, objects (i.e. agents, meta-agents, places) are not necessarily instances of classes in the object-oriented sense and the focus is on message sending and migration only.

7   Conclusions

We discussed the objectives of introducing a meta-agent protocol to communicating mobile agents. Meta-agent protocols can help to provide a clear separation between application level and meta level. Communication, dynamic change of behaviour as well as fault-tolerance, monitoring and dynamic performance optimization can be isolated from the pure application relevant parts of an agent-based system, thus leading to modular and portable application components.

Clearly, not all of the potentials of meta-agent protocols have been discussed here. However, we believe, the provided specification is helpful to explore the design space when developing meta-agent protocols or introducing reflection to communicating mobile agents in general. The protocol is intentionally vague in aspects, like message semantics and concurrency, in order to achieve a general applicability.

References

1. G. Agha. *Actors—A Model of Concurrent Computation for Distributed Systems*. The MIT Press, 1986.
2. G. Agha and C. Hewitt. Actors: A conceptual foundation for concurrent object-oriented programming. In B. Shriver and P. Wegner, editors, *Research Directions in Object-Oriented Programming*, pages 49–74. MIT Press, 1987.
3. American National Standards Institute and Information Technology Industry Council. *American National Standard for Information Technology: programming language — Common LISP*. American National Standards Institute, 1996.
4. D. G. Bobrow, L. G. DeMichiel, R. P. Gabriel, S. E. Keene, G. Kiczales, and D. A. Moon. Common LISP object system specification X3J13 document 88-002R. *ACM SIGPLAN Notices*, 23, 1988. Special Issue, September 1988.
5. A. Goldberg and D. Robson. *Smalltalk-80: The Language and its Implementation*. Addison-Wesley, 1983.
6. C. Hewitt. Viewing control structures as patterns of passing messages. *Artificial Intelligence*, (8):323–364, 1977.
7. G. Kiczales, J. des Rivières, and D. Bobrow. *The Art of the Metaobject Protocol*. MIT Press, Cambridge, Massachusetts, 1991.
8. P. Maes. Concepts and experiments in computational reflection. In *Proceedings of the Conference on Object-Oriented Programming Systems, Languages, and Applications (OOPSLA)*, pages 147–155. ACM Press, December 1987.
9. S. Matsuoka, T. Watanabe, and A. Yonezawa. Hybrid group reflective architecture for object-oriented concurrent reflective programming. *Lecture Notes in Computer Science*, 512:231–??, 1991.
10. H. S. Nwana. Software agents: An overview. *Knowledge Engineering Review*, 11(3):205–244, September 1996.

11. J. Padget and G. Nuyens (Eds.). The EuLisp Definition. Version 0.99; available from ftp://ftp.maths.bath.ac.uk, 1992.

12. J. Padget, G. Nuyens, and H. Bretthauer. An overview of EuLisp. *Lisp and Symbolic Computation*, 6(1/2):9–98, August 1993.

13. J. A. Rodríguez, P. Noriega, C. Sierra, and J. A. Padget. FM96.5 A Java-based Electronic Auction House. In *Second International Conference on The Practical Application of Intelligent Agents and Multi-Agent Technology: PAAM'97*, 1997.

14. B. C. Smith. Reflection and semantics in Lisp. In *Conference Record of the Eleventh Annual ACM Symposium on Principles of Programming Languages*, pages 23–35. ACM, January 1984.

15. T. Watanabe and A. Yonezawa. Reflection in an Object-Oriented Concurrent Language. In *Proceedings of the OOPSLA '88 Conference on Object-oriented Programming Systems, Languages and Applications*, pages 306–315, November 1988. Published as ACM SIGPLAN Notices, volume 23, number 11.

16. J. White. Mobile agents white paper. Technical report, General Magic, 1996.

A   Specification of the Meta-Agent Protocol

This appendix specifies the meta-agent protocol as described in Sections 2 and 3.

The arguments can be thought of as typed with the convention m is a request or reply message; r is a reply message; pl is a place; a is an agent; ma is a meta-agent and fun is a function.

In keyword lists values are preceded by keywords (e.g. (key1: 42 key2: "abc")).

Function:	`make-request`
Arguments:	`inits`
Result:	request message object
Description:	The keyword list `inits` is used to create a request object. The keywords `subject:` and `body:` are accepted. The keyword `subject:` is required. A message identification (see `message-id`) is generated.
Function:	`make-reply`
Arguments:	`inits`
Result:	reply message object
Description:	The keyword list `inits` is used to create a reply object. The keywords `to:` and `reply:` are accepted. The keyword `to:` is required must be followed by a request message object. The created reply has the same identification, subject and body as the supplied request.
Function:	`message-id`
Arguments:	`(m)`
Result:	identification of message m
Function:	`message-subject`
Arguments:	`(m)`
Result:	subject of message m
Function:	`message-body`
Arguments:	`(m)`
Result:	body of message m
Function:	`message-reply`
Arguments:	`(r)`
Result:	reply of message r

Table 1. *Message Interface*

Function:	make-place
Arguments:	inits
Result:	place object
Description:	The keyword list inits is used to create a place object. The keywords **name:** and **function:** are accepted. The value after the keyword **function:** must be a function with one argument and determines the initial function of the place. The function is applied to the created place on a new thread of execution.

Function:	place-name
Arguments:	(pl)
Result:	name of place pl

Function:	agents
Arguments:	(pl)
Result:	list of agent objects visiting place pl

Function:	add-agent
Arguments:	(pl a)
Result:	pl
Description:	Add agent a as visiting agent to place pl.

Function:	remove-agent
Arguments:	(pl a)
Result:	pl
Description:	Remove agent a as visiting agent from place pl.

Function:	neighbour-places
Arguments:	(pl)
Result:	list of place objects which are neighbours to place pl

Function:	add-neighbour-place
Arguments:	(pl1 pl2)
Result:	pl1
Description:	Add place pl2 as neighbour to place pl1.

Function:	remove-neighbour-place
Arguments:	(pl1 pl2)
Result:	pl1
Description:	Remove place pl2 as neighbour from place pl1.

Function:	start-place
Arguments:	(pl)
Result:	pl
Description:	Start thread with function specified with **make-place** and argument place pl.

Function:	shutdown-place
Arguments:	(pl)
Result:	pl
Description:	Send visiting agent home and suspend remaining threads at place pl.

Table 2. *Place Interface*

Function:	make-agent
Arguments:	inits
Result:	agent object
Description:	The keyword list inits is used to create an agent object. The keywords name: and home: are accepted. The value after the keyword home: must be a place object. The agent is assigned a meta-agent object using make-meta-agent (see Table 4).

Function:	agent-name
Arguments:	(a)
Result:	name of agent a

Function:	agent-meta
Arguments:	(a)
Result:	meta-agent object linked to agent a

Function:	home
Arguments:	(a)
Result:	place object where agent a was initially created
Description:	The function uses meta-home (see Table 4).

Function:	place
Arguments:	(a)
Result:	place object which agent a is currently visiting
Description:	The function uses meta-place (see Table 4).

Function:	behaviour
Arguments:	(a)
Result:	list of functions which constitute the behaviour of agent a
Description:	The function uses meta-behaviour (see Table 4).

Function:	add-behaviour
Arguments:	(a fun)
Result:	a
Description:	The function fun is added to the list of functions that define the behaviour of agent a. The function uses meta-add-behaviour (see Table 4).

Function:	remove-behaviour
Arguments:	(a fun)
Result:	a
Description:	The function fun is removed from the list of functions that define the behaviour of agent a. The function uses meta-remove-behaviour (see Table 4).

Function:	send
Arguments:	(a1 a2 m . fun)
Result:	a1
Description:	Agent a1 sends message m to agent a2. If m is a request message and a function fun is supplied, a reply behaviour is added. The reply behaviour is automatically removed after the first matching reply for m arrives, i.e. the identification of m and the reply message are identical. The function send uses meta-send (see Table 4).

Function:	migrate
Arguments:	(a pl)
Result:	a
Description:	Agent a is moved from its current place to place pl. The function uses meta-migrate (see Table 4).

Table 3. *Agent Interface*

Function:	make-meta-agent
Arguments:	inits
Result:	agent object
Description:	The keyword list inits is used to create a meta-agent object. The keywords agent: and home: are accepted. The value after the keyword agent: must be an agent object. The value after the keyword home: must be a place object. The function is used by make-agent (see Table 3).

Function:	agent
Arguments:	(ma)
Result:	agent object linked to meta-agent ma

Function:	meta-home
Arguments:	(ma)
Result:	place object where the agent of the meta-agent ma was initially created
Description:	The function is used by home (see Table 3).

Function:	meta-place
Arguments:	(ma)
Result:	place object which the agent of the meta-agent ma is currently visiting
Description:	The function is used by place (see Table 3).

Function:	meta-behaviour
Arguments:	(ma)
Result:	list of functions that define the behaviour of the agent of the meta-agent ma
Description:	The function is used by behaviour (see Table 3).

Function:	meta-add-behaviour
Arguments:	(ma fun)
Result:	ma
Description:	The function fun is added to the list of functions that define the behaviour of the agent of the meta-agent ma. The function is used by add-behaviour (see Table 3).

Function:	meta-remove-behaviour
Arguments:	(ma fun)
Result:	ma
Description:	The function fun is removed from the list of functions that define the behaviour of the agent of the meta-agent ma. The function is used by remove-behaviour (see Table 3).

Function:	meta-send
Arguments:	(ma1 ma2 m . fun)
Result:	ma1
Description:	The agent of the meta-agent ma1 sends message m to the agent of the meta-agent ma2. If m is a request message and a function fun is supplied, a reply behaviour is added. The reply behaviour is automatically removed after the first matching reply for m arrives, i.e. the identification of m and the reply message are identical. The function meta-send is used by send (see Table 3).

Function:	meta-migrate
Arguments:	(ma pl)
Result:	ma
Description:	The agent of the meta-agent ma is moved from its current place to place pl. The function is used by migrate (see Table 3).

Table 4. *Meta-agent interface*

Examples of Fuzziness in Compilers and Runtime Systems

Angela C. Sodan

GMD FIRST, Rudower Chaussee 5, 12489 Berlin, Germany

Abstract. In this paper, we review some techniques used in compilers and runtime systems for parallel and distributed computation, involving aspects of fuzziness. Fuzziness is in a general sense considered as being present if the techniques applied classify, rate or otherwise handle information with some range of tolerance, if they operate with similarities, uncertainties, or do not seek for perfect/optimal solutions (but apply heuristics or approximations). In many cases, fuzziness, in this sense, is already used but may need a better theoretical basis; and in others, its integration may improve approaches, opens up new perspectives or become relevant for future applications, as in distributed computing. In this paper, we focus on the potential application of fuzzy theory, providing a simplified – but in many cases sufficiently accurate – approach on sound theoretical principles. Other important theoretical approaches – as far as they are applied in compilers for dealing with approximateness – are the determination of bounds guaranteeing minimal quality or maximal runtime, or statistics providing means and variances. As a spin-off, so to speak, the paper investigates – from the point of the user – the various forms and benefits of fuzziness, concluding with a brief philosophical discussion of fuzziness.

1   Introduction

In compilers, much of the information we deal with has to be exact and certain. For example, language syntax and semantics have to be precise and unambiguous. And compilers are required to compile programs in such a way that their semantics are completely preserved, despite any transformations or optimizations that may be applied internally. This is true of compilers in general, and for parallelization in particular it means that sequential code can only be transformed into parallel code, if the absence of conflicting data and control dependencies can be guaranteed. Thus, on the one hand, verification is a desirable goal, support being increasingly provided by theory and formal methods. On the other hand, it means that the basic principle in compiler construction is to perform certain and safe actions with respect to the application semantics. Furthermore, decisions should be taken from a discrete – and crisp – set of possibilities, applying or not applying a specific transformation or implementation strategy.

However, fuzziness – used here in the general sense of uncertainty and approximateness – is or may be frequently involved. In principle, fuzziness can be

J.A. Padget (Ed.): Human and Artificial Societies, LNAI 1624, pp. 43–61, 1999.

applied if it does not result in faulty behavior. Thus, fuzziness is often appropriate where performance is the "only" concern. It appears, then, most frequently in connection with some kind of discrete optimization, e.g. in code generation or static task scheduling: the optimization criteria are relaxed – heuristics often then being applied – thus potentially reducing the runtime complexity of the compiler significantly, perhaps even by several orders of magnitude. The reduction in the efficiency of the resulting code may, on the other hand, be acceptably low, e.g.10% of the optimal program runtime. Currently, discrete optimization is becoming even increasingly relevant as the number of these kinds of problems grows, e.g. task or data mapping to parallel machines, complex transformations, or configuration in distributed systems. Other examples of the potential involvement of fuzziness are: abstracting classifications (e.g. of application-characterizing data), allowing decision making at a higher – and usually more effective – level, fuzzy weighing of trade-off decisions, and fuzzy transitions between different implementation strategies by variations in their realization.

In this paper, we give several examples of the presence or application of fuzziness in compiler and runtime systems. In doing so, we also discuss the different ways in which fuzziness occurs and can be exploited to advantage. Our considerations are mainly concerned with fuzzy theory, which is quite promising as regards the provision of a good theoretical framework. Fuzzy theory has already been practically applied with great success in fuzzy control and is currently being extended to logic reasoning in terms of its theoretical framework, this being what is mostly required in the context of compilers and runtime systems. Our own experience with a fuzzy inference system (based on fuzzy pre-selection rules) for a specific configuration task demonstrated that fuzzy theory can really be very helpful in the compiler field. Theoretical approaches currently in use are the derivation of bounds for runtime complexity or minimal quality of the result. Although this constitutes an important basis, more subtle ratings of the intermediate ranges are often desirable as well. Fuzzy theory is a promising approach here, but other approaches like statistics, neural networks, or special constraint-solving techniques [3] may in many cases also be applied or may actually be superior. In any case, domain-specific metrics that quantify the attached fuzziness are then required.

We begin by briefly introducing the basic ideas of fuzzy theory, and then give examples of the different kinds of fuzziness occurring in the compiler and runtime system. We then go on outline the philosophical background of fuzziness. A summary concludes the paper.

2   Fuzzification of Theories

Fuzziness is always attached to some crisp, sound theory. One of the original motivations of Zadeh [23] – who introduced fuzzy theory in 1965 – was the recognition that reality never matches the ideal, and that some means for bridging the gap is needed. In Western thinking, the crisp/logical view was long time predominant, the introduction of fuzziness being considered some sort of paradigm shift. On the other hand, the crisp theories now offer the essential basic skeleton to which fuzziness is attached.

Fuzzy sets form the basis of fuzzy theory. They are a generalization of ordinary sets, allowing us to define degrees of membership – and thus degrees of certainty – as a number in the interval [0,1], see Fig. 1. Usually, we have a core with membership 1, borders with 0 values, and a gradual, smooth transition between the 0 and 1 areas. Thus, the distinguishing characteristic of fuzzy sets is that they are defined by membership functions, mapping values of arbitrary input-domain metrics' scales to the interval [0,1].

Fig. 1. Rectangular and triangular membership functions – the simplest and most frequently used ones.

Theories are fuzzified by their variables' or symbolic terms' becoming fuzzy sets. Fuzziness can be quantified and explicitly dealt with by carrying it along in the argumentation of the basic theory to which it is attached. The main application of fuzzy sets is fuzzy logic, defining the logical operators AND, OR, NOT, and IMPLICATION on fuzzy sets by determining specific operations for combining the fuzzy sets. There is no one single way to do this, but rather a variety of possibilities, each having its own rationale. Fuzzy inference is defined on the basis of these fuzzy-logic operators. Furthermore, fuzzy inference includes fuzzification of input data and a defuzzification of the internal data to deliver the output. The input data is fuzzified by mapping the input value using the fuzzy membership functions to their degrees of membership. Then, these are combined in antecedents of rules, and again the obtained fuzzy values of consequences in fired rules are combined – all according to the operators defined. Finally, the value obtained is defuzzified, i.e. it is mapped by a defuzzification function to a crisp value in the output domain, e.g. a yes/no decision or a specific real value (like a control parameter). For more basic information on fuzzy theory see the excellent textbook of Klir and Yuan [7]. A brief introduction to and overview of its current successful practical application in the form of fuzzy control is given by Munakata and Jani in [12]. For a basic discussion of fuzzy-theory benefits see also [13] or [5].

Generally, fuzzy theory enables us to explicitly deal with and quantify the respective degree of uncertainty, and handle transitions and overlapping in membership.

3   Examples of Fuzziness

3.1   Classification of Quantitative and Qualitative Application Characteristics

My co-researcher Vicenc Torra and I defined a (fuzzy) inference system for automating configuration of strategies in a system offering multiple implementation strategies of which those best suited to the application characteristics can be selected (for details, see next section) [19,21]. Examples of application characteristics considered in our specific context (mapping dynamic tree-like control structures to a parallel machine) are, for example, runtime in potential processes, argument sizes, the amount of data allocated, or the degree of irregularity in the tree. These characteristics are quantifiable by metrics on continuous scales like seconds or bytes. The characteristics' values are then classified in symbolic terms to allow the construction of rules and the taking of higher-level configuration decisions. For example, symbolic classifications of arguments are "small" or "large", being fuzzy in nature. This involves – as some kind of integrative function — **abstraction from potentially different input domains** (such as seconds and bytes). The input domains then are either a continuous scale or lower-level terms (in the case of hierarchical characteristic composition). **As a basic application and benefit of fuzzy sets, such classes can be defined with fuzzy and overlapping membership** (see Fig. 2). Drawing hard boundaries would be a rather questionable undertaking – not only because input data might be uncertain to some degree, but mainly because minimal differences in data might have completely different consequences. However, at least in our system context, slight changes in application parameters usually have only a minor impact on overall performance. In such cases, there are often fuzzy transitions with respect to the appropriateness of strategies, meaning that within specific characteristic ranges different strategies result in acceptable – or even not greatly different – performance (see also [17]). Furthermore, because the final global configuration usually consists of several strategies and – as is well known – the locally best decisions do not necessarily lead to the global optimum, the final selection should be made on the basis of more than one criterion and more than one applicable rule. In other words, a more or less holistic, context-related view should be taken. Thus, all acceptable possibilities should be left open, no hasty decisions being made on the basis of individual reductive subconsiderations. **Fuzzy inference has the significant benefit that rules can be fired on a usually larger scale, and with fuzzy degrees of certainty, and that the consequences of the fired rules can be combined, considering all acceptable possibilities in relation to each other and selecting the globally best – or a globally good – solution.** It thus helps us overcome to some degree the deficiency of reductive rule systems, as criticized e.g. by Minsky [11].

While the configuration in our example considered only one specific machine context, in extensions to configuration in distributed systems, different target characteristics may have to be considered. Especially in this extended application context, we are often faced with decisions based on qualitative char-

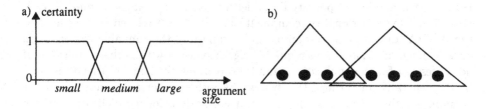

Fig. 2. Classification of a) quantifiable and b) qualitative parameters by means of fuzzy sets and their membership functions.

acteristics. In other words, characteristics may also be crisp (or discrete). When considering different potential target systems, crisp classifications may be, for example, processor type (quantifications like processor speed may be desirable as well), whether memory is shared or distributed, which basic software packages and communication systems are available, or structural information (like network topologies). To find a matching assignment, the requirements for target characteristics may be crisp or fuzzy, e.g. that a floating-point CPU be highly recommended or that the memory be shared. Finding matching assignments **inherently has the potential for applying fuzzy similarity (to match the requirements) or applying fuzzy classifications again, performed also on qualitative information and discrete objects**. For example, generalized processor or memory-system classes may be formed. In this case, gradual membership and fuzzy transitions between classes may be important, too. Fuzzy membership can then be defined on the elements of sets of discrete objects (see Fig. 2). Conceptually, from the point of view of using fuzzy sets, there is not much difference – whether something is continuous or discrete can even be considered a matter of observation distance.

Fuzzy classification on discrete objects may also have an important application in the analysis phase, such as for the automatic recognition of specific program patterns (for which efficient implementation techniques may then be exploitable), as performed by the Vienna FORTRAN compiler [4].

3.2   Configuration in Multiple-Strategy and/or Multiple-Application/Multiple-Target Environments

In the current phase of the synthesis and growing complexity of applications, multiple-strategy systems are becoming increasingly important. No single strategy performs well for all kinds of application, and if there are generalizing theories, they still need – for optimal performance – different specialized implementations, chosen according to the characteristics of the application in hand. Examples of multiple-strategy systems are: the above-mentioned mapping system, offering several strategies for dynamic granularity determination and load balancing [17]; the PEACE parallel operating system [6], consisting of a small kernel and a number of potentially added packages (e.g. single or multithreading) of varying functionality, complexity and – closely related – efficiency; or the APPLY Lisp system compiling and configuring the runnable system with only as much functionality as required (e.g. dispensing with garbage collection if not necessary for the application) and thus avoiding the large overhead imposed by the generality of earlier LISP systems. Another important – more general – example are the various existing loop transformations for parallelization, which may provide different benefits in different contexts and may even conflict with one another [1]. These systems all basically refer to a single-target environment. Distributed systems – becoming increasingly important with growing world-wide interconnection – are another example basically posing the problem of mapping multiple applications with potentially different requirements to multiple heterogeneous targets (which may still offer multiple implementation strategies). However, despite the growing significance of multiple-strategy systems, there is still a lack of solutions for automatic configuration, one example being the work of Berman and Wolski [2].

Configuration is basically a combinatorial, i.e. discrete, optimization problem of high complexity. Thus, it is essential to apply domain knowledge to limit search complexity. In the mapping system, we extracted a set of rules (see Fig. 3) incorporating such knowledge about criteria for selecting strategies in relation to application characteristics and a single target environment. Final configurations usually consist of several strategies that must fulfill some – certain – compatibility constraints. The theoretical goal is to find the configuration that provides globally optimal performance (maximum speedup or minimal runtime) for the application in question – or, in practical terms, a close-to-optimum configuration.

(correlation-arg $(DARG_{in,task}, DT_{subtree,task})$ **AND**
    NOT **(correlation-depth** $(DRD, DT_{subtree,task})$ = *strong*) $\Rightarrow$
    granularity-by-argument
(arg-size $(DARG_{task})$ = *small*) **OR shrink-sublinearly** $(DARG_{task})$ $\Rightarrow$
    (distributed-creation = *high-prob*)

Fig. 3. Examples of rules in the fuzzy inference system for mapping.

For the mapping system, the rules are based on mostly quantified fuzzy application characteristics, as described in the previous section. The rules also contain fuzziness in their consequences in the form of preference values. As mentioned earlier, there may be gradual transitions between strategies with respect to their performance. Furthermore, a global cost function (i.e. a unifying formula describing the performance of all strategies and substrategies and their potential compatible combinations) is not (yet) available in this field, and the rules thus express partial knowledge with respect to e.g. partial cost relations or theoretical complexity investigations (such as the fact that load balancing must be hierarchically structured in order to be scalable for large numbers of machine nodes).

Fuzzy logic allows us to represent such a gradual appropriateness or vague knowledge. The configuration was automated by a fuzzy-inference system based on the formalized rules mentioned above [19]. Several strategies are selected as candidates by firing the rules and configurations are formed combinatorially from (only) them with the potential of selecting a globally good configuration, as discussed in the previous section. However, fuzziness and the flexibility available during combination had to be limited by stagewise defuzzification to avoid undesirable intermixing of the fuzzy conclusions and to properly reflect causal-logical chains [21]. The fuzzy values attached to the selected strategies (values resulting from the combination of the propagated fuzziness in antecedents and the basic fuzziness in the conclusion) are ultimately used to rank the global configurations obtained (based on the value distances to the ultimately made defuzzification yielding a crisp strategy). In other words, **the fuzziness carried along the rule application can quantify the quality of the obtained solutions.** However, this rating itself is rather fuzzy in our application context, because the performance of strategies depends to some degree on their parameterizations (such as granularity sizes or load-balancing thresholds) – performed after configurations have been composed – and ranges of good performance may then overlap. Thus, several configurations are delivered, their order, however, providing some indication of their appropriateness.

Configuration in multiple-application/multiple-target contexts is of increased complexity because of the higher dimensionality of the decision space, and there may be a large set of – potentially conflicting – requirements to be met. Thus, it may be important to relax the requirements and introduce as large as possible a tolerance range for each individual requirement in order to increase the chance of finding a globally satisfactory solution. **Here, fuzzy sets allow the description of tolerance ranges, but also enable us to distinguish different degrees of desirability.** Note that, in this respect especially, some specific weak-constraint-solving techniques offer solutions, too.

3.3   Performance Ranges

In the configuration described above, the optimization criterion was performance. Assuming that full estimations are possible for the parameterized configurations, their speedup curves may overlap, and more than one configuration may perform well within specific parameter ranges. If rules do not yet sufficiently prune the search space, we may refrain from trying to find the optimal solution – a perfect speedup is usually not necessary, just a sufficiently good one (e.g. it does not usually matter much whether speedup is, say, 18.2 or 18.5) – and use the knowledge about the performance ranges to reduce the search effort (see Fig. 4a). Then, the minimal speedup (and also potentially a desirable speedup in combination with a search-time limit) can be used to stop the search when a reasonably good solution has been found. Note that the minimal speedup value can make the search space narrower or broader. The application may influence settings by its sensitivity to performance differences or specific constraints such

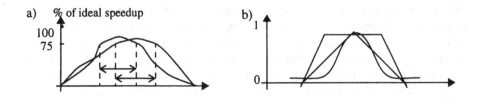

Fig. 4. Performance ranges as a) acceptable-speedup ranges in solutions and b) variation ranges including lower/upper bounds.

as possible granularities (often formable in specific discrete steps only and limited by the problem size). Note that, unlike the example in the previous section, relaxing requirements here refers to the quality of the global solution. **Fuzzy sets are used to obtain an approximate solution (instead of insisting on the optimal one), while reducing the effort required to obtain the solution, thus allowing us to express again both ranges and different degrees of acceptability.** The approximate solution can, however, not normally estimate the difference from the achievable optimum (dependent on the characteristics of the application and the system, and requiring – if no rough overall estimation can be made – that all relevant configurations be tried), but only the distance from the ideal speedup.

If performance ranges are calculable in advance, independently of a specific application, they can also be used for determining the ratings of the configurations. More generally, in hierarchical systems with multiple layers of strategies, ratings may summarize performance ranges at the lower level and allow preselections of configurations worth investigating further and are being refined by considering the subconfigurations or parameterizations.

Another form of performance ranges occurs when there is performance indeterminacy, e.g. in the hardware, in the application behavior (such as varying task runtimes and numbers, sizes of dynamic data structures, or garbage-collection initiation and running times) or subtle unpredictable interactions between the components of a system (e.g. when application behavior and dynamic load balancing affect each other). Such indeterminacy has to be dealt with, for example, in rating algorithms, in real-time control, and in the configuration of parallel systems. The potential variations in runtime are important in performance (cost) estimations for making decisions in compilers between different implementations, for guaranteeing reaction times in real-time systems, or for rating the quality of algorithms, implementation strategies, or network communication systems. Variation should be limited, and bounds should be certain and as narrow as possible here, because this increases the degree of predictability (the broader the range, the more indeterministic and fuzzy is performance behavior). This, of course, has to be dealt with and ensured at the implementation and modeling levels. However, fuzzy theory may be useful when rating and selecting global solutions composed of several – potentially hierarchical – subsystems that inherently contain some indeterminacy. **The potential overall spread of fuzziness can be quantified by the fuzzy-set intervals, membership functions being able to model both bounds and varying degrees of probability within bounds. Thus, distribution functions can be approximated, while a closed form is created by the establishment of hard boundaries** (see Fig. 4b).

3.4 Data Distributions

Data-distribution problems involving fuzziness occur in different forms, e.g. hardware caching, Virtual Shared Memory (VSM – similar to Virtual Memory on sequential machines – performs automatic, implicit transfer and software caching of data), dynamic remapping or dynamic load balancing. On distributed-memory parallel machines, proper data distribution is important, significantly influencing performance. It becomes an especially difficult problem if data structures are irregular and dynamic, as in adaptive grid calculations. In some cases, it is quite impossible to solve this problem statically; in others, it may be partly solvable with increased compiler effort. Dynamic self-organizing techniques such as those mentioned above are then often applied. However, these impose extra overhead – e.g. in dynamic load balancing, the exchange of status and sending requests – and make runtimes less predictable (i.e. fuzzier). Thus, the compiler should perform data distribution statically, where possible, with acceptable effort (again, complexity may make perfect solutions impractical) while leaving the rest – where certainty about data accesses is not available or too costly to obtain – to the dynamic approaches. Thus, compilers may perform proper cache or page alignment to minimize the data transfer (avoiding thrashing). Generally, there may be a trade-off between compiler effort (if analysis is in principle possible) and the efficiency of the generated code. Furthermore, a gradual transition may be possible, not only in the current choice, but also as an evolutionary process during users' program or the compiler development. For example, VSM allows easy porting of programs from shared to distributed memories, first applying the dynamic approach and later on rewriting the programs or adding more analysis in the compiler, when more effort can be invested or understanding increases. Similar arguments apply to fine-grained multithreading, which is less sensitive to an imperfect mapping (thanks to their fast remote access times and latency hiding) but which nevertheless achieves even better performance with proper mapping. Generally, hybrid approaches are likely to perform best.

Fuzzy trade-offs also occur in many compiler and runtime-system decisions, as well as in dynamic load balancing or dynamic remapping, i.e. periodic global data redistributions such as used in problems like adaptive grid calculation with dynamic refinement of specific mesh area (see Fig. 5). Dynamic-remapping cost may be quite high and must be weighed against the cost of tolerating some imbalance (see [8]). A fuzzy membership function with varying degrees of desirability may be defined, but currently only interval boundaries are used as thresholds for remapping initiation. Similar arguments apply to dynamic load balancing where too fine-grained balancing may be too costly. Thus, in all these examples, **fuzziness occurs in terms of trade-offs for weighing alternative decisions with fuzzy transitions, seeking the global optimum and the switching point at which one or the other decision is of greater benefit**.

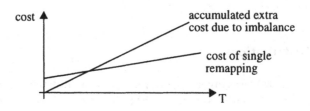

Fig. 5. Trade-offs for remapping.

Another context in which fuzziness may occur is adaptive dynamic load balancing, where parameter settings – and potentially even specific substrategies – may be changed dynamically in accordance with changing application behavior. Here, there is some similarity to **fuzzy control, which operates with one-stage rules in a recurrent mode** using feedback from the controlled system and proved quite stable, i.e. not overly sensitive to minor variations in the controlling parameters. Similarly, in adaptive load balancing, criteria may be evaluated by simple fuzzy rules (that have to be kept extremely simple to be fast enough), mutual influences between strategies and application behavior may require that the control parameters settle at a specific value.

3.5   Classification of Approaches

In many cases, approaches used in compilers or runtime systems also have fuzzy transitions with respect to the features they offer, their performance, and their

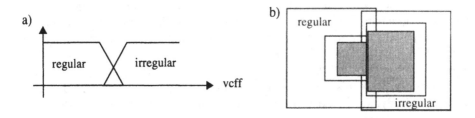

Fig. 6. a) Fuzzy transitions between dual characteristics quantified by the variation coefficient of some parameter. b) Subsets of regular and irregular applications taking advantage of fine-grained multithreading (dark grey), subsets having fuzzy transitions (light grey).

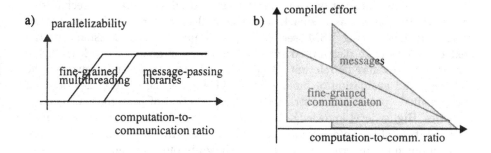

Fig. 7. a) Fuzzy transitions between the capacity of two communication approaches for parallelizing applications depending on the computation-to-communication ratio. b) Fuzzy transitions between the effort required in compilers (or by users) for aggregating communications or computations and performing appropriate mappings.

apppropriateness for specific kinds of applications. Dual classifications are often applied to system approaches and the application behavior. For example, application behavior may be irregular or regular; or for data-transfer either remote-data access in fine-grained multithreaded systems or message passing may be used. Instead of a crisp differentiation, it is more appropriate to consider fuzzy transitions between the poles – as shown in Fig. 6a. Similarly as shown in Fig. 7a, cases in which one or the other system approach is appropriate depending on the application characteristics – may have fuzzy transitions and overlappings. Figure 7b shows similar transitions for the related compiler effort. And there may also be fuzzy transitions in the related subsets (see Fig. 6b) when matching application characteristics and system approaches, this view being more realistic than the usual rigid one that binds multithreading to irregular applications.

In many cases of this sort, full quantifications are not yet possible, but even a briefly sketched classification may be helpful for taking rough decisions. **Basing our view on the existence of fuzzy transitions can generally help to improve qualitative understanding** and, more specifically, **relax the contrariness of dual approaches**. Qualitative understanding is the step usually preceding quantification – since for quantification we need to know what to quantify. In the context of classification, fuzzy sets may also be used to **express different personal preferences and expert opinions, i.e. allowing us deal with subjectivity and to abstract from it to some degree**. Figure 6b also shows that fuzzy theory defines not only varying degrees of membership, but also **the degree to which one set is a subset of another one**.

3.6 Performance Monitoring

Performance monitoring is used to obtain information about performance behavior that is not amenable to static estimation (or too costly to extract, cf.

Sect. 3.4). This information can then be used to adapt dynamic mechanisms or – more typically – as feedback to the compiler or user to help find bottle-necks (e.g. when using VSM, see [22]) or to improve static decisions for the next compilation. In distributed systems, information about network traffic or user preferences may be relevant. Basically, monitoring potentially involves the collection and evaluation of bulks of data. Of interest here are either detailed event chains – potentially abstracted for the detection of patterns – or general statistics. Higher-level knowledge-based tools may be built on top for automatic interpretation of the information, as is the case in automatic concept detection [4] or in our mapping system. As we have shown in our approach, in such cases it can be helpful to apply fuzzy inference. Fuzziness may also be used here as a partial **tolerance of uncertain input**. It is important to note that infor-mation is not only obtained by bottom-up evaluation; most current tools offer selective abstract specifications controlling, from the higher-level semantics of the program, which information is to be collected or filtered.

Another important fact – adding a new aspect of fuzziness – is the uncertainty potential involved, namely that – similar to the uncertainty law in physics – the observation can influence the observed, known in monitoring as the probe effect. For example, communication or cache behavior may be changed by the insertion of monitoring code. In some cases, the sensitivity to disturbance depends on the degree of indeterminacy in the program (in a well-designed program, indetermi-nacy should be limited), but in most cases – like the cache behavior – the granu-larity of the observation in relation to the observed code has the most significant influence. Generally, then, **uncertainty is introduced by monitoring, and it is the greater, the smaller the granularity of the observation**. This not only means that monitoring code has to be carefully designed, but also that **relative details cannot be measured and uncertainty about them has to be accepted** (see Fig. 8). Note that here a special case of trade-offs occur – as discussed in Sect. 3.4. Fuzzy theory may help us to quantify this trade-off. Furthermore, even a generalization of the uncertainty law of quantum mechanics to other systems with canonically conjugated variables and their measurement may be possible.

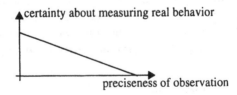

Fig. 8. Trade-offs in monitoring.

3.7 Reliability

Much effort is expended on making software development safer, i.e. on obtaining reliable software. An important branch of research here is formal specification. Tools are available for verifying software by analysis and model checking. Furthermore, testing is applied either additionally or on its own, preferably based on a proper theory. Systematic testing and progress toward incrementally increasing reliability during the stepwise testing procedure should be ensured, and the degree of reliability that can be guaranteed should be quantifiable. Although it is not yet clear whether fuzzy theory can be applied here, there is a fuzzy transition from unreliable to reliable software (cf. Fig. 9), i.e. a **fuzzy transition in the degree to which an objective is achieved**. Note that this is very similar to quantifying the quality of a result in a configuration problem while limiting the search effort.

Another aspect of reliability is proper language design, preventing errors and increasing safety by abstract descriptions, functional programming, or similar restrictive mechanisms. On a practical level, however, such languages that are restricted to one specific paradigm are often not properly accepted and may not meet the requirements of the problem in hand or be too inefficient for specific time-critical problems. Thus, market forces were probably not the only reason for the success and survival of languages like C or C++; their flexibility also played a role here. Although the main solution path would appear to be the provision of multiple-paradigm languages (perhaps best integrated in object-oriented approaches), the preservation of flexible low-level procedural processing may also be essential – as in the case of Common Lisp, which still provides LISP's original low-level features despite incorporating more abstract mechanisms. Another example: Posix Threads on shared-memory UNIX machines are implemented in user space, this offering high efficiency, but also opening up the possibility that faulty application code will destroy the unprotected thread-maintenance structures. **Here, then, fuzziness may mean abandoning the goal of total control and guaranteed automatic safety** and dealing with degrees of safety. A degree of automatically provided safety may be defined, for example, as the amount of safe component's code. In the case of lack of automatic safety-mechanisms, of course, still higher levels can establish a high degree of safety (for safety critical programs, ideally 1) by compilation from abstract languages, by using specification, and/or by intensive testing. However, even when relaxing safety maintenance and deferring it to higher-level code, for complex environments or programs it is nevertheless important to automatically limit the spread of potential errors by lower-level mechanisms, e.g. by checking the meeting of module specifications and protocols, or by assigning specific address ranges to specific programs or program parts.

3.8 Multiple Passes and Hierarchical Organization

Compilers are usually structured in several passes which perform, step by step, analysis, transformation, and code generation. There is usually a bottom-up part

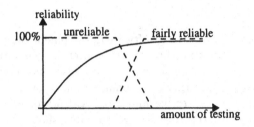

Fig. 9. Degrees of reliability.

analyzing lexical entities, syntax and, potentially, data and control dependencies. Transformations for optimization are then mostly applied in the top-down part, leading to the generation of code. In the automatic detection of parallelism, the analysis phase has a very high impact, its importance being much less if parallelism is explicitly specified. Part of automatic parallelization may then be the recognition of concepts (programming patterns), as already mentioned in Sect. 3.1. In this case, the top-down phase is simplified because the patterns already suggest specific ways of efficient implementation. Thus, we find again fuzzy transitions in how to draw boundaries and how much work to perform in each part. At any rate, several abstraction levels are involved, and in the bottom-up phase a mass of information may be abstracted (summarized, generalized) – if structuring is not already provided by language mechanisms – and, conversely, any single item of information may expand into a mass of data at a lower level (see Fig. 10a). The advantage of having different abstraction levels is well accepted because some transformations and optimizations can be better performed if high-level structural knowledge is available, whereas fine-grained tuning, like peephole optimization, operates at the level of or very close to, the ultimately generated code. Peephole optimization may work well, then, in a narrow context, potentially with **varying amounts of context and with overlapping ranges with respect to higher-level features from which the current-level code was generated**. Thus, again, some fuzziness is involved (see Fig. 10b) However, the hierarchical procedure – intentionally – sets a focus, this providing another way of reducing the search for solutions. The theoretical range of optimization is limited, the optimum not usually being attainable, but problems become practically solvable within a reasonable time-frame and – provided the compiler is good – the difference between the delivered solutions and the theoretical optimum might actually be insignificant.

Similarly, all system design is usually structured in multiple hierarchical layers, e.g. machine, runtime system, compiler, programming languages, and applications (see Fig. 11a). Here as well, drawing boundaries and introducing abstraction levels is essential to make complexity manageable, even if this rules out absolutely perfect solutions. The convenience of higher-level languages – in sequential as well as parallel languages – and other abstractions is indispensable with respect to development time, and there are often no important drawbacks as regards execution time. There are, on the other hand, fuzzy transitions that blur the boundaries of the layers. A well-known example here is that some small but often-used subroutines may be tuned by (re-)writing them in machine code if they are critical for overall performance. Or directives may be given by the user to help the compiler select efficient implementations while basically performing this task automatically. Furthermore, besides the more abstract generalized approaches that can be used in different contexts and for different purposes, but have to be paid for by some overhead, specialized solutions – e.g. specialized routines for typical communication patterns like broadcasts – may be offered for use in typical and frequent recurring cases, providing better performance in such cases (this again showing a trade-off and fuzzy transition between the cost we are willing to invest in software development by adding specializations or tuning, and the software efficiency we may obtain). Another aspect of the fuzziness between layers is the fact that features or performance may overlap. Thus, message passing and fine-grained multithreaded systems [20] offer different mechanisms for communication at different abstraction levels, but message-passing libraries may be extended to provide some lower-level features as well, and fine-grained multithreaded systems may be enhanced by abstract mechanisms built on top of the basic ones. Furthermore, the convenience of use offered by the different approaches – for the compiler or the programmer – may overlap, or a good implementation of a general communication library may outperform a bad implementation of a fine-grained multithreaded system, even if only standard features are provided (see Fig. 11b). If modeling layers by weights, this would mean having a basic weight per layer, modulated by the weight of the specific instance, such that the ranges of layers overlap.

Fuzziness and hierarchical abstraction are thus two essential ways for making complexity manageable, and they are closely intertwined, i.e. every abstraction involves some fuzziness and means abandoning perfectionism in details. Furthermore, not only classes at the same level, but also those at different abstraction levels may overlap as regards their characteristics – e.g. features, convenience of use or performance – in a fuzzy manner, and gradual transitions may be created

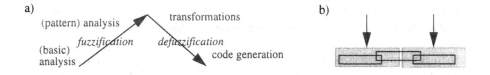

Fig. 10. a) Analysis, transformation, and code generation in compilers, potentially involving a kind of fuzzification in the bottom-up pass and defuzzification in the top-down pass. b) Overlapping ranges in lower-level features created from higher-level ones, e.g. in peephole optimization.

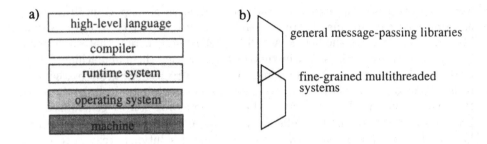

Fig. 11. a) Layered software design and b) overlapping performance and functionality or solutions at different abstraction levels.

by specializations. Ultimately, this means that **hierarchical levels overlap, though they have a basic orientation.**

4 Philosophical Excursion

Some ancient philosophies – like the Egyptian Hermetic philosophy, the Jewish Kabbala or the Japanese/Chinese Yin-Yang philosophy – teach that there are two opposite and complementary – i.e. dual – poles to each aspect, and that this constitutes a basic principle pervading the whole universe (i.e. not just relating to the biological level). The ultimate goal, then, is full development of both poles and their harmonious integration. The Hermetic philosophy postulated polarity as another basic principle of the universe (although it was investigated by the Hermeticians mostly with respect to growth of consciousness), polarity meaning that there are different poles located on the same scale, with gradual transition between them. Current results in the field of neuropsychology [16] to some extent confirm these philosophical postulations. The two hemispheres of the brain have been shown to possess different, complementary qualities with respect to several tasks (laterality). Basically, this means that the brain's full potential – with respect to the diversity, quantity and quality of task performance – can only be exploited if both hemispheres are fully developed and operate in an integrated manner. Although, for many tasks, one or the other hemisphere is more important, both always seem to contribute. The currently most widely accepted model is thus the relative dominance of one hemisphere for a specific task.

Minsky [11] has already called for the combination logical and analogical methods to mimick human intelligence in computers. And, in [18], we have pointed out that the concept of dual poles and exploiting their integration in hybrid solutions can generally be applied well to computer science, this view acquiring greater importance, the more complex systems become. We have also presented a model of fractally nested dual poles. In fact, the concepts of crisp and fuzzy are themselves dual poles. Integrating fuzziness in crisp theories – as is currently being done – thus meets the postulated goal of integration. Furthermore, the relative dominance of one of the brain's hemispheres is reflected here as well. Fuzzy logic was first successfully applied in fuzzy control, where some simple rules are established and applied in a one-stage system, the feedback loop in the recurrent system allowing dynamic adaptation and balancing out the status. Such a procedure would appear more related to what the right brain usually does, just as fuzziness would seem basically more related to the right brain (it is not surprising, then, that fuzzy logic was so successful here). On the other hand, the more left-brain-oriented logical reasoning – as we have seen in the configuration problem – also involves fuzziness, but here the application of fuzziness seems to be more limited, the spread of fuzziness controlled, and the sequential chaining of rules dealt with by defuzzification in multiple stages.

Closely related to the idea of relative dominance is the fact that the fuzzy/crisp pair itself gradual with respect to membership, a system potentially involving more or less fuzziness: different numbers of its variables may be fuzzy or crisp; the fuzzy ranges may be tight or broad; or the extent of their effects may be highly local or globally spread. In fact, there is hardly anything (perhaps nothing at all) that is completely one-sided. Schröder [15] points out that, as a direct consequence of the uncertainty law, there can never really be nothing at the physical level (one factor being 0, the uncertainty relation cannot be fulfilled). We may assume that more generally nothing is ever really certain, we having at best a low/high degree of evidence. Similarly, the philosopher Popper [14] defines the evolution of science and consciousness as a process of falsification (dropping theories that are shown to not reflect reality properly). This also means that we never have complete certainty and cannot eliminate fuzziness; we can only reduce it by an evolutionary increase in understanding and insight. But this raises the question of whether fuzziness is really fully quantifiable (as is claimed by fuzzy theory) or whether this is a contradiction in itself – perhaps quantification is possible for well-understood systems (where fuzziness occurs e.g. as ranges of variation in behavior).

Assuming the ancient philosophies to be right, we may find applications of fuzziness everywhere. In the past, awareness of fuzziness and its relevance have traditionally been greater in the East, but it is currently growing in the West in all aspects of life [10]: the overlapping of research disciplines evolves in interdisciplinary work; fuzzy transitions from working life to retirement are under discussion; and fuzzy working hours with part-time employment are on the increase. In computer science, not only does the evolution of fuzzy theory reflect this trend, but also the growing impact of other so-called soft-computing approaches like genetic algorithms, statistics and dynamic chaotic systems, fuzzy ranges occurring in the latter as attractors.

5   Summary and Future Prospects

We have presented several examples of fuzziness occurring in compilers and runtime systems. In fact, in a very general sense, fuzziness is omnipresent. It occurs in the classification of quantitative or qualitative features in applications, strategies or target systems; it allows the flexible integration of individual items of knowledge to form a global view; it permits the description of performance ranges and of the similarity between requirements and solutions, the conceptualization of transitions between approaches (horizontally and vertically), the description of trade-offs like efficiency or reliability and the effort to be invested, or of the degree of detail measurable. Basically, fuzzy theory allows us to express fuzzy transitions, overlapping ranges, mixtures of bounds, and degrees of desirability, and a compromise-enabling integration of information. However, quantification of the fuzziness involved requires domain-specific metrics. Furthermore, fuzziness – and this is probably its most significant benefit (although related to others) – is often used for pruning search spaces and performing approximations rather than seeking perfect solutions. Optimization problems are often NP-hard, and optimal results from specific parameters are therefore too time-consuming to calculate or may not even be practically computable (cf. Bremermann's limit stating that problems requiring more than 1093 bits of information are transcomputational). What is more, perfectionism often fails to pay off with respect to the quality of the results, improvement being insignificant. In the form of heuristics (pruning search spaces on the basis of domain knowledge), fuzziness is in wide-spread use in compilers, but it often requires more theoretical foundation. Generally, fuzziness and hierarchical abstraction constitute essential means for mastering the complexity of the real world, and – as was indicated above – they are closely intertwined.

It is worth noting, though, that it is not always fuzzy theory that is best suited for describing fuzziness. Statistics, neural networks, and genetic algorithms are other means – and they may even be more precise. In fact, fuzzy theory, in its basic form, is itself fuzzy: triangular and trapezoidal membership functions are only rough approximations (e.g. when describing a statistical distribution). While fuzzy theory is currently being extended to incorporate more complex and more accurate mechanisms, the fuzziness in basic fuzzy theory has – not surprisingly – the advantage of being easy to use and fast in computation.

Generally, the significance of fuzzy approaches (or so-called soft computing) and of the integration of fuzziness into crisp theory and approaches can be expected to grow, this reflecting the general trend toward the convergence of contrary approaches. Crisp theory offers a skeleton structure and domain knowledge and may be relaxed in practical application by attaching fuzziness to it in a theoretically sound manner.

Acknowledgment

This paper evaluates and expands the knowledge gained from this collaboration with the fuzzy-theory expert Vicenc Torra on a specific compiler configuration task. The work was also influenced to some extent by the constraint-solving research of Armin Wolf. My thanks go to Phil Bacon for polishing up my English.

References

1. Bacon, D. F., Graham, S. L., and Sharp, O. J.: Compiler Transformations for High-Performance Computing. ACM Computing Surveys **26**(4) (Dec. 1994) 345–420
2. Berman, F. and Wolski, R.: Scheduling from the Perspective of the Application. Proc. HPDC'96 (1996)
3. Borning, A., Duisberg, R., Freeman-Benson, B., Kramer, A., and Woolf, M.: Constraint Hierarchies. Proc. ACM OOPSLA'97 (October 1987)
4. Di Martino, B. and Chapman, B.: Program Comprehension Techniques to Improve Automatic Parallelization. Proc. Workshop on Automatic Data Layout and Performance Prediction, Rice University, Houston/USA (Apr. 1995)
5. Dubois, D. and Prade, H.: What Does Fuzzy Logic Bring to AI? ACM Computing Surveys **27**(3) (1995)
6. Giloi, W.K., Brüning, U. and Schröder-Preikschat, W.: MANNA: Prototype of a Distributed Memory Architecture With Maximized Sustained Performance. Proc. Euromicro PDP96 Workshop (1996)
7. Klir, G. J. and Yuan, B.: Fuzzy Sets and Fuzzy Logic – Theory and Applications. Prentice Hall (1995)
8. Hambrush, S. E. and Khokhar, A. A.: Maintaining Spatial Data Sets in Distributed-Memory Machines. Proc. IPPS (April 1997)
9. Maeda, H.: An Investigation on the Spread of Fuzziness in Multi-Fold Multi-Stage Approximate Reasoning by Pictorial Representation – Under Sup-Min Composition and Triangular Type Membership Function. Journal Fuzzy Sets and Systems **80** (1996) 133–148.
10. McNeill, D. and Freiberger, P.: Fuzzy Logic. Simon&Schuster, New York (1993)
11. Minsky, M.: Logical Versus Analogical or Symbolic Versus Connectionist or Neat Versus Scruffy. AI Magazine **65**(2) (1991) 34–51
12. Munakata, T. and Jani, Y.: Fuzzy Systems – An Overview. Communications of the ACM **37**(3) (March 1994) 69–76
13. Pearl, J.: Decion Making under Uncertainty. ACM Computing Surveys **28**(1) (March 1996)
14. Popper, K. R. and Eccles, J. C.: The Self and Its Brain – An Argument for Interactionism. Springer Verlag, Heidelberg, Berlin, London, New York (1977)
15. Schröder, M.: Fraktale, Chaos, und Selbstähnlichkeit – Notizen aus dem Paradies der Unendlichkeit (German). Spektrum Akademischer Verlag, Heidelberg etc. (1994)
16. Springer, S. P. and Deutsch, G.: Left Brain, Right Brain. W.H. Freeman and Company, New York (1981)
17. Sodan, A. C.: Mapping Symbolic Programs with Dynamic Tree Structure to Parallel Machines. Oldenbourg Verlag, München/Wien (1996)
18. Sodan, A. C. The Dichotomies of the Left and Right Brain – Yin and Yang in Computer Science. Communications of the ACM (Apr. 1998) 103–111
19. Sodan, A. C. and Torra, V.: Configuration Decisions for Mapping by Fuzzy Inference. Proc. IEEE ICA3PP, Melbourne/Australia (Dec. 1997)
20. Sodan, A.C., Gao, G. R., Maquelin, O., Schultz, J.-U., and Tian, X.-M.: Experiences with Non-numeric Applications on Multithreaded Architectures. PPoPP'97, Las Vegas/USA (June 1997)
21. Torra, V. and Sodan, A. C.: A Multi-Stage System in Compilation Environments. Accepted for Journal Fuzzy Sets and Systems (to appear)
22. Xu, Z., Larus, J. R., and Miller, B. P.: Shared-Memory Performance Profiling. PPoPP'97, Las Vegas/USA (June 1997)
23. Zadeh, L. A.: Fuzzy Sets. Information and Control **8**(3) (1965)

Towards Rigorous Compiler Implementation Verification

Wolfgang Goerigk and Friedemann Simon

Institut für Informatik und Praktische Mathematik, Christian-Albrechts-Universität
zu Kiel, Preußerstraße 1-9, D-24105 Kiel, Germany.
{wg|fs}@informatik.uni-kiel.de

Abstract. This paper sketches a rigorous correctness proof of a compiler executable. We will emphasize the central rôle of partial program correctness and its preservation, which captures the intuitive correctness requirements for transformational programs and in particular for compilers on real machines. Although often left out of sight, implementation verification is definitely necessary, not only but also for compilers. We will show that a rigorous compiler correctness proof also for the final binary compiler machine program is possible and feasible. Verified compiler implementations guarantee correctness properties for generated executable program implementations; we need them, not only in safety critical systems, but also for security in e.g. network computing.

1 Introduction

The purpose of this paper is to show that rigorous verification of compilers down to their machine code implementation is possible and feasible. The key ideas are *preservation of partial correctness* as implementation correctness notion, and *bootstrapping* with an a posteriori *code inspection* as compiler implementation technique. We use a subset of Common Lisp (COMLISP) as source and implementation language [7]. An initial fully correct Lisp compiler implementation will provide a sound execution basis for Lisp application programs [3]. This is important for further compiler development as well as for the correct implementation of e.g. compiler generators or system software.

The work presented here is part of the *Verifix*[1] project on *Correct Compilers* [5] and has been supported by the VIM[2] research network. The goal is to develop methods for correct realistic compiler construction for practically relevant source languages and concrete target machines, and to completely verify them down to their binary machine code implementations, in order to guarantee a correct, safe and secure execution basis for application programs and system software.

---

[1] *Verifix* is a German joint project on *Correct Compilers*. Research groups at the universities of Karlsruhe, Ulm and Kiel cooperate, funded by the Deutsche Forschungsgemeinschaft (DFG) under the grant La 426/15-1,2.

[2] The VIM research network – A Virtual Multicomputer for Symbolic Applications – is funded by the EC HCM programme under the grant CHRX-CT93-0401.

J.A. Padget (Ed.): Human and Artificial Societies, LNAI 1624, pp. 62–73, 1999.
© Springer-Verlag Berlin Heidelberg 1999

Motivation

The use of computer based systems in safety critical applications justifies and requires the verification of software components. Correct program execution, however, depends crucially on the correctness of the binary machine code executables, and, therefore, on the correctness of compiler programs. This is definitely true for security as well, in particular if code, downloaded from somewhere in a computer network, is to be executed on a local machine.

At least two different questions arise w.r.t. security in network computing. First, the user wants to trust the application program or applet downloaded and executed on his or her local machine. Techniques like *proof-carrying code* [24], *certifying compilers* [25], or *byte-code verification* [31] have been proposed in order to solve this problem. But finally, any such technique relies and depends on correctness and security of the execution of e.g. a virtual machine implementation, a just-in-time compiler, or a plug-in, which have to run locally in order to execute the applet. The user wants to trust these tools as well. Both problems relate our work very closely to the VIM project, to modern world-wide network computing, to virtual multicomputers, or to software agents.

In 1984, Ken Thompson, the inventor of Unix, devoted his Turing Award Lecture [30] to security problems due to Trojan horses intruded by compilers and compiler implementations. He shows in detail how to hide a small piece of virus code, a Trojan horse, completely in the binary implementation of a concrete C compiler, not visible in the compiler source code, but reproducing itself when this source code is recompiled in a bootstrapping process. The virus then generates a back door into the executable for the Unix login command, allowing to use a special password for hacking into the system.

No source code inspection, no source code verification will ever find such an intentional error, and it seems unlikely that compiler validation can help. Ken Thompson closed his lecture:

> You can't trust code that you did not totally create yourself. (Especially code from companies that employ people like me.) No amount of source-level verification or scrutiny will protect you from using untrusted code.

A lot of questions arise, and in this paper we want to sketch our approach to answer one of them. We want to show that a rigorous compiler correctness proof down to the binary machine code executable of the compiler is possible and feasible.

In order to guarantee full compiler correctness, we have to verify carefully both, the compiling specification and the compiler implementation. Chirica and Martin [1] have first described this explicitly. In 1988, J Moore [19] pointed out that full compiler verification has to verify the compiler implementation as well. He verified a compiler program, written in Boyer/Moore-Lisp, but not its binary implementation. Unfortunately, for the final compiler executable, the literature gives no sufficient solution so far.

Rigorous Compiler Verification

The compiler correctness proof can be modularized into separate proofs for

- compiling specification correctness,
- correctness of the compiler construction as a high level program, and
- implementation correctness of the final compiler executable.

Due to vertical compositionality of L-simulation or preservation of partial correctness (cf. section 2), each of the proofs may again be modularized into different layers of abstraction using adequate intermediate languages. This makes compiling verification, compiler construction and in particular the implementation correctness proof of the binary executable much easier. Furthermore, horizontal compositionality allows for separate proofs for different program parts. We will show that preservation of partial correctness captures the intuitive correctness requirements and that it enables us to combine small proof modules using adequate proof strategies to complete the entire correctness proof.

In order to construct and to verify an initial fully correct compiler implementation, we proceed in four steps:

Step (a) is to define an appropriate notion of *correct compilation* for sequential imperative languages. It has to guarantee sufficient correctness properties of the target program even for concrete target processors with their finite resource limitations. We use *preservation of partial correctness*, which corresponds to L-simulation (cf. section 2).

Step (b) is to define a compiling specification C, a relation between source and target programs, and prove semantically, that it preserves partial correctness (*compiling verification*, cf. section 3.1).

Step (c) is to construct a compiler program π_C in the source language and prove, that π_C is a *refinement* (correct implementation) of C in the sense of preserving partial correctness (*correct compiler construction*, cf. section 3.2).

Step (d) uses an existing (unverified) implementation of the source language to execute π_C. We apply π_C to itself and bootstrap a compiler executable m_C. We check syntactically, that m_C is correct, i.e. that it actually has been generated according to C (*compiler implementation verification*, cf. section 3.3).

Since the correctness of m_C depends on an initial unsafe compiler execution, we have to check once syntactically that the target program m_C has actually been generated according to the correct compiling specification C. If this a posteriori code inspection finally succeeds, we can guarantee that the resulting compiler executable m_C actually preserves partial correctness.

In particular, binary code inspection guarantees the absence of Trojan horses as follows: the virus could either be part of or generated by m_C, or both, like in Ken Thompson's scenario. In step (d) above we checked m_C not to contain it. C and π_C are both proved correct (steps (b) and (c)), and m_C is proved to be generated from π_C according to C (step (d)). Thus, m_C neither generates nor contains the virus. The binary executable m_C is correct.

2   Preservation of Partial Correctness

Our implementation and compiler correctness notion is *preservation of partial program correctness* or L-simulation [5,22,10]. We prefer to define this notion in a relational setting for imperative programs, because in this setting we can give the most intuitive definition. Programs denote relations between *state* domains, i.e. non deterministic error strict state transformations. In the *Verifix* project we use operational semantics and weakest liberal precondition semantics as well.

A relation $R \subseteq Q \times Q$ is said to be *error strict*, if for any $\sigma \in Q$: $(error, \sigma) \in R \Leftrightarrow \sigma = error$ holds (assuming only one *error* element in Q). This means, that programs will not recover from error states. For binary relations R_1 and R_2 we define $R_1; R_2 =_{def} \{(a, c) \mid \exists b \text{ s.t. } (a, b) \in R_1 \text{ and } (b, c) \in R_2\}$ to denote the relational composition of R_1 and R_2.

Let us consider imperative programs π resp. π' of a source language SL or target language TL, respectively. Let $\mathcal{M}(\pi)$ and $\mathcal{N}(\pi')$ denote the semantics of

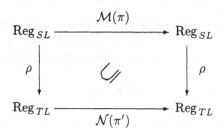

Fig. 1. Compiling Correctness: Preservation of Partial Correctness

π and π', state transformers (error strict relations on the domain Q_{SL} and Q_{TL} of SL and TL states (or data). Let $\text{Reg}_{SL} \subseteq Q_{SL}$ and $\text{Reg}_{TL} \subseteq Q_{TL}$ be the subsets of *regular* (non *error*) states and let $\rho \subseteq \text{Reg}_{SL} \times \text{Reg}_{TL}$ denote a data representation function or relation between source and target language states or data. Figure 1 shows the general setting and we define π' to be a *correct implementation* of π, if and only if

$$\rho; \mathcal{N}(\pi') \subseteq \mathcal{M}(\pi); \rho . \tag{1}$$

Our definition captures the following intuitive requirements:

1. If a target program execution, i.e. π', ends in a regular final state without resource violation, then the source program π can end in a corresponding final state. Every regular target program result is also correct w.r.t. the source program.
2. If the source program π can only end in error states, then the target program π' must not end in a regular final state.

3. If the source program π diverges, i.e. cannot terminate, then the target program π' must not be able to end in a regular final state. In the deterministic case this means that divergent source programs may only be compiled into target programs which either are divergent or end in irregular resource errors.

The definition (1) is equivalent to the more elementary requirement

$$\forall\, i_1 \in \text{Reg}_{SL}, i_2 \in \text{Reg}_{TL}, f_2 \in \text{Reg}_{TL} :$$
$$(i_1, i_2) \in \rho \,\wedge\, (i_2, f_2) \in \mathcal{N}(\pi') \tag{2}$$
$$\implies\; \exists\, f_1 \in \text{Reg}_{SL} :\quad (f_1, f_2) \in \rho \,\wedge\, (i_1, f_1) \in \mathcal{M}(\pi) \ .$$

A compiling specification $\mathcal{C} \subseteq SL \times TL$ is said to be *correct* in the sense of preservation of partial correctness (*preserves partial correctness*), if, for every $(\pi, \pi') \in \mathcal{C}$, π' is a correct implementation of π.

Preservation of Partial Correctness is Compositional

For our purposes, in particular for *vertical* compiler decomposition into subsequent compilation phases, it is crucial that L-simulation or preservation of partial correctness guarantees compositionality. Suppose π_1 is compiled correctly to π'_1

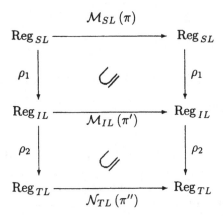

Fig. 2. Vertical Compositionality of L-simulation

and further on to π''_1 using two different compiler phases with π'_1 as an intermediate program. Let ρ_1 and ρ_2 denote the corresponding representation relations (cf. figure 2). Then the little calculation

$$\rho_1; \rho_2; \mathcal{N}_{TL}\,(\pi'') \subseteq \rho_1; \mathcal{M}_{IL}\,(\pi'); \rho_2 \subseteq \mathcal{M}_{SL}\,(\pi); \rho_1; \rho_2 \tag{3}$$

shows vertical compositionality, using associativity of relational composition and the fact, that each single diagram commutes in the sense of preservation of

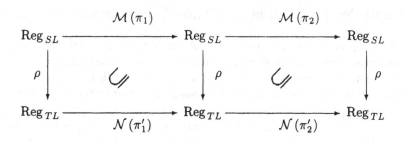

Fig. 3. Horizontal Compositionality of L-simulation

partial correctness. A similar proof shows horizontal compositionality: Suppose π_1 is correctly compiled to π_1', and π_2 is correctly compiled to π_2' (figure 3), then correct compilation of $\pi_1 ; \pi_2$ to $\pi_1' ; \pi_2'$ (horizontical compositionality) is shown as easily by

$$\rho; \mathcal{N}(\pi_1'); \mathcal{N}(\pi_2') \subseteq \mathcal{M}(\pi_1); \rho; \mathcal{N}(\pi_2') \subseteq \mathcal{M}(\pi_1); \mathcal{M}(\pi_2); \rho \qquad (4)$$

Preservation of partial correctness is adequate, essential and sufficient for our purposes, for rigorous compiler verification and compiler implementation verification for sequential imperative languages, as we will see. It is guided by the intuition that program execution on real hardware must not deceive the user with respect to correctness of results.

Since we do not want to rule out concrete finite target hardware processors, we have to admit that target program execution always may end in a resource violation, that it fails with e.g. memory or arithmetic overflow [29]. Whenever a target program execution gives a regular result (does not abort), however, this result is guaranteed to be correct. Thus, partial source program correctness is preserved, whereas total correctness is not in general.

On the other hand, a compiler, that preserves partial program correctness, has to generate code that detects and signals every possible runtime error (finite error), due to e.g. array index boundary violations or division by zero. If not, e.g. if the target program π' would possibly generate a regular result, say $f_2 \in \text{Reg}_{TL}$, for an input, say $i_1 \in \text{Reg}_{SL}$, although the source program π is undefined on i_1, i.e. although there is no $f_1 \in \text{Reg}_{SL}$ with $(i_1, f_1) \in \mathcal{M}(\pi)$, then the target program would not be a correct implementation in our sense, because $(i_1, f_2) \in \rho; \mathcal{N}(\pi')$, but $(i_1, f_2) \notin \mathcal{M}(\pi); \rho$.

Correct implementation in our sense guarantees, that the target program, which is actually executed on the machine, signals an error and aborts observably in any irregular (runtime error) situation. Otherwise the target program could give a result not allowed by the source program. This is important for security: Hacking into software or computer systems often succeeds, because programs can be forced into an irregular state, which then is exploited in order to run program parts in a privileged mode.

3   Compiler and Implementation Correctness

After defining an appropriate notion of correct compilation in the previous section, we now proceed according to steps (**b**) - (**d**) (see section 2) in order to prove full compiler correctness. We will not go into much detail here. A more detailed description of the compiler implementation verification is given in [8].

We follow Chirica and Martin [1] and decompose the full compiler correctness into compiling specification correctness and compiler implementation correctness. The latter again may be proved separately for the implementation as a high level program and the binary implementation of that program as an executable machine program. We will see below how these different proof parts are combined, exploiting the vertical compositionality of L-simulation.

3.1   Compiling Verification

Compiling verification has to establish the fact that a compiling specification $C \subseteq SL \times TL$, a syntactical mapping from source to target programs, is semantically correct, i.e. that C preserves partial correctness in our case. Compiling verification has a very long history starting in the mid-60's with the work of McCarthy and Painter [18]. A good overview of the research work performed so far and the results achieved since then is given by Jeffrey J. Joyce in [15]. Vertical and horizontal compositionality ease this proof because it can be modularized into different compilation steps and into separate compilation theorems for different language constructs. This fact coincides both with experiences from practical compiler construction and with necessities which come up if we want to prove compiler implementation correctness.

In this paper we have defined compiling correctness in an intuitive relational setting. In our concrete proofs, however, we use operational semantics and simulation proofs as well as monotonic predicate transformers [23,22] and weakest liberal precondition semantics. Predicate transformers generalize relations and form a richer semantical basis allowing for more elegant and modular proofs. We prove an appropriate set of algebraic refinement laws for programs with respect to their semantics and the correctness proof essentially uses algebraic refinement theory [12,13].

Compiling specifications for our concrete COMLISP compiler are defined in [9]. Denotational semantics for COMLISP and the first stack intermediate language are defined in [4]. We use PVS [27] for additional formalization, proof checking and mechanical proof support. Some formalizations including the necessary fixed point theory, for instance for the proof sketched in [10], is available and has been documented in [28].

3.2   Compiler Implementation Correctness

At this point, the compiling specification C, a mathematical definition of a relation $C \subseteq SL \times TL$ between source and target programs, is far away from an implementation as a binary machine program executable. In the following, we will construct or generate more concrete correct implementations step by step, decomposing the full implementation problem into smaller ones.

The crucial idea is, that L-simulation (or preservation of partial correctness) is the notion of correct implementation in every single refinement step, for manual compiler construction as well as for bootstrapping using a compiler which preserves partial correctness. Correctness follows from vertical compositionality.

We shall reach an intermediate layer where further manual refinement will become inadequate, where we should use a compiler to generate low level implementations. At this point, we are suddenly left alone with our rigorous correctness requirement, because there is no fully verified compiler available yet. Fortunately, we are just on the way to produce one which, again fortunately, indeed preserves partial correctness. The question arises how we can make use of our own compiler to help us to mechanically generate low level implementations correctly, although we have not yet finished the correctness proof.

We will show, that this is possible, if we observe some requirements from the very beginning. We have to use an existing programming language, for instance COMLISP, both as source and implementation language, because we want to run the compiler once applied to itself. It has to preserve partial correctness and we must be able to check the results of the initial compiler bootstrapping.

Let us assume a correct compiling specification $\mathcal{C} \subseteq SL \times TL$ between source and target programs. Let $m_{\mathcal{C}}$ be an implementation of $\mathcal{C}$ on the target machine written in the target machine language TL. Then $m_{\mathcal{C}}$ is said to be a *correct implementation* of $\mathcal{C}$, if the diagram in figure 4 commutes in the sense of L-simulation (or preservation of partial correctness). D_{TL} is the domain of target machine data, and $\rho_{\mathrm{TL}}^{\mathrm{SL}}$ and $\rho_{\mathrm{TL}}^{\mathrm{TL}}$ are data representation relations for proper source and target programs, respectively.

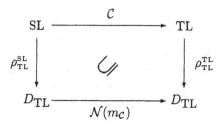

Fig. 4. Compiler Implementation Correctness

3.3 Compiler Construction and Bootstrapping

Let us now decompose the diagram in figure 4 vertically into two steps (figure 5 below): The upper part corresponds to manual correct compiler construction as high level (recursive) program π_C, and the lower part corresponds to bootstrapping of π_C to m_C using our own compiler π_C. The correctness of the entire implementation is guaranteed by vertical composition, if every single diagram commutes in the sense of preservation of partial correctness. Note, that we use two completely different approaches in order to establish L-simulation or preservation of partial correctness in the two parts of figure 5.

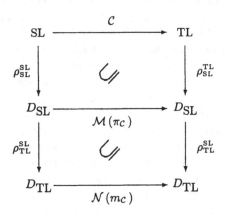

Fig. 5. Implementation Correctness by Vertical Composition

Again, D_{SL} and D_{TL} are the source and target languages data domains, and ρ_{SL}^{SL}, ρ_{TL}^{SL}, and ρ_{SL}^{TL} are the corresponding data representations.

But how can we establish the lower commuting diagram? It appears that, if we could execute π_C, which is a proved correct implementation of C written in its own source language, and apply it to π_C itself, we would obtain a binary implementation m_C. In fact, the lower diagram in figure 5 would commute, and m_C would be correct. The problem is, however, that we cannot execute π_C directly, which is a COMLISP source program. We have to implement it.

Since π_C is also a Common Lisp program, we can use an existing Common Lisp system to execute π_C and to generate m_C. But is the compiler implementation m_C now correct? Unfortunately, in our situation no mathematically precise propositions are known about the correctness of the Common Lisp system. Even if it would have been officially validated, correctness can not be guaranteed. Moreover, due to sophisticated optimization, existing Common Lisp systems will probably not preserve partial correctness. However, since we used our own compiler in order to generate m_C, we can check it to be in compliance with our correct compiling specification. If this syntactical code inspection (checking) succeeds, correctness of C and π_C imply the final correctness of the machine executable m_C. This finishes our proof.

In [8] we give a more detailed description of this a posteriori (double) checking proof for our concrete COMLISP compiler. Our most recent implementation uses four compilation phases and consists of 237 usually very small Lisp-functions. The complete printed output for the double-checking for the largest function covers about 14 pages of program text. Only very few functions (13) need substantially more than one page.

In addition, a more sophisticated argument [14,5,17] allows for saving a lot of work while checking especially low level code. This *diagonal* argument makes use of the fact that the compiler is applied to itself. The compiler works in separate phases, but most its code is also only used in one of the phases and, hence, only has to be checked down to its own target code. Lower level implementations will be generated by other parts of the compiler which have already been checked to be correctly implemented in their own target code. Following the strategy to do less complex tasks in lower level translation phases, we can therefore minimize the double check proof work.

4   Conclusions and Related Work

The idea to separate compiling specification correctness from compiler implementation correctness and to prove both of them in order to gain full correctness has first been described explicitly by Chirica and Martin [1]. J S. Moore [19,20] also distinguishes these tasks. He uses the Boyer/Moore prover nqthm to prove the correctness of a compilation function from Piton into FM8501-Code. More recently, the VLisp project reports [26,11] also express the necessity of proving the compiler implementation correct. In the VLisp and in the CLInc project however, this task has explicitly been left out. Our work is very closely related to Paul Curzon's work on compiler verification, in particular on the verified Vista implementation [2]. One crucial difference is, that he uses and trusts a theorem prover (HOL) both to carry out the proofs and to execute the compiling specification.

We have described our approach to completely verify specification and implementation of a realistic initial fully correct compiler executable. The subset COMLISP of Common Lisp has carefully been selected as a bootstrapping kernel, as both source and implementation language. Its applicative part (the pure functional sub-language of COMLISP) also coincides with the logic of the new Boyer/Moore prover ACL2 [16,21]. This links mechanical program correctness proofs to the work described here [3,6], allowing for partial correctness proofs of executable programs.

We have implemented the COMLISP compiler as a COMLISP program. The complete compiler has been bootstrapped successfully as executable machine program on a Transputer T400 single board computer with 1 MB of memory. The output which is necessary to perform the correctness proof by double checking the results has been generated. The efficiency of the generated code is acceptable: the complete bootstrap takes about one hour, mostly because all input/output-operations for all intermediate program representations have to be piped character by character through one Transputer link. We have also implemented code-generators for i386, DEC α, and MC 68000 processors, as well as for C and Forth.

References

1. L.M. Chirica and D.F. Martin. Toward Compiler Implementation Correctness Proofs. *ACM Transactions on Programming Languages and Systems*, 8(2):185–214, April 1986.
2. Paul Curzon. The Verified Compilation of Vista Programs. Internal Report, Computer Laboratory, University of Cambridge, January 1994.
3. Wolfgang Goerigk. An Exercise in Program Verification: The ACL2 Correctness Proof of a Simple Theorem Prover Executable. Technical Report Verifix/CAU/2.4, CAU Kiel, 1996.
4. Wolfgang Goerigk. A Denotational Semantics for ComLisp and SIL. Technical Report Verifix/CAU/2.8, CAU Kiel, December 1997.
5. Wolfgang Goerigk, Axel Dold, Thilo Gaul, Gerhard Goos, Andreas Heberle, Friedrich W. von Henke, Ulrich Hoffmann, Hans Langmaack, Holger Pfeifer, Harald Ruess, and Wolf Zimmermann. Compiler Correctness and Implementation Verification: The *Verifix* Approach. In P. Fritzson, editor, *Proceedings of the Poster Session of CC '96 – International Conference on Compiler Construction*, IDA Technical Report LiTH-IDA-R-96-12, Linköping, Sweden, 1996.
6. Wolfgang Goerigk, Thilo Gaul, and Wolf Zimmermann. Correct Programs without Proof? On Checker-Based Program Verification. In *Proceedings ATOOLS'98 Workshop on "Tool Support for System Specification, Development, and Verification"*, Advances in Computing Science, Malente, 1998. Springer Verlag.
7. Wolfgang Goerigk and Ulrich Hoffmann. The Compiler Implementation Language ComLisp. Technical Report Verifix/CAU/1.7, CAU Kiel, June 1996.
8. Wolfgang Goerigk and Ulrich Hoffmann. Rigorous Compiler Implementation Correctness: How to Prove the Real Thing Correct. In *Proceedings FM-TRENDS'98 International Workshop on Current Trends in Applied Formal Methods*, Boppard, 1998. To appear.
9. Wolfgang Goerigk and Ulrich Hoffmann. The Compiling Specification from ComLisp to Executable Machine Code. Technical Report Nr. 9713, Institut für Informatik, CAU, Kiel, December 1998.
10. Wolfgang Goerigk and Markus Müller-Olm. Erhaltung partieller Korrektheit bei beschränkten Maschinenressourcen. – Eine Beweisskizze – Technical Report Verifix/CAU/2.5, CAU Kiel, 1996.
11. J. D. Guttman, L. G. Monk, J. D. Ramsdell, W. M. Farmer, and V. Swarup. A Guide to VLisp, A Verified Programming Language Implementation. Technical Report M92B091, The MITRE Corporation, Bedford, MA, September 1992.
12. C. A. R. Hoare. Refinement algebra proves correctness of compiling specifications. In C.C. Morgan and J.C.P. Woodcock, editors, *3rd Refinement Workshop*, pages 33–48. Springer-Verlag, 1991.
13. C.A.R. Hoare, He Jifeng, and A. Sampaio. Normal Form Approach to Compiler Design. *Acta Informatica*, 30:701–739, 1993.
14. Ulrich Hoffmann. Über die korrekte Implementierung von Compilern. In *Workshop "Alternative Konzepte für Sprachen und Rechner"*, pages 94–105, Bad Honnef, 1996. Also available as Technical Report Verifix/CAU/3.1.

15. Jeffrey J. Joyce. Totally Verified Systems: Linking Verified Software to Verified Hardware. In M. Leeser and G. Brown, editors, *Hardware Specification, Verification and Synthesis: Mathematical Aspects*, volume 408 of *Lecture Notes in Computer Science*, 1990.

16. M. Kaufmann and J S. Moore. Design Goals of ACL2. Technical Report 101, Computational Logic, Inc., August 1994.

17. Hans Langmaack.   Softwareengineering zur Zertifizierung von Systemen: Spezifikations-, Implementierungs-, Übersetzerkorrektheit. *Informationstechnik und Technische Informatik it-ti*, 97(3):41–47, 1997.

18. J. McCarthy and J.A. Painter. Correctness of a compiler for arithmetical expressions. In J.T. Schwartz, editor, *Proceedings of a Symposium in Applied Mathematics, 19, Mathematical Aspects of Computer Science*. American Mathematical Society, 1967.

19. J S. Moore. Piton: A verified assembly level language. Technical Report 22, Comp. Logic Inc, Austin, Texas, 1988.

20. J S. Moore. *Piton, A Mechanically Verified Assembly-Level Language*. Kluwer Academic Publishers, 1996.

21. J S. Moore and M. Kaufmann. ACL2: An industrial strength version of Nqthm. In *Proceedings of COMPASS '96*, June 1996.

22. Markus Müller-Olm. Three Views on Preservation of Partial Correctness. Technical Report Verifix/CAU/5.1, CAU Kiel, October 1996.

23. Markus Müller-Olm. *Modular Compiler Verification*, volume 1283 of *Lecture Notes in Computer Science*. Springer-Verlag, Berlin, Heidelberg, New York, 1997.

24. George C. Necula. Proof-carrying code. In *Conference Record of POPL '97: The 24th ACM SIGPLAN-SIGACT Symposium on Principles of Programming Languages*, pages 106–119, Paris, France, 15–17 January 1997.

25. George C. Necula and Peter Lee. The design and implementation of a certifying compiler. In *Proceedings of the ACM SIGPLAN'98 Conference on Programming Language Design and Implementation (PLDI)*, pages 333–344, Montreal, Canada, 17–19 June 1998.

26. Dino P. Oliva and Mitchell Wand. A Verified Compiler for Pure PreScheme. Technical Report NU-CCS-92-5, Northeastern University College of Computer Science, Northeastern University, February 1992.

27. S. Owre, J. M. Rushby, and N. Shankar. PVS: A Prototype Verification System. In Deepak Kapur, editor, *Proceedings 11th International Conference on Automated Deduction CADE*, volume 607 of *Lecture Notes in Artificial Intelligence*, pages 748–752, Saratoga, NY, October 1992. Springer-Verlag.

28. Holger Pfeifer, Axel Dold, F.W. von Henke, and Harald Rueß. Mechanized Semantics of Simple Imperative Programming Constructs. Ulmer Informatik-Berichte 96-11, Universität Ulm, December 1996.

29. W. Polak. Compiler specification and verification. In J. Hartmanis G. Goos, editor, *Lecture Notes in Computer Science*, number 124 in LNCS. Springer-Verlag, 1981.

30. Ken Thompson. Reflections on Trusting Trust. *Communications of the ACM*, 27(8):761–763, 1984. Also in ACM Turing Award Lectures: The First Twenty Years 1965-1985, ACM Press, 1987, and in Computers Under Attack: Intruders, Worms, and Viruses Copyright, ACM Press 1990.

31. Frank Yellin. Low level security in java. In *Fourth International Conference on the World-Wide Web*, MIT, Boston, December 1995.

Shifting the Focus from Control to Communication: the STReams OBjects Environments Model of Communicating Agents [1]

Stefano A. Cerri

Dipartimento di Scienze dell'Informazione, Università di Milano, Via Comelico 39
20135 MILANO, Italy
cerri@dsi.unimi.it

Abstract. The paper presents the computational model underlying new agent communication languages. The model, called STROBE, has been identified and two prototypical languages inspired by the model have been implemented. In order to describe unambiguously the STROBE model we have chosen to use a formal programming language, i.e. Scheme. STROBE shows how generic communication may be described and implemented by means of STReams of pragmatically marked messages to be exchanged by agents represented as OBjects interpreting messages in multiple Environments. The model, therefore, is at the same time a software architecture and a proposal for a lexicon potentially useful for exchanging efforts in emergent agent technologies. An outline of the expected functionality's of the languages under development may allow to appreciate if and how they may fit the expected ones, i.e. cognitive simplicity for designing and controlling multi-agent generic dialogues, including human and artificial communication facilities.

1. Introduction

Communication among intelligent agents is one of the popular research issues at the moment. In [1] many of the current efforts are reported, together with an extended bibliography. In spite of the impressive, convincing research advancements, at the application level we do not notice yet a major impact. As it was the case for Artificial Intelligence applications, possibly once more the real problem is complexity, not so much for the equipped machine to perform according to well designed software, but rather for the designer and implementers to conceive and realize the suitable application by using available methods and tools.

Within the Artificial Intelligence and Education community [2] we notice a major concern that reaches the same conclusion, i.e. complexity in AI & ED research makes

---

[1] This paper is a revised version of the one appeared in the Proceedings of JFLA97, Journées francophones des langages applicatifs, Collection Didactique de l'INRIA, Marc Gengler et Christian Queinnec (eds.), pag. 145-168 (1997) with the title: A simple language for generic dialogues: "speech acts" for communication.

J.A. Padget (Ed.): Human and Artificial Societies, LNAI 1624, pp.74 -101, 1999.
© Springer-Verlag Berlin Heidelberg 1999

it almost unviable for AI & ED real applications. Even worse: research does not cumulate because neither the description nor the implementation languages are somehow common. Self's proposal was to go back to logic for expressing issues such as mutual beliefs or planning the moves in a dialogue. A hypothesis that fits trends in the AI community for the same foundational purpose, but at the same time is challenged by arguments such as those reported in this paper.

At the moment, AI & ED programs choose more and more object / agent (or actor) - based architectures, considering off the shelf languages as implementation tools (e.g. [3] reviews most of them). What occurs, is that those languages offer primitives and virtual machine models that are not really matching those required by the applications, or either, if they do, that they are too complex to learn and use. Cognitive simplicity in the conception and design of new applications becomes a must for any concrete dissemination of research results as well as for most applicative efforts.

We have chosen cognitive simplicity and composition of primitives as our main purpose. As we were skeptical that abstract logical formalisms would provide for cognitively simple models of dynamic processes, we have instead adopted a representation of communicative processes based on a formal, programming language suitable for process reification and visualization. Among all languages, Scheme [4] was chosen for its abstraction power associated with its formal foundations[i] and for the simplicity of its underlying evaluation mechanism (e.g. the environment model of evaluation). The criticism that Scheme is sequential and therefore unable to model multi-agent interactions is challenged by active research in concurrent languages.

In the following, we will describe:

a. Why educational applications require generic communicative processes, and therefore why advances in educational software are enabled by advances in models and languages supporting communication and, conversely, the requirements of educational dialogues support efforts in the design of new communication languages. The educational metaphor, therefore, pushes technologies of a much wider applicability, such as those claimed to be (almost) mature by industrial initiatives such as FIPA (http://drogo.cselt.stet.it/fipa/).

b. How a simple agent-to-agent communication model[ii] may be described by three powerful Scheme primitives, i.e. STReams, OBjects and Environments.

c. What can be borrowed from a modern artificial agent communication language, i.e. KQML [7] , that may be integrated in the STROBE model, but, at the same time, what are its limitations to model dialogues where humans participate, thus why multiple viewpoints (or cognitive environments) are required.

d. Why multiple communicating agents of generic types (humans and artificial agents) require functionality's typically associated to enhanced operating systems or actors and how we think to model them by means of Scheme extensions. Finally how the high level (Scheme) descriptions and prototypes may be integrated with lower level ones, by means of interpreting / integrating Scheme with Java, thus offering machine independent resource management utilities to be used in the net.

2.   Learning as a side effect of communication

One fundamental reflection for anybody interested in Education is that the goal of Education is that learners learn, i.e. change state during / after a communicative process. The process does not per se need to be "educational". That term applies eventually after an evaluation of the new state reached by the learner as a result of communicating. Communication is the real issue for learning and therefore for Education; learning may occur as a side effect (as it was agreed in the workshop reported in [8]). Educational software, then, is nothing else as highly interactive software. Whether or not communication stimulates learning in the learner is not primarily a property of the software managing the communicative process but a relation between the process and its effects on the learner[iii].

For instance, in [9] there is an example of learning outcomes from dialogues with a simulator. The author's assertion that "there is an urgent need to further research in this area and it is one of our aims to try to model these different styles computationally" supports our assumption that formal (computer) languages for dialogues are missing. Looking back in the literature (see, e.g. [10]), we notice that the foundations for languages representing human dialogues were laid down years ago, but still the need is not satisfied.

Other authors (e.g. [11] that developed the reflective actor language ReActalk on top of Smalltalk) claim with good reasons that "models developed for agent modeling are of relevance for practical applications, especially for open distributed applications". Among these applications, Intelligent Tutoring Systems play a major role (cf. [12]). We have shown in [3] and [37] where we used the actor languages ABCL/1 and Rosette, that when the chosen actor's granularity fits the components of the problem to be solved, then the conception and implementation of actor-based software may be relatively simple, and so their abstraction and generalization. However, the global, concurrent message exchange control process is not easily conceived. The transition from a sequential, synchronous to a concurrent, asynchronous mental model of computation (control and communication) is a hard process for any human player engaged in the technological arena today. In order to contribute, we have decided to start from understanding and modeling human-system dialogues, thus the processes in the machine that eventually are suitable to control a dialogue with a human.

Those "dialogue control processes (DCPs)" are the ones definitely interesting for understanding and enhancing primarily human-to-system communication, but, as we will see, also generic agent-to-agent communication, up to many-to-many participants. Therefore we need to make DCPs as transparent as possible by choosing an adequate underlying virtual machine model and a visible "granularity" of agents and messages that allows us to reason also in terms of human dialogues. Tradeoffs between controlling joint variables (versus actor's replacements and "pure" functional languages) and the higher level perception of the human agent's exchanges in the dialogues are exactly the issue that we try to address with our research described here in its foundational results.

2.1. Types of communication

There exist many types of communication among humans. The discipline that studies it - pragmatics - has made remarkable advancements (cf. [13] for an extensive presentation). In human-to-system communication, similarly, software layers in the system manage various communicative processes with the user.

Among those types, even if we risk to oversimplify, we will select three types that we assume fit best with past and current human-computer communication systems: information systems, design systems and tutorial systems. Each type is characterized by two properties: the initiative taken (human or computer) and the type of speech acts [14] involved.

Assume that U is the user, and C is the computer, playing the role, on turn, of an Information, a Design or a Tutoring system committed to manage dialogues with the user.

Information systems (when they are mature) consist mainly of communication exchanges where U asks questions to C and C answers to U. During the construction of an Information system, U tells C new information that C stores in its archive. Design exchanges (e.g. programming environments) consist mainly of orders from U to C and the execution of those by C. Finally (strictly) tutoring systems consist of exchanges where C asks U questions, U answers to C and C decides what to do on the basis of U's answer. In that case, C is not interested in knowing what U believes just for updating C's knowledge - as it is the reciprocal case of U asking questions to C in informative exchanges -, but instead for deciding about what initiative to take during the dialogue in order to accomplish essentially an evaluation task leading to the next phase of the conversation. From this simplification we may assume that what we called "strictly tutorial User-Computer exchanges" are basically those where the Computer tests the knowledge of the User. In order to avoid confusion, we may call the systems supporting those exchanges: Testing systems.

From various sources in the literature dedicated to Educational software, we may conclude that Tutoring Systems (and / or Learning Environments) do engage in dialogues with the learner that include Information, Design and Testing phases. Therefore educational applications require managing dialogues with the human user of generic types. Any student may interrupt his teacher to ask for information. Any student wishes to engage in an exercise on a simulated environment where he may play with situations by ordering the simulator to run under his / her control. Information systems and design systems may be considered part of any really effective educational system of the future. What these systems need is controlling dialogues with the user in a fashion that is compatible with the user's needs, intentions, preconceptions, goals...

Notice that in testing exchanges C takes the initiative, while in Information and Design exchanges U takes the initiative. Human-to-human dialogues are such that any of the two may take the initiative at any time, so that a swap of initiative is a common feature. Assuming to aim at more flexible and powerful artifacts, it is clear that also in human-to-computer dialogue models, informative, design and testing exchanges should be allowed and embedded within each other, at the initiative of either partner. This requirement, if respected by our proposed solutions, will allow to generalize the models to generic agent-to-agent dialogues, where each agent, human or artificial, is associated to a role (caller, called...) in each exchange, while roles may be swapped during the dialogue[iv].

Models of agent-to-agent communication require explicit roles, further to an explicit association of agents to physical entities participating to the communicative process. A type and a role associated to each partner, at least, will define then each exchange in communication.

2.2.   Communication is not transmission

As one may easily notice, communication is very different from transmission, and therefore we are not just interested here in phenomena at the (low) transmission level (e.g.: active sockets, busy channel, synchronization, queue scheduling) but instead mainly at the high level of active agents (available knowledge, intentions, preconditions, effects, etc.). Certainly (high level) communication between agents (human or artificial) must be founded ultimately on reliable transmission of the messages. But the last is not the major concern; it is just an important enabling factor that we assume to be able to guarantee. For instance, we assume not only that communicative messages include pragmatic aspects (e.g. sender, destinations, intention, role...), but also that these aspects may be used by the receiver to process the message (e.g. to process the queue of incoming messages).

Assuming that messages are correctly transmitted, communication is successful if the rules associated to the pragmatics of the communicative process have been respected. Agent communication languages, such as KQML [7] , do address the issues of communication among intelligent information agents, under the hypothesis that these agents are artificial and that they "serve" information to clients asking for it. Their pragmatic level solves most of the transmission and interoperability problems, but lack substantial components in at least two situations. One concerns the case that human agents are part of the multi-agent conversation and the other when the conversation is generic, i.e. includes all three types of exchange cited above (and perhaps other ones, such as those including commitments by a participating agent).

One weak aspect of KQML is related to multiple viewpoint [18], that we address by using cognitive environments as Scheme first class ADT [19] . Another one concerns the choice of the primitives. Regarding this, we are designing primitives that fit specifications deduced from available research on the pragmatic classification of human dialogues (such as the one reported in [9]). A third weakness concerns reflection, as most researchers point out (e.g. [2, 12]).

2.3.   Agent communication languages: KQML

The "Knowledge Sharing Effort" community, in particular concerning the language KQML[v], has recently produced significant advancements. This is a language for specifying dialogues among artificial agents by means of primitives that allow queries and directives expressed in various "content languages" (e.g. SQL, Prolog) to be embedded into KQLM messages. These primitives are "performatives", such as evaluate, ask-if, reply, tell, advertise, etc. and the types of the speech acts associated to the performatives are: assertion, query, command "or any other mutually agreed upon speech act". Both choices are quite similar to our ones. The distinguishing property of KQML with respect to traditional languages is the supposed independence of the "pragmatic level" from the language of the embedded "content message". This allows an important level of interoperability. We share also this view.

A KQML application to Authoring Educational software is described in [20] , where the concern is mainly software reuse. We are encouraged by this and similar results concerning the productivity of software, but we are not sure that the application of tools developed for a specific context of applications - interoperability among data and knowledge bases for informative purposes - will allow to express easily issues typical of a quite different context, i.e. human-computer generic dialogues. One of those issues consists of user modeling. In [21] we may find an attempt to customize KQML primitives for learner modeling. We will see if and how the results of this attempt will cross / complement our own ones.

We believe that the limitation of KQML with respect to generic dialogues is the assumption that mutual beliefs of agents are correct: in the general case, this assumption may not be true. In our model, we try to model exactly those more general cases of dialogue that occur frequently in educational applications and, more in general, in multi-agent interactions.

3. The STROBE model[vi]

In [22] we have outlined a model of communication between agents that is based on the three primitive notions of stream, object and environment. The environment component of the model has been discussed in [19]. We have shown there that the desiderata emerging from the analysis of realistic agent-to-agent dialogues induce two requirements concerning the computational formalism adopted:

Requirement #1: the environment[vii] for evaluating procedures and variables is a first class abstract data type.

Requirement #2: multiple environments are simultaneously available within the same agent-object.

Looking at KQML, we have noticed that our first requirement may fit their virtual architecture. Basically, labeling a message with the explicit language in which the message is expressed, is equivalent - in our functional terms - to forcing the partner to use an environment for the evaluation of the query where the global frame binds the language symbols to the evaluation and application functions corresponding to a simulator (or an interpreter, or a compiler including run time support) of the chosen language. The KQML expression

(ask-one :content	(price IBM ?price)
:receiver	stock-service
:language	my-prolog-like-query-language
	;; (corresponding to theirs LPROLOG)
:ontology	NYSE-TICKS)

may be simulated by our architecture as a request to the receiver agent to use the environment including the definitions of the *my-prolog-like-query-language* available. Further, the KQML expressions specify also an ontology, i.e. consider a specific environment among many possible ones where terms are defined in a coherent way suitable to represent - independently from the application - a domain of discourse assumed to be valid for the receiver agent, and known to the queerer. The natural computational manner to describe the evaluation of a KQML message like the one above is therefore to send a message with content *(price IBM ?price)* to agent *stock-service* where the evaluation environment of the agent is the composition of a global frame containing *my-prolog-like-query-language* 's bindings and a local frame containing the definitions available in *NYSE-TICKS*.   But what if the receiver's ontology - even if it has the same name - would be different from the queer's?

What we have added to KQML is the second requirement, i.e. the opportunity to model the evaluation of the same query within environments that are different from the one supposed to be correct. That is necessary in order to experiment on responses from the receiver different from the ones expected by the sender.

3.1. Basic description of dialogues between two partners

3.1.1.   Agents as interpreters

Each dialogue is basically a set of message exchanges E among two agents each with a private memory. Each message exchange may be considered as one or more pairs of moves M, sometimes called acts. Each move is performed by one agent on turn that accepts a message, executes a set of internal actions and sends a message to the partner in the dialogue. In each pair of moves, we may distinguish an agent that takes an initiative, sending a move to the partner, and an agent that reacts to the other agent's initiative. Agents may take the initiative when they wish, but we assume initially to respect the turn-taking rule that agents wishing to take an initiative may do that only after they have reacted to the partner, with the exception of the very first move. Therefore a swap of the "initiative" role among partners is allowed during the dialogue process[viii], even if the "turn-taking rule" is assumed to be respected. Further, we assumed (initially) full synchronization: an agent waits to react until he has received the other agent's message.

In computational terms, each agent's operation in a single move may therefore be modeled by a REPL: *"read - eval - print - listen"* loop, similar to the cycle of an interpreter. If agent P sends a move M to agent Q, then Q "reads" M; "evaluates" M to obtain a response, "prints" (sends to P) the response and "listens" to the next move. This is Q's REPL cycle. P's REPL cycle is shifted with respect to Q's. P "prints" first, then it "listens", then it "reads" Q's response, then it "evaluates". In this turn-taking P was the initiator, Q the responder. Let's now concentrate on a single initiative dialogue, even if the model is valid for mixed initiative dialogues.

3.1.2.   Informal description of interactions

In case the input move is an assertion, it is reasonable to assume that the expected result is the extension of the receiver's environment by a new binding that reflects the assertion 's content. Therefore, when the input message is an assertion, the expected behavior of the receiver will be to <u>define</u> (or <u>set!</u>) a new name-value binding, that extends / modifies the receiver's environment, and to acknowledge the partner of the success of the operation. When the input move is a query, the expected reaction of the partner will be either a search for a value in the private memory or the execution (application) of a procedure, according to the nature of the query. In the latter case, the query is in fact an order. A search in the environment is performed in Scheme by calling the <u>eval</u> on the expression included in the move. If that is a variable, a search in the environment will find the corresponding value, else, if that is an expression indicating functional application, the <u>apply</u> is invoked on the value of the first sub-expression after the evaluation of each parameter.

The querying agent may predict the answer - in case he is able to make hypotheses about the partner's private environment, i.e. the partner's knowledge or beliefs -, but the success of the prediction is not certain.

In dialogues involving humans the search for a cause of a mismatch constitutes the traditional issue of cognitive diagnosis [2]. Cognitive diagnosis must cope with the problem that one cannot make a closed-world assumption in a human and therefore one should identify strategies for the testing of hypotheses empirically selected [3] .

The same, unfortunately, occurs also when the assumption may superficially be considered valid; even if it is not, as it is sometimes the case of dialogues among artificial agents. For instance, in debugging hardware microcircuits many assumptions are made in order to reduce the search space, because an exhaustive search of the inconsistencies may not be tractable, thus introducing potential errors (in case one or more assumptions was incorrect). Agents searching for information available on the web, for instance the cheapest available book or stock share available, cannot foresee unpredictable interactions with the external world[ix] (e.g. an offer suddenly available in a server in Tokyo), so that, contrary to what we may assume, the dialogue situation may be unpredictable and thus is inherently open. Basically, all situations where new events may change the search space during the time needed for exploring it are inherently open.

3.1.3.   The lexicon

Let us call:

P	the agent initiating the dialogue;
Q	the partner;
i_0	the initiating message sent - conventionally - by P to Q at time 0;
$o_0 , ... o_n , ...$	the sequence of outputs of agent Q, each corresponding to an input;
$g_0 , ... g_n , ...$	the sequence of procedures applied by Q;
$f_0 , ... f_n , ...$	the sequence of procedures applied by P
	to its inputs $o_0 , ... o_n , ...$, yielding $i_1 , ... i_{n+1} ...$;
t	the variable denoting the discrete time, i.e. the turn-taking index;
	$t = 0, 1, ..., n, n+1, ...$.

Adopting a syntactic notation for the application of a function to its argument that consists in simple juxtaposition, we may assume that:

$$o_n = (g_n \ i_n) \qquad \text{and} \qquad i_{n+1} = (f_n \ o_n).$$

3.1.4. STReams

According to this lexicon, the set I (including the messages of P, the initiating agent in the dialogue) is <u>build dynamically</u> during the process of message exchange. In other words, P evaluates (generates) the next message to be send to Q only after P has received Q's answer, i.e. P delays the evaluation of the next message.

An abstract data type that represents this mechanism of delayed evaluation is the stream. Streams are optimal data structures as they model sequences that do not yet exist, but eventually may exist at the time they are needed.

This property is essential in dialogue exchanges: one cannot "undo" the effects of a sequence of moves between autonomous agents retrospectively. Backtracking and their associated belief/truth revision techniques, are notions that are associated to search in closed systems, not to interactions with open systems. Time cannot be reversed.

Streams model nicely the fact that planning in autonomous, interactive systems is different from planning in closed systems. An agent in STROBE may plan ahead only the next move, because the second next move will possibly be generated by another planner, different from the previous one, that we cannot know before. Even the Scheme evaluation model may be modified from one time to the other.

This observation forces us to consider the issue of reflection, widely debated within the AI & ED [2] and within the Programming Languages research (see, e.g. reflection in LISP-like languages reported extensively in [23]). We agree with the requirements outlined in [2] and the criticisms to interoperability in actor languages like Actalk reported in [11] . The last author solved the issue of generic MOC (Model of Computation) in Actor Languages by designing his ReActalk reflective actor language. We have the ambition to provide even more evidence for the need of reflection in dialogue modeling languages, but wish also to keep our basic MOC as simple as possible. In order to do that, we have taken an example of a simple, interactive, reflexive interpreter built in Scheme by slightly modifying the eval primitive designed in Continuation Passing Style [24] and plan to integrate a revised version of it into our prototypical language.

3.1.5. OBjects

The notion of private memory is crucial in generic dialogues. Some knowledge may be shared other knowledge is necessarily private. Encapsulation of variables and methods (information hiding), among other features of objects in object-oriented programming (OOP), make them attractive for modeling private knowledge in each agent, but do not explain what occurs when agents exchange real messages in an autonomous fashion.

To keep the architecture simple, we will not include here any in-depth consideration about objects, such as (multiple) inheritance, virtual methods, meta-object protocols and the like. These - more advanced - opportunities offered by objects might all be modeled by using the standard primitives of the language. For an extended discussion about objects in Scheme defined only on the basis of first class functions (and therefore the basic MOC of the language) see [25] .

3.1.6.   Environments

We will call eQ_0 ... eQ_n the private environments of Q and eP_0 ... eP_n the private environments of P as they are generated at subsequent phases of the dialogue. Each environment includes a set of local frames - modeling a private, non shared memory - and possibly other higher level frames modeling a memory shared with the partner, up to the global environment that is supposed to be shared. This shared environment models the agreement among agents about the syntax and semantics of the Scheme expressions that are part of the moves. Because agents are instances of the same object class, they may share also the functionality's concerning how to react to a partner's move, i.e. they share the pragmatic rules of the dialogue[x].

Table 1. The dialogue process with explicit environments

Exchanges						Moves
E_0 :	i_0		->	$((g_0\ i_0)eQ_0)=>$	o_0	M_0P
	i_1	$<=((f_0\ o_0)eP_0)$	<-		o_0	M_0Q
E_1 :	i_1		->	$((g_1\ i_1)eQ_1)=>$	o_1	M_1P
	i_2	$<=((f_1\ o_1)eP_1)$	<-		o_1	M_1Q
E_2 :	i_2		->	$((g_2\ i_2)eQ_2)=>$	o_2	M_2P
	i_3	$<=((f_2\ o_2)eP_2)$	<-		o_2	M_2Q
....						
E_n :	i_n		->	$((g_n\ i_n)eQ_n)=>$	o_n	M_nP
	i_{n+1}	$<=((f_n\ o_n)eP_n)$	<-		o_n	M_nQ

3.1.7.   Simple classification of moves

Moves in STROBE belong to an abstract data type consisting of a move type and a move expression. Move types are recognized by the agent that receives the move and consequently performs the corresponding activities, such as updating the private environment, activating a diagnosis, generating an answer or generating the next move. Move types, in this simple version of the model, include the intention of the sender.

Table 2. Move classification and interpretation, single initiative

move type	move subtype	initiating move: examples	effect on receiver	Reacting move: Examples (type)
assertion	definition of a variable	(define a 3)	environment modified	ok (ack)
assertion	definition f a procedure	(define (square x) (* x x))	environment modified	ok (ack)
request	value of a variable	a	(eval a) in environment	▪ 3 (answer) ▪ unknown (answer) ▪ error (answer)
request	value of a procedure	square	(eval square) in environment	▪ (lambda(x) (* x x) in <definition environment >) (*answer*) ▪ unknown (*answer*) ▪ error (*answer*)
order	application of a procedure to arguments	(square a)	(apply (eval square) (eval a))	▪ 9 (*executed*) ▪ unknown (*answer*) ▪ error (*answer*)
ack	Acknowledge positive	ok	update partner's model	Generate next move
ack	Acknowledge unknown	don't know	update partner's model	Generate next move
ack	Acknowledge negative	error	update partner's model	Generate next move
answer	value	3	start diagnosis	Generate next move
answer	procedural value	(lambda (x) (* x x) in <definition environment >)	start diagnosis	Generate next move
executed	value (plus potential side effect)	9	start diagnosis	Generate next move

3.2. Cognitive environments

In the environment model of evaluation, the environment is responsible for what usually is called the memory (or the state or finally the context). We have chosen initially to represent explicitly four such contexts, to be interpreted as the private environment and the partner's model for each of the two agents. For the moment, the private environment is used for the evaluation of the partner's moves while the partner's model is only used for activating a (primitive) diagnosis. Environments are modified during the dialogue process, according to the common pragmatic principles governing each agent's behavior reacting to the partner's moves.

We have defined Cognitive Environment a first class Abstract Data Type (ADT) that is made of a set of one or more labeled contexts. Each context is an environment ADT in traditional terms, i.e. a sequence of frames each of which is a sequence of bindings. Contexts are assumed to be coherent internally, but not necessarily one with another. A binding is a pair name-value, where names are identifiers and values are objects in the domain of discourse, i.e. in our case in the domain of the formal language Scheme itself.

In [27] we may find a precise treatment of first class environments in Scheme and, due to their limitations in lexically scoped languages, first class extents. The capturing problems described by the authors, do not seem to be of immediate concern for our experimental context, even if that may become the case at a maturer phase of the project. Therefore we agreed with them that adding environments as first-class values can greatly enhance the expressiveness of a language [19] and consider their first class extents for a potential subsequent refinement of our model, eventually stimulated by their finding that once first class extents are introduced, it is simple to consider environments in Scheme as the natural data structure for representing components of objects (and classes at the same time).

3.2.1. Multiple contexts

Dialogues are processes occurring between agents that are based on the REPL cycle on turn by each agent. The set of move types reported in Table 2 might be used to model any interaction among two agents conventionally called P and Q.

The effect of any move of P on Q is modeled by the evaluation of the move of P in the Q's private environment. Here we have the problem: the private environment of Q may not be the one expected by P. As a consequence, the value (the effect) of P's move on Q may be different from the value/effect expected by P. This fundamental phenomenon occurs because P and Q are assumed to be autonomous, i.e. P does not have direct access to bindings in Q's cognitive environment. If P knew all that Q knows, P would foresee Q's behavior all the times. The reaction of Q to a move from P would be "expected" by P. Expected does not mean specified. For instance, in traditional Information Systems, even if one does not know the answer to a query, one foresees properties of the answer that make it relevant for the informative needs of the queerer.

3.2.2. Emerging functionality's

The cognitive environment notion enhances the traditional access, in the environment, to a value from its name. Thanks to cognitive environments, agents may possess quite powerful search + access functionality's similar to the one available in temporally evolving, advanced information systems. Our cognitive environment is in fact a set of databases plus the update and query language consisting of constructors and selectors. Each database is progressively build during the dialogue as a side effect of pragmatic markers as denoted by move types, and searched in the moments an agent needs it.

In the following, a preliminary list of foreseen functionalities is presented. The list is not exhaustive, but it gives an idea of the potential properties of first class, cognitive environments associated to agents in the STROBE model.

Multiple access

Access by name: this is the traditional update / query that looks for the first instance of the identified variable in the nearest frame. Access by value: one may ask for the first available name of a concept associated to a specific value. Access by name and value: one may ask for the first available binding name-value of a concept.

Access to the history of the bindings

The above accesses may be recursively repeated onward in a single context (environment) up to the global frame. A query may sound like: give me all the names of variables with value <value> that are available in the set of frames belonging to <context>. Eventually, one may introduce versioning, i.e. labeled traces of variable updates, so that the "historical" state changes may be saved and queried.

Access to multiple contexts

As contexts are environments in traditional Scheme terms, one may perform multiple evaluations of the same expression in order to check if any of the contexts may justify some unexpected behavior. Any set operation (intersection, union, etc.) on environments may produce a new environment that may justify an unexpected behavior. As we will see, one may associate to an agent several labeled environments, one each partner agent so that expressions are evaluated in the context established during each sub-dialogue.

Search • access

Information systems of the future will be able to be more adapted to the needs of the human user. For instance, search of the information will answer questions such as: "given the following need: <a formalized need>, where in a networked set of knowledge sources (humans, databases eventually not homogeneous...) may I find probably even a partial response to my need?" while access follows (or does not follow, if the results of the search phase make access irrelevant or not enough interesting for the queerer) with a significant saving of resources. We have solved the problem in a non trivial application domain [28] by building a kind of shared ontology - a common lexicon - that meta-describes each knowledge source in the net, and applying a concurrent, distributed search strategy. If cognitive environments are first class data structures, these techniques may be applied.

4. STROBE agents communicating by KQML-like messages

In the preliminary version of STROBE described above, there were many limitations that we discuss hereafter.

Firstly, the pragmatic markers associated with messages were quite elementary, i.e. the six basic performatives representing speech acts: assert, query, order, acknowledge, answer and executed. We wanted those performatives to be extended and extensible, as we know that the range of "speech acts" occurring in real dialogues is much wider.

Secondly: message exchange between agents was synchronous and sequential. Mixed initiative dialogues, i.e. role exchange (or, in the two-agent case - swapping) required the introduction of a coordinator agent, a kind of interface with an external observer. Multiple autonomous agents[xi] were not supported at the level of the language.

Thirdly: no provision was made for an explicit identification of the language of messages, that was assumed to be constantly Scheme, in other words there was no mean - at the level of the language - to denote any "content language abstraction".

Some of these features are available in KQML, but that agent communication language does not include other properties that we consider necessary for our scenarios. Let us just mention those limits of KQML.

Concerning the variety of performatives available in KQML, these are mainly concerned with transmission of messages, interoperability and buffering[xii]. All these are enabling conditions for multi-software-agent communication, but they are insufficient for dialogues that include humans, such as the ones we envision in our scenario (cf. [31] for an example of classification of pragmatic components of educational dialogues)

Concerning concurrency, KQML includes broadcasting and the management of queues of messages. However, there is no effort in KQML to model agents with multiple viewpoints. Further, KQML does not need reflection, as it is not concerned with "real autonomy" such as, for instance, the one shown when an agent takes the initiative.

Finally, concerning the content language abstraction, KQML indeed allows to separate the content of messages (including their language syntax and semantics) from the pragmatics. Even if we know that natural languages and also, in some way, formal languages do mix pragmatic aspects with semantic and syntactic ones, this separation is useful for our purposes and thus we have included it in our design.

4.1. Our KQML extension: supporting richer pragmatic primitives

An improvement of the STROBE architecture has been achieved by implementing an interpreter of KQML messages in Scheme. The interpreter has been written in STk 3.0[xiii] using the object extension available. Agents in our new prototype belong to an agent class and communicate with each other by means of KQML messages that are also objects.

The STk implementation of agents required extending STk with a set of functionalities for the management of sockets [xiv]. These allow messages among agents to be buffered and handled by the agents at due time. Once any of those messages is read by the KQML agent, the corresponding performative activates the actions required by the semantics of the performative as described in [30] .

Because a KQML object is also a Scheme object, our agents may be easily associated to cognitive environments modeling multiple viewpoints.

The current actions associated to the performatives are quite simple: the design of actions adequate for realistic dialogues, including educational dialogues, is the next step of our research plan to be performed together with experiments on selected domains[xv].

4.2.   Code excerpts

Agents are defined as members of the class <Agente>, partially defined in STk as shown in the excerpt below:

```
;;;;;;;;;;;;;;;;;;;;;;;;;;;;;;;;
;;; Class that generates agents
;;; communicating by means of KQML messages.
;;; Notice that KQML messages are STk objects.
(define-class <Agente>
  ()
  ((name                       ;;; class name
    :initform '<Agente>)
   (my-name                    ;;; instance name
    :initform '()
    :getter %get-name
    :setter %set-name!)
   (kqml-object   ;;; kqml object managing communication
    :initform '()
    :getter %get-kqml
    :setter %set-kqml!)
   (environments   ;;; Set of environments available,
          ;;; one for each partner in the communication.
    :initform '((env))          ;;;
    :accessor %env)
   (pipe                        ;;; active pipes
    :initform '((pipe))         ;;;
    :accessor %pipe)
   (forward                     ;;;
    :initform '((forward))      ;;;
    :accessor %forward)
   (standard-handler            ;;;
    :initform %standard-eval
    :accessor %standard-handler)
   (handlers                    ;;;
    :initform '((handlers))     ;;;
    :accessor %handlers)))       ;;;
;;;;;;;;;;;;;;;;;;;;;;;;;;;;;;;;;;;;;;;;;;
```

KQML messages are instances of the Class <KQML> as briefly indicated in the excerpt below:

```
;;;;;;;;;;;;;;;;;;;;;;;;;;;;;;;;;;;;;;;
(define-class <KQML>
  ()
  ((name                        ;;; class name
    :initform '<KQML>)
   (my-name                     ;;; instance name
    :initform '()
    :getter %get-name
    :setter %set-name!)
   (direct-connections;;; connections with other agents
    :initform '((direct));;;list of pairs:
                         ;;;(agent-name . socket)
    :accessor %dir-con)
   (p-socket       ;;; socket for accepting connections
    :initform #f
    :accessor %passive)
   (received-connections    ;;;
    :initform '((received))  ;;;
    :accessor %ric-con)
   (ports                   ;;;
    :initform '((ports))     ;;;
    :accessor %ports)
   (messages            ;;; messages awaiting to be sent
    :initform '()            ;;; queue
    :accessor %msg)
   (pipe                    ;;; active pipes
    :initform '((pipe))      ;;;
    :accessor %pipe)
   (broadcast   ;;; received "broadcast" performatives
    :initform '()            ;;;
    :accessor %broadcast)
   (automatic-functions     ;;;
    :initform '((functions))  ;;;
    :accessor %func)))
;;;;;;;;;;;;;;;;;;;;;;;;;;;;;;;;;;;;;;;;;;;;;;;;;;;;;;;;;;;;;;;;;;;;
```

It is clear to us that these excerpts give just a vague idea of our prototype. A complete description, however, would not only be too long for this paper, but also not particularly beneficial for the reader because the current prototype mixes features at the level of implementation with higher level ones that denote properties at the dialogue (pragmatic) level.

What seems to us more relevant here is a discussion concerning our planned enhancements of STROBE according to the goals that we have outlined previously[vi].

5.   Feasible requirements for modeling multiple communication

5.1.   Autonomous agents are not just pair-wise communicating

Agents as they have been modeled in the first STROBE prototype are sequential agents that exchange messages each with one other agent at a time. The introduction of a coordinator-agent allowed introducing a minimal level of initiative in the dialogue among agents: at the end of each exchange, the coordinator may give the initiative for the next exchange to the agent that previously responded. The coordinator agent is an interface with the external (human) experimenter, but also a means of simulating mixed initiatives[xvii].

Now: if any agent consists only of the information assumed to be available during the dialogue with one single partner agent, and if the initial state of both agents is known to each other (they are both instances of the same agent class), as it occurred in our preliminary experiments [19, 22] , there is no reason for any of the two agents to suspect that the partner's reaction to any of its moves will not coincide with the expected one. If the dialogue occurs between two artificial agents that know each other at the beginning and communicate only with each other the situation is not an open one. Each agent may fully reconstruct the partner's state. Real situations are quite different, they are inherently open.

An open situation for an agent, say A communicating with a partner B is a situation such that at any time B is unable to predict the behavior of the partner. One case may be that B does not know fully the initial state of the partner A. Another one is that A is allowed to react to messages sent by other agents (for instance, another agent called C) while it keeps also active the conversation with B. Even if the phenomenon is certainly not new, from a purely "shared variable" viewpoint, it may help understanding to recall it in detail within our communication model because we may include explicit pragmatic information that is usually not considered in other frameworks.

Initiating messages reaching an agent may basically consist of assertions, queries and orders. Assume that assertions are the only messages that certainly modify the agent's environment. Queries are usually non-invasive, while orders may be but not necessarily are. Therefore our agent A communicating with B and with C may only "wonder" B or C in case its dialogues with C or B respectively, did have side effects on its (A's) private environment - e.g. as a consequence of assertions -, as we see easily hereafter.

For instance, an agent A that communicates with B up to a certain moment, then with C and then again with B may be - for B - an open system, Taken at the extreme consequences: if B has sent the message (assert (define x 3)) to A, and A has acknowledged, and then C has sent to A the message (assert (define x 4)) and A has acknowledged; then B sends A (request x): B will receive (answer 4) instead of (answer 3) from A as it would have expected.

B -> A	A -> B	C -> A	A -> C
(assert(define x 3))			
	(ack)[env_A (x 3)]		
		(assert(define x 4))	
			(ack)[env_A (x 4)]
(request x)			
	(answer 4)		

In STROBE the situation is controlled by assuming each dialogue to be situated within a pair of environments: one private to the agent and the other reflecting the *current* partner's model. Extending the hypothesis to multiple partners, it is natural to think extending the environments available to each partner with a labeled environment for each partner reflecting the partners assertions "historically". If that is true, then A should answer 3 to B's request because the value of the variable x required by B is to be found in A's environment reserved by A to B : env_{AB}. This holds for every assertion of type *define*.

B -> A	A -> B	C -> A	A -> C
(assert (define x 3))			
	(ack)[env_{AB} (x 3)]		
		(assert (define x 4))	
			(ack)[env_{AC} (x 4)]
(request x)			
	(answer 3)		

But: what about *set!* (i.e. real assignments) potentially modifying any local or global variable? In case x is global, A will not be able to reset the value B believes A knows (x 3) because x - a global variable for A -, was later assigned by C during the dialogue.

In order to behave properly, A should protect also the global variable x, for instance generating two sub-environments env_{ABg} and env_{ACg} of the global where to keep the values of x assigned by B and C [xviii]. We have adopted this approach in the new version of STROBE.

Our intuition, and the preliminary experiments on multi-agent dialogues, suggest that differences with similar protection mechanisms known in the literature, will have to do with the pragmatics of communication, i.e. exactly those roles, goals, intentions etc. that allow to distinguish agents from programs, and agent communication languages from network protocols. In the following section, we further elaborate on similarities and differences between our work and other ones.

5.2.   The coordination of message exchanges in multi-agent dialogues

The following transcript concerns three STROBE agents A, B, C communicating by means of KQML-like messages. It shows how an inconsistency may occur when agent B "is told" by agent A a value for the variable create-rational that is inconsistent with the value subsequently "told" to B by agent C, even if both definitions of the function create-rational are semantically correct.

```
AB ;;; Messages from A to B
(achieve :content (define create-rational (lambda (x y)
(cons x y))) :sender A :receiver B)
(achieve :content (define numerator (lambda (x) (car x)))
:sender A :receiver B)
(achieve :content (define denominator (lambda (x) (cdr x)))
:sender A :receiver B)
(achieve :sender A :receiver B :content (define plus (lambda
(x y) (create-rational (+ (* (numerator x) (denominator y))
(* (numerator y) (denominator x))) (* (denominator x)
(denominator y)))))))
(evaluate :content (create-rational 1 2) :sender A :receiver
B :reply-with d1)
BA ;;; Messages from B to A
(tell :content (1 . 2) :sender B :receiver A :in-reply-to
d1)
AB(evaluate :content (plus (1 . 2) (create-rational 1 3))
:sender A :receiver B :reply-with d2)
BA(tell :content (5 . 6) :sender B :receiver A :in-reply-to
d2)
Continues with a third agent C.
CB ;;; Message from C to B
(achieve :sender C :receiver B :content (define create-
rational (lambda (x y) (cons (/ x (gcd x y)) (/ y (gcd x
y))))))
AB (evaluate :content (plus (1 . 2) (1 . 6)) :sender A
:receiver B :reply-with d3)
BA (tell :content (2 . 3) :sender B :receiver A :in-reply-to
d3)
For A this is an unexpected response, as A taught B a
definition of rational numbers that did not include the
reduction of numerator and denominator by their greatest
common divisor. The example shows that assignement of a
variable (create-rational) private for B, but accessible to
both A and C may cause A (or either C) to perceive B as
behaving unexpectedly (or incorrectly).
```

The availability of a cognitive environment in B allows A to eventually understand B's unexpected behavior by querying B about the reason for its belief that (plus (1 . 2) (1 . 6)) is (2 . 3) instead of (8.12). Agent A may therefore activate a diagnostic procedure that queries B to provide for an answer to the query (plus (1 . 2) (1 . 6)) not only in B's current environment , but also in B's environment dedicated to A. If this answer fits A's expected one, then A understands that env$_{BA}$ is different from env$_{BC}$. A subsequent query about the values of plus put by A to B will not find the cause of the difference, but a query about create-rational will, so that A may come to the conclusion that C has asserted B a version of the create-rational function that simplifies numerator and denominator of rational numbers by dividing both by the gcd. Perhaps A did not use gcd in its definition of create-rational because it did not possess any gcd concept; therefore A may ask B or C for such a concept and finally resolve B's ambiguity by re-asserting A's view on rational numbers as equal to C's.

This kind of diagnostic process has been implemented in its essence in our system, so that we may conclude that, from our preliminary work, cognitive environments [xix] and pragmatically marked messages support effectively (and simply) the run time generation of dialogues among autonomous agents that map onto realistic dialogues among human or artificial agents communicating asynchronously in a fashion potentially including inconsistencies.

5.3. STROBE agents versus Actors

The discussion concerning concurrency - parallelism in programming languages reported in [34] highlights the foundations of the problems we find in our communication model. Basically, Agha identifies three approaches:

-sequential processes, i.e. processes transforming states;

-functions, i.e. stateless procedures processing streams of values;

-actors, i.e. objects exchanging asynchronous messages and able to transform dynamically their own behavior (eventually generating new private data / methods) and the topology / behavior of the net (by generating new actors).

The last solution is shown to subsume the previous ones. We assume Agha is right, and therefore assume Actors as a basis for our own discussion about STROBE agents.

Actors are equipped with handlers of buffers of asynchronously incoming messages. We adopt the same solution. Actors do not really maintain a "self" because they may modify their own behavior in a principled, fundamental way (cf. [34] , page 9, note 1: "sequential processes may activate other sequential processes and multiple activations are permitted, but the topology of the individual process is still static" differently from the case of Actors). We do not exclude, in STROBE, to generate new agents dynamically. Agents are objects, objects are functions and Scheme may define or set! functions dynamically. However, that is not the only way our agents are allowed to react to messages.

Our cognitive environments already represent a kind of dynamic generation of new actors / actor's behaviors. Consider, for instance, agent B of the previous example. When B receives from C the message

```
(achieve :sender C :receiver B :content (define create-rational (lambda (x y) (cons
(/ x (gcd x y)) (/ y (gcd x y))))))
```

B updates a newly created environment env$_{BC}$ dedicated to C thus becoming a single agent that behaves in two different ways. The "self" of B, however, is not lost: B has two "selfs", from that moment on; one that reflects B's dialogues with A and one that reflects B's dialogues with C. Agha's actors would split into two. Our B agent behaves as two different actors, still maintaining control over its own history and therefore the origins of its behavior. Therefore B may answer A (or C or any other agent) questions concerning any labeled subenvironment available.

5.4.   Metaphors for communication: telephone versus mail

The telephone system was cited in [34] as a real world metaphor possibly associated to systems with synchronous communication (like Hoare's Communicating Sequential Processes and Milner's Calculus of Communicating Systems).

STROBE is clearly adopting the asynchronous model, thus the metaphor of the postal system, as attributed in [34] to the dataflow and the actor models of computation. Dataflow models are not adequate for us, because their functional behavior exclude dependency from the history of interactions, which is for us a requirement. But the Actor model is as well limited for our purposes. Let us give two reasons.

Firstly, as we briefly described before, actors modify their behavior (or generate new actors) forgetting their history. Our cognitive environment allows our agents to possess multiple behaviors emerging from different interaction histories with other agents but keeping the historical reasons of that multiple behavior.

Secondly, actor's buffered asynchronous communication model fits the mail system metaphor only in a limited way. Mailboxes in actors include messages in the actor language itself, not distinguishing between the content of the message and its pragmatic level. It is like a real world postal mailbox containing only the letters, without envelopes or an electronic mailbox containing only the messages, not an overview of sender, title, etc. of each incoming electronic mail. As a consequence, actor's "arbiters", i.e. the schedulers of priorities in the processing of messages by actors, dispose of limited information with respect to the needs of a really autonomous agent such as a human (or even an artificial but autonomous one). KQML-like messages and the explicit description of pragmatic information separated from the content allow, instead, our agents to be equipped with schedulers of incoming messages that fit much better realistic behaviors of autonomous agents[xx].

For instance, suppose we receive in our electronic mail system EUDORA (or any other one) two messages such that their effects on our plan of what to do today may be inconsistent: one from a colleague, chairperson of a Conference where we have an accepted paper that has to be revised and sent for publication before tomorrow, and one from the Director of our Department. The first message urges us to commit our delivery of the paper on time; the second one urges us to participate to an important, unforeseen meeting. Now: the scheduling of activities and answers is fully under our own control, and EUDORA helps us to tailor our behavior by providing pragmatic information - different from the pure content of the messages - that is useful for deciding what to do, even if we are free to adopt a behavior that - a posteriori - may result to be the worse one. We may, for instance, decide either

a. to look first to all messages before committing us with an acceptance either for the paper or for the meeting (this solution resembles the periodic "synchronization" in distributed databases: no real change occurs before the effects of all, possibly inconsistent, proposed changes, periodically, are evaluated; the same buffering mechanism we have described and implemented when we talked about set! operations in global variables) or either (e.g. if messages to read are too many so that our estimated time to read all of them would exclude us to spend the afternoon in finishing the paper or attending the meeting):

b. we commit ourselves to the paper - and later discover that we can't go to the meeting - (or vice versa, according to which message we opened first).

In both cases we notice that the scheduler of our activities concerning the access to the electronic mailbox belongs to us and that decisions taken by that scheduler are influenced by meta-level information on the messages.

Cognitive environments AND pragmatically marked messages seem to offer us all the opportunities to model a realistic "postal", asynchronous message exchange computational paradigm where agents are equipped with full autonomy, including the scheduling of actions in response to incoming messages.

Agents behaving this way are like operating systems, equipped with interpreters, compilers, ontologies (to be stored in their environments) and are autonomous in the sense that they do not just react to incoming buffered messages (like actors, that represent the asynchronous concurrent version of a client-server model of computation) but proact by planning what to do next, including the strategy of reaction to messages, according to a scheduler that is in itself a dynamic, evolutionary program, the kernel of the agent's behavior. For a recent, excellent introduction to the fundamental aspects of actors and agents, see [39] .

5.5.   The explicit representation of state changes in STROBE agents

Let us now reflect briefly on how to represent state changes in agents in our model. In [30] the authors propose / use ATN-like grammars to describe state changes as a result of performatives exchanged by agents. They also explicitly talk about "dialogue grammars" that describe the conversation polices. Their remark that the paradigm of parsing <<differs from the usual one in that the "sentence" (the set of messages exchanged, seen as terminals) might well be unfinished, meaning that the thread might not be complete>> is correct.

We have proposed quite long ago [35, 36] to use ATN grammars to describe dialogues, in particular educational dialogues. The DART [xxi] system, built on PLATO, was designed and implemented with this purpose. However, we now see clearly a danger in such an approach, and understand in the same time why Labrou and Finin's ATN proposal is correct, while for STROBE agents this approach would not be correct. We recall that KQML agents do have a unique "self", as KQML is designed for dialogues among software agents that assume consistency among agents. Our agents equipped with cognitive (multiple) environments, in order to cope with multiple viewpoints in human communication, do not possess a unique "self". ATN grammars do not foresee, in their original definition, multiple co-existing, eventually inconsistent states[xxii].

5.6.   Future developments

A pre-emptive operating system in Scheme is an illuminating exercise if one wishes to familiarize with continuations and engines [4]. We have done the exercise. The operating system functionalities may be integrated within STROBE, i.e. merged with the ones of the KQML interpreter. Such a task scheduler has been implemented in order to separate the control of the allocation of resources considered available within a single agent from the control of KQML message exchanges with partner agents. Single agents may activate their own resources in a pre-emptive, time-shared fashion like a traditional operating system, but events occurring externally and producing messages at the input require a scheduling regime that is associated to the semantics of KQML performatives, i.e. the pragmatics of communication. The latter will require substantial modifications to the previous task scheduler.

Finally, KQML is a large-scale project aiming at interoperability between heterogeneous systems. STROBE is a model and a small scale project aiming at performing experiments with realistic agent-to-agent dialogues in order to refine the semantics of performatives, i.e. define higher level primitives that allow to design and implement systems for human-computer communication according to better pragmatic principles as the ones currently used. Therefore STROBE is at the moment monolingual (Scheme) but also highly compositional. The requirement of (relative) cognitive simplicity in the design advises us to focus on functionalities even at the costs of efficiency and robustness. However, three aspects were beyond the immediate scope of STROBE, i.e. interfaces, networking and platform independence.

For these reasons we have constructed a language integrator, called JASCHEMAL that allows Scheme code to be compiled by Java programs into Java Byte Code, and facilitates also mutual calls. The prototype is currently developed for a significant subset of Scheme standard primitives, including procedural objects and continuations.

6.   Conclusions

Recent developments in Computing (e.g. networks, multimedia interfaces) have produces an extraordinary acceleration in the applicative needs for truly interactive, human-computer communication systems for various purposes. For instance, Education is an area of rapid growth of demand, Information another one. Object oriented technologies, considered to be an AI exclusive domain in the 70ties, are current state of the art and objects operate by exchanging messages. The shift from programs/algorithms within a single machine to processes/objects exchanging messages among various cooperating agents is perhaps the major current challenge in applicative Computing. It reduces basically to consider communication as driving control, not vice versa. The mental model of the underlying virtual machine is necessarily different from the previous one.

Human communication by exchanging messages shows that the pragmatic aspects of communication (goals, knowledge, intentions...) drive the success of the communicative processes. Emerging mainly from the needs of the AI community, in particular interoperability between knowledge bases for informative purposes, the Knowledge Sharing Effort has produced in the US a first mature language - called KQML - that incorporates pragmatic primitives, its performatives. From the needs of advanced educational applications, we have proposed a model and architecture called STROBE that shares the same objectives but suggests slightly different paths for achieving them.

Scheme is considered in STROBE both as a description and a prototyping language. Message exchange is viewed as a dynamic process where agents decide the next move by assembling / selecting it after evaluating the stream of previous messages exchanged with the partners. Agents are equipped with cognitive environments, i.e. trees of frames labeled according to the history and the partner's messages. Scheduling of tasks in agents occurs in a fashion similar to that of operating systems, but unlike them (and actors) is influenced by the explicit pragmatic layer that belongs to messages. When an agent processes a message, it is seen by its partners as an enhanced interpreter of KQML-like messages, that includes as a component an interpreter of the content language indicated in the message.

The integration of the proposed architecture with available networks, interfaces and platforms, i.e. most of the "lower level" technologies necessary for a realistic experimentation is achieved by coupling Scheme with Java.

Even if the work done is far from being complete, its properties become progressively clearer. One concrete result is that the concept is feasible. Another, to be debated, hypothesis is that it is also helpful for studying complex communicative phenomena by experimentation. Finally, the most important claim - yet only partially justified - is that it is relatively simple. If this were true, we would have reached our goal, as complexity of languages, tools and systems too often has hindered the accumulation of results in the research and a sensible utilization of them in practical applications.

7.   References

1.   Woolridge,M., Muller, J. P. and Tambe, M. (eds.): Intelligent Agents II. Agent Theories, Architectures, and Languages. In: Carbonell, J.G. and Siekmann, J. (eds.) Lecture Notes in Artificial Intelligence, Vol. 1037. Springer-Verlag, Berlin Heidelberg New York (1996) XVIII- 437

2.   Self, J.: Artificial Intelligence in Education: Towards Computational Mathetics. University of Lancaster, Lancaster, UK, Unpublished draft, May 1995.

3.   Cerri, S.A. and Loia, V.: A Concurrent, Distributed Architecture for Diagnostic Reasoning. Journal of User Modeling and User Adapted Interaction 7 (1997) 69-105.

4.   Kent Dybvig, R.: The Scheme Programming Language; ANSI Scheme. Prentice-Hall, Inc., (1996)

5.   Queinnec, C.: Les langages LISP. InterEditions, Paris (1994)

6.   Abelson,H. and Sussman,G:J.: Structure and Interpretation of Computer Programs. 2nd edn. MIT Press, Cambridge, Mass. (1996)

7.   Mayfield,J., Labrou,Y. and Finin,T.: Evaluation of KQML as an Agent Communication Language. In: Woolridge,M., Muller,J.P. and Tambe,M. (eds.) Intelligent Agents II. Agent Theories, Architectures, and Languages, Lecture Notes in Artificial Intelligence, Vol. 1037. Springer-Verlag, Berlin Heidelberg New York (1996) 347-360.

8.   Cerri,S.A.: Models and Systems for Collaborative Dialogues in Distance Learning. In: Verdejo,M.F. and Cerri,S.A. (eds.) Collaborative Dialogue Technologies in Distance Learning, Computer and Systems Sciences, Vol. 133. Springer-Verlag, Berlin Heidelberg New York (1994) 119-125.

9.   Pinkilton,R. and Parker-Jones,C.: Interacting with Computer-Based Simulation: the role of dialogue. Computers Educ. 27 (1996) 1-14

10. Bunt, H.C.: Dialogue analysis and speech act theory. Institute for Perception Research, Eindhoven 330/II (1978)
11. Giroux,S.: Open Reflective Agents. In: Woolridge,M., Muller,J.P. and Tambe,M. (eds.) Intelligent Agents II. Agent Theories, Architectures, and Languages, Lecture Notes in Artificial Intelligence, Vol. 1037. Springer-Verlag, Berlin Heidelberg New York (1996) 315-330.
12. Leman,S., Marcenac,P. and Giroux,S.: A Generic Architecture for ITS based on a MultiAgent Model. In: Frasson,C., Gauthier,G. and Lesgold,A(eds.)Intelligent Tutoring Systems. Lecture Notes in Computer Science, Vol 1096. Springer-Verlag, Berlin Heidelberg New York (1996) 75-83
13. Moeschler,J. and Reboul,A: Dictionnaire encyclopédique de pragmatique. Editions du Seuil, Paris (1994)
14. Searle,J. R.: Speech acts. An essay in the philosophy of language. Cambridge University Press, Cambridge, UK (1969)
15. Guin,D.: Towards Models of Interaction Between an Artificial Agent and Human one. In: Verdejo,M.F. and Cerri,S.A. (eds.) Collaborative Dialogue Technologies in Distance Learning, Computer and Systems Sciences, Vol. 133. Springer-Verlag, Berlin Heidelberg New York (1994) 170-180
16. Reitz,P.: Contribution à l'étude des environments d'apprendissage. Conceptualization, spécification et prototypage. PhD Thesis. Departement d'Informatique. Université de Montpellier II (1992)
17. Cerri, S. A.: The "Natural Laboratory" Methodology Supporting Computer Mediated Generic Dialogues. In: Verdejo,M.F. and Cerri,S.A. (eds.) Collaborative Dialogue Technologies in Distance Learning, Computer and Systems Sciences, Vol. 133. Springer-Verlag, Berlin Heidelberg New York (1994) 181-201
18. Self,J.: Computational Viewpoints. Computing Department, University of Lancaster, Lancaster, UK AI Report n. 44, March 1990.
19. Cerri,S.A.: Cognitive environments in the STROBE model. Presented at EuroAIED: the European Conference in Artificial Intelligence and Education, Lisbon, Portugal (1996)
20. Cheikes,B.: Should ITS Designers Be Looking For A Few Good Agents? Presented at AI-ED Workshop on Authoring Shells for Intelligent Tutoring Systems, Washington, DC, 1995.
21. Paiva,A.: Learner Modelling Agents. Presented at EuroAIED: the European Conference in Artificial Intelligence and Education, Lisbon, Portugal (1996)
22. Cerri,S.A.: Computational Mathetics Tool kit: architecture's for dialogues. In: Frasson,C., Gauthier,G. and Lesgold,A(eds.)Intelligent Tutoring Systems. Lecture Notes in Computer Science, Vol 1096. Springer-Verlag, Berlin Heidelberg New York (1996) 343-352
23. Friedman,D.P. and Yonezawa,A.(eds.): Special issue on Computational Reflection. LISP and symbolic computation. An International Journal. 9, 2/3, Kluwer, Dordrecht (1996) 151-257
24. Jefferson,S. and Friedman, D. P.: A Simple Reflective Interpreter. LISP and symbolic computation. An International Journal. 9, 2/3, Kluwer, Dordrecht (1996) 181-202
25. Noermark,K.: Simulation of Object-Oriented Concepts and Mechanisms in Scheme. Institute of Electronic Systems, Aalborg University, Aalborg, DK R 90 01, ISSN 0106-0791 (1991)
26. Garrod,S.C. and Doherty,G.: Conversation, co-ordination and convention: an empirical investigation of how groups establish linguistic conventions. Cognition 53, (1994) 181-215
27. Lee,S-D. and Friedman,D.P.: First-Class Extents. Computer Science Departement, Indiana University, Bloomington, Indiana (August 1992)
28. Fabiano,A.S. and Cerri,S.A.: Concurrent, asynchronous search for the availability of knowledge. Applied Artificial Intelligence Journal 10 (1996) 145-161

29. Ferber,J.: Les systèmes multi-agents. Vers une intelligence collective. InterEditions, Paris (1995)

30. Labrou,Y. and Finin,T.: A semantics approach for KQML - a general purpose communication language for software agents. Presented at Third International Conference on Information and Knowledge Management (1994)

31. Pinkilton,R.: Analyzing Educational Discourse: The DISCOUNT Scheme. Computer-Based Learning Unit, The University of Leeds, Leeds, UK, TR n. 96, (April 1996)

32. Brusilowsky,P., Schwartz,E. and Weber,G.: ELM-ART: An Intelligent Tutoring System on World Wide Web. In: Frasson,C., Gauthier,G. and Lesgold,A(eds.)Intelligent Tutoring Systems. Lecture Notes in Computer Science, Vol 1096. Springer-Verlag, Berlin Heidelberg New York (1996) 261-269

33. Cerri,S.A.: Learning Computing: understanding Objects by understanding Variables and Functions. Object Currents: The first Online Hypertext Journal on Internet concerning Object Oriented Programming, 1, (1996) http://www.sigs.com/objectcurrents/

34. Agha,G.: Actors: A Model of Concurrent Computation in Distributed Systems. The MIT Press, Cambridge, Mass. (1986)

35. Cerri,S.A. Mattijsen,P. and Van Dijk,M.: Computer Aided Design of Didactic Software. In: Interactive Techniques in Computer Aided Design, ACM-Italian-Chapter (ed.) IEEE Computer Society (1978) 195-203

36. Cerri,S.A. and Breuker,J.: A rather intelligent language teacher. Presented at Artificial Intelligence : Proc. AISB-80 Conference, Amsterdam, NL (1980)

37. Cerri,S.A. Gisolfi,A. and Loia,V.: Towards the Abstraction and Generalization of Actor-based Architectures in Diagnostic Reasoning. In: this volume.

38. Dionisi,G.: AL: un linguaggio per descrivere la comunicazione tra agenti. Tesi di laurea in Scienze dell'Informazione, Università di Milano, (october 1998)

39. Kafura,D. and Briot,J.P.: Actors & Agents. IEEE Concurrency 6,2 (1998) 24-29

8.   Acknowledgements

I am particularly grateful to Antonio Gisolfi, who invited me several times to conferences of an outstanding professional level, organized by him in Ravello, including the one where I presented an extension of this work. Vincenzo Loia is the only person that has succeeded in convincing me to dedicate efforts in writing scientific papers, in particular recently when we had clear evidences that performing experimental research in Computing within Universities may be considered loosing your time. Erick Gallesio has contributed in a significant way to enhance my knowledge of Scheme, and is co-author of our joint presentation at the VIM Conference in Ravello. Julian Padget, finally, was always supportive and patient, particularly in accepting my delays. Thank you.

---

[1] In Queinnec's book [5] , chapter 5 is entirely dedicated to the relations between Scheme, Denotational semantics and lambda calculus.

[ii] Model and architecture are used as synonyms: a computational model is the abstract view of a computational architecture, i.e. the set of expressions in a language, together with the underlying virtual machine (the evaluation method of the expressions) that describes the solution to a class of problems. We also share the view of those [6] that believe that a program is a language for a class of problems. As an abstraction, STROBE is a model and an architecture. The (prototype) Scheme programs supporting STROBE functionality's, together

with the semantics of Scheme constitute a (prototypical) programming language embedded in Scheme.

[iii] Whether this effect is measurable and how, is an important, but still open issue.

[iv] Role exchange in Educational applications has been described in [15] as an application of a model developed for machine learning reported in [16] . The NAT*LAB project reported also in [17] was exploring experimentally the potential advantages of role exchanges in educational dialogues according to the Natural Laboratory methodology.

[v] See: http://www.cs.umbc.edu/kqml/ for most KQML papers emerging from the Knowledge Sharing Effort.

[vi] This section is a revision from [19, 22]. As these Conferences were for the AI in Education community, it seems necessary for us to survey here at least a minimal information. Notice that STROBE was initially concerned with synchronous, two-human-partner communication, even if mixed initiative was allowed by introducing a third partner called coordinator.

[vii] Environment means here the set of frames that bind variables to values; i.e. the meaning is the one common in Programming Language research. In agent's research the meaning of environment may be associated to the set of stimuli external to the agent.

[viii] By introducing a third "coordinator" agent that decided, at the end of each exchange, which partner agent between the two will be allowed to take the initiative for the next exchange.

[ix] (called "environment" in the Agent's literature)

[x] Concerning cognitive studies on shared meanings, we find in [26] that cooperation between humans is established after a long process negotiating a common "vocabulary".

[xi] The notion of autonomous agent is controversial (cf. [29] for a comprehensive presentation). The minimal level of autonomy that dialogues require is the one that allows any agent to take spontaneously the initiative. That may occur asynchronously. An agent, even processing another agent's query, may feel the need to put a query on turn, in order to use the results of the last one for the benefit of assembling an answer to the first one. This observation allows deducing that scheduling of activities within agents should occur internally to the agent. That would be excluded if agents would communicate with each other according to queued messages, where scheduling of message processing is external to the single agent and proprietary of the shared communication language. Actors, e.g., do have this common scheduling property and therefore we suspect that they may not easily be applied to modeling autonomous agent's dialogues.

[xii] Even if KQML papers refer to "cognitive states of agents" [30] it is clear that the "cognitive" property of KQML agents refers only to software agents, e.g. knowledge bases, assumed implicitly to be consistent and persistent.

[xiii] STk 3.0 is freely available via anonymous ftp at ftp.unice.fr . It has been developed and is currently maintained by Eric Gallesio: eg@ unice.fr . The current version available is 3.99 .

[xiv] These are: active-socket for creating an active socket; wait-input-socket for waiting until at least a socket receives a message, passive-socket to create a passive socket awaiting requests for connection, passive-socket-accept that accepts a connection request on a passive socket and restitutes a new socket to be used for communication; select-input-socket selecting which sockets do have available messages. The current version of STk supports sockets nicely.

[xv] At the time of writing, a third implementation of the STROBE architecture is available with the name AL (Alice Language) [38]. In AL there is a reduction of primitive performative types to three, while any other one may be constructed from these by designing the behavior associated to new performatives in the form of a finite state automaton associated to each agent. Experiments with AL are currently ongoing, mainly in the area of electronic commerce. AL is freely available on request.

[xvi] As this paper is a revised version of one written earlier, most of the enhancements have been realized and are going to be published in due time.

[xvii] In [9] , for instance, two experiments were performed: the first analyzed protocols from experimenter - learner interactions, including the common phenomenon of mixed initiatives, and the second from experimenter - student1 - student2 interactions. From their results, even a "simple" statistical analysis of the types of moves used in the two different dialogues may allow to draw conclusions concerning the learning outcomes, that may be used as requirements for subsequent applications.

[xviii] The solution is the one commonly used when accessing shared variables in Distributed DBMS.

[xix] Remarkably, partner-labeled environments are proposed also in important applicative situations where WWW servers manage interactions with clients interleaved with each other and requiring non purely functional computations on the server (e.g. using a CL-HTTP server or MIT Scheme server remotely, as shown in [32] and also in [33]). That was in fact the architecture of the PLATO system (Un. Illinois, then CDC) in the 60ties, when PLATO was able to manage in real time up to 500 - 1000 simultaneous users (students and teachers!) with a centralized computing power of the order of a few MIPS. The historical note is not folklore, because current developments in the WWW will require substantial progress in "centralized" operating systems supporting threads of communications with users, if WEB computers will become diffused. A trend that is opposite to the one, typical of the 80ties, that consisted in distributing computing power and control to PCs and workstations.

[xx] At the moment of writing, the second prototypical language implementing the STROBE architecture is available with the name JASKEMAL. The scheduler of messages in JASKEMAL is indeed proprietary of the agent, thus offers the opportunity to build really autonomous agents, each behaving as an operating system with a dynamic, proprietary scheduler.

[xxi] Didactic Augmented Recursive Transition Networks.

[xxii] While a description of a dialogue among autonomous agents may hardly be described by a single ATN or a single Petri Net (see, for example, [29]) – a result already available in [35, 36] – we believe that each agent may suitably be described by a finite state automaton FSA (or an ATN or a Petri Net). We agree with [38] that a FSA is simpler as a Petri net, even if an ATN has more representational power, as it is an extension of a FSA with sub-nets and actions on registers.

Direct Manipulation, Scalability and the Internet

Don Cruickshank and Hugh Glaser

Department of Electronics and Computer Science, University of Southampton,
Highfield, Southampton, Hants SO17 1BJ, UK
{dgc96r,hg}@ecs.soton.ac.uk

Abstract. UNIX has provided us with a tried and tested set of shell utilities. The associated shells provide rich languages for generating scripts to automate common tasks using pipelines, sequences, conditionals and iterations. These facilities are also used to compose components in complex user-defined systems. Unfortunately, the shell-like facilities are inaccessible to the growing majority of users who have never experienced a command-line interface. These users are only familiar with directing computers in a visual manner. The Psh project is an attempt to provide similar functionality to the UNIX shell in a visual context. In this paper, we consider how the project relates to the existing desktop metaphor as found in the Macintosh Finder or a modern Microsoft Windows system. In a separate thread, we also integrate the desktop with the internet by using the URL as the general identifier instead of the traditional UNIX style identifier.

1 Introduction

The desktop metaphor has only a basic subset of the functionality of the UNIX shell. It offers a convenient interface for the casual user, but it is usually limited to simple job control. The desktop, as found in the Apple Macintosh computer, contains iconic objects that resemble items found in the office, such as a folder, document or the trashcan, and they are presented to the user in a direct manipulation environment. This system depicts the current state of the computer, but it displays few visual cues about what has happened, or what is going to happen.

Direct manipulation of graphical icons is intuitive; an icon can have a pictorial representation that describes its behaviour. For example, dragging a document into the trashcan implies that the document will be lost when the trashcan is emptied. Such systems are easy to learn, especially when compared to the environment offered by a typical UNIX shell. The problem with the current desktop metaphor is that the direct manipulation becomes labour intensive when the user has more demanding requirements. In particular, as typical disks have grown from less than a gigabyte to tens of gigabytes, the user requires the larger-scale tools from larger-scale interfaces, such as UNIX or VMS. Apple attempted an answer to this deficiency with AppleScript[12]. It adds scripting ability to the

J.A. Padget (Ed.): Human and Artificial Societies, LNAI 1624, pp. 102–112, 1999.
© Springer-Verlag Berlin Heidelberg 1999

Finder, but requires the user to switch to a text based programming language. For many users, whose experience of file management is only through the desktop metaphor, this can be an insurmountable task.

In this paper, we discuss the Prograph SHell project, "Psh". The primary objective of Psh was to augment the desktop metaphor with scripting ability, whilst remaining in the visual domain of the desktop. The development of Psh focused on the similarities and differences between the Macintosh Finder and the visual programming language of Prograph [11]. A Finder window contains a set of icons, representing files and folders, with almost no visual programmability. A Prograph method window contains a bag of icons, with dataflow arcs, that represent a visual program. Psh is an attempt to merge these two concepts by using Prograph as a mock desktop environment.

Another aspect that we will consider is that internet services are becoming part of the modern desktop. With a suitable tool, such as Anarchie, FTP access via the URL [7] has already been integrated into the language of the Finder. Recently, Microsoft Windows has also moved towards removing the distinction between URLs and local files. This is important, because a considerable amount of time is spent using the internet/intranet to communicate, and we will consider a system in which the only file identifier is the URL.

2   Problem Definition

In the Finder, actions can be sequenced and stored as a script by *recording* from the AppleScript editor. Most systems have an equivalent facility; in a Windows environment the user must use a DOS shell. However, control flow such as iteration and conditionals have to be programmed using a text based editor, such as AppleScript. This breaks the desktop metaphor, and the user is forced to program the system from "behind the scenes".

The typical use of the desktop metaphor is for job control. For example, an application is started by opening the application's icon, or by opening a document that was created with the application. The documents are just entities that are simply passed onto the relevant application. To improve the facilities, the current range of desktop objects must be enhanced to cater for general purpose processing.

One of the main drawbacks of the desktop metaphor is that there is only a small number of gestures available, such as the mouse click, double click, drag, etc. Due to the lack of gestures, some operations are accomplished with the same gesture. In the Finder, moving a folder to the trashcan and ejecting a disk share the same gesture. In contrast, the UNIX interface has many gestures, which are denoted by special characters, such as the backtick for command substitution and "$" for variable substitution.

As an example of the lack of gestures in the current desktop environment, consider a compressed document. The icon of the compressed document indicates that double clicking it will decompress the document. In the Finder, the decompression utility has a choice between deleting the original (compressed) document or not. In either case, the only gesture that makes sense in the current Finder environment to invoke the decompression process is the *Open Document* gesture. Both cases are plausable, and decompression utilities on the Macintosh typically have a flag in their preference file to select either behaviour.

Turning to the issue of file system access, we note conceptual and technical problems when using URLs as a general identifier. Conceptually, the problems relate to giving the user consistent views of local and remote (HTTP) file systems. Technically, HTTP [9] puts constraints on access methods. With URLs, a document can be specified by the path of the document and the name of the document itself. However, we cannot be certain that we are able to examine the contents of the directory that the document is stored in, because most HTTP servers allow for a "default" page. For example, consider a server that assumes the default document for each directory to be named index.html. If a particular directory, http://www.foo.com/, contains an index.html document, then specifying the directory name will actually return the default document, http://www.foo.com/index.html. This masks the contents of the directory away from the client side user, and HTTP/1.1 does not support directory reading by any other method.

If a directory listing *is* returned, we are then faced with the problem of parsing it. The "directory" that is returned is a document containing links, and HTTP servers are free to structure this document in their own way. Unfortunately, there is no method to reliably determine if the returned document is a virtual directory listing, a default document, or even a document informing us that the directory does not even exist. This inhibits the user, from the client side, from reliably seeing what the directory contains.

This problem is part of a greater confusion that arises in accessing data using different transfer protocols (TPs), since there is not a clear separation between type and access method. For example, accessing a file of characters that are structured as HTML will be displayed as text or rendered differently according to the server, the TP (http, ftp, ...) and the browser, each making almost independent decisions.

3   Related Work

The typical UNIX shell is a powerful environment for process management, but string manipulations are often relegated to utilities, such as *sed* or *awk*. Although powerful in their own right, this forces the user to switch between different languages, each with their own special processing abilities and peculiarities. The Scheme Shell [6] is an attempt to remedy this. The author of [6] noted that the UNIX shell is a command environment accompanied by a mixture of specialised languages, and then attempted to build a shell with a single programming language. The implementation involved taking an implementation of scheme, and tacking on process management commands and an interface to the UNIX system functions. This work is of special interest to us, as both the Scheme Shell and Psh are built on an interpreted language environment, and then specialised towards the UNIX shell.

IShell [4] is a tool for building visual pipelines. It is a close analogy to the UNIX pipeline, and similarly does not cope with conditionals. It describes an environment where the user can inspect the flow of data through an arc. The IShell environment is based on the concept of process control. Processes in the pipeline are executing in parallel, and the rate of flow can be modified by the user to fine-tune the efficiency of the pipeline. IShell uses the dataflow metaphor, but unlike Prograph, it executes the commands simultaneously and thus models the implementation of the UNIX pipeline more closely than Psh. WebVM [5] is a distributed virtual machine where nodes communicate via the world wide web. It is the underlayer to WebFlow [5], a visual tool for pipelining processes across the web.

Pursuit [1] is a "program by demonstration" shell that uses the comic strip metaphor. Scripts are built by recording the user's actions in the desktop environment and displaying them as a sequence of processes. To specify different cases, the user demonstrates the different cases to the PBD system. When Pursuit produces the visual script, it makes an abstraction of the user's actions on the behalf of the user. However, the inference engine is certainly prone to error. To avoid the wrong assumptions, the inference engine asks the user to confirm the abstractions that it makes. SILK/JDI [2] also uses a PBD inferencing technique, but instead of recording operations from a desktop environment, it attempts to interpret the behaviour of hand drawn user interfaces, from the raw pen strokes.

4   The Psh System

With Psh, we are building a visual shell based on a subset of the UNIX shell utilities. The system can be programmed using visual scripts (Prograph methods). Psh merges the local file system with the internet by using URLs to access objects instead of the traditional UNIX style file identifiers.

An early version of the Psh system has been reported elsewhere [3], and a reader familiar with UNIX will gain sufficient understanding from the Psh command shown in Figure 2.

In the command shown, the command *cat* reads the contents of the file bar.txt. The file's contents are passed to the *head* command, which returns a number of lines from the start of the given text. The *wc* operation then counts the number of lines, words and characters of its input and makes the results available on three separate outputs. Finally, we elect to show only the number of characters. In effect, this command displays the number of characters contained in the first three lines of the file bar.txt. In a UNIX shell, we might use the following to achieve the same effect:

```
cat bar.txt | head -3 | wc -c
```

To give a flavour of the facilities available in Psh, we can turn a command into a script by parameterisation. In Psh, a script can receive parameters from the *input bar* (the long horizontal shaded bar at the top of the window pane). In this example, we could allow the user to specify the input file by removing the `bar.txt` constant, and drawing an arc from the input bar to the top of *cat*. In effect, we can develop a command, and place abstractions on it when the need arises. The dataflow metaphor aids the process of parameterisation, as we can directly trace the use of constants.

To represent access methods and file types, the nucleus of Psh consists of two class hierarchies: *access* and *data*. The *access* classes generalise the access to the resources available to the shell. A currently used small hierarchy is shown in Figure 1. We have chosen to refer to these resources via the URL, although any similar scheme would work equally as well. The *data* classes (example in Figure 4) generalise the types of data that the shell can manipulate. An object of this class contains both the value of the data, and the methods to manipulate them. The access class gives us the freedom to apply Psh scripts on different URL schemes. For example, in the UNIX shell, we could write a simple command to print all documents in a particular directory starting with the word `foo`. If that directory is only available via the FTP protocol, then our UNIX shell command becomes non trivial. Such a command is much easier to write in our scheme, since the data class distinguishes between files by content type, and allows us to use *data-direct dispatching* to call the relevant implementation of a particular utility. We expand on this later on in this section.

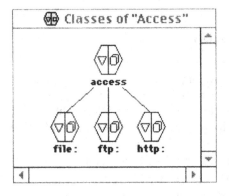

Fig. 1. The access class hierarchy

4.1   Choice of Metaphor

In this paper, we regard visual programming to be the process of writing programs using a visual representation. To give the scope of visual programming,

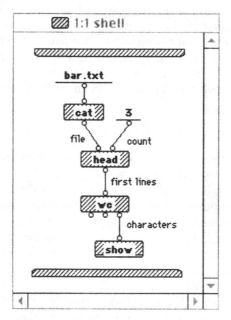

Fig. 2. An example Psh command

we give a brief account of two metaphors that have been used in visual shells: the *dataflow* metaphor and the *comic strip* metaphor.

The dataflow metaphor is based on a directed acyclic graph. The nodes of the graph describe changes that happen to the data on its journey through the graph, and the arcs show the paths of dataflow. The execution order is relaxed; the main criteria is that a node can only be executed when data is available on all of its input terminals. This is the metaphor used in Prograph [11], IShell [4] and WebFlow [5]. The nodes in a dataflow graph can have multiple inputs and outputs, and the user is able to use output from a single node as input to several other nodes. To support conditionals, a dataflow function can consist of a set of graphs, each depicting a possible outcome of the function as a whole. The dataflow model used in Prograph has control flow semantics similar to Prolog, and has the separate cases shown in different "panes".

The comic strip metaphor is based on a sequence of pictures, which represent a sequence of changes to the data. Although it is simple in concept, it is a convenient way to show output from a simple macro recording. This feature has been utilised in Pursuit [1] and Silk/JDI [2]. To denote control flow, Pursuit has used annotated arcs between different comic strips. In this form, the comic strip metaphor is equivalent to a flowchart.

With the dataflow metaphor, the semantics of a gesture initiating decompression (mentioned in Section 2) is clear. The decompression utility receives the contents of the compressed document via a dataflow arc, and thus is not directly associated with the original document. Deleting the original document does not make sense, as we have only examined its contents. If we are to permanently store the decompressed copy, we then move it back to the file space.

It is also worth noting that each process in the comic strip metaphor processes only a single input and output. If we need to split the data, process only part of it and rejoin the results to produce a single result later in the strip, we need to temporarily store the portion of data that is not to be processed elsewhere.

4.2   Flags

The behaviour of many UNIX commands can be modified by specifying flags on the command line. In our visual shell, we separate the flags into two classes. The first class are those which enable or disable parts of the output. For example, we can represent the output of *wc* by three output terminals. If we decide to ignore some of the outputs, the values on the remaining output terminals are not affected. The second class of flags are those which modify the behaviour. For example, the comparison algorithm in *sort* can be reversed.

It is useful to make this distinction, as Psh commands can produce multiple outputs just as easily as single outputs. In Figure 2, the first two outputs of *wc* are ignored. In a UNIX, we would either have to specify a flag with *wc* to select only the character count, or use a separate utility to strip the unwanted values from the output. By providing multiple outputs, we can implement desktop utilities with fewer flags than their UNIX counterparts.

4.3   Model of Access

In the Psh project, we have chosen to use the URL (Universal Resource Locator) to reference objects. This system will provide transparent access to the local file system, FTP sites and web sites.

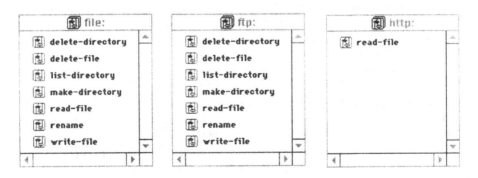

Fig. 3. Methods defined for each URL access scheme.

The access to local and remote files is generalised with the access class. This class is specialised with sub-classes which correspond to URL schemes. The availability of services that a scheme offers is defined by the methods defined in its class, although it might be more accurate to say that a scheme is defined by the methods that it offers. Figure 3 shows the sub-classes *file*, *ftp* and *http*. Naturally, the classes will contain only the methods that are supported by the relevant URL scheme. For example, deleting a directory using the HTTP protocol is not usually supported. Note that the existence, or otherwise, of access methods is orthogonal to file access permissions, which are a function of the server or file system.

Using URLs instead of traditional UNIX file identifiers changes the semantics of the perceived file system. The most notable is the lack of directory structure. The UNIX file system makes a distinction between file and directories, whereas the URL itself only refers to files. Directories may be used as part of the identifier, but a document, or file, is always returned. Most HTTP servers will generate a pseudo directory listing, if a directory is retrieved without a default page. Thus, you cannot get a listing of a directory that has a default page. The second important difference is that there is no "parenting" facility to HTTP space. It is the responsibility of the web client to process ".." entries in the relative URL [8] before it is sent to the HTTP server. This means that the parent of a soft-linked directory may differ in HTTP space and the UNIX file system.

4.4   Model of Data

Each document type in the Psh system is sub-classed from the *data* class. Note that the data class is orthogonal to the access class. We expect a document to behave in a consistent manner, regardless of which URL scheme was used to retrieve it. Most document types will support at least *open*, *close*, *show* and *print*. The envisaged desktop environment contains diverse datatypes, such as pictures and sound. We would expect a good word count package to use techniques similar to OCR and speech recognition on those types. An example population of the *data* class hierarchy is shown in Figure 4. The example shows a *Text* datatype and also a *Text List* datatype. Many utilities, such as *grep*, process lines of text and also generates lines of text.

Part of our design is to allow utilities to deliver their output in a datatype that is most convenient. As most UNIX shell utilities process a single datatype, a binary stream, the UNIX utilities often have to convert their output back into a form which is useful for the next utility to process. In the case of a *grep* followed by *head*, this results in unnecessary conversions taking place, because if *grep* was allowed to leave its output as a list of lines, *head* would only need to return the first n elements of that list. Data-directed dispatching allows us to perform this coercion between datatypes, by dispatching the relevant version of a utility depending on the given datatype. For *grep*, we might decide to implement a *grep* for the *Text List* datatype, and have the *Text* implementation of *grep* use the *Text List* implementation after applying a standard coercion function. In both cases, the output is a *Text List*. Now, if we run two *grep* utilities in sequence, we avoid converting the data back into a text stream between the two *greps*. In effect, utilities should not perform conversions after processing their data. Conversions should only occur on demand, via the data-directed dispatching mechanism.

Note that the UNIX shell does appear to perform some data-directed dispatching, by reference to file extensions and magic numbers, but the dispatching is performed within the commands, not the shell. The Macintosh Finder does perform data-directed dispatching, as does modern Windows with the registry, but we consider that our approach in a proper class hierarchy provides a clean and more powerful model.

When a document is referenced from a remote medium, we either have to examine the contents of the document to determine the type or rely on an external typing system. MIME [10] is a common classification system used on the internet, and is given with a document from an HTTP server.

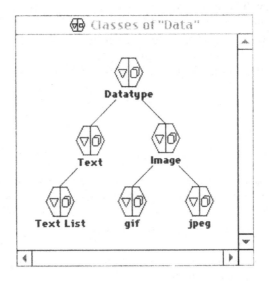

Fig. 4. An example population of the data classes.

5   Implementation Status and Future Work

A working prototype of the Psh system has been implemented on the Apple Macintosh computer, using the Prograph CPX environment. We have integrated the system with Netscape Communicator and Anarchie to provide access to web servers and FTP sites. We are able to execute scripts on URL schemes of our choosing, provided that the transport protocols involved support the requested operations. We are integrating Psh with the Macintosh Finder, by using Apple Events, to provide a visual alternative to the AppleScript language.

There are a number of future directions that we are considering for this research.

5.1   Password Persistence

As Psh allows the user to create scripts that do not explicitly state a URL access scheme, it is feasible that the user might use scripts on files via authenticated FTP access. There is a conflict between user convenience and password security. It is unreasonable to expect the user to enter a password for every operation performed on the FTP site, but the user also needs to know when the password has been 'forgotten' by the system.

5.2   Identify a Useful Set of Desktop Commands

A continuation of this project will be to identify a useful set of desktop commands. For general text based operations, we can look back in hindsight at the successful utilities from the UNIX environment. However, with datatypes such as pictures and sounds, we would need to reconsider how many of those utilities would operate with diverse datatypes.

5.3   Implications of Psh to Text Based Shells

Psh was designed and implemented as a visual shell. A possible direction would be to examine the implications of the design issues that this might have to a traditional command line shell, and build a prototype of such a shell. For example: in Psh, we can apply a command separately to each item in a list and collect the results into another list, much like the functional *map*.

6   Conclusions

In this paper, we have presented the design of a system that can be used automate tasks without leaving the iconic desktop. We have indicated how the use of data-directed dispatching offered by object-oriented facilities can be used to generalise and simplify the mapping of data to applications. The paper also considers the role of the URL in data access. We propose and describe the implementation of a clean separation between access type and content type.

A prototype of the Psh system has been developed with Prograph CPX. We have integrated the system with common applications, and have provided HTTP and FTP access in addition to the local file system.

References

1. Modugno, F., Corbett, A.T. and Myers, B.A. *Evaluating program representation in a demonstrational visual shell.* In Human Factors in Computing Systems (CHI) - Conference Proceedings. 1995.
2. Landay, J.A. *SILK: Sketching Interfaces like krazy.* In Conference on Human Factors in Computing Systems - Proceedings. 1996.
3. Glaser, H. and Smedley, T. J. *Psh - The Next Generation of Command Line Interfaces.* In IEEE Symposium on Visual Languages, Proceedings. 1995.
4. Borg, K. *IShell: A Visual UNIX Shell.* In Proceedings of ACM CHI'90 Conference on Human Factors in Computing Systems. 1990.
5. Fox, G. and Furmanski, W. *Towards Web/Java based High Performance Distributed Computing - an Evolving Machine.* In Proceedings of the Fifth IEEE International Symposium on High Performance Distributed Computing. 1996
6. Shivers, O. *A Scheme Shell.* MIT Laboratory for Computer Science Technical Report 635. 1994.
7. Berners-Lee, T., Masinter, L. and McCahill, M. *Uniform Resource Locators.* RFC 1738. 1994.
8. Fielding, R. *Relative Uniform Resource Locators.* RFC 1808. 1995.
9. Berners-Lee, T., Fielding, R. and Frystyk, H. *Hypertext Transfer Protocol.* RFC 1945. 1996.
10. Freed, N. and Borenstein, N. *Multipurpose Internet Mail Extensions.* RFC 2045. 1996.
11. Prograph International. *Prograph CPX Users Guide.* 1993.
12. Apple Computer Inc. *AppleScripting and Apple Events.* 1994.

Part II

Agents and Capabilities

Towards the Abstraction and Generalization of Actor-Based Architectures in Diagnostic Reasoning

Stefano A. Cerri[1], Antonio Gisolfi[2], and Vincenzo Loia[2]

[1] Dipartimento di Scienze dell'Informazione, Università di Milano
Via Comelico 39, 20135 Milano, Italy
cerri@dsi.unimi.it
[2] Dipartimento di Matematica ed Informatica, Università di Salerno
84081 Baronissi, Salerno, Italy
{gisolfi, loia}@dmi.unisa.it

Abstract. Research in multimodel based diagnosis stresses the role of a centralized diagnostic agent in a computational framework made of different models. Each of these models provides knowledge according to a given representation of the system to diagnose: structural, behavioral, functional and teleological aspects are each embodied into a different model. According to this approach, various proposals have been formulated in terms of cooperation among different views without comprehensively addressing the issues of concurrency and collaboration, in particular the effect of asynchronous message passing in software design. We present here the use of a distributed and concurrent architecture in which different models collaborate in order to achieve a global diagnosis through a set of independent actors. The paper reports about two experiences: a distributed architecture representing a user model in an intelligent tutoring system (ITS) and a diagnostic engine for troubleshooting a physical system. In spite of the difference of the two applications, we may abstract from the two architectures important common patterns that constitute the core of the distributed management of the multiple knowledge sources.

1 Introduction

Programming techniques have evolved from the machine-level style dominating in the 50ties up to the agent-level one in the 90ties. Important milestones have characterized this progress: e.g. structured programming (1970) and object-oriented programming (1980). The currently fashionable agent-based approach to software design and implementation derives from the development of methods oriented to distribute geographically groups of objects each actively committed to perform independent computations and to exchange asynchronous messages by means of suitable communication protocols. In other words: agents, though proposed much earlier,

J.A.. Padget (Ed.): Human and Artificial Societies, LNAI 1624, pp.115 -132, 1999.
© Springer-Verlag Berlin Heidelberg 1999

have acquired importance in proportion to the growth of the WWW and the need for really distributed computations. This evolution has lead to a radical change of the traditional approach of designers involved in software construction: from action-based, algorithmic systems to interaction-based systems. The rationale behind, is not just efficiency but instead the need to capitalize from the opportunities - throughout the entire life cycle of complex systems - offered by the alternative, inherently interactive, behavioral models of the systems, especially when the interactions occur in a distributed, concurrent environment.

Artificial Intelligence research has strongly relied on non-algorithmic approaches to the design and implementation of intelligent systems. A significant part of the recent research interests in AI adopts approaches different from the ones in traditional centralized knowledge-based systems, i.e. "new" architectures where different knowledge-sources are physically and logically distributed so that separate problem-solving activities cooperate in order to accomplish a common goal. The entities that individually contribute to the overall process are usually named agents. About the difference between agents and actors, a recent report [15] confirms that the distinction is more an issue of convenience than a fundamental principle.

Our research focuses in the adoption of the actor model [2] as a computational metaphor of cooperative distributed problem solving (CDPS). In this work we present our research experiences reported in the integration of heterogeneous knowledge sources in distributed environments in order to support diagnostic reasoning. We show how a concurrent architecture designed to model the student behavior during a learning session [7] has been extended in order to perform diagnostic reasoning about physical systems [17]. In spite of the different application domain, the two architectures present common issues, in particular the role of the knowledge-based sources and the concurrent reasoning model.

The paper is organized as follows. Section two discusses the role of diagnostic reasoning as an adequate example of a complex problem that can be formulated in terms of CDPS. Section three presents critically the basis of the Actor Model of computation adopted by us. Section four discusses the concurrent model of diagnostic reasoning designed to diagnose mental states of a student attempting to solve a simple algebra problem. Section five describes the abstraction and generalization of the architecture in order to perform diagnosis about physical systems. Section five closes the paper with conclusive remarks and future research ideas.

2 DAI Approach to Problem Solving

Many efforts in Distributed Artificial Intelligence (DAI) emphasize the role of distributed search on separate knowledge sources. The state space search is organized into independent sub-domains, each of them explored by local sub-searches: possible collaborative strategies can be useful if there is the need to share intermediate results.

In general it is possible to distinguish three kinds of distributed search [16]:

- *Fine-grained decomposition.* The partition of the state space involves large collections of small and independent sub-problems. This means that simple computations are sufficient to support control and data operations. Fine-grain processors optimize this situation: processors are numerous, simple and can support limited information and control. This approach is very close to connectionism and is particularly useful to treat well-defined problems in terms of a reduced representation of knowledge.

- *Large-grained decomposition.* The state space is divided in a relatively small set of independent/dependent subsets of states. This means that the role of problem solving in each subset is more significant and thus the possible target architecture becomes more complex: the processors are expected to support robust computational entities (e.g.: processors as evaluators, such as a LISP processor), and complex collaboration strategies must be used to organize rich interaction protocols. The more sophisticated is the collaboration among concurrent entities, the more knowledge is required for the protocols to be adequately managed.

- *Hybrid situations.* Hybrid situations occur when the granularity originated from the decomposition of the state space may change dynamically, hence making it difficult to map it directly onto a processor-based organization. In this case it is preferable to use a general computational model that provides a dynamic topology of computational entities, independently from the mapping on processors, or either foresee mobile code, thus introducing extra difficulties.

Cooperative Distributed Problem Solving (CDPS) is generally viewed by the DAI community as large-grain search space decomposition on a large-grain processor organization. In contrast with distributed (parallel) processing, where the main problem is to realize (transparently, for the end user) the parallel execution of multiple tasks that share common resources, CDPS aims to solve a common goal by designing explicitly a distribution of tasks and duties in a network of cooperative entities.

Diagnostic reasoning is a good candidate for being treated as a CDPS. In fact, diagnostic reasoning is strictly linked to model-based reasoning, as it aims to capture reasoning on a representation of how a device works. This goal requires building a model that reflects in a "complete" way the structure and the behavior of the device. Diagnostic reasoning has attracted the interest of many researchers in the last three decades and some important lessons have been learned. Here we list just two of them that we consider more relevant for our work, reminding the reader to [8] for a more extended discussion:

- the design of a model-based diagnostic system should distinguish carefully between structure and behavior. The system should provide multiple descriptions of the structure, modeling it in terms of physical and functional information. In this way the models are capable of both simulation and inference, and can be organized hierarchically;

− effective model-based diagnosis faces with the tradeoff of completeness and specificity: if all possible answers are considered then diagnosis becomes indiscriminant, but omitting any one means that an entire class of faults will be out of reach.

Multiple-modeling diagnosis process [12] is a recent effort devoted to integrate several models of the same system in order to improve the effectiveness and efficiency of the reasoning.

This research, strongly motivated by cognitive arguments, requires defining how multiple models cooperate. In a centralized, synchronous (or blackboard-based) architecture the design and the management of this cooperation does not seem easy. By moving to an appropriate distributed, concurrent and asynchronous architecture we have been able to design and manage the cooperation for diagnosis among multiple knowledge sources in a simple and elegant way. We have operated in two apparently different scenarios of diagnostic reasoning, one related to cognitive diagnosis and the other to troubleshooting of a physical device.

− *User/student reasoning.* Student modeling aims at diagnosing what is wrong with a student's method of performing a task and at transferring this information to other modules which compose the tutoring system [4]. In this way the student can receive an "intelligent" guide because the tutorial module may adapt the initiative of the system with a new balance of didactic actions on the basis of the student's necessity [20].
− *Physical troubleshooting reasoning.* In this well studied scenario, the main task is to localize the parts of the technical systems responsible for the abnormal behavior. In order to optimize the diagnostic search, a multimodeling approach [6] may be followed, constituting in an abstract framework in which different knowledge components and representations coexist. Focus-based mechanisms [18] are introduced in order to reduce the size of the complexity.

In both application domains, we have achieved the design and implementation of a truly concurrent architecture able to represent diagnostic reasoning. The architecture does not assume any shared memory or any necessary synchronization among concurrent processes. By distributing knowledge and tasks we obtain a powerful framework for representing the knowledge underlying a skill. By organizing different categories of intelligent actors, we obtain an efficient medium-grained model able to depict the numerous levels of the diagnostic activity. Our framework of distributed computation is similar to that defined in [2], augmented by additional communication schemes available as primitives from object-based concurrent languages [24]. Before entering in the details of the architecture we briefly describe the fundamental issues of the Actor Model.

3 Using Actor Model

Designing software in terms of distributed, cooperative entities could be viewed as a natural evolution of object-level languages. Object-oriented programming is based on a philosophy of software development through progressive refinements, strengthening the abstraction level as a result of the use of abstract data types and information hiding. However, the "classical" notion of object is not adequate to support real distribution of control and therefore concurrency: it is known that message exchanges in objects are variants of procedure calls, and therefore the mental model for the design of application is still a centralized one. The execution of methods in large objects may occur in parallel, but is limited by the parallelism available and does not modify the centralized mental model underlying the design. In other words: parallel execution is not distributed control in the absence of synchronization or shared memory.

The actor model, on the contrary, assumes distribution of control, asynchronous concurrency and the absence of a shared memory as its axioms. It satisfies the two requirements of high-level programming and efficiency. Actors combine object-oriented and functional programming in order to make the management of concurrency easier for the user.

The actor model can be so synthesized:

- the universe contains computational agents (or entities, if you prefer), called actors;
- actors perform computation through asynchronous, point-to-point message passing;
- each actor is defined by its state, a mail queue to store external messages and internal behavior;
- an actor's state is defined by its internal data, not sharable by other actors. These local variables are named acquaintances, according with the actor model terminology;
- an actor reacts to the external environment by executing its procedural skills, called scripts.

The actor model is at the basis of the so-called object-oriented concurrent programming (OOCP) which constitute one of the most important paradigms employed to realize DAI architectures. Furthermore, actor-based languages are computationally practical; they can be efficiently compiled and implemented on distributed multiprocessor architectures [3].

The term "agent" has also become widespread over the past few years. Agents possess autonomous, local duties that increase their ability in reasoning, accepting or refusing orders, negotiating commitments. Agents are not just servers of clients. To improve the intelligence of their behavior, it is often necessary to equip the agents with appropriate knowledge, such as belief, negotiation schemes, or the intention. In the literature, agents are active computational entities described more with respect to their behavioral properties – say: top down - as to their structural, linguistic founda- tions or specificities – say: bottom up -. People report about reactive and cognitive agents, implemented in object oriented languages or scripting languages or even actor languages. Despite the considerable effort spent on this topic, a consistent defi- nition of the minimal linguistic components of an agent has not yet been achieved, even if there are attempts to reach a common "standard" view. On the contrary, the notion of actor evolves from a clear "bottom up" linguistic foundation that we have preferred in this research, even if we believe that the two notions will eventually converge soon.

Our interest here is mainly focused on experimenting the actor paradigm as a lan- guage able to express more naturally complex problems (such as the design of soft- ware architectures). We are interested in the re-usability of the conceptual design, more than in the efficiency of the code. For this purpose, we will be justified if our realizations just simulate concurrency on a single processor machine even if we do not have precise performance evaluations on multi-processor hardware.

4 Concurrent Diagnostic Reasoning about Mental States

The first domain that we discuss is essentially composed of a student that tries to solve simple high school algebraic problems. This case study is characterized by a remarkable complexity, due to the heterogeneity of the required knowledge and to the richness of problem solving activities [5] [21]. The main objective of the Diag- nostic Module (DM) inside an intelligent tutoring system (ITS) architecture is the building of a complete model containing the "significant" correct/wrong student's strategies used to solve the proposed exercise. This model is continuously sent to the other components of the system, in order to guide an appropriate teaching session. The overall architecture of the DM is composed of four categories of actors, as shown in Figure 1.

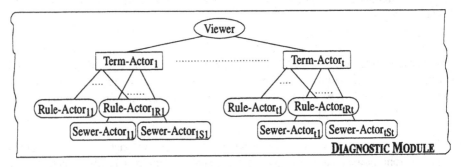

Fig. 1. The Diagnostic Module.

Each actor population is designed to accomplish specific tasks, as synthetically described in Table 1.

4.1 TermActors

A Term-Actor embodies active knowledge about how the student can manipulate the corresponding term in solving the equation. The possible operations the student can apply on a term, depend strongly on its "form", intended as a set of characteristics of the single term and as a set of relationships with the close terms. Each Term-Actor knows, at its creation, the term that it represents: this initial knowledge is expanded during the diagnostic activity, thanks to a full collaboration with other Term-Actors generated for the remaining terms. During this collaboration a Term-Actor infers all the possible "associations" which can be established with the other terms.

This information is crucial to lead the search for the student's strategies of resolution. Table 2 shows the Term-Actors adopted in our DM and, for each of them, some of the corresponding strategies.

The Term-Actors NT-SUM and NT-MULT manage sum/subtraction and multiplication of constant terms (referred by "N"), while XT-SUM and XT-MULT manage the same operation on variables (referred by "X").

Table 1. The actors of the DM and their main tasks.

Actors	Description
Term-Actors	They are generated directly from the data to analyze (the terms of the equation). They possess information necessary to direct the process of diagnosis.
Rule-Actors	They are specialized in recognizing a particular strategy of a student's problem-solving practice, be it correct or incorrect.
Sewer-Actors	Each of them is able to produce a micro diagnosis; all together can be viewed as an association of experts that eventually produce complete diagnostic models.
Viewer-Actors	This actor accomplishes the functions of a coordinator among the other modules of the instructional system. It is also involved in arranging some top-level activities of the DM.

Table 2. The Term-Actors and some of the corresponding resolution strategies.

Term-Actors	Rule-Actors
NT-SUM	NULL, N-ADDSUB, N-L-TO-R, N-L-TO-SIGN-ERR
NT-MULT	NULL, PREC-ERR, TERM*TERM
XT-SUM	NULL, X-ADDSUB, X-R-TO-L
XT-MULT	NULL, PREC-ERR, TERM*TERM

4.2 Rule-Actors

For each Term-Actor we have several Rule-Actors, which represent a possible, correct/wrong utilization of the related term in the equation. Generally, for any Term-Actor we have different strategies which are tested concurrently. Table 3 shows some of the most important Rule-Actors.

Table 3. Some of the most important correct/wrong rules.

Rule-Actors	Strategies
X-ADDSUB	to apply ADDition/SUBtraction of the variable terms (X-terms)
N-ADDSUB	to apply ADDition/SUBtraction to the Numeric-terms (N-terms)
N-L-TO-R	to move a N-term from Left TO Right
X-L-TO-R	to move an X-term from Left TO Right
N-L-TO-R-	wrong rule applied for a N-term from Left
SIGN-ERR	TO Right without changing the sign

Each time that a Rule-Actor succeeds in the execution of the corresponding rule, it evaluates if the form obtained as a result is useful to better understand the student's behavior. In the positive case, the actor sends such information, enriched with other data, to its caller (Term-Actor).

4.3 Sewer-Actors

Once that all the Rule-Actors have returned their answers to the corresponding Term-Actor, this actor is ready to combine the answers in a unique pattern, that represents a possible justification about the student's reaction on that term. This situation occurs for each of the Term-Actors, in such a way that, by unifying their knowledge, we obtain a global explanation about the student's cognitive actions. The Sewer-Actors have the task to assembly in parallel this "local diagnosis". Their goal is to lead to a complete diagnostic model (CDM), i.e. a model that contains all the cognitive explanations about the student's actions. This model is built in an iterative way, by re-launching, at each new step of the analysis, a new diagnostic reasoning phase. Each Sewer-Actor manages a little part of the overall diagnostic model, but, thanks to an active collaboration, it tries to completely explain all the logical links from the initial equation, provided by the tutor, to the one, provided by the student. We name this little component of diagnostic knowledge *partial diagnostic model* (PDM).
A Sewer-Actor terminates its activities in two situations:

– all the terms of the initial equation have been used and all the terms of the student's answer have been justified;

– the Sewer-Actor is unable to provide a CDM; the Sewer contains a local failure diagnosis. In this case the Sewer builds a Final Incomplete Diagnostic Model (FIDM).

The management of a FIDM is performed using other techniques, such as heuristic, fuzzy and non-monotonic logic, but we do not discuss these extensions in this paper.

4.4 Viewer

The Viewer-Actor plays a role of supervisor. The main activity of the Viewer consists in collaborating with the previous actors, in order to evaluate all the possible diagnostic solutions, eliminating partial models, up to the discovery of the diagnostic model.

4.5 Example

We illustrate here a simple example of the actor interaction. Let us suppose to have two equations: $3x+4-5x=6$ **(eq1)** $-2x=6+4$ **(eq2)**

The first is provided by the Tutor, the second one is the student's answer to the Tutor's assignment that asks the student to simplify the equation. The "active" representation of (eq1) is shown in Figure 2.

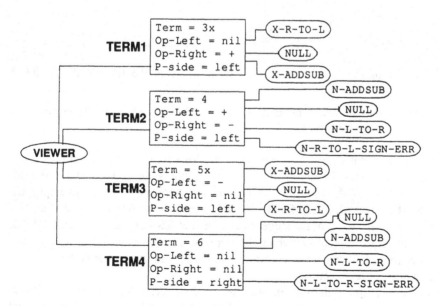

Fig. 2. The active representation of the equation: $3x+4-5x=6$

We notice that each Term-Actor contains some basic data: the represented term, the associated left and the correct operators, the side of the equation where the term belongs to. Moreover, we highlight for any Term-Actor the associated "pool" of Rule-Actors. The Term-Actors, thanks to the collaboration activity, acquire additional knowledge about possible aggregations of terms; each term contacts all the other ones in order to know just those with whom it may be (mathematically) combined. Afterwards, each Term-Actor cooperates with "its" pool of Rule-Actors in order to obtain the local diagnosis. On the basis of (eq2), each Term-Actor in (eq1), produces a local diagnosis (local resource `mic-diagn` in Figure 3).

Let us consider the state of the local diagnosis related to the Term-Actor

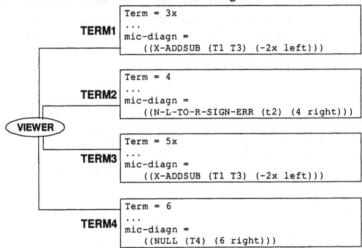

TERM1

```
Term = 3x
...
mic-diagn =
    ((X-ADDSUB (T1 T3) (-2x left)))
```

TERM2

```
Term = 4
...
mic-diagn =
    ((N-L-TO-R-SIGN-ERR (t2) (4 right)))
```

VIEWER

TERM3

```
Term = 5x
...
mic-diagn =
    ((X-ADDSUB (T1 T3) (-2x left)))
```

TERM4

```
Term = 6
...
mic-diagn =
    ((NULL (T4) (6 right)))
```

TERM1.
As shown in Figure 3, `mic-diagn` takes as value the list `(X-ADDSUB(T1 T3)(-2x Left))`.

Fig. 3. After the application of the strategies tried by the Rule-Actors, the Term-Actors acquire new knowledge about the justified terms.

The first element `X-ADDSUB` represents the Rule-Actor that justified the action; the second element - the sub-list `(T1 T3)` - contains the Term-Actors of the initial equation (eq1) which have been used in the justification (in the example, the terms **TERM1** and **TERM3**); finally, the last element - the sub-list `(-2x LEFT)` - contains the term `-2x` of the student's answer that has been justified, and the side LEFT of the equation (eq2) in which the element lies. The existence of local micro-diagnoses in each Term-Actors constitutes a intermediate step towards the construction of a diagnostic model.

For each of these micro-diagnoses, the involved Term-Actor creates a Sewer-Actor, in order to construct a new "pattern" to analyze, including only those original terms of (eq1) and (eq2) that were not explained in the previous phase. Figure 4 shows the creation and the internal status (starting from the Term-Actor **TERM1**) of the Sewer-Actors which successfully construct a CDM. Following Figure 4, the diagnosis process starts from the Viewer: after all the parallel execution of the Rule-Actors, the four Term-Actors receive asynchronously their feedback. **TERM1** creates the Sewer-Actor **SEWER1** containing:

- the applied Rule-Actor (X-ADDSUB);
- the representation of the justified term (-2x) in (eq2) and the side (left) in which the term lies;
- the Term-Actors (T1, T3) on which the Rule-Actor (X-ADDSUB) has been applied;
- the Term-Actors (T2, T4) in (eq1) which have not been used for the justification;
- the part of the student's answer (eq2) which remain not justified, by specifying the left hand side ( ) and the right hand side (6 + 4);
- the partial diagnostic model ((X-ADDSUB (T1, T3) (-2x left)).

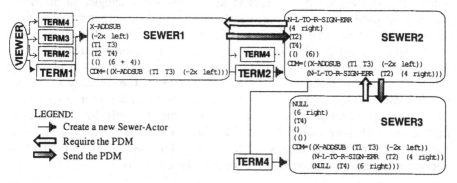

Fig. 4. A CDM is found. Now it is possible to explain all the student's actions .

Each new Sewer represents an additional knowledge acquisition. In the last sewer (**SEWER3**) we notice that a complete diagnostic model is obtained. In this frame, the resource CDM contains a plausible explanation from equation (eq1) to (eq2):

- (X-ADDSUB (T1 T3) (-2x left)): sum the terms 3x and -5x and obtain as result the term -2x present in the left side of (eq2);
- (N-L-TO-R-SIGN-ERR (T2) (4 right)): move the term 4 in (eq1) from left to right with a wrong sign and obtain as result the term 4 in the right side of (eq2);
- (NULL (T4) (6 right)): no operation on the term 6 in (eq1), thus the same term on the right part of (eq2).

Let us stress that each Sewer characterizes a branch of the overall diagnostic tree, which is built in parallel and asynchronously with respect to the other branches. The example depicts a naive situation, but the complexity of the diagnostic reasoning (due to a richer generation of different Sewer-Actors for the same Term-Actor) does not affect the final performance thanks to the utilization of concurrent, asynchronous management of diagnostic paths. The management of concurrency, in other words, is ensured by the language, and the designer's efforts are concentrated on the description of collaborative activities among actors.

5 Concurrent Diagnostic Reasoning about Physical States

Expert reasoning in the domain of physical diagnosis often faces a high degree of complexity [1] [14]. In a faulty system, the abduction process from symptoms to potential faults causing the symptom to occur, several observations may be applied with different standpoints. For this reason the integration of multiple knowledge-based sources seem to represents an important improvement in terms of completeness and soundness of the diagnostic reasoning [6] [10]; this approach fits the natural human habit to use and amalgamate different problem solving tactics and information [12, 13]. Pioneering attempts to apply DAI methodologies in diagnostic reasoning appeared in [11] for speech analysis. In [19] the distributed diagnostic is based on a blackboard that serves as a globally shared database. The question that remains with blackboard models is how much the "shared memory" and the consequent synchronization really simplify the cognitive load in the design phase, and further what are the implications in terms of efficiency. The diversity of our approach consists in using the actor computational model as a higher level tool to define with appropriate precision and completeness the task definition and the coordination issues that are essential for the architecture . Table 4 reports a short description of the main actor classes, while Figure 5 illustrates the overall diagnostic process by stressing the cooperation among the different actors.

For improving the simplicity of our description, we divide the overall process in two principal phases. The first phase (represented in Figure 6), consists in the construction of the focus-of attention, e.g., a collection of Structural-Agents which are candidates to justify the malfunctioning(s). This task is an important optimization that allows the reduction of the complexity of the diagnostic search. The second phase (represented in Figure 7) explains the collaboration activity that leads to the generation of the CDP.

We show the correspondence ($\leftrightarrow$) between the collaboration activities (1-9) shown in Figure 5 and the actions executed in the first phase (denoted by a single quote) and in the second phase (double quote).

(1) $\leftrightarrow$ (1'),(13'')	(4) $\leftrightarrow$ (7'),(11')	(7)$\leftrightarrow$(2''),(3''),(4''),(6'')
(2) $\leftrightarrow$ (2'),(3'),(4'),(6')	(5) $\leftrightarrow$ (8'),(9')	(8) $\leftrightarrow$ (9''),(10'')
(3) $\leftrightarrow$ (5')	(6) $\leftrightarrow$ (1''),(7''),(8'')	(9) $\leftrightarrow$ (11''),(12'')

In the first part of the diagnostic reasoning (Figure 6), after having reported a mal-functioning, the user activates the diagnostic reasoning (1') on a given domain. This request is captured by the Arbiter. This actor starts a collaboration (2') with the Teleological-Actor in order to establish the portion of the domain, named teleological-focus, where, most probably, the malfunctioning is present having reported the given symptoms (3'). Thus, the responsible Teleological-Actor interacts with the Arbiter (4') and with the user (5') in order to decide if the anomaly is due to a user's mistake.

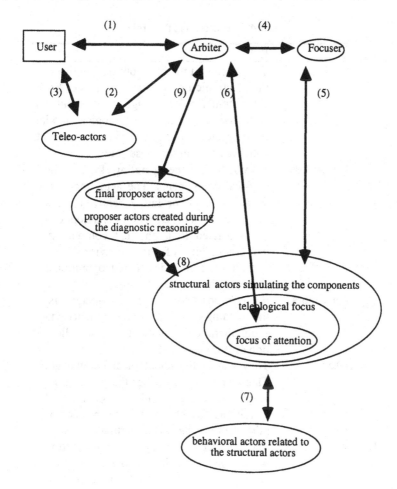

Fig. 5. The framework and the collaboration among actors.

If no human error is found then an actual diagnostic search is activated from the Teleological-Actor to the Arbiter (6'). In this case, the Arbiter interacts with the Focuser-Actor (7') in order to obtain a focus of attention (a sub-set of the teleological focus). The cooperation between the Focuser and Structural-Actor (8',9') inside the teleological-focus (see Figure 5) accomplishes the recognition of the focus of attention (10') that is sent from the Focuser to the Arbiter (11').

Now the second phase begins (Figure 7): the Arbiter asks the Structural-Actors belonging to the focus of attention to activate (in parallel) their behaviors (1''). The cooperation between these Structural-Actors and each of the corresponding Behavioral-Actors starts (2''): possible micro-diagnosis are deduced (3'',4'') by comparing them with the symptoms. The Behavioral-Actor, for each new (compatible) local diagnosis, creates a Proposer-Actor identifying the micro-diagnosis (5'') and sends the new diagnostic information to the corresponding Structural-Actor (6'').

Table 4. The actors and their role.

Actors	Role
Structural-Actors	They represent the basic physical entities of the electronic or mechanical device. Each actor contains knowledge only about its structure: the complete topological model of the system is achieved via a concurrent collaboration among these actor.
Behavior-Actors	They represent the operating skills of the physical components. The actor may express a correct, or faulty behavior for a given component. Different behaviors can be associated to a physical component: the community of the Behavior-Actors provide an active distributed operational model of the physical system
Proposer-Actors	Each Proposer handles a micro-diagnosis: the building of a CDP is accomplished via a collaboration protocol inside a collection of Proposer-Actors.
Teleo-Actors	They handle the teleological knowledge. This knowledge describes the goals of the diagnosed system and the operational conditions which enable their accomplishment via the correct settings
Focuser-Actor	The Focuser speeds up the identification of a subset of the Structural-Actors representing the most probable fault components. This subset is called the *focus*.
Arbiter	The role of this actor is to coordinate the actor categories and to provide the CDM to other components of the system.

When all the Behavioral-Actors have communicated their local diagnoses to their Structural-Actor, the latter can start a new justification; this action is performed in parallel and conducted by the Arbiter (7'') (8''). The global diagnostic reasoning is assured by the cooperation of the Proposer-Actor: each Structural-Actor informs the corresponding Proposer-Actor to pursue the search (9'') with an updated focus of attention. Each Proposer continues the justification by considering the symptoms not yet justified and the Structural-Actor not yet used in the justification - notice the similarity with the cognitive reasoning - (10''). The cooperation strategies (9'') and (10'') are thus repeated until all the symptoms are justified. If the reconstruction of the diagnostic path is complete, then a CDP is returned: the Proposer-Actors send the CDP to the Arbiter (11''); otherwise an incomplete diagnosis is returned (12'').

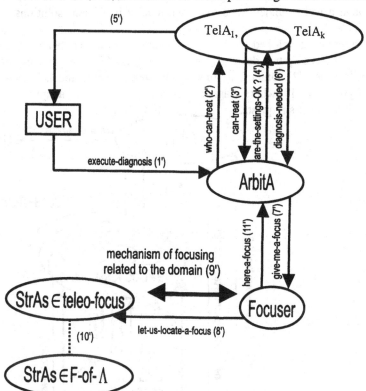

Fig. 6. Collaboration activities involved in the building of the focus of attention.

6   Conclusions

This paper reports about our experience in designing a cooperative distributed problem solving method suitable for diagnostic reasoning. The main results support the initial intuition that actors exchanging asynchronous messages allow to design relatively simple solutions to a class of complex and (apparently) different problems such as those associated to cognitive diagnosis and troubleshooting of physical devices.

The two architectures described in this paper present meaningful similarities, such as the active representation of the domain under diagnosis (Term-Actors and Structural-Actors), the asynchronous application of different problem-solving rules (Rule-

130   Stefano A. Cerri et al.

Actors and Behavior-Actors), and the distributed management of micro-diagnosis (Sewer-Actors and Proposer-Actors). The additional actor categories introduced for physical diagnosis (Teleo-Actors and Focuser) are used to optimize the diagnostic reasoning. We conclude that the Actor model of asynchronous, concurrent computation simplifies the task for designing diagnostic systems. Even if we do not have concrete data, since the model maps naturally on a distributed hardware architecture, we have a well founded hope that traditionally inefficient solutions may become tractable.

The architecture developed for the user/student modeling has been implemented in ABCL/1 [23]. The system designed for the diagnosis of physical systems has been realized in Rosette [22]. Other experiments have been done in the field of adaptive hypertext/hypermedia [9] where diagnostic deduction is useful to adapt contents and interfaces to new user's requests.

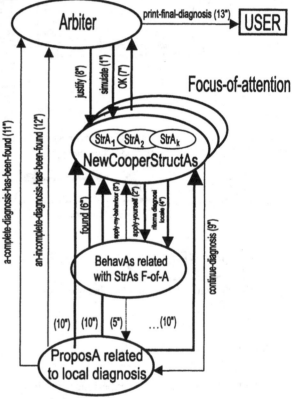

Fig. 7. Control flow scheme for a complete diagnostic activity.

References

1. Abu-Hanna, A., R. Benjamings, and W. Jansweijer, 'Device understanding and modeling for diagnosis', *IEEE Expert*, **6**, 26-31, 1991.
2. Agha, G, '*Actors: A Model of Concurrent Computation in Distributed Systems*', MIT Press, Cambridge, MA, 1986.

3. Agha, G., C. Houck and R. Panwar, 'Distributed Execution of Actor Programs', *Languages and Compilers for Parallel Computing*, LNCS 586, pp. 1-17, Springer-Verlag, 1992.
4. Anderson, J. R., C. F. Boyle, A.T. Corbett, and M. W. Lewis, 'Cognitive modeling and intelligent tutoring', *Artificial Intelligence*, **42**: 7-49, 1990.
5. Brown, J. S. and R. R. Burton, 'Diagnostic Models for Procedural Bugs in Basic Mathematical Skills', *Cognitive Science*, **2**:155-192, 1978.
6. Chittaro, L., G. Guida, C. Tasso, and E. Toppano, 'Functional and teleological knowledge in the multimodeling approach for reasoning about physical systems: a case study in diagnosis', *IEEE Transaction System, Man, Cybernetics.*, **23** : 1718-1751, 1993.
7. Cerri, S. A. and V. Loia, 'A Concurrent, Distributed Architecture for Diagnostic Reasoning', *User Modeling and User Adaptive Interaction*, **7**:69-105, 1997.
8. Davis, R., 'Retrospective on Diagnostic Reasoning based on Structure and Behavior', *Artificial Intelligence*, **59** : 149-157, 1993.
9. Dattolo, A and V. Loia, 'Active distributed framework for adaptive hypermedia, *Int. Journal of Human-Computer Studies*, **46**(5):605-626, May 1997.
10. Damasio, C.V., W. Nejdl, L. Pereira, and M. Schroeder, 'Model-based diagnosis preferences and strategies representation with meta logic programming', *Meta-logics and Logic Programming*, K. R. Apt and F. Turini (Eds.), pp. 269-311. MIT Press, 1995.
11. Fennel, R. D. and V. Lesser, 'Parallelism in Artificial Intelligence Problem Solving: A Case Study of Hearsay II', *IEEE Transaction on Computers*, **26**: 98-111, 1977.
12. Fröhlich, P., W. Nejdl, and M. Schroeder, 'Strategies in Model-based Diagnosis', in *Journal of Automated Reasoning*, **20**(1,2):81-105, 1998.
13. Fröhlich, P., I. Móra, W. Nejdl, and M. Schroeder, 'Diagnostic Agents for Distributed Systems', *Proceedings of ModelAge97* Sienna, Italy, January 1997.
14. Hamscher, W. C., 'Modeling digital circuits for troubleshooting', *Artificial Intelligence*, **51**: 223-271, 1991.
15. Kafura, D. and Briot, J.P., 'Introduction to Actors and Agents', *IEEE Concurrency*, Special Series on Actors and Agents, Summer 1998, pp. 24-29, 1998.
16. Lesser, V., 'An Overview of DAI: Viewing Distributed AI as Distributed Research', *Journal of Japanese Society of AI*, Special Issue on DAI, vol. 5, num. 4, R. Nakano and S. doshita (Eds.), pp. 392-400, 1990.
17. Loia, V. and A. Gisolfi, 'A Distributed Approach for Multiple Model Diagnosis of Physical Systems', *Information Sciences*, **99**(3-4):247-288, 1997.
18. Noteboom, P. and G. B. Leemeijer, 'Focusing based on the structure of a model in model-based diagnosis', *Int. J. Man-Machine Studies*, **38**: 455-474, 1993.
19. Rissland, E.L., C. Basu, J.J. Daniels, J. McCarhty, Z. B. Rubinstein, and D. B. Skalak, 'A Blackboard-Based Architecture for Case-Based Reasoning', *Proceedings of Case-Based Reasoning Workshop*, Washington D.C., pp. 77-92, Morgan Kaufmann Pub., 1991.
20. Self, J, 'Model-based cognitive diagnosis', *User Modeling and User Adapted Interaction* **3**, 89-106, 1993.
21. Sleeman, D., 'Assessing aspects of competence in basic algebra', in *Intelligent Tutoring Systems*, D. Sleeman and J. S. Brown (Eds.) 185-199, 1982.
22. Tomlinson, C. , Scheevel, M., and Singh, V., '*Report on Rosette 1.1*', MCC TR ACT-OODS-275-91, MCTC, Austin, TX, July 1991.
23. Yonezawa, A., '*ABCL: an Object-Oriented Concurrent System*', MIT Press, 1990.
24. Yonezawa, A. and M. Tokoro (Eds.):, '*Object Oriented Concurrent Programming*', MIT Press, 1987.

Converting Declarative into Procedural
(and Vice Versa)

Iain D. Craig

Department of Computer Science
University of Warwick
Coventry CV4 7AL, UK EU
idc@dcs.warwick.ac.uk

Abstract. Procedural and declarative are often seen as two irreconcilable extremes. In this paper, we show how a reflective rule system can move between declarative and procedural interpretations with relative ease. We outline a new way to interpret these shifts, one which is more principled than the usual dichotomy. We also show that some relatively small changes in rule structure allow different dynamics to be assigned to rule components and to entire rules. This serves not only to show that description plays a critical role in reflection, but also to show that different kinds of dynamics can be supplied when required. Alternative dynamics can be provided by rule sets encoded in the same representation. The new structure can be used in exactly the same way as the ELEKTRA interpreter that is the main focus of this paper's attention.

1 Introduction

Procedural and declarative are often seen as two irreconcilable extremes of computational interpretation. The conversion from declarative to procedural has been a major theme in Computer Science for many years, but has achieved only limited success. This is of some interest because intermediate points are seldom considered possible. The points are also related asymmetrically; the declarative end is more desirable than the procedural one. The declarative end is seen as better because it can more easily be described using established parts of mathematics. Moreover, procedural aspects are often seen as 'dirty,' characterised by many little details which are often claimed to be of a machine-specific nature. This detail is not amenable to direct description in terms of mathematical logic and relies upon some kind of 'mental simulation' [1] of the operations. Unfortunately, it is only by applying procedures that a genuine dynamic results; declarative representations need processors (or interpreters) to animate them; the declarative end of the spectrum relies upon notions that are different from those at the procedural end. The declarative end of the spectrum exhibits a dynamics that cannot necessarily be inferred from the text.

This paper describes part of a reflective production rule interpreter (called ELEKTRA) that blurs the distinction between procedural and declarative; what we see instead is that different dynamics are involved in different processes, and

J.A. Padget (Ed.): Human and Artificial Societies, LNAI 1624, pp. 132–141, 1999.

these processes can be inter-converted and even mixed in various forms. We will present arguments drawn from experience with reflective programs in support of our position.

The paper is organised as follows. In the next section, we will briefly describe ELEKTRA, a reflective production rule interpreter. ELEKTRA allows rules to interpret other rules and makes its internal structure available to rules in order to permit them to function in sophisticated ways. As part of the system, there is a pre-processor which converts rules into assertions which describe their structure and content. These assertions are stored in working memory and are used to optimise the process of reflection. It has been shown that ELEKTRA can, itself, be completely interpreted by two meta rules. ELEKTRA can be thought of as an implementation of the reflective tower concept. This concept allows us to change perspectives on objects, as we argue in section three.

As a central metaphor, we adopt the concept of the reflective tower [6].

At one level in the reflective tower, we have rules that are just executed to produce changes in working memory. At higher levels of the tower, such rules can be handled as if they were data; this is a characteristic of any reflective system, but there is no explicit reification operator in ELEKTRA because it relies upon an implicit quotation mechanism. We also see how the procedures that implement actions in ELEKTRA rules can be given a declarative interpretation; we also see that certain condition elements naturally have a procedural interpretation, but this can also be treated in a declarative fashion when appropriate. What we see is that the interpretation of the components of ELEKTRA rules depends upon how they are used. We finally consider a slight alteration to ELEKTRA in which additional dynamics can be introduced. This is done by making rule syntax considerably cleaner and more uniform and then by attaching rules which determine the way in which rules and their components are to be interpreted. This allows many dynamics to be expressed, and, moreover, expressed in a context-sensitive fashion (this is because rules can inspect the local state and decide what to do). The section ends with some comments about the possibility of multiple, concurrently active interpretations.

The paper ends with a short summary.

Before progressing, the reader should note that we have chosen production rules as a means to an end; our primary interest is in the properties of computation, not in programming languages of any particular kind. We have chosen the production rule representation of programs because they are conceptually very simple; thus, we hope, it will be easier to make our points clear without recourse to complex computational apparatus. More importantly, production rule systems (Post systems) Turing-equivalent, hence we can express any computable function in terms of rules. It is the latter property that is most valuable to us in this paper for we are interested in the semantic distinction between declarative and procedural interpreations of programs.

2   Elektra—a Review

ELEKTRA is basically a production rule interpreter of the forward-chaining variety. Its rules have the standard format: a collection of pattern-matched condition elements (interpreted as a conjunction) and a sequence of actions. Rules also have a unique identifier and a small integer value whose interpretation will be explained below. Rule conditions are represented by elements consisting of relation, function and constant symbols, and of variables; they are similar to atomic formulae in logic.

ELEKTRA's basic architecture is the same as all classical forward-chaining interpreters and contains all the familiar components:

- A long-term memory, called production memory (PM). PM stores long-term knowledge in the form of rules.
- A short-term memory, called working memory (WM). WM stores intermediate results of problem-solving activity and serves as an attention focusing mechanism.
- A pattern matcher for testing rule applicability. The matcher determines which rules have condition parts which are satisfied by the contents of WM; these rules are eligible to have their actions executed to cause changes to WM.

During the matching process, variables in rule conditions become bound to values derived from the WM elements that match them. The variables are collected to form *bindings*; a collection of bindings and a reference to the rule in which they occur is called a *rule instance*. Rule instances are collected to form the *conflict set*, to which selection operations are applied in order to choose a rule whose actions are to be executed (or *fired*).

The ELEKTRA interpreter can be used as a normal forward-chaining interpreter of a kind similar to the OPS family (e.g., [5]); it can be made to perform conflict resolution in the usual way. This mode of operation is a default mode; it is considered to be less important than the mode in which the interpreter executes rules at different levels of a hierarchy starting with object-level rules and including a potentially infinite number of meta levels. This is where the integer, called the *tag*, enters the picture:

1. When a rule is assigned to the object level, it is assigned a tag value of zero.
2. When a rule is assigned to the first meta level, it is assigned a tag value of one.
3. When a rule is assigned to the kth meta level, it is assigned a tag value of k.

It is possible to run the interpreter in a mode in which rules have additional primitive actions similar to those proposed by Davis [4]. In this mode, rules at a level less than n, for some value of $n \geq 0$, are given preference by the conflict resolution and other control components. In this scheme, meta rules are used to suggest rules to interpret.

The use of meta rules just outlined is, however, somewhat inflexible. Meta rules must be constructed for each object-level rule-set and omissions can easily occur. Moreover, this use of meta rules is restricted to control structures that cannot be altered dynamically. ELEKTRA, therefore, employs another scheme which is considerably more flexible. This scheme, described in more detail in [2, 3], depends upon the introduction of a rule pre-processor and a collection of additional primitives; in addition, it requires parts of the rule interpreter to be made accessible to the rules in the form of predicates and actions.

The rule pre-processor is used to convert every rule in a rule program into a collection of assertions which are loaded into WM at the same time as the program is loaded into PM. The assertions derived from the pre-processor describe the structure and contents of each rule in the program. This information includes information about the rule's tag value, the length of the condition part, the length of the action part, relations describing the contents of condition elements (for example, the contexts in which relation and constant symbols appear)—see [2, 3] for more detail. By describing rule structure and contents in WM, it becomes possible to employ the usual matching process in reasoning about rules (otherwise expensive operations on rules must be performed at runtime). Rules that reason about (or process) rule content or structure cost the same to execute as rules that manipulate ordinary, problem-related WM elements.

Although rules are completely described in WM, they are also held in PM in their normal form. The reason for the duplication is that it can be easier to interpret (match and fire) a rule in its standard form, while it is invariably easier to reason about a rule using an assertion.

The additional primitives fall into two sets. One set contains primitives that form and manipulate sets, sequences and bags; this set's primitives are completely general and can be used in any rule. The second set contains primitives that manipulate structures that are internal to the ELEKTRA rule interpreter. These primitives operate on such things as sets of variable bindings, rule instances and sets of rule instances. These are structures that are normally hidden from view by the interpreter, but in ELEKTRA, the interpreter is 'open' software. Unlike traditional software which attempts to place abstraction barriers to prevent access, ELEKTRA and other 'open' software permits access to its internals.

The ELEKTRA interpreter is made open to avoid duplication of code. ELEKTRA meta rules can directly invoke matching routines to match either a condition or a condition part against WM; they can also invoke the action execution procedures that are used to fire rules. The matching primitives are intended to be used as condition elements in meta rules, and the action execution primitives are intended for use in meta rule actions (the term 'intended' is intentional: the pre-processor allows us also to include execution primitives in condition parts and match primitives in actions—see the next section).

Access to bindings, sets of bindings, rule instances and sets of rule instances allows rules to take over the role of the rule interpreter itself. For complete reasoning about rules, however, it is still necessary to have the ability to match arbitrary conditions and to execute arbitrary actions. Rules, using this mechanism, can be tested on a 'what if?' basis to see if they are potentially satisfied in a given context provided by WM. (ELEKTRA also allows matches to be performed against sets of condition elements that are outside WM. This allows rules to construct hypothetical contexts and to see how rules respond to them).

In [3], it is shown how the forward-chaining rule interpreter can be implemented as a pair of meta rules. An interpreter for backward chaining has also been constructed as a set of rules. In each case, the meta rules perform functions such as matching and action execution; they also manipulate sets of rule instances in order to decide which rule next to execute. It is possible to construct collections of rule interpreters and to schedule their activity as a function of WM content.

3   Declarative and Procedural in Elektra

In this section, we will attempt to show that the differences between procedural and declarative can be blurred in a reflective system such as ELEKTRA. We will see that it is possible to give the same object both a procedural and a declarative interpretation, depending upon how one *uses* it. It might be claimed that all we are doing is to show that procedural attachment works. This is certainly the case, but we are also, particularly in two of the examples, showing that entire structures can be treated in both procedural and declarative fashion. The claim that we are 'merely' showing that procedural attachment works is mistaken, however, for the whole point of procedural attachment *is* to permit multiple interpretations, a fact which has not been sufficiently expressed in the literature. In addition, we will also see that it is possible to mix procedural and declarative interpretations within a single structure; this challenges the notion that a single structure must have a single interpretation, another proposition that has slipped between the floorboards. If we can have procedural, declarative, procedural and declarative interpretations of the same structure, it would appear plausible, at least in principle, to ask whether it is possible to find yet more interpretations with which to make richer mixes.

In ELEKTRA, it is possible for rules to operate on rules. Rules can be both active and passive in the sense that they can be executed for their effect and also treated as data by other rules. Normally, we think of rules as being executed in order to change working memory, thus altering the system's state. This is a procedural interpretation of rules. Yet, in ELEKTRA, it is possible to regard rules as declarative objects because they are totally described in working memory. As we have seen, the pre- processor converts each rule in the system into a collection of assertions which describe its structure and content. These assertions can be used by rules to reason about rules, both about structure and content; rules and their components (condition elements, relation and constant symbols, action symbols, condition parts, action parts, etc.) can be treated as data supplied to the matching process, and can be passed as data between condition elements, actions, and so on. This dual treatment of rules, both in terms of executable elements and a domain of discourse, reduces the distinction between procedural and declarative.

The condition parts of ELEKTRA's rules can contain special elements whose standard interpretation is to be executed; sometimes, these elements return values, sometimes only a truth value (actually, the equivalent). These elements can also be matched by the standard pattern matcher to bind variables in the normal way. For example, if an instance of one of these elements is stored in working memory, it is matched in the usual way and it receives the predicate satisfaction interpretation. When rules are matched against working memory, such an element, when it occurs as a condition element, it receives the procedural interpretation. These special elements are interpreted sometimes in a procedural way, sometimes in a declarative one; the interpretation that is actually given depends upon how the element is being used, not on some *a priori*, uniform interpretation.

What we see in condition elements is that it is possible to assign condition elements different interpretational processes depending upon how we want to use them. It is possible for an application to specify new matching processes, it need not rely upon the standard match method and upon the mechanisms for procedural attachment, although it might make use of them. In an application, the elements that, as standard, receive a procedural interpretation might receive a declarative one (predicate satisfaction); it is possible to do this (and relatively easy because we can use procedural attachment at a higher level of the reflective tower), so we can change the interpretation of an element as and when we wish. The temporal qualification is necessary in the last sentence because it is possible to switch between different interpreter processes in ELEKTRA, an interpreter being just a set of rules.

The interpretation of the condition part of a production rule in a conventional interpreter such as OPS5 [5] can be accurately described as having a declarative semantics. In ELEKTRA, this cannot be stated because of the possibility that some elements have a procedural interpretation.

In an identical fashion, the semantics of the action parts of rules is amenable to a dual interpretation. Here, however, we can usually give a procedural interpretation to this rule component because actions must be executed in order to change working memory contents. The declarative interpretation enters the picture when it is remembered that actions are also stored in working memory as assertions. In a way identical to condition elements, actions can be passed as data values between rule condition elements, and they can be asserted and retracted by other actions.

Reasoning can clearly be performed on actions. For example, if it is known that a rule makes a particular assertion, other things can be inferred about it; if there are rules that assert instances of two particular predicates, inferences can be made about them. We can also represent actions (and we can increase the repertoire of actions by means of procedural attachment) as collections of working memory elements. This allows us, inter alia, to consider that we are manipulating instances of classes, so we can include information about how the action is to be handled. In other words, we can provide complex descriptions for actions and to include information about how to execute, match, or otherwise

treat an action; furthermore, this description might include information about
the pre- and post- conditions of actions, thus making reasoning about state transformations possible. (It should be noted that such description is also possible for
condition elements of all kinds, as well as for predicate, function and constant
symbols; we have a completely general mechanism). With such descriptions in
place, we can, of course, have rules of the form:

$$if \ldots then \; print(\text{``foo''})$$

and we can equally have rules of the slightly less usual form:

$$if \ldots print(?x) \ldots then \ldots$$

as well as:

$$if \ldots arity(print, ?n), \; P(print, ?x), \; R(?x, ?n) \; then \ldots$$

where '?' introduces a pattern variable.

The second and third forms indicate that reasoning can be performed on
elements that usually receive only a procedural interpretation; of course, this is
something we expect from reflective systems, but it also displays another way in
which procedural and declarative interpretations can be exchanged. (By means
of reflection, we can also introduce various kinds of higher-order rule: this is an
aspect for further research.)

What we are seeing here is that we have two kinds of dynamic being expressed, the particular dynamic depending upon how an element is used. If we
use elements as if they have a procedural interpretation (behaviour), they can
express it. Many condition elements do not have a procedural interpretation,
so we must take a little care—or we assign them a default behaviour which
involves the execution of the pattern-matching procedure (yet again a pun!),
thus showing that, in principle, we *could* assign a procedural interpretation to
every element. Conversely, whenever an element has a declarative interpretation
(this includes everything in the ELEKTRA universe), that dynamic—predicate
satisfaction—is expressed. What is more, we are free to mix the interpretations
almost as we wish. (We need to say 'almost' because our interpretation of rules
requires us to interpret action parts as essentially procedural.) We can, though,
adjust our interpretation of rules slightly, as we will now consider.

The form of rules in ELEKTRA is somewhat asymmetric. The fundamental
interpretation of condition parts is that a declarative dynamic is required, while
action parts are essentially procedural. Syntactically, actions are composed of the
application of action (function or procedure) symbols to arguments, while condition elements are negated or not. Our syntactic change is to permit negations
to occur on both sides of a rule. Thus, what we formerly considered to be actions
can have a prefixed negation symbol. We will also remove many of the action
symbols, in particular those dealing with working memory addition and removal.
In an action part, if an element is negated, it has the removal interpretation; if
it is un-negated, it has the semantics of working memory assertion.

In most rule interpreters, there are two operations for altering working memory, one to add and one to remove elements; in ELEKTRA, we provide an additional action which is used to remove all instances of a relation (this is inherited from Prolog), but we can provide the same functionality by means of a little polymorphism. We will allow sets of atomic formulae to occur as elements of rules (on either side of the rule). If a negation symbol prefixes such a set, the contents of the set are removed from working memory; otherwise, they are added. If a negated set has a cardinality of one and its unique member is non-ground, all matching instances will be removed. Conversely, when matching, a match is successful if and only if all elements of the set match working memory, and, given that we assume the CWA, negation is handled in the obvious way (all elements must fail).

Once we have these changes in place, we have rules whose 'condition' part (antecedent) and 'action' part (consequent) are now identical. We are now in a relatively nice position, for we are able to specify how the two parts of rules are to be interpreted. It makes no difference whether we move from consequent to antecedent or from antecedent to consequent; indeed, our rules now have more of the feel of assertions for all hints of enforced procedural interpretation has been removed. We can specify that antecedents are to be interpreted procedurally and that consequent parts are to be assigned a declarative interpretation unless otherwise indicated.

The assignment of interpretations required by the previous paragraph can be done in a number of ways. Again, we are in the pleasant position in which we can choose which approach to adopt; we will shortly see that we can allow ourselves considerable freedom while maintaining full control.

The first way in which we can assign interpretations (dynamics or behaviours) is to fix it in the control structure of some interpreter like the OPS5 or ELEKTRA default interpreters. This is fine as a default, but inflexible in the extreme. We might prefer to allow one or two of the possibilities to be coded and allow the user to set a switch to tell the interpreter program of the required method. This last approach has a slight advantage, but it is still inflexible: in particular, what do we do if we want to switch between interpretations while the system is running, or when a particular subset of its rules are being processed (interpreted, animated).

The above methods ignore the fact that we are dealing with an extension to ELEKTRA. What we can do in order to preserve all of ELEKTRA's benefits is something along the following lines. We process each rule in the normal fashion. For each rule, we can specify how it is to be interpreted. This specification takes the form of assertions in working memory. This provides a first step towards flexible interpretation. Next, we can associate each rule with a class of rules. Each rule belongs to a class in exactly the way that an instance belongs to a class in an object-oriented language; this serves to associate parameters with the rules in the class in a richer way than simple assertions permit. We can also associate rules with the classes with the intention that the rules perform the interpretation of the class' instances. These rules can take into account the contents of working memory (the system state) and can select the interpretation method that is most appropriate for the moment; sometimes going forwards, sometimes backwards, sometimes treating a rule element procedurally, sometimes declaratively.

The above scheme also affords possibilities for different kinds of dynamic to be introduced. Rules can be used to interpret the elements of rules on an individual basis; this is a new kind of dynamic that allows different behaviours to be introduced, perhaps even on the basis of the system's current state, and other factors. It must be remembered that whenever a meta rule is matched, it can test *anything* that is in working memory and at *any* level of the reflective tower; nothing need be excluded from a meta rule's attention. Thus, by means of rule attachment, new dynamics, for example those associated with procedure call (and perhaps co-routines and threads), can be associated with rule elements.

If we have this extended form of interpretation, it is necessary to find some kind of bottom-level behaviour. It might be thought that we have to resort to the fixed approach we considered above. This is not so, for we can make use of assertions and classes just as we can for other kinds of rules. The bottom-level behaviour can be expressed in terms of rules, just as ELEKTRA currently expresses forward chaining in terms of two meta rules [3]. What we have in ELEKTRA is two rules that apply to themselves (this is the technique, some might say 'trick,' which drives reflection); this should be quite possible within the scheme that we are proposing. It might be objected that the current scheme depends upon the assertion and retraction of working memory elements to control the basic ways in which rules are interpreted; this can be achieved by the bottom-level rules themselves. These rules will be more complex than the corresponding ones in ELEKTRA (this is necessary because they deal with more structure and more information, and they admit of more possibilities). Even when we have a class structure, we can still use rule attachments; this is for the same reasons.

As a result, we can have a rich system in which different kinds of dynamics can be mixed within a single structure. Furthermore, the dynamics of these elements can be changed over time and with the state of the system. This is an interesting possibility.

We can now see that what is initially treated as procedural can be treated as declarative at higher levels in the reflective tower. Higher levels can treat lower levels as if they are data. However, even though higher levels can treat lower ones in a declarative manner, the procedural interpretation is still available; a rule from a lower level can be interpreted both procedurally and declaratively by rules at higher levels and at the same time! The sense in which a rule or a component of a rule is purely procedural or purely declarative is clearly blurred. We can also see that we can associate rules describing completely different dynamics with entire rules and with rule elements; thus, the sense in which we have a unique interpretation is further weakened.

The distinction between procedural and declarative is, perhaps, harder to see in ELEKTRA because it employs a single calculus approach to reflection; that is, it employs the same notation for describing procedural and declarative elements. We make puns on structures (this is one of the requirements for single calculus reflection). If there were two calculi, one each for procedural and declarative, the distinction could be more easily seen and, moreover, maintained, but it would still be amenable to the kind of mixing process that we are describing in this section. This is for the reason that descriptions must be reduced to executable elements; conversely (this is something that ELEKTRA does not yet do, except in its pre-processor), descriptions must be constructed from executable elements. If both operations are provided, it becomes possible to mix procedural and declarative in precisely the way that we describe in this section. In any case, procedural attachment is a technique, *not* a semantics.

4   Conclusions

We have seen that a reflective processor is able to convert between declarative and procedural representations. Indeed, it is possible to mix the two kinds of interpretation within a single context. This is possible because a meta rule can treat any rule or other structure below it in the tower of meta levels in any way it chooses. In particular, a meta rule can inspect a lower rule and treat it as a declarative item. Alternatively, a meta rule can treat a declarative item that occurs lower in the tower as a procedural item, provided that the latter aspect is available in one way or another (either in the form of an interpreting rule or of an interpreting procedure in some other language).

In a similar fashion, meta rules are able to take descriptions of computations and execute them as procedural elements while retaining the ability to regard the descriptions as declarative objects.

Reflection is a mechanism which is able to convert between these two extremes in interpretation (or dynamics).

The procedural/declarative distinction can be further blurred by slight changes in syntax and allowing additional mechanisms determine the semantics of rules. This is interesting because it allows more flexibility in rule interpretation, but it also shows how a slight change in the form of a description allows considerable change in semantics and in behaviours.

References

1. Backus, J., Can programming be liberated from its von Neumann style? A functional style and its algebra of programs, *Communications of the ACM*, Vol. 21, No. 8, pp. 613-41, 1978.
2. Craig, I. D.,. A Reflective Production System, *Kybernetes*, Vol. 23, No. 3, pp. 20-35, 1994.
3. Craig, I. D., Rule Interpreters in ELEKTRA, *Kybernetes*, Vol. 24, No. 3, pp. 41-53, 1995.
4. Davis, R., Meta-rules: Reasoning about Control, *Artificial Intelligence Journal*, Vol. 15, pp. 179-222, 1980.
5. Forgy, C. L., *The OPS5 User's Manual*, Technical Report No. TR CMU-CS-81-135, Department of Computer Science, Carnegie-Mellon University, 1981.
6. Smith, B. C.,*Reflection and Semantics in a Procedural Language*, Ph. D. dissertation, Computer Science Dept., MIT, Report No. MIT/LCS/TR-272, 1982.

Reflective Reasoning in a Case-Based Reasoning Agent

Miquel Sànchez-Marrè[1], Ulises Cortés[1]♠, Javier Béjar[1], Ignasi R.-Roda[2], and Manel Poch[2]

[1]Secció d'Intel·ligència Artificial. Dept. de Llenguatges i Sistemes Informàtics.
Universitat Politècnica de Catalunya. Campus Nord-Edifici C5.
C/ Jordi Girona 1-3. E-08034 Barcelona. Catalonia, Spain
{miquel, ia, bejar}@lsi.upc.es
[2]Laboratori d'Enginyeria Química i Ambiental.
Universitat de Girona.
Campus de Montilivi. E-17071 Girona. Catalonia, Spain
{ignasi, manel}@lequia1.udg.es

Abstract. As a Case-Based Reasoning agent (CBR) evolves over time, and solves new problems based on previous experiences, there are some pitfalls that can appear in the problem-solving task. When those troubles arise, is the time to start some reflective reasoning tasks to overcome those problems and to improve the CBR performance. Our proposal is to extend the basic reasoning and learning cycle with some new added reflective tasks such as forgetting cases, learning new cases, updating the case library organisation or re-exploring the case library, and including other strategies such as building meta-cases.

1 Introduction

Over the last decade an important progress has been made in the Case-based Reasoning (CBR) field. Specially, because problems are more clearly identified, and research results have led to real applications where CBR performs well. As noticed by Althoff & Aamodt [2] in this situation, it has also become clear that a particular strength of CBR over most other methods is its inherent combination of problem solving with sustained learning through problem solving experience.

The real environment within our CBR-agent has emerged is the Wastewater Treatment Plants (WWTP) supervision domain. It is a clear example of a real-world complex process where AI techniques are needed and where applications give not only fair results but also open new lines of research [9,16]. Particularly, we have proposed CBR architecture to model the experiential specific knowledge about a concrete WWTP. CBR is a flexible paradigm that supports the implementation of a dynamic learning environment. Within the frame of a Case-based reasoning agent,

---

♠ Currently at the Ecole Fédérale Polytechnique de Lausanne. Enjoying the CLUSTER chair of 1998-1999.

J.A. Padget (Ed.): Human and Artificial Societies, LNAI 1624, pp. 142 -158, 1999.
© Springer-Verlag Berlin Heidelberg 1999

we can model the actual operating situations of a WWTP through cases, and organise all the cases into the case library.

1.1 The CBR Agent Environment: Wastewater Treatment Plants

Wastewater Treatment Plants (WWTP) provide a necessary buffer between the natural environment and the concentrated wastewater from urban and industrial areas. But their goals are not yet achieved when WWTP is built. Only when their operation is successful, these WWTP achieve their objective of returning good quality water to the natural environment. The correct control and operation of WWTP is not an obvious task. There are many operations from different nature meeting in a WWTP: mechanical, electrical, chemical, biological, physical operations, *etc.* All of them can originate failures that can guide the plant to a bad operation state, for example, a bad outflow water quality.

Classical control methods, such as feedback [18], feed-forward [6], adaptive [7] and optimal control [20], have been used to improve and optimise WWTP operation. However, this classical approach, based on mathematical modelling, shows some limitations when trying to control the activated sludge process –the main used biotechnological technique in WWTP–, mainly when the plant is not working under the ideal state. Some aspects that difficult the success of classical control methods are the following:

- The complex, and often unknown, behaviour of the micro-organisms
- The lack of on-line sensors and signals
- The ill-structure of the WWTP domain
- The uncertainty of some variables or instruments
- The dynamic state of the process
- The use of subjective information
- The relevance of many qualitative variables
- The delay of the analytical information from the laboratory

In spite of these circumstances, the use of mathematical models and control algorithms improves WWTP operation and general management. However, it is necessary to find a deeper approach that let us detect some unforeseen situations such as mechanical faults or cope with a toxic shock. Also to take advantage of the subjective knowledge accumulated through years of experience by the experts [27], to use the objective information provided by years of WWTP operation, or to use the available but incomplete information to solve a specific problem.

1.2 The Target System: A Hybrid Multi-knowledge Supervisory Architecture

The integrated AI framework developed is called DAI-DEPUR [28,29], that stands for distributed and integrated supervisory multi-level architecture. It was developed for the WWTP domain, but is clearly a general framework for complex real-world process supervision.

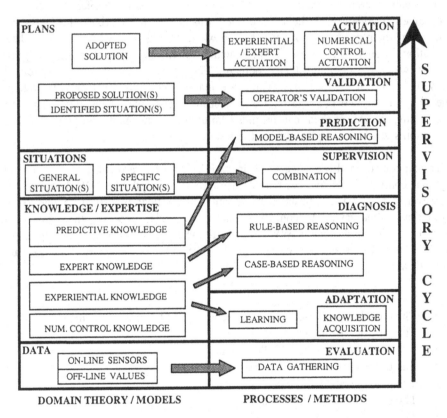

Fig. 1. The integrated AI framework: DAI-DEPUR architecture

DAI-DEPUR is an *integrated* architecture (see figure 1). It joins in a single framework several cognitive tasks and techniques such as learning, reasoning, knowledge acquisition, distributed problem solving, *etc*. Four levels are distinguished from the domain models [31] point of view: data, knowledge, situations and plans. On the other hand, taking into account the supervision tasks, 7 levels are considered.

It is possible to describe the behaviour of our CBR-agent and its application to the WWTP domain as *problem solving + learning*. It is also possible to describe these two elements in terms of the *goals* to be achieved by the system, the *tasks* that need to be solved, the *methods* that will led to accomplish those tasks and the *background knowledge* or the specific knowledge of the application domain that those methods require.

1.3 Overview

This paper proposes a set of reflective tasks and strategies to overcome some CBR competence and performance problems. These tasks can be included in the general cycle of a CBR agent. In this introductory section it has been briefly presented the WWTP domain, where our CBR approach was originated and where the hybrid multi-knowledge supervisory architecture DAI-DEPUR was developed. Section 2 describes the main design decisions of a CBR system, and in special, those of our approach. Dynamic problems that can appear in the evolution of a CBR system, and our introspective tasks to overcome those problems are explained in section 3. In section 4, it is outlined the final CBR reasoning cycle with the new reflective tasks introduced in section 3. The conclusions and future work are discussed in section 5.

2 Static Problems with a CBR Agent

CBR systems have been used in a broad range of domains to capture and organise past experience and to learn how to solve new situations from previous past solutions. CBR systems have been applied to planning (PRECEDENTS [21], CAPLAN/CBC [32], CHEF [10]), design (NIRMANI [22], JULIA [11]), classification (PROTOS [4]), diagnosis (CASEY [14]), understanding and analysis (AQUA [23,24]), interpretation (HYPO [3]), troubleshooting detection (CASIOPÉE, LADI [17]) and explanation (SWALE [13]). For Case-based Reasoning in continuous situations, there are (CIDA [12]), an assistant for conceptual internet work design, and (NETTRAC [5]) for planning and execution monitoring in traffic management in public telephone networks.

In the WWTP domain, Case-based Reasoning has been used for designing most suitable WWTP operations for a set of determined input contaminant [15].
The basic reasoning cycle of a CBR agent can be summarised by a schematic cycle (see figure 2). In Aamodt and Plaza [1] they adopt the four REs schema:

• *Retrieve* the most similar case(s) to the new case.
• *Reuse* or *Adapt* the information and knowledge in that case to solve the new case. The selected best case has to be *adapted* when it does not match perfectly the new case.
• *Revise* or *Evaluate* the proposed solution. A CBR-agent usually requires some feedback to know what is right and what is wrong. Usually, this is performed by simulation or by asking to a human oracle.
• *Retain* or *Learn* the parts of this experience likely to be useful for future problem solving. The agent can learn both from successful solutions and from failed ones (repair).

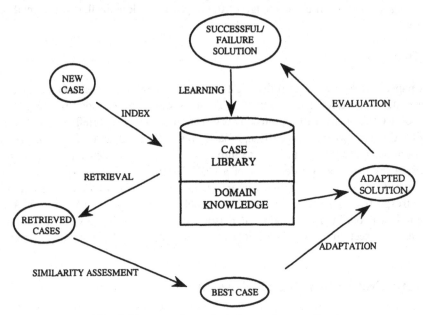

Fig. 2. The general case-based reasoning paradigm

The quality of the new case(s) extracted by the CBR-agent depends upon some of the following criteria:

- The *usefulness* of the case(s) extracted and selected
- The *ease* of use this (these) case(s)
- The *validity* of the reasoning process
- The *improvement* of knowledge through experience

When setting a CBR-agent one has to take into account some design decisions or static problems such as:

- How to describe the domain problems
- The case structure
- The case library structure
- The missing information problem
- The indexing of the case library
- The similarity assessment between cases

2.1 Our CBR Approach

In our approach [26,29] we have chosen a domain independent implementation by means of a table of attributes. This option eases the use of raw data coming from sensors and allows the connection of the CBR-agent with other modules as shown in figure 1. Those attributes are considered relevant by the experts at beginning of the process. And represent the use of *intensive knowledge* about the domain coming from experts. This fact could be considered as the incorporation of their *preferences* in the decision making about the set of alternatives that appear in the application domain. The attributes can be ordered or not, and are discretized also by the experts. The case structure is a record-like structure or template with some slots such as in the following example:

(:identifier CASE-64

  :situation-description ((Water-inflow 35,000 m^3/day)
                             (Inflow-Biological-Oxygen-Demand 280 mg/L)
                             (Biomass-IVF 320 mL/mg)
                          . . .)
  :diagnostics BULKING-SITUATION
  :actuation-plan   ((1 Microbiological-Observation)
                    (2 Identification-of-main-filamentous-microorganism)
               . . .)
  :case-derivation CASE-16
  :solution-result SUCCESS
  :utility-measure 0.74
  :distance-to-case 0.2103)

The case library is implemented as a prioritised discrimination tree, in order to get a CBR agent with good performance in time, thus only assessing the similarity of some retrieved cases. A prioritised discrimination tree means a tree where each node matches with a prioritised attribute. The expansion of this tree follows a lazy strategy. This implementation facilitates the case extraction when the case library grows as the attributes represent the relevant aspects that constitute the base for the search in the case library. The goal of the retrieval task of our CBR-agent is to search for similar precedents from the case library.

The case library has at each node as many branches as different discretized values are defined for the attribute. It supports missing information by means of some frequency values associated to each branch in the tree. The indexing of the case library in the retrieve phase is made taking into account the predictive discriminant checklist of attributes, and following the path into the case library that best matches the input values of the new case. The similarity assessment of retrieved cases is made through a new similarity measure based on a new defined distance function: *L'Eixample* distance [25].

L'Eixample distance is sensitive to weights, in the sense that, for the most important attributes, those with weight $> \alpha$, the distance is computed using their qualitative values. That is maintaining or amplifying the differences between cases, and for those less relevant ones, those with weight $\leq \alpha$, the distance is computed using their quantitative values, i.e. reducing the differences between cases. *L'Eixample* distance is used to rank the best cases:

$$d(C_i, C_j) = \sum_{k=1}^{n} e^{Wk} * d(A_{ki}, A_{kj}) \, / \sum_{k=1}^{n} e^{Wk}$$

(1)

where,

$d(A_{ki}, A_{kj}) = |quantval(A_{ki}) - quantval(A_{kj})| \, / \, (upperval(A_k) - lowerval(A_k))$
      if A_k is an ordered attribute and $W_k \leq \alpha$

$d(A_{ki}, A_{kj}) = |qualval(A_{ki}) - qualval(A_{kj})| \, / \, (\#mod(A_k) - 1)$
      if A_k is an ordered attribute and $W_k > \alpha$

$d(A_{ki}, A_{kj}) = 1 - \delta_{qualval(Aki), qualval(Akj)}$
      if A_k is a non-ordered attribute

and,

C_i is the case i; C_j is the case j; W_k is the weight of attribute k; A_{ki} is the attribute k in the case i; A_{kj} is the attribute k in the case j; $quantval(A_{ki})$ is the quantitative value of A_{ki}; $quantval(A_{kj})$ is the quantitative value of A_{kj}; A_k is the attribute k; $upperval(A_k)$ is the upper quantitative value of A_k; $lowerval(A_k)$ is the lower quantitative value of A_k; α is a cut point on the weight of the attributes; $qualval(A_{ki})$ is the qualitative value of A_{ki}; $qualval(A_{kj})$ is the qualitative value of A_{kj}; $\#mod(A_k)$ is the number of modalities (categories) of A_k. $\delta_{qualval(A_{ki}), qualval(A_{kj})}$ is the δ of Kronecker.

The adaptation of the best similar case is based on interpolation parameter adjustment. If the retrieved case is *close enough* to the new case, the original solution (*i.e.*, the control actions) only needs few adaptation changes. In this domain we can assume that most times the retrieved cases are so similar to the new ones that they only need *parameter adjustment* to derive the new solution.

For each important difference between the attributes of the new case and the retrieved one, the system adjusts the parameters pointed by these differences. These adjustments are done by means of a linear interpolation between the values of the attributes of the situation and the values of the actuation parameters. In other cases, special-purpose adaptation heuristics must be developed. Our approach to the adaptation process can be summarised as follows:

      if distance(C_{NEW}, C_{RETR}) $\leq \beta$ **then**
            solution-parameters-interpolation(C_{NEW}, C_{RETR})
      else
            special-purpose-adaptation-heuristics(C_{NEW}, C_{RETR})
      endif

where β is a cut point on the distance value.

3 Dynamic Problems with a CBR Agent

Although a CBR agent can be well designed for problem solving in a given domain, as it evolves over time, and solves new problems based on previous experiences, there are some pitfalls that can appear in the performance of its dynamic problem-solving task. Some of the basic troubles are:

- Bad performance in space
- Bad performance in time
- Unsuccessful search in a hierarchical case library

The solution can be obtained by analogy with the human beings. As a case-based system learns and evolves over time, it could reason about itself by *reflection* or *introspection*, about its cognitive tasks, and about the organisation of its memory. Thus, it can refine all these features and try to solve these problems, as stated in [8].

3.1 Bad Performance in Space

The size of the case library (*efficiency in space*) could be growing as the CBR agent is learning new cases without an extensive improvement in the performance of the system, as pointed out in [19]. Two natural human cognitive tasks appear as the solution to these problems: *forgetting* [30] and *sustained learning* [25].

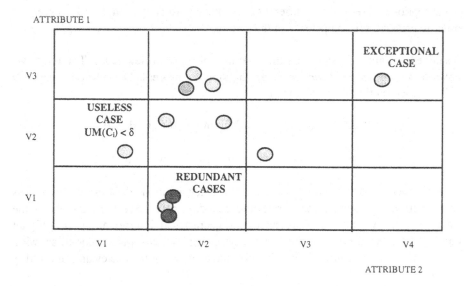

Fig. 3. Ontology of cases

Human beings forget facts they do not use. And hopefully, what it is not used is what is useless for their goals. Bearing in mind this analogy, we claim that there can be some *useless* cases stored in the case library that can be removed from it, with a significant increase in the performance. The *normalised utility measure* we have defined is:

$$UM\ (C) = ((\#\ UAS(C)\ /\ \#\ S(C)\ ) - (\#\ UAF(C)\ /\ \#\ F(C)\ ) + 1\ )\ /\ 2$$
(2)

where,

C is a retrieved case. $\#\ UAS(C)$ is the number of times that the case C was used and its application was a success when C was among the retrieved cases. $\#\ S(C)$ is the total amount of successes when the case C was among the retrieved cases. $\#\ UAF(C)$ is the number of times that the case C was used and its application was a failure when C was among the retrieved cases. $\#\ F(C)$ is the total amount of failures when the case was among the retrieved cases.

Thus, when the $UM(C)$ is 0 means that the case C is useless, and on the other hand, when it is 1 it means that the case C is very useful. We propose to *forget* the unuseful cases:

$$\text{Forget a case C} \Leftrightarrow UM(C) < \delta \text{ and it is not an exceptional case}$$

An exceptional case is a very different case, that has to be kept in the case library in order to preserve the competence of the system.

Sustained learning is focused on the retaining of relevant new cases. Therefore, we have to introduce a *relevance measure* to guide the process. The relevance measure will be based on the similarity measure:

$$\text{Learn a new case } C_i \Leftrightarrow \text{Minimum } \{d(C_i, C_k)\} \geq \gamma\}$$

Where C_k are the cases in the same leaf of the case library tree than C_i

To this objective, our proposal is to build a categorisation of cases: useful/useless cases, normal/exceptional cases, relevant/redundant cases. See the example in the figure 3 with two attributes for an easier geometrical interpretation. In [25] an ontology of cases was established, and a set of experiments were reported showing the goodness of this approach and the advantages in using both relevance and utility measures.

3.2 Bad Performance in Time

The search time (*efficiency in time*) in the retrieval step increases due to a bad case library organisation. For example, if the case library is organised in a hierarchical way, such as a discrimination tree or network, some straight paths that end with a leaf node could appear. In these paths, there are no branches at all.

If the hierarchical structure can be arranged in such a way that the depth of the structure becomes smaller than the current one (*compactness*), then the average retrieval time of cases can be reduced. This reflexive task will be named as *updating the case library organisation*. This task is to be performed off-line and only when then library has been in use during a time and the learning process is considered as stable.

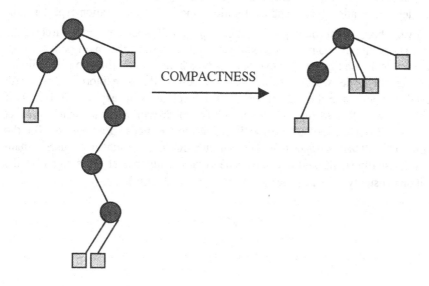

Fig. 4. Updating the case library organisation

Then system can look in the structure for straight and deep paths that end with a leaf node with more than one case (see left side of figure 4). If that path has expanded all the available discriminating attributes, then the two cases are not distinguishable one from the other. Therefore, that path can be shorted by pruning the unnecessary nodes -non discriminating attributes- , and climbing up the cases up to find the first attribute on this path (see right side of figure 4).

Other kind of compaction could appear if a path has been frequently visited and its use has been successful, in the sense defined in section 3.1, the unnecessary nodes can be pruned. If the path is considered useless it is removed. In other cases the path remains the same, as there is not enough evidence.

3.3 Unsuccessful Search in the Case Library

Re-exploration. In this section we describe a method to re-explore the hierarchical case library. This method has been implemented in [28] and the basic idea underlying the process is to prevent from the fact that some potentially good cases could not be reached in the retrieval process. Such an *unsuccessful search* in the case library will lead to an impasse situation. Among the causes that cause these failures we can mention: a) wrong choice at a high node in case library as an effect of the discretisation process of the attribute's values or b), if the hierarchy of nodes does not correspond to the importance of the features, as for example a bad discrimination order of the attributes, *etc*.

The re-exploration task searches the case library again with two exploration techniques: exploration-type 1 and exploration-type 2. The exploration-type 1 means that only the best[1] child (main path) will be explored. It is the common search of the case library in the previous unsuccessful retrieval, following the main path through the hierarchical case library. The exploration-type 2 means that the two best children of the current node will be explored. The best child is explored again with exploration-type 2, and the second best child is explored with exploration-type 1, if possible. If we call n to the maximum number of discriminant attributes, then at most n paths from the root are explored, and at most n^2 nodes are explored. So, the searching time, $T(n)$, is upper bounded by a function of the number of discriminant attributes, usually small, and does not depend on the number of cases stored in the case library, usually bigger as the system grows: $T(n) \in O(n^2)$.

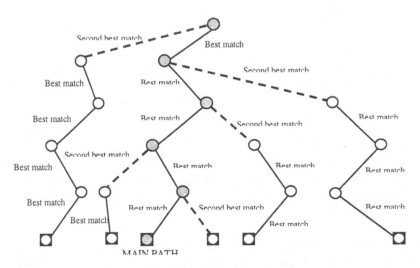

Fig. 5. Partial-matching re-exploration

---

[1]The most similar values to the new case value or most frequently used values.

Thus, the cases retrieved are all the cases stored in the memory that differ at most in one attribute's value from the new case (see figure 5). Therefore, this partial matching strategy allows to recognise subparts of cases as a *possible* solution to the actual problem.

Meta-cases. Another strategy to improve the CBR agent's performance, could be the splitting of the case library into several case libraries with different hierarchical structures. In the retrieval phase, first, the CBR-agent will search within a previously established classification to identify which kind of case(s) it is coping with. For each established class (*meta-case*) there will be a set of specific discriminating attributes and a different case library.

The meta-cases are in a way syntactic patterns that contain aspects considered as relevant. These relevant aspects (attributes) constitute the basis for the search in the case library and the use of these relevant aspects is in fact equivalent to using declarative bias during the identification phase. This fact will allow implementing clearer and more flexible retrieval mechanisms for real-world applications. Thus, there will be a partition of the cases by means of its similarity to previous established *meta-cases*. See the figure 6.

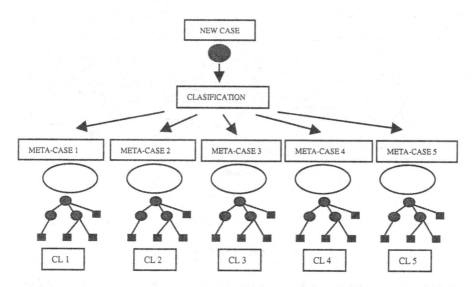

Fig. 6. Meta-reasoning by means of meta-cases

4 The Extended CBR Agent Cycle

We have stated that adding some reflective tasks and a new strategy to the basic reasoning cycle of a CBR agent can overcome some possible troubles. This introspective reasoning can be included in the general CBR reasoning paradigm.

Thus, the CBR agent can reason about itself and its performing capabilities, and decide to start some tasks to maintain or restore the good performance and competence of the system.

The new added tasks are:

- Sustained learning: learn only those relevant cases
- Forgetting: forget the useless cases
- Updating the case library organisation: compact the case library
- Re-exploration: search again the case library with partial-matching criterion
- Meta-reasoning: reasoning about what kind of case (meta-case) it is coping with

The extended CBR reasoning cycle is showed in figure 7. The new reflective tasks are depicted in the figure labelling dashed lines and the new strategy of meta-reasoning labels a full line, and the symptoms that can start those reflective tasks are depicted as rhombus.

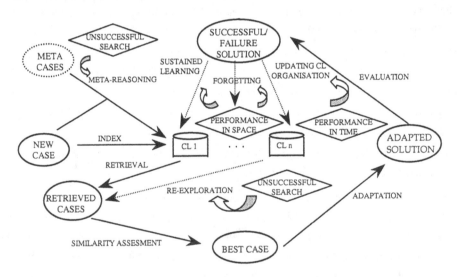

Fig. 7. The extended CBR agent cycle

The proposed new extended CBR cycle starts with a *meta-reasoning* task that selects the best case library suited for coping with the new case. This selection is made in basis of the similarity of the new case and the pre-defined meta-cases. For each meta-case there is an associated case library. Next, the case library is *indexed* and the common *retrieval* process of the most similar cases is started. Then the next task is the *similarity assessment* of the retrieved cases in order to select the best case. But if the most similar case is not enough similar, then a the *re-exploration* task can be started, trying to gather some other cases more similar to the new case than the previous ones. The *adaptation* task follows to get an adapted solution from the solution of the best retrieved case. Then, the *evaluation* of the proposed solution gets a feedback on how the solution has been applied. If this new case is enough relevant, it can be learned through a *sustained learning* task. Moreover, if the performance in space of the system is degrading, a *forgetting* task can be started to remove the useless cases from the case library. Also, if the system detects that the performance in time is decreasing, it can try to solve it by means of an *updating the case library organisation* task, to compact the case library.

These new capabilities enhance the adaptive and flexible characteristics of the case-based reasoning paradigm. They complement the basic REs scheme in the sense that they are mostly reflective tasks that only will be activated when the system reason that they will improve its performance and competence. It seems reasonable that they will be more useful when the system has enough information about the domain, i.e. when the learning and reasoning processes of the system gain stability over time.

5 Preliminary Experimental Evaluation

We had implemented the *sustained learning*, *forgetting* and *re-exploration* tasks described in section 3 to provide the DAI-DEPUR Case Based Reasoning agent with these reflective tasks improving its performance. About these tasks we had very good results producing a moderate but significative increasing of the case library without loosing the recovery capabilities and reducing the involved time and resources.

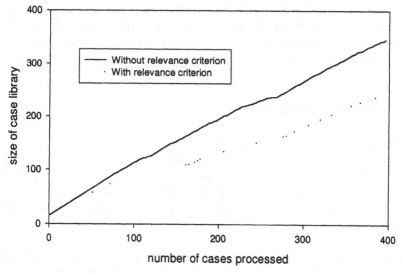

Fig. 8. Size evolution of the case library in both experiments

In [25] we show the results of the application of the sustained learning, forgetting tasks and re-exploration of the case library. In that experiment, the cases were described with 11 attributes, after a selection process of 41 initial attributes based on the relevance assigned by the experts.

We present a double experiment to show how the performance in space and the successful search can be improved with our proposed new tasks, based on the relevance and utility criteria. In the first experiment the case library was seeded with a representative set of 15 initial cases from a previous classification built-up by Linneo[+] [27], taken from real data of operation of the Girona's WWTP during the 1996-1997 period. The experts carried out the selection of these cases. We consider this set as a declarative *bias*. This set was tested against all the 396 real operation cases from the whole period, with a final case library size of 346 cases (87.3 % of cases processed), with the common CBR techniques.

The second experiment included the use of our added tasks. The case library was seeded in the same way than in the previous experiment, but in this case, only 14 of the 15 initial cases were stored due to the relevance criterion used. The new seed set was tested against the stream of all the 396 real operation cases from the whole period, with a final size of the case library of 242 cases (61 % of cases processed), with the new added tasks. See figure 8 for a detailed description of the compared case library size evolution.

For a detailed discussion about the results you can see [25].

We are just now experimenting with the *meta-reasoning* task, and we are working in progress   on the *updating of the case library organisation* task through the integration of tree compaction techniques using relevance, utility, discriminating power of attributes criteria.

6 Conclusions and Future Work

In this paper we have considered the revision of the basic RE[4] cycle of a CBR agent to include new reflective tasks and a new strategy aiming to increase the performance of the system and that do not overload its daily execution. In practice, reflective tasks can be expensive but they are only started when an impasse appears. First, each one of these tasks has been explained, and finally, the extended basic CBR cycle has been presented.

Sustained learning, forgetting and *re-exploration* tasks are implemented in DAI-DEPUR, and the preliminary results are good. The evaluation of the improved performance and competence, by the experts and by empirical testing is very promising.

The implementation of these techniques in the CBR agent leads the case library towards an optimal configuration of cases, maximising *competence* and minimising size and response-time (*performance*) of the system.

We are still working in progress on the *meta-reasoning* and *updating of the case library organisation* aspects and testing the system against simulated data that may give an improvement of the variety of cases to be treated.

Acknowledgements

This research is been partially supported by the Junta de Sanejament de la Generalitat de Catalunya and the Spanish CICyT projects TIC96-0878 and AMB97-0889, and EEC project VIM ERBCHRXCT 930401. Also the authors wish to acknowledge the co-operation of Gabriela Poch, manager of the Girona's wastewater treatment plant.

References

1. Aamodt, A., Plaza, E.: Case-based reasoning: fundamental issues, methodological variations and system approaches. AI Communications Vol. 7(1) (1994) 39-59
2. Althoff, K.D., Aamodt, A.: Relating case-based problem solving and learning methods to task and domain characteristics: towards an analytic framework. AI Communications Vol 9(3) (1996) 109-116
3. Ashley, K.D.: Modelling legal argument: reasoning with cases and hypotheticals. The MIT Press (1990)
4. Bareiss, E.R.: Exemplar-based knowledge acquisition: a unified approach to concept representation, classification and learning. Academic Press (1989)
5. Brandau, R., Lemmon, A., Lafond C.: Experience with extended episodes: cases with complex temporal structure. In Proc. of Workshop on case-based reasoning (DARPA). Washington D.C. (1991)
6. Corder, G.D., Lee, P.L. Feedforward control of a wastewater plant. Water Research Vol. 20 (1986) 301-309
7. Dochain, D.: Design of adaptive controllers for non-linear stirred tank bioreactors: extension to the MIMO situation. Journal of Process Control Vol. 1 (1991) 41-48
8. Fox, S., Leake, D.B.: Using introspective reasoning to refine indexing. Proc. of 14th Int. Joint Conference on Artificial Intelligence (IJCAI95), Montréal (1995) 391-397
9. Gimeno, J.M., Béjar, J., Sànchez-Marrè, M., Cortés, U.,R.-Roda, I.: Discovering and Modelling Process Change: an Application to Industrial Processes. Proc. of 2nd Int. Conference on the Practical Application of Knowledge Discovery and Data Mining (PADD 98), London (1998) 143-153
10. Hammond, K.: Case-based planning: viewing planning as a memory task. Academic Press (1989)
11. Hinrichs, T.R.: Problem solving in open worlds: a case study in design. Lawrence Erlbaum (1992)
12. Joh, D.Y.: CBR in a changing environment. Procc. of 2nd Int. Conf. On Case-based Reasoning (ICCBR'97). LNAI-1266 (1997) 53-62

13. Kass, A.M., Leake, D.B.: Case-based reasoning applied to constructing explanations. Proc. of Workshop on case-based reasoning (DARPA). Clearwater, Florida (1988)

14. Koton, P.: Using experience in learning and problem solving. Ph. D. dissertation. Dept. of Computer Science. MIT (1989)

15. Krovvidy, S., Wee, W.G.: Wastewater Treatment Systems from Case-Based Reasoning. Machine Learning Vol. 10 (1993) 341-363

16. Lenz, M., Bartsch-Spörl, B., Burkhard, H.-D., Wess S., (eds.): Case-Based Reasoning Techniques. LNAI 1400 (1998.)

17. Lenz, M., Burkhard, H.-D, Pirk, P., Auriol E., Manago, M.: CBR for diagnosis and decision support. AI Communications Vol. 9(3) (1996) 138-146

18. Marsilli-Libeli, S.: Optimal control strategies for biological wastewater treatment. Environmental Systems Analysis and Management., S. Rinaldi (editor). North-Holland Publishing Co. (1982) 279-287

19. Miyashita, K., Sycara, K.: Improving system performance in case-based iterative optimization through knowledge filtering. Proc. of 14th Int. Joint Conference on Artificial Intelligence (IJCAI'95) Montréal (1995) 371-376

20. Moreno, R., de Prada, C., Lafuente, J., Poch, M., Montague, G.: Non-linear predictive control of dissolved oxygen in the activated sludge process. ICCAFT 5 / IFAC-BIO 2 Conference, Keystone (CO) (1992.)

21. Oxman, R., Voß, A.: CBR in design. AI Communications Vol. 9(3) (1996) 117-127

22. Perera, S., Watson, I.: NIRMANI: an integrated case-based system for strategic design and estimating. Progress in Case-Based Reasoning. LNAI #1020 (1996) 186-200

23. Ram, A.: Indexing, elaboration and refinement: incremental learning of explanatory cases. Machine Learning Vol. 10(3) (1993) 201-248

24. Ram, A., Hunter, L.: Goals for learning and understanding. Applied Intelligence Vol. 2(1) (1992) 47-73

25. Sànchez-Marrè, M., Cortés, U., R.-Roda, I., Poch, M.: Sustainable Case Learning for Continuous Domains. Environmental Modelling and Software. In press. To appear in 1999.

26. Sànchez-Marrè, M., Cortés, U., R.-Roda, I., Poch, M., Lafuente, J.: Learning and Adaptation in WWTP through Case-Based Reasoning. Special issue on Machine Learning of Microcomputers in Civil Engineering Vol. 12(4) (1997) 251-266

27. Sànchez-Marrè, M., Cortés, U., Béjar, J., de Gràcia, J., Lafuente, J,. Poch, M.: Concept Formation in WWTP by means of Classification Techniques: a Compared Study. Applied Intelligence Vol. 7(2) (1997) 147-166

28. Sànchez-Marrè, M., Cortés, U., Lafuente, J., R.-Roda, I., Poch, M. DAI-DEPUR: an Integrated and Distributed Architecture for Wastewater Treatment Plants Supervision. Artificial Intelligence in Engineering Vol. 10(3) (1996) 275-285

29. Sànchez-Marrè, M.: DAI-DEPUR: an Integrated Supervisory Multi-level Architecture for Wastewater Treatment Plants. Ph.D. Thesis. Software Department Universitat Politècnica de Catalunya (1996) http://www.lsi.upc.es/~miquel

30. Smyth, B., Keane, M.T.: Remembering to forget. Proc. of 14th Int. Joint Conference on Artificial Intelligence (IJCAI'95) Montréal (1995) 377-382

31. Steels, L.: Components of expertise. AI Magazine Vol. 11(2) (1990) 28-49

32. Veloso, M., Muñoz-Avila, H., Bergmann, R.: Case-based planning: selected methods and systems. AI Communications Vol. 9(3) (1996) 128-137

Modelling Rational Inquiry in Non-ideal Agents

Antonio Moreno[1], Ulises Cortés[2], and Ton Sales[2]

[1] Departament d'Enginyeria Informàtica - Universitat Rovira i Virgili (URV)
Carretera de Salou, s/n. 43006-Tarragona, Spain
amoreno@etse.urv.es

[2] Dep. de Llenguatges i Sistemes Informàtics - Universitat Politècnica de Catalunya
C/Jordi Girona, 1-3. 08034-Barcelona, Spain
{ia,sales}@lsi.upc.es

Abstract. The construction of *rational agents* is one of the goals that has been pursued in Artificial Intelligence (AI). In most of the architectures that have been proposed for this kind of agents, its behaviour is guided by its *set of beliefs*. In our work[1], *rational agents* are those systems that are permanently engaged in the process of *rational inquiry*; thus, their beliefs keep evolving in time, as a consequence of their internal inference procedures and their interaction with the environment. Both AI researchers and philosophers are interested in having a formal model of this process, and this is the main topic in our work.

Beliefs have been formally modelled in the last decades using *doxastic logics*. The *possible worlds model* and its associated *Kripke semantics* provide an intuitive semantics for these logics, but they seem to commit us to model agents that are *logically omniscient* and *perfect reasoners*. We avoid these problems by replacing possible worlds by *conceivable situations*, which are all the situations that the modelled agent is capable of considering.

In this paper we show how this notion of *conceivable situations* may be used to model the process of rational inquiry in which a non-ideal rational agent is engaged. We define a wide class of agents, called *rational inquirers*, which are a general abstraction of any kind of non-ideal agent. We show how the beliefs of this kind of agents evolve in time as a consequence of a multi-dimensional belief analysis, and we use the framework of *conceivable situations* in order to model this evolution.

1 Aim of the work

1.1 Introduction

Artificial Intelligence (AI) has pursued the goal of constructing *rational agents* for a long time. This kind of agents may be defined ([15]) as *systems that have some kind of perception and try to act upon the environment so as to achieve*

---

[1] Research partially supported by projects *VIM: A Virtual Multicomputer* (Human Capital and Mobility, ERBCHRXCT930401) and *SMASH: Multi-agent systems and its application to medical services* (CICYT, TIC 96-1038-C04-04).

J.A. Padget (Ed.): Human and Artificial Societies, LNAI 1624, pp. 159–181, 1999.
© Springer-Verlag Berlin Heidelberg 1999

their goals, given their beliefs; thus, beliefs somehow guide their behaviour (*e.g.* they may be used to choose between alternative courses of action available to the agent). The architecture of such agents usually includes a knowledge base (that stores relevant facts about the agent and its environment) and modules that may perform inferences from those facts, interact with the agent's environment, create and evaluate different plans, *etc.* In the last decade it has been argued that, if the agent is to display a rational behaviour, it needs to have a module capable of handling its beliefs.

In this document we take the expression *"rational agents"* to refer to those agents that, apart from complying with the previous definition, are permanently engaged in a process of *rational inquiry* (defined by Brandom in [14] as *the [rationally controlled] transformation of belief over time*). Intuitively, these agents are constantly trying to make their beliefs as similar as possible to the facts that hold in the real world. They keep trying to expand their beliefs (by including facts that are true in their environment) and to get rid of wrong beliefs (those that do not reflect the state of the actual world). The classical philosophical tradition has considered ([14]) two components in this process: a *rational* one, that consists in the application of some inference procedures to the actual beliefs (resulting in the addition of inferred beliefs or the discovery of some incompatibility in them), and an *empirical* one, which adds or removes beliefs according to the result of observations performed in the agent's environment. An important concern both in AI and in Philosophy is how to *build a formal model of rational inquiry*; this is the aim of our work.

1.2   Possible worlds and Kripke semantics

The natural start point in our work was to consider *logics of knowledge and belief* (epistemic and doxastic logics, [5]). These modal logics are used to analyse in a formal way the reasoning about knowledge or belief performed by an agent. In the literature of doxastic logics the universal modal operator ($\Box$) is usually called B. If several (m) agents are taken into account, a family of subscripted operators (B_1, B_2, ..., B_m) is considered (where $B_i\varphi$ is read as *"Agent i believes φ"*). The usual language of propositional doxastic logic for m agents contains a set of primitive propositions (P, Q, R, ...), the basic logical operators ($\neg$, $\vee$, $\wedge$ and $\Rightarrow$) and the modal belief operators B_1, B_2, ..., B_m. The formulas of this language are the primitive propositions and the applications of the logical operators or the modal operators to other formulas of the language.

The semantic model traditionally adopted as a basis in doxastic logics is the *possible worlds model* ([6]). This model is based on the assumption that there is a set of possible states (or *possible worlds*) in which the agent can be in any moment; when the agent is in a possible world, there is a set of possible worlds which are compatible with the actual world, in the sense that the agent cannot distinguish these worlds from the actual one. The usual semantics given to the formulas of the doxastic language described above is the *Kripke semantics* ([10]), that states that the agent believes a formula iff it is true in all the worlds that the agent cannot tell apart from the actual world.

A *normal Kripke structure* is a tuple of the form $(S, \pi, R_1, ..., R_m)$, where S is the set of possible worlds, π is a truth assignment to each primitive proposition in each world and R_i is the accessibility relation between worlds for agent i (*i.e.* $(s, t) \in R_i$ iff s and t are indistinguishable worlds for agent i). Given a normal Kripke structure M, the relation $M,s \models \varphi$ (read "φ *is true (or satisfied) in state s of model M*") is usually defined in the following way:

- $M,s \models$ P, being P a primitive proposition, if $\pi(s, P) = true$
- $M,s \models \neg\varphi$ if $M,s \not\models \varphi$
- $M,s \models (\varphi \vee \psi)$ if $M,s \models \varphi$ or $M,s \models \psi$
- $M,s \models (\varphi \wedge \psi)$ if $M,s \models \varphi$ and $M,s \models \psi$
- $M,s \models (\varphi \Rightarrow \psi)$ if $M,s \models \neg\varphi$ or $M,s \models \psi$
- $M,s \models B_i\varphi$ if $M,t \models \varphi$ $\forall t$ such that $(s, t) \in R_i$

The last clause formalizes the conception of beliefs previously stated: an agent i believes a proposition φ when it is true in all the worlds considered possible by the agent, *i.e.* in all the worlds that the agent cannot tell apart from the actual world. That means that φ has to be true in all the worlds connected to the actual world through R_i, which is the accessibility relation between worlds for agent i.

There exists ([5]) a *sound and complete axiomatization* of the class of all normal Kripke structures for m agents. An axiomatic system S is *sound* with respect to a class of structures C if every formula provable in S is true in every structure of class C. S is *complete* with respect to C if every formula which is true in every structure of class C can be proved in S. An axiomatic system *characterizes* a class of structures when it is a sound and complete axiomatization of the class. The axiomatic system that characterizes the set of all normal Kripke structures for m agents has two axioms and two inference rules, which are the following:

- A1. All the instances of tautologies of propositional calculus.
- A2. $(B_i\varphi \wedge B_i(\varphi \Rightarrow \psi)) \Rightarrow B_i\psi$ (axiom K)
- R1. From $\vdash \varphi$ and $\vdash (\varphi \Rightarrow \psi)$ infer $\vdash \psi$ (*Modus Ponens*)
- R2. From $\vdash \varphi$ infer $\vdash B_i\varphi$ (*Necessitation*)

This axiomatic system is known as system K_m (or K if only one agent is considered), and it is the simplest one used to model logics of knowledge and belief.

1.3 Logical omniscience and perfect reasoning

Axiom A1 (all the instances of all propositional tautologies) and rule R1 (*Modus Ponens*) are taken directly from classical propositional logic. The problems to be addressed in this work derive from axiom K and the rule of necessitation: they (seem to) commit us to model agents that are

- **logically omniscient**, because they believe all tautologies (since all of them are true in every world), and

- **perfect reasoners**, because they also believe all logical consequences of their beliefs (*e.g.* if an agent believes P and (P $\Rightarrow$ Q) in a state s, it means that these two propositions are true in all the worlds compatible with s (all states R_i-accessible from s); therefore, Q will also be true in all of these worlds, and the agent will also believe Q).

These facts imply that an agent with the basic arithmetic axioms would have to know whether the Fermat theorem is indeed a theorem or not, or that an agent that knew the rules of chess would have to know whether White has a winning strategy or not ([9]). The union of these problems is usually referred to in the literature as the problem of *logical omniscience* (even though some authors prefer to call it *closure under logical consequence* ([9]) or *tautological closure* ([16])). We will distinguish between logical omniscience and perfect reasoning, as described above.

Obviously there are many circumstances in which these conditions are unacceptable; that would be the case when the agent is supposed to be able to compute its knowledge or to take actions based on it. This would be an *internal* view of knowledge, as something that is acquired after a computation. It is clearly not a realistic model of either human agents (who are not logically omniscient) or computational agents (which have resource limitations that can prevent them from being perfect reasoners). In summary ([13]), omniscience is irreparably out of line with the needs of any real reasoning agent.

We may now state a more refined version of the aim of this work: to develop a way to *model the process of rational inquiry* (the evolution of a rational agent's set of beliefs over time as a consequence of its interaction with the world and its internal inferential processes), *keeping the flavour of the possible worlds model and the Kripke semantics* (because, after all, they seem a very natural and intuitive semantics for modal logics of belief) *but trying to avoid the problems of logical omniscience and perfect reasoning* (in order to take into account non-ideal agents).

2   Modelling tools

2.1   Conceivable situations

Several authors have tried to solve (or, at least, partially alleviate) the problems of logical omniscience and perfect reasoning, both in AI and in Philosophy (see [12] for a detailed review of the most relevant approaches). A particularly interesting suggestion was made by Hintikka in [7], where he proposed the idea of considering *[logically] impossible [epistemically] possible worlds*; he seems not to have pursued this idea, though. This is the path followed in our work, as will be apparent in the rest of the paper.

The main roots of these problems are the assumptions of *completeness* and *consistency* that underlie the possible worlds model. As McArthur notes in [11], since worlds are *complete* the agent is forced to have beliefs about the way that everything would be in all of the accessible worlds; moreover, since worlds are *consistent* as well, everything that follows from the agent's beliefs must also be believed. Therefore, a natural solution to these problems could be reached by dropping these assumptions. This suggestion has been dismissed by most of the logicians and logically concerned philosophers of the Western tradition since Aristotle's time. Nevertheless, this possibility can be seriously entertained (some philosophers have indeed argued for the feasibility of this kind of worlds, *e.g.* Rescher and Brandom in [14]).

The *partiality* or *incompleteness* of possible worlds has been traditionally accepted in the AI literature, the most common justifications being the following:

- The agent can be unaware of certain facts (Fagin and Halpern tried to take this fact into account in their *logic of general awareness*, [2], see [12]).
- The agent can have limited resources (*e.g.* the time required or the space needed to perform a given inference). This is the most evident justification, if rational agents have to be implemented at all in a real computer.
- The agent can ignore some relevant rules (*e.g.* the agent may have not been told what the rule of *Modus Tollens* is). This view was clearly considered by Konolige in his Ph.D. thesis ([9]), where each agent was modelled with a base set of beliefs and a (possibly incomplete) set of inference rules (see [12]).

Inconsistency is a totally different matter. It can be argued in its favour with a number of ideas:

- The agent can be unable to take all its beliefs into account in every inference; if it focuses in a subset of them (call that a *context*), it can draw conclusions which are consistent within the context but inconsistent if all the beliefs are considered.
- It is indeed possible to define arguably interesting procedures of inquiry over inconsistent belief sets (as shown *e.g.* in [14]).
- These kinds of world are perfectly conceivable (and even depictable in pictures, as Escher proved so many times - see *e.g.* [8]).
- Some theories have been considered acceptable for a certain period of time (*e.g.* Frege's set theory) for many people, but they have been proved to be inconsistent later (as Russell did with Frege's theory). This inconsistency does not mean that the theory has been useless and that all the work made on it has been wasted (many interesting insights can be gained even with the inconsistency proof).
- If a theory is expressed in first-order logic, it is not even decidable in general whether it is consistent or not, so these theories would be pretty useless if they could be used only in case they were previously proved to be consistent.
- A modified version of the analytic tableaux method is going to be used to perform the logical analysis of the agent's beliefs, as will be explained below, and the conception of possible worlds as (possibly) inconsistent sets induces a nice relationship between a tableau and the set of possible worlds that it represents (note that an open tableau can contain an inconsistent set of formulas, *e.g.* if the logical development of the tableau has not (yet) shown the contradiction that may be hidden in the set, waiting for further analysis to appear).

Therefore, we are going to avoid the classical logicians' reluctance towards (possibly) incomplete and (possibly) inconsistent possible worlds; they will be considered as (epistemologically and even ontologically) possible as the good old complete and consistent possible worlds. Consider the positive side of this move: if worlds are incomplete and inconsistent, both logical omniscience and perfect reasoning seem to vanish before our very eyes. The agent can clearly fail to believe some tautologies, and it does not have to believe any logical consequence of its beliefs. These facts will be easier to grasp later, when these worlds are used to model rational inquiry.

In fact, the expression *"possible world"* does not convey exactly the idea that we have of what a doxastic alternative is; in our framework, we will call them *"conceivable situations"*, rather than *"possible worlds"*. A *conceivable situation*, as its name suggests, is any scenario that the modelled agent may think of, irrespective of its partiality or its consistency. It may be a situation that it has experienced, that it has been told of, or even a situation that it has just imagined as possible. The only condition for an scenario to qualify as a conceivable situation is that the agent considers it so; it does not have to be either consistent or physically realizable. The main point is that a conceivable situation is *not* a model (in the logician's sense of the term). In the rest of the paper the notion of conceivable situation will be considered as primitive, and will correspond to what the modelled agent considers as *"realities"*, be they experiential or just imagined.

2.2   Modelling the evolution of beliefs

Recall that the goal of this research is the definition of a general model of the process of rational inquiry, so something must be added to the classical possible worlds model (assuming that one indeed intends to keep the general conception of the model and the Kripke semantics). A very natural idea to model dynamic beliefs is to have some kind of *variability* in the main ingredients of the possible worlds model: the (assumed fixed) set of possible worlds W and the (also assumed fixed) accessibility relation R.

Imagine that the agent's beliefs in world w have to be analysed. This world is R-connected to worlds w_1, w_2 and w_3. A certain proposition P is true in w_2 and w_3, but not in w_1; therefore, P is not believed in w. If the content of the accessible worlds could be variable and not fixed, the following situation could arise: the agent could (for instance, as a consequence of an observation performed in the real world) notice that P holds indeed. This observation could be included in all the accessible worlds (w_1, w_2 and w_3), producing a modification of w_1 (which, in turn, would cause a modification in the agent's beliefs in w, which now would include P). This simple example shows that a variability in the contents of the possible worlds could account for experiences performed in reality, and could model the changes of beliefs produced by such observations. This is the kind of belief modification that will be used in the experimental dimension of analysis (see section 6).

Imagine that in the previous situation (P is true in w_2 and w_3, not in w_1, so P is not believed in w), a certain proposition Q is true in w_1 but false in w_2 and w_3 (therefore, it is not believed in w either). The agent, in the course of an inferential process performed on its beliefs, could reach the conclusion that Q is clearly unacceptable (e.g. it contradicts a large set of other actual beliefs). Therefore, it could conclude that the accessible worlds that contain Q are not viable alternatives to its present world, and thus they don't have to be considered accessible any more. This fact would imply that $(w \, R \, w_1)$ would no longer hold, and that the set of doxastic alternatives to w would be reduced to $\{w_2, w_3\}$. But these two worlds contain P, and thus, via the standard Kripke semantics, the agent would now believe P in w. This example shows how a modification of the accessibility relation (e.g. a restriction in the set of possible doxastic alternatives) can indeed model a modification of the beliefs caused by an internal inferential process of the agent (other sources could have been considered; e.g. the agent could have observed the impossibility of Q as a result of an observation in its environment).

In summary, we think that the process of *rational inquiry* (including the consideration of observations made by the agent and the results of its own inferential processes) *can be modelled within the possible worlds model, keeping the Kripke semantics, but allowing dynamic changes in the content of possible worlds and in the accessibility relation between them.*

3   Multi-dimensional belief analysis

3.1   A syntactic representation of conceivable situations

A *conceivable situation* is (partially) *represented* by a set of propositional formulas in a doxastic language. There are no conditions imposed on this set, so it can be both partial (most facts about the actual world will probably not be contained in each conceivable situation) and inconsistent (although perhaps the inconsistency is not apparent in the set, it may be hidden in its deductive closure). This characterization of conceivable situations implies that they can fail to contain some (even all) tautologies, and that the set of formulas that represents one of them does not have to be necessarily deductively closed. As mentioned above, this is a way of avoiding the problems of logical omniscience and perfect reasoning.

In fact, it has been repeatedly proposed in the literature to consider *impossible* possible worlds, in the sense of having possible worlds where the usual logical connectives do not behave in the usual way, or tautologies may not be true, or inconsistent formulas may hold (see [12]). The drawback of these approaches is that, although they alleviate the problems of logical omniscience and perfect reasoning, they cause different problems. Basically, their main inconvenient is that they are very limiting, in the sense that the agent has not got a minimal set of inference capabilities (e.g. it can believe P and $(P \Rightarrow Q)$ and not believe Q, or it can believe $(P \wedge Q)$ without believing either P or Q). In summary, there seems to be ([4]) no way to make a knowledge-based analysis of the agent's beliefs (and also recall that our final aim is to model the evolution of beliefs over time, not a static set of beliefs in a certain point in time). The rest of the paper defines a particular class of non-ideal agents and shows how the evolution of their beliefs may be modelled in the framework of conceivable situations.

3.2   Multi-dimensional belief analysis in rational inquirers

In this paper we are concerned with a special class of non-ideal agents, that will be called *rational inquirers*. These agents are permanently engaged in the process of *rational inquiry*; i.e. they keep trying to modify their beliefs, in order to make them as similar as possible to the facts in the real world. They try to get rid of those beliefs that do not reflect the state of the actual world, and to logically refine those that are discovered to be true[2]. Thus, the belief set of this kind of agents is constantly being modified. Our aim is to give a formal model of the evolution of the beliefs of this kind of agents.

Rational inquirers try to make their beliefs as similar as possible to the actual world by performing a *multi-dimensional analysis of their beliefs*. The different dimensions of analysis that we consider are the following:

- A *logical* dimension, in which the agent will carry out some inferential (strictly deductive) processes.
- An *exploratory* dimension, in which the agent will be allowed to have *doubts*, to wonder whether it believes a given formula.
- An *experimental* dimension, in which the agent will perform tests in its environment, in order to obtain information that might be useful to refute doubtful beliefs or to confirm uncertain ones.

Moreover, the agents's beliefs will also change in response to data received directly from the external environment. The following sections describe the main ideas underlying each of these interwoven strands, and the final section summarizes the paper.

4   Logical dimension

4.1   Dynamic accessibility between conceivable situations

The agent's beliefs are expressed in a language $\mathcal{L}$, which is the language traditionally used in propositional modal logics of belief, restricted to standard propositional formulas prefixed by a (possibly empty) sequence of modal operators (e.g. $\neg(P \wedge (Q \vee R))$, BQ, $BB(P \Rightarrow (\neg Q \vee R))$). $\mathcal{L}_p$ is the strictly propositional part of $\mathcal{L}$.

In each conceivable situation (henceforth, a *cosi*) there are some propositions which are true and some propositions which the modelled agent believes. A *cosi*

---

[2] Note the implicit rationality in this process: the closer beliefs are to the real facts, the more successful will be the plans generated by the agent in order to achieve its goals.

is (possibly partially) represented with a set of propositional formulas. Furthermore, no restriction is imposed on this set (it does not have to be consistent, it may be not deductively closed, it may fail to contain some tautologies, etc.). Intuitively, as explained above, a *cosi* can be envisioned as *any situation that the agent may consider as real*. It can be a situation that has happened to the agent, or maybe something it has imagined. It is useful to bear always in mind that they can be logically inconsistent or physically unrealizable, so they must not be confused with "possible worlds" or with logical (complete, consistent) models.

The standard Kripke semantics ([10]) for modal logics of knowledge and belief is used throughout the logical analysis: a formula ϕ is believed by the agent in *cosi* w iff ϕ appears in all the doxastic alternatives to w (all the *cosis* related to w by the accessibility relation R). In the classical approaches the accessibility relation between "possible worlds" is predetermined, so the set of beliefs is constant. This fact implies that these approaches are unsuitable to model changing beliefs. In this new framework the aim is to model the evolution of the agent's beliefs over time. This evolution can be due to different facts, such as internal logical analysis of the agent or incorporation of data derived from tests performed in the environment in which the agent is located.

In the logical analysis the agent's set of beliefs in a *cosi* changes over time; this evolution will be formally modelled with a change in the accessibility relation between *cosis*, as suggested in section 2.2. In this model, a sequence of accessibility relations will be *generated*; each of them (*via* the standard Kripke semantics) will define a different set of beliefs. In the next section we present a modified version of the analytic tableaux method, that is used by rational inquirers to perform a limited logical analysis of their beliefs.

4.2   Generation of the sequence of accessibility relations

The evolution of the agent's beliefs in a *cosi* will be described with an example. Assume that the agent's initial set of beliefs in a *cosi* w_e is the following:

$$Beliefs(w_e) \equiv \{\ BP,\ B(P \lor Q),\ B(\neg Q \lor R),\ BBP,\ BB(\neg Q \lor R),\ BB(\neg P \lor Q)\ \}$$

The initial set of beliefs is just a set of formulas of $\mathcal{L}$; therefore, it is composed only by positive beliefs (however, in the course of the logical analysis the agent may attain negative beliefs, as will be shown later). Notice also that nested beliefs (at any level of nesting) may be considered.

The evolution of the agent's set of beliefs will be modelled with a sequence of accessibility relations. The initial accessibility relation, R_0, is obtained by applying the standard Kripke semantics in a *backwards* fashion; if the agent has a certain belief α, it will consider as doxastic alternatives all those *cosis* that contain α[3]. If it believes that it believes a formula β, it will consider that it

---

[3] This is a sufficient (but not necessary) condition for believing α. We start the analysis considering the most general case, in which *all cosis* that contain α are considered as possible; in the course of the analysis, we will get rid of all those *cosis* that do not satisfy other conditions (*e.g.* if $(P \lor Q)$ is an initial belief, during the analysis we will discard all those *cosis* that contain this formula but do not contain either P or Q).

believes β in all its doxastic alternatives, and that means that it will consider all the *cosis* that contain β as doxastic alternatives of its doxastic alternatives, and so on. In the example used in this section, the following result would be obtained: $\forall w' \epsilon\ W, (w_e\ R_0\ w') \leftrightarrow \{$ P, (P $\vee$ Q), ($\neg$Q $\vee$ R) $\} \subseteq w'$.

Let's define $\overline{w_\alpha}$ as the class of all *cosis* that are R_0-accessible from w_e. The *cosis* R_0-accessible from (all the *cosis* in) $\overline{w_\alpha}$ would be those having the following property: $\forall w' \epsilon\ \overline{w_\alpha}, \forall w''\ \epsilon\ W, (w'\ R_0\ w'') \leftrightarrow \{$ P, ($\neg$Q $\vee$ R), ($\neg$P $\vee$ Q) $\} \subseteq w''$.

A *cosi* w is R_0-accessible from w_e iff every proposition which is believed by the agent in w_e appears in w. A *cosi* w is R_0-accessible in two steps from w_e iff every proposition which is believed to be believed by the agent in w_e appears in w. The generation of the initial accessibility relation would continue until the deepest nested beliefs had been taken into account. The ontology of *cosis* just defined is represented in figure 1. In that figure, and in all the odd-numbered figures along the paper, each class of *cosis* $\overline{w}$ is represented by a rectangle that contains four columns[4], that have the following meaning (from left to right):

- α appears in the first column if $\forall w \epsilon \overline{w}\ \alpha \epsilon w$ ($\alpha \epsilon \mathcal{L}_p$)
- α appears in the second column if $\forall w \epsilon \overline{w}\ \alpha \notin w$ ($\alpha \epsilon \mathcal{L}_p$)
- α appears in the third column if $\forall w \epsilon \overline{w}\ \alpha$ is believed in w
- α appears in the fourth column if $\forall w \epsilon \overline{w}\ \alpha$ is not believed in w

The last two columns are included in an inner rectangle, to reinforce its doxastic interpretation.

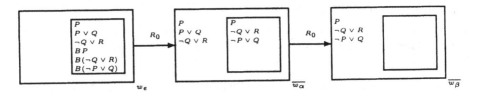

Fig. 1. World w_e and its doxastic alternatives

w_e is R_0-related to all the *cosis* in class $\overline{w_\alpha}$. $\overline{w_\alpha} = \{\ w_{\alpha_1}, w_{\alpha_2}, \dots\ \}$, where $w_{\alpha_i} = \{$P, (P $\vee$ Q), ($\neg$Q $\vee$ R)$\} \cup \Delta_{\alpha_i}$. According to the above definitions, every proposition believed in w_e appears in all the *cosis* $w_{\alpha_1}, w_{\alpha_2}, \dots$ Each *cosi* in class $\overline{w_\alpha}$ is R_0-related to all the *cosis* in class $\overline{w_\beta}$; this class is formed by all those *cosis* that contain (at least) the formulas P, ($\neg$Q $\vee$ R) and ($\neg$P $\vee$ Q).

The logical analysis of the agent's beliefs is performed using a modified version of the analytic tableaux method. The formulas contained in a tableau are divided into two sets, called *left column* and *right column*. Each tableau represents a set of *cosis*: all those *cosis* that contain the formulas of its left column and do not contain any of the formulas of its right column. The analysis may start

---

[4] Do not mislead by the fact that the four columns are not used in any of the rectangles in figure 1; they are used e.g. in the representation of $\overline{w_{\alpha_2}}$ in figure 5.

e.g. with a tableau T_0 representing the class of *cosis* $\overline{w_\alpha}$, i.e. a tableau containing in its left column the formulas P, (P ∨ Q) and (¬Q ∨ R). Notice that T_0 not only represents the class of *cosis* $\overline{w_\alpha}$; it is also a representation of the initial first-level beliefs of the agent in w_e.

The splitting rule[5] of the analytic tableaux method has also been modified: when it is applied to analyse a disjunction ($\phi \vee \psi$) contained in the left column of a tableaux T, it generates three subtableaux: the first one has ϕ and ψ in its left column, the second one has ϕ in its left column and ψ in its right column, and the third one has ψ in its left column and ϕ in its right column. Thus, with this rule the agent explores all the possibilities of accounting for the truth of the disjunction, namely that one (or both) of its members are true. The three subtableaux also keep all the formulas contained in T. The semantic meaning of the generation of these subtableaux is the following: the class of *cosis* represented by T is partitioned into four subclasses. These subclasses are formed taking into account the presence or absence of each of the two disjuncts of the analysed formula (e.g. if ($\alpha \vee \beta$) is analysed, one of the subclasses that will be considered will contain all the *cosis* of the original class that contain α but do not contain β). The three subtableaux represent three of those four subclasses in which the original class is partitioned (the unrepresented subclass is composed by all those *cosis* of the original class that do not contain any of the disjuncts of the analysed formula).

After the application of this rule to analyse (P ∨ Q) in T_0, the state shown in figure 2 (see next page) is reached.

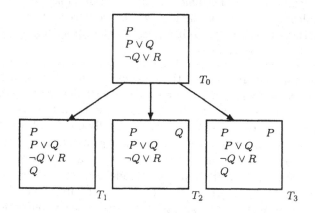

Fig. 2. Splitting rule applied to (P ∨ Q) in T_0

---

[5] The logical analysis suggested in this paper contains several rules for dealing with the logical operators in both columns of tableaux; nevertheless, in the example shown in this section the only rule that shall be needed is the one that analyses disjunctions contained in the left side of tableaux; this rule will be referred to as *the splitting rule*.

One can wonder now which class of *cosis* is represented by T_1, T_2 or T_3. Recall that T_0 represents the class of *cosis* $\overline{w_\alpha}$. Consider the following partition of class $\overline{w_\alpha}$:

- $\overline{w_{\alpha_1}}$: *cosis* of $\overline{w_\alpha}$ that contain P and Q.
- $\overline{w_{\alpha_2}}$: *cosis* of $\overline{w_\alpha}$ that contain P but do not contain Q.
- $\overline{w_{\alpha_3}}$: *cosis* of $\overline{w_\alpha}$ that contain Q but do not contain P.
- $\overline{w_{\alpha_4}}$: *cosis* of $\overline{w_\alpha}$ that do not contain either P or Q[6].

It is clear that the tableau T_1 represents the class of *cosis* $\overline{w_{\alpha_1}}$, T_2 represents $\overline{w_{\alpha_2}}$ and T_3 represents $\overline{w_{\alpha_3}}$. The *cosis* in class $\overline{w_{\alpha_4}}$ are not even considered by the analytic tableaux method, because it looks for models of the initial set of formulas, and it is not possible to have a model of the set $\{P, (P \vee Q), (\neg Q \vee R)\}$ in which both P and Q fail to be true.

In the classical analytic tableaux method, those tableaux that contain an atom and its negation are *closed*, and thus dismissed from the logical analysis (because they cannot represent a model of the initial set of formulas, which is the aim of the method); the agent eliminates them from the analysis by *closing* them. In the tableaux analysis that is being considered in this paper, the conditions that a tableau must satisfy in order to be eligible to be closed are the following:

- *The tableau contains a formula and its negation in its left column.*
  The tableau is representing a class composed by *cosis* that contain an explicit contradiction. They are considered as *logically impossible* and eliminated from the analysis by closing the tableau that represents them.
- *The tableau contains the same formula both in its left and right columns.*
  The tableau represents a class in which every *cosi* must contain and not contain the given formula, so it represents the empty set of *cosis* and can be dismissed from the analysis.

An important difference with the classical method is that a tableau is *not* closed automatically when one of these conditions holds. The agent *must* explicitly notice one of the above conditions and close it on purpose, after realising that the tableau represents an empty or a logically impossible class of *cosis* (e.g. a *cosi* may contain a lot of formulas and the agent may not have noticed that it contains a contradiction, even if it is as obvious as the presence of a formula and its negation). This fact permits to model agents that have contradictory beliefs (*BP* and *B¬P*) or even agents that are not sure about their beliefs (*BP* and *¬BP*). The former class of agents may have received contradictory information from different (maybe equally reliable) sources. The latter class of agents could, for instance, only be able to focus on a subset of their beliefs at each point of time; in one of these *contexts* they could believe a given formula, while not believing it in other *contexts*. Note that the presence of contradictions does not prevent us from keeping our view of a tableau as the representation of a class of

---

[6] Note that both $\overline{w_{\alpha_3}}$ and $\overline{w_{\alpha_4}}$ are empty classes, because P is contained in every *cosi* in $\overline{w_\alpha}$.

cosis because, as explained above, *cosis* do not have to be logically consistent, physically realizable entities. They only have to be conceivable by the agent, but not *real*, in any wider sense of the word.

In the example, T_3 contains P both in its right and left columns, so it represents an empty set of *cosis*. If the agent decides to close it, the class of *cosis* represented by it is dismissed from the analysis. The remaining tableaux tree contains only T_0, T_1 and T_2. Thus, the effect of the analysis of the formula (P ∨ Q) in T_0 is the restriction of the doxastic alternatives of w_e, that shrink from $\overline{w_\alpha}$ to its subclasses $\overline{w_{\alpha_1}}$ and $\overline{w_{\alpha_2}}$. The application of the splitting rule is modelled with the generation of a new accessibility relation, R_1, that restricts the set of R_0-accessible *cosis*. This restriction is shown in figure 3.

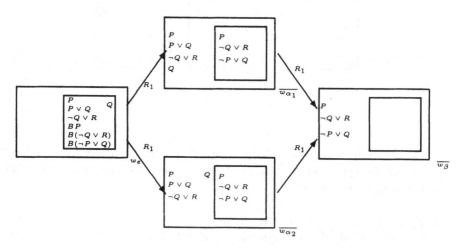

Fig. 3. Generation of R_1

w_e was R_0-related to all the *cosis* in class $\overline{w_\alpha}$, but is R_1-related only to the ones in classes $\overline{w_{\alpha_1}}$ and $\overline{w_{\alpha_2}}$. The change of the accessibility relation implies a (possible) change in the agent's beliefs. The first-level beliefs in w_e at this point would still be { P, (P ∨ Q), (¬Q ∨ R) }, because these are the only formulas common to both classes of doxastic alternatives. However, notice that the restriction of the doxastic alternatives has caused the addition of a new (negative) belief, ¬BQ. This formula is a new belief because there are *cosis* accessible from w_e that do not contain Q (the ones in class $\overline{w_{\alpha_2}}$). This fact is reflected in figure 3, with the addition of Q in the fourth column of the representation of w_e. The second-level beliefs in w_e have not changed because the set of *cosis* accessible in two steps from w_e has not changed (it is still $\overline{w_\beta}$). Thus, the complete list of (positive and negative) beliefs held by the agent at this point in w_e would be the following: { BP, B(P ∨ Q), B(¬Q ∨ R), ¬BQ, BBP, BB(¬Q ∨ R), BB(¬P ∨ Q) }.

If the agent wants to pursue the logical analysis, it can consider now e.g. the tableau that represents the class of worlds $\overline{w_\beta}$. This tableau (T_4) contains in its left column all the propositional formulas known to be included in all the *cosis* in this class, namely P, (¬Q ∨ R) and (¬P ∨ Q). Analysing the disjunction (¬Q ∨ R) in this tableau, the result shown in figure 4 is obtained.

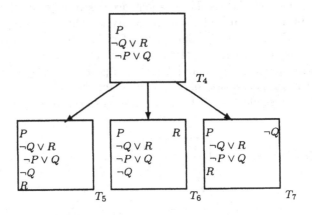

Fig. 4. Analysis of (¬Q ∨ R) in T_4

The semantic counterpart of this syntactic analysis can now be considered. Recall that T_4 represents the class of *cosis* $\overline{w_\beta}$. This class can be partitioned into the following four subclasses:

- $\overline{w_{\beta_1}}$: *cosis* of $\overline{w_\beta}$ that contain ¬Q and R.
- $\overline{w_{\beta_2}}$: *cosis* of $\overline{w_\beta}$ that contain ¬Q but do not contain R.
- $\overline{w_{\beta_3}}$: *cosis* of $\overline{w_\beta}$ that contain R but do not contain ¬Q.
- $\overline{w_{\beta_4}}$: *cosis* of $\overline{w_\beta}$ that do not contain either ¬Q or R.

The tableaux generated in the last analysis (T_5, T_6 and T_7) represent the subclasses $\overline{w_{\beta_1}}$, $\overline{w_{\beta_2}}$ and $\overline{w_{\beta_3}}$, respectively. This analysis may be modelled with the generation of a new accessibility relation, R_2, in which accessibility has been restricted again, because the *cosis* in class $\overline{w_{\beta_4}}$ are no longer accessible from the ones in classes $\overline{w_{\alpha_1}}$ and $\overline{w_{\alpha_2}}$, as they were with R_0 and R_1. This restriction is shown in figure 5 (see next page).

The agent would now notice that there are *cosis* accessible from those in classes $\overline{w_{\alpha_1}}$ and $\overline{w_{\alpha_2}}$ that do not contain ¬Q (the *cosis* belonging to class $\overline{w_{\beta_3}}$), so this formula would not be believed in any of the *cosis* of these classes. The same situation happens with R, which is not contained in any of the *cosis* in class $\overline{w_{\beta_2}}$ and therefore is not believed in the previous level either. This situation is shown in figure 5, where ¬B¬Q and ¬BR appear in the first level (in the fourth column of both $\overline{w_{\alpha_1}}$ and $\overline{w_{\alpha_2}}$). The information in the first level is transmited to w_e by the standard Kripkean procedure; as all the doxastic alternatives of this *cosi* contain ¬B¬Q and ¬BR, these formulas must be believed by the agent in w_e, as shown in figure 5.

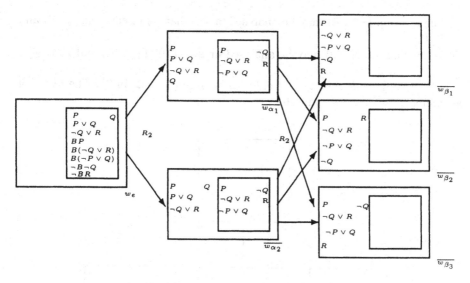

Fig. 5. Generation of R_2

The main idea in the model of the logical analysis is the following: to keep a (direct or indirect) access to all those classes of *cosis* represented by all open tableaux. There is a tableaux tree to be considered for each level of nesting of the initial set of beliefs. When a disjunction is analysed in an open tableau, a new accessibility relation is generated. In this new accessibility relation, there is no longer access to the class of *cosis* represented by that tableau, but to some subclasses of that class of *cosis* (those represented by the generated subtableaux that have not been closed). In the following list you can find a brief summary of the relationship between the syntactic tableaux analysis and its semantic counterpart (*cosis* and the accessibility relation between them, that define the agent's beliefs via the Kripke semantics):

- Tableau ≡ Class of *cosis*.
- Closed tableau ≡ Special type of tableau, that is discovered by the agent to represent either an empty set of *cosis* or a class of (logically impossible) *cosis*.
- Application of a splitting rule ≡ Generation of a new accessibility relation between *cosis*.

Following the example, the agent's beliefs at this point are { BP, B(P ∨ Q), B(¬Q ∨ R), BBP, BB(¬Q ∨ R), BB(¬P ∨ Q), $B¬B¬$Q, $B¬B$R, ¬BQ }. The agent may now decide to proceed with the logical analysis, because there are still open tableaux that contain formulas that have not been analysed yet. The five possibilities of analysis at this point are:

- The formula $(\neg Q \vee R)$ may be analysed in T_1 (that represents class $\overline{w_{\alpha_1}}$) and T_2 ($\overline{w_{\alpha_2}}$).
- The formula $(\neg P \vee Q)$ may be analysed in T_5 ($\overline{w_{\beta_1}}$), T_6 ($\overline{w_{\beta_2}}$) and T_7 ($\overline{w_{\beta_3}}$).

Let's assume that the agent decides to analyse $(\neg P \vee Q)$ in T_5. The result of this analysis is shown in figure 6.

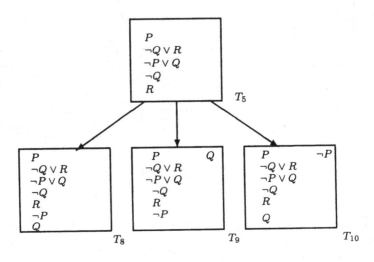

Fig. 6. Analysis of $(\neg P \vee Q)$ in T_5

As usual, $\overline{w_{\beta_1}}$ can be partitioned into four subclasses, taking into account the absence or presence of $\neg P$ and Q. Three of these subclasses are represented by the three subtableaux generated in the analysis of $(\neg P \vee Q)$ (T_8, T_9 and T_{10}), while the fourth one is not even taken into account (that would be the class of all those *cosis* in $\overline{w_{\beta_1}}$ that contain the disjunction but do not contain any of the disjuncts).

It can be noticed that T_8 and T_9 contain both P and $\neg P$ in their left columns, and therefore the classes of *cosis* represented by these tableaux may be considered by the agent as logically impossible and dismissed from the analysis by closing those tableaux. T_{10} contains Q and $\neg Q$ in its left column, so it may also be closed and the class of (logically impossible) *cosis* that it represents is no longer taken into account. This argument shows that all the subtableaux generated in this analysis are closed; that means that the agent has no longer access to the *cosis* of class $\overline{w_{\beta_1}}$, which were those *cosis* represented by T_5. In summary, the agent has explored all the subclasses of $\overline{w_{\beta_1}}$ and has discovered that none of them is logically possible. Thus, in our model we would now generate a new accessibility relation, R_3, shown in figure 7, in which that class of *cosis* is no longer accessible. It can also be noticed that this elimination does not imply any change in the positive and negative beliefs of previous levels. The positive beliefs in the first level are still P, $(\neg Q \vee R)$ and $(\neg P \vee Q)$, because these are still the only formulas known to appear in all its doxastic alternatives (the *cosis* in classes $\overline{w_{\beta_2}}$ and $\overline{w_{\beta_3}}$); the negative beliefs in the first level do not change either (¬Q and R), because for each of these formulas there are accessible *cosis* that do not contain it (¬Q is not contained in $\overline{w_{\beta_3}}$ and R is not contained in $\overline{w_{\beta_2}}$). If the situation has not changed in classes $\overline{w_{\alpha_1}}$ and $\overline{w_{\alpha_2}}$, it cannot have changed in w_e either, because these two classes contain all those *cosis* that are accessible from w_e.

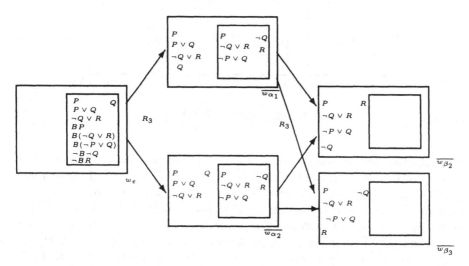

Fig. 7. Generation of R_3

A similar situation arises when the agent analyses (¬P ∨ Q) in T_6, which is the tableau that represents the class of *cosis* $\overline{w_{\beta_2}}$ (see figure 8 in the next page), because the three subtableaux generated in this analysis also contain contradictions in their left columns, so all of them may be closed (T_{11} and T_{12} contain P and ¬P, whereas T_{13} contains Q and ¬Q).

Recall that T_6 is the representation of the class of *cosis* $\overline{w_{\beta_2}}$. As T_{11}, T_{12} and T_{13} are generated from the analysis of a formula in T_6, they represent subclasses of $\overline{w_{\beta_2}}$. All of these subtableaux are closed, so all these subclasses are considered as logically impossible and eliminated from the analysis. That means that the agent has no longer access to any *cosi* in class $\overline{w_{\beta_2}}$, as shown in figure 9, that represents the accessibility relation generated as a consequence of the last tableau analysis, R_4.

The change of the accessibility relation from R_3 to R_4 models a change in the agent's beliefs. Now the only *cosis* accessible from $\overline{w_{\alpha_1}}$ and $\overline{w_{\alpha_2}}$ are those in class $\overline{w_{\beta_3}}$. All of these *cosis* contain P, (¬Q ∨ R), (¬P ∨ Q) and R, and therefore these four formulas are believed in all the *cosis* contained in the classes $\overline{w_{\alpha_1}}$ and $\overline{w_{\alpha_2}}$. The first three formulas were already believed in all of these *cosis* from the beginning of the analysis, but notice that R was explicitly *not* believed in

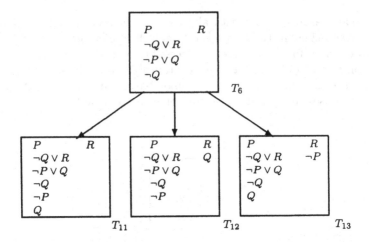

Fig. 8. Analysis of ($\neg$P $\vee$ Q) in T_6

those *cosis* when the previous accessibility relation, R_3, was considered. It is easy to see that if a formula is positively believed at some point of the analysis, it will continue to be considered as a positive belief in the rest of the analysis, whereas if a formula is a negative belief at some point of the analysis, it may be the case that it is transformed into a positive belief at a later stage of the logical analysis. This result is due to the fact that the sequence of accessibility relations is increasingly restrictive. If a formula is a positive belief, it means that it is true in all doxastic alternatives; no matter how these alternatives are restricted, the formula will still be true in the remaining accessible *cosis*. If a formula is a negative belief, that means that there are accessible *cosis* which do not contain that formula; if the set of accessible *cosis* is restricted in such a way that these *cosis* are eliminated (as has happened in the example), the formula will be contained in all remaining doxastic alternatives and it will be considered as a positive belief.

The agent could keep analysing other formulas. If it performed an exhaustive logical analysis, its final beliefs would be $\{BP, B(P \vee Q), B(\neg Q \vee R), BBP, BB(\neg Q \vee R), BB(\neg P \vee Q), BBR, BBQ, B\neg B\neg Q, B\neg B\neg P, \neg BQ, \neg B\neg Q, \neg BR\}$.

In summary, the logical analysis causes the evolution of the agent's beliefs due to internal deductive procedures. This evolution is modelled with the generation of a sequence of accessibility relations, $R_0, R_1, R_2, \ldots$, in which every accessibility relation is more restrictive than the previous one (and thus, the agent's beliefs increase in this process).

5   Exploratory dimension

In the logical analysis of beliefs the classical analytic tableaux method has been modified in a number of ways. There is another important difference with respect to the classical method: *the agent is not allowed to add to an open tableau any*

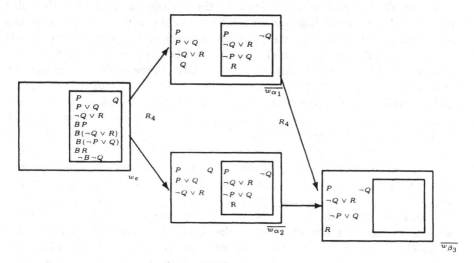

Fig. 9. Generation of R_4

tautology. If tautologies could be freely added into the tableaux, the problem of logical omniscience could not be avoided. This prohibition is based on the idea that a tableau is just a partial representation of a set of *cosis*, and it cannot be modified with no apparent reason.

In the exploratory dimension of analysis, the agent is allowed to introduce some formulas in the open tableaux; more specifically, the agent may pose itself questions, may introduce *doubts* in the analysis, may wonder whether a certain formula ϕ is or not the case. Technically, this idea is implemented by allowing the introduction of instances of the *Axiom of the Excluded Middle* ($\phi \vee \neg\phi$) in the open tableaux of the logical analysis. The use of this particular tautology seems a natural way to allow the agent to have *doubts*, to wonder whether it believes some formula (ϕ) or its negation ($\neg\phi$). This exception permits the introduction of the formula ($\phi \vee \neg\phi$) in a tableau, which is later split into two subtableaux containing ϕ in one column and $\neg\phi$ in the other. In this way, the agent can explore both alternatives independently, and the logical analysis can guide the search of examples or counter-examples needed to give more credence to one side of the doubt than to the other. In fact, the possibility of adding this kind of tautologies in the analytic tableaux is a well-known idea in the tradition of classical proof theory (see *e.g.* [1]).

The introduction of self-posed questions (by the agent, *via* Excluded Middle) and the consequent splitting of tableaux, suggest a simple explanation of two hitherto unrelated fenomena. One is purely logical: the closing of all tableaux generated by a set of statements (representing *e.g.* one's beliefs) now means, simply, that all the conceivable situations potentially contained in (or derived from) the given set are impossible; the immediate consequence is that the agent, after having explored all the open possibilities, ceases to believe in the set (a process discovered with much fracas by the Pythagoreans, and usually called *reductio ad absurdum*). The second lies more in the province of epistemologists or even philosophers of science: suppose (considering predicate logic for a second) that the agent doubts of the validity of a general law such as *All birds fly* (i.e. $\forall x$ $(Bird(x) \Rightarrow Flies(x))$). It adds to its set of beliefs (in the exploratory dimension of analysis) the formula $\forall x(Bird(x) \Rightarrow Flies(x)) \lor \neg\forall x(Bird(x) \Rightarrow Flies(x))$ and, when it analyses this disjunction (in the logical dimension), it will have access to two classes of conceivable situations: in the first class the law will hold, while the second will contain $\neg\forall x(Bird(x) \Rightarrow Flies(x))$, from which by standard (first-order) tableaux processing the agent would get $Bird(a)$ and $\neg Flies(a)$ (for some (undetermined) a). At this point, the agent can notice that it can increase its beliefs if it can dismiss this class of *cosis*; if the agent looks *actively* in the real world for an individual a such that $Bird(a)$ and $\neg Flies(a)$ and it cannot find it, then it can conclude that an individual with these properties does not exist; when this conclusion is finally reached, the agent can declare this class of *cosis* as *physically impossible*, and so the agent will have grounds not to consider it any more as a conceivable, realizable alternative. Then the tableau that represents this class of *cosis* would be closed and dismissed from the analysis. At that moment all the *cosis* accessible by the agent would contain $\forall x(Bird(x) \Rightarrow Flies(x))$ so, by definition, the agent would believe this law. This is an example of how the agent may combine different dimensions of analysis in order to refine its set of beliefs.

6   Experimental dimension

In the experimental dimension of analysis the agent is allowed to make experiments in its environment and to incorporate the resulting propositions (externally obtained, as opposed to the internally obtained propositions of the logical analysis previously described) in all open tableaux of the logical analysis. Thus, this dimension models the agent's acquisition of data in the actual world (obtained *via* experiences, tests, *etc.*). The root of this dimension can be traced as far as Kant, who argued in his *Critique of pure reason* that Reason has to take into account observations of the environment; he thinks that Reason must not approach Nature as a student, that takes everything that its teacher chooses to say, but as a judge who formulates questions and compels the witnesses to answer them. Nature has to be constrained to give answers to questions of Reason's own determining.

This dimension is very much related to the logical dimension. The logical analysis can guide the experimental analysis, suggesting which experiences or tests the agent can perform in the actual world to gain knowledge. The agent may find out whether its actual set of beliefs is accurate by trying to confirm its predictions by experience.

7   External inputs

We also allow the agent to incorporate into the analysis information that it receives from the environment. These new pieces of information are added to the analysis by introducing them in the open tableaux of the logical analysis. This incorporation may cause a tableau to be closed, if it fulfills any of the tableau closing conditions and the agent realizes that fact. Thus, a tableau may be closed by different reasons:

– As a result of the logical tableaux analysis, the tableau may describe a contradictory class of *cosis* or an empty class of *cosis*; if the agent notes this fact, it will close that tableau (a purely *logical closing*) and it will cease to take that class of *cosis* into account in the rest of the analysis.

– As a result of information received from the environment (as a direct external input or in the experimental dimension of analysis), one of the closing conditions may hold in a tableau; thus, if the agent realizes that situation, it will close the tableau (a logical closing due to empirical reasons).

– The agent may fail to find in the real world a set of individuals that satisfy the properties stated in a tableau. Thus, it may consider the class of *cosis* represented by the tableau as *physically impossible* and it may close that tableau in order to eliminate them from further analysis.

One important issue arises here, namely the difference between monotonic and non-monotonic beliefs. The former are the ones obtained from the purely logical closing of tableaux, while the latter are those derived from the *empirical* closings of tableaux, caused by the other dimensions of analysis, that may be defeated later (*e.g.* the agent can later notice that a fact (received directly from another agent) was not true, or that the environment's answer to a question, in the experimental dimension, was not correct, or that there indeed exists an individual with a desired set of properties). This means that this work will have connections with the AI field of *belief revision*, which has received much attention in recent years (see *e.g.* [3]).

8   Limited belief analysis

There are several aspects of the belief analysis that limit the reasoning capabilities of *rational inquirers*, and prevent them from being *ideal agents*:

– Tableaux are not closed automatically in the logical analysis. The agent must explicitly note the appearence of one of the closing conditions before closing the tableau.

– Tautologies may not be freely added to tableaux (with the exception of the instances of the Axiom of the Excluded Middle that may be used in the exploratory dimension of analysis, see section 5).

- The classical analytic tableaux method is refutative, in the sense that, in order to prove that α is a consequence of a set I, it tries to fail in building a model of $I \cup \{\neg\alpha\}$, by *exhaustively* analysing the tableau containing I and $\neg\alpha$ and closing all the subtableaux in the analytic tableaux tree. Our analysis has an important difference: the agent is *not* obliged to exhaustively analyse any tableau. In this way we can model imperfect reasoning due to a lack of resources, whereas with the previous differences we were modelling those agents that do not have a perfect deductive power. The agent may decide to stop the logical analysis at any point of the derivation tree, and to proceed with other tasks (*e.g.* to make some experimental tests in order to corroborate or falsify the current beliefs obtained in the logical analysis, or to pose itself a question in the exploratory analysis).

9   Summary

- The main aim of this work is to provide a way of modelling the process of rational inquiry, unlike the standard approach of modelling an agent's belief set in a certain fixed point in time.
- This process of rational inquiry is modelled within the possible worlds framework and its classical Kripke semantics. To avoid the problems of logical omniscience and perfect reasoning that appear in this semantics, two important changes to the classical approaches are made:
    - We consider *conceivable situations* (*cosis*) as the primitive semantic entities; they include all the situations that the modelled agent is capable of imagining or considering, regardless of their partiality or inconsistency. A *cosi* is partially represented with a set of propositional formulas.
    - Both the set of *cosis* (W) and the accessibility relation between them (R) are not constant, fixed, but variable. This variability accounts for the evolution of the agent's beliefs over time (through the usual Kripke semantics).
- We define a class of non-ideal rational agents, called *rational inquirers*, that perform a multi-dimensional dynamic analysis of their beliefs, in order to make them as similar as possible to the facts in the real world. This analysis includes:
    - A logical dimension, in which the agent makes some (limited) deductive inferences in its belief set, using a modified version of the analytic tableaux method.
    - An experimental dimension, that allows the agent to take into account all the data that it can obtain from the actual world. The agent performs tests in the real world in order to increase its knowledge. The tests to be performed are suggested by the logical analysis (linking in a novel fashion the rational and empirical components of the classical notion of inquiry).
    - An exploratory dimension, where the agent is allowed to have doubts, to wonder whether a formula is true or not.

- Moreover, the agent may also receive data from the environment and incorporate this information into its belief set.

Acknowledgements

We would like to acknowledge the interesting comments made by an anonymous referee, which have helped to improve the quality of the paper.

References

1. J. Bell and M. Machover. *A course in Mathematical Logic*. North Holland, 1977.
2. R. Fagin and J. Halpern. Belief, awareness and limited reasoning. In *International Joint Conference on Artificial Intelligence*, pages 491–501, 1985.
3. P. Gärdenfors. *Knowledge in flux*. Cambridge University Press, 1988.
4. J. Halpern. Reasoning about knowledge: an overview. In J. Halpern, editor, *Theoretical Aspects of Reasoning about Knowledge*, pages 1–17, 1986.
5. J. Halpern and Y. Moses. A guide to completeness and complexity for modal logics of knowledge and belief. *Artificial Intelligence*, 54:319–379, 1992.
6. J. Hintikka. *Knowledge and belief*. Cornell University Press, Ithaca, N.Y., 1962.
7. J. Hintikka. Impossible possible worlds vindicated. *Journal of Philosophical Logic*, 4:475–484, 1975.
8. D. Hofstadter. *Gödel, Escher, Bach: an Eternal Golden Braid*. Basic Books Inc. Publishers, 1980.
9. K. Konolige. *A deduction model of belief*. Morgan Kaufmann, San Mateo, CA, 1986.
10. S. Kripke. A semantical analysis of modal logic i: normal modal propositional calculi. *Zeitschrift für Mathematische Logik und Grundlagen Mathematik*, 9:67–96, 1963.
11. G. McArthur. Reasoning about knowledge and belief: a survey. *Computational Intelligence*, 4:223–243, 1988.
12. A. Moreno. Avoiding logical omniscience and perfect reasoning: a survey. *AI Communications*, 8:101–125, 1998.
13. D. Perlis. Logic for a lifetime. Technical Report CS-TR-3278, Computer Science Dept., University of Maryland, 1994.
14. N. Rescher and R. Brandom. *The logic of inconsistency*. Rowan and Littlefield Eds., 1979.
15. S. Russell and P. Norvig. *Artificial Intelligence. A modern approach*. Prentice Hall Series in Artificial Intelligence. Prentice Hall, 1995.
16. Y. Shoham. Agent-oriented programming. *Artificial Intelligence*, 60:51–92, 1993.

On the Process of Making Descriptive Rules

D. Riaño

Departament d'Enginyeria Informàtica,
Universitat Rovira i Virgili,
Carretera de Salou s/n, 43006 Tarragona, Spain

Abstract. The automatic inductive learning of production rules in a classification environment is a difficult process which requires several considerations and techniques to be studied. This is more noticeable when the learning process is applied to real world domains. Our goal is to focus and study some of the most important problems related to the automatic learning of production rules as well as to provide some tools for dealing with these problems. We first consider the data representation problem. Four different types of data are proposed. We then deal with the unsupervised case in which the data are observations of objects in the world and we pose three alternative mechanisms for clustering. If the data set contains examples and counter examples of some world concepts, the learning is called supervised. Within supervised learning we find the data redundancy problem. Two sorts of redundancy are studied: the one which is concerned with the set of examples, and the one which is concerned with the set of example descriptors.

Before we generate rules that describe the domain which is represented by the input data, we analyze the set of conditions which will be the basis of our rules. These conditions are called selectors and they enable us to control more directly the semantics of the induced rules. We have implemented several algorithms that generate selectors automatically and we have tested them together with four new rule generation algorithms. The results obtained are compared with those other results produced by other classical rule learning methods such as CN2 and C4.5RULES.

1   Introduction

Within the framework of symbolic inductive learning, the automatic construction of descriptive rules is a complex process that makes up several important problems. Many of these problems are the consequence of the logical evolution of inductive learning when we want to learn domains of increasing complexity (e.g. unsupervised domains, large data sets, redundant data, missing values, noisy information, uncertain data, etc.), or when we want learning to be near the human understanding (e.g. uncertainty, concept induction, integrating knowledge and data, etc.), or when we are limited by some practical requirements (e.g. accelerating the reasoning process, compacting the knowledge base, etc.).

The above problems are mentioned to justify the necessity of different mechanism that can be used to design inductive learning algorithms which can come

J.A. Padget (Ed.): Human and Artificial Societies, LNAI 1624, pp. 182–197, 1999.

to grips with difficult environments in which expertise is not easily found. In this paper we present a new inductive learning system which learns descriptive rules from an unsupervised data set. The system transforms raw data into rules by means of a sequence of stages and, therefore, from an engineering point of view we can describe the learning process as a multi-processing system. Some of these stages (e.g. data representation, data clustering, feature and instance selection, learning selectors, rule induction, and rule compaction) are studied, solved, and the solutions compared with other published solutions.

Figure 1 shows a diagram with the stages of the production rule learning process GAR which we propose in this paper. In the diagram we distinguish in blocks the entities of the learning process (i.e. static component) which are reached by means of the processes indicated in the arrows (i.e. dynamic component).

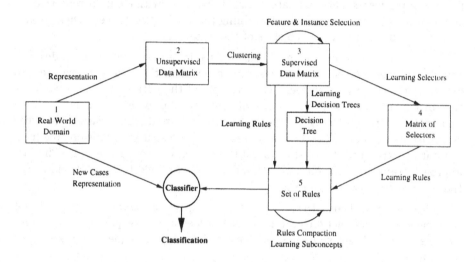

Fig. 1. The process of making descriptive rules with GAR.

The learning process starts with the *Real World Domain* which we are going to study. The first step is to observe the domain and then represent these observations by means of both defining a set of attributes and taking a list of cases from the domain. The defined attributes are used to describe the cases or observations which are used as a sample of the domain that we want to learn. After the representation stage, an unsupervised data matrix contains all the information that the process has about the real world domain. Each case is saved in a row and each column contains the values of all the cases for a certain attribute.

Clustering is the second step in figure 1. It is used to transform unsupervised representations of the target domain into other representations which are called supervised when some expert validates them. Broadly speaking, the clustering process transforms a set of observations into a set of clusters, each one containing a subset of observations which are interpreted as instances of the concept or class that the cluster represents. In machine learning there are several clustering models. Some of them are reported in section 3.

When all the clusters are identified with world situations, concepts, or classes, the data becomes supervised. Then, redundant information can be isolated and removed. Feature selection and instance selection are the processes that reduce the number of attributes and instances respectively. Langley [1] proposes several criteria to classify these processes; however, we will only discuss two of them in detail, which are the searching strategy criterion and the evaluating strategy criterion. In section 4, we propose five searching strategies: exhaustive, greedy, heuristic, iterative, and probabilistic, and three evaluation strategies [2]: embedded, filter, and wrapper.

Regardless of the strategy selected, after the feature and instance selection process, a reduced supervised data matrix is available with columns representing the relevant attributes and rows containing the relevant instances. There is also an extra column indicating the class of the instances.

Rule learning is a process that transforms a data matrix into a set of descriptive if-then rules. As far as this system is concerned, these rules which are also called production rules represent the concepts of the data matrix as a conjunction of restrictions about the values of some attributes. Figure 1 shows three approaches to rule learning. In the first one, rules are directly learned from the supervised data matrix [3]. The second approach constructs a decision tree from the data matrix and, then, transforms the tree into a set of rules [4]. The last approach transforms the data matrix into a matrix of selectors and, then, learns the set of rules from the matrix of selectors [5].

When we have learned the descriptive rules, we can transform the rule set by means of a compaction process whose immediate consequence is to reduce the size of the rule set which a classifier uses later to catalogue new cases in the domain.

To sum up, the learning process starts with an unsupervised data matrix which describes some cases of the target domain (e.g. patients in a hospital), learns the set of concepts which are important in that domain (e.g. diseases), and generates a set of rules which are used to classify the new cases in one of the above concepts (e.g. medical diagnosis). All the stages of the process have been implemented and integrated in one system called GAR which can be used to carry out the complex inductive learning process depicted in figure 1 automatically.

The paper is organized as follows. Section 2 briefly introduces the sort of data that the learning process is able to manage. Section 3 addresses the clustering phase and introduces *Sedàs* [6], the numerical taxonomy clustering system which we use to transform unsupervised data into supervised data. In section 4, the feature and instance selection problem is considered. Section 5 is about the process of transforming data matrices into matrices of selectors which we use to construct rules in section 6. Rule compaction is dealt with in section 7. In section 8 we describe an example of the sort of problem that we can solve with the system being discussed. Finally, section 9 deals with some considerations about the implementation of the system.

2   Representing the real world domain

In figure 1 the learning process starts with a representation stage standing for the process that observes the domain that we want to study and that generates a data matrix containing a set of observations (i.e. rows) which are the elements from which the target domain is learned. In order to make the data matrix as homogeneous as possible a set of attributes (i.e. columns) is given so that all the observations in the matrix are described according to the same features. Two important problems arise from the process of filling the data matrix: choosing a *descriptive* set of attributes (we must be sure that the attributes can describe the domain) and taking a *representative* set of observations (we must be sure that the domain is well represented with those observations). Both are hard problems which are solved with some expert criterion, if it is available, or otherwise by considering as many attributes and observations as possible.

From a numerical point of view, Kerlingen [7] introduces four attribute types: numeral, ordinal, interval, and ratio. The numeral type represents numbers whose values have no meaning, the ordinal type represents order relations, the interval and the ratio types represent numbers whose values have a meaning. Depending on whether or not the zero value has a special meaning we are considering a ratio or a interval type, respectively. In machine learning, numerical attributes are usually extended with symbolic attributes. Here, we present a system which is able to work with continuous, numeric, symbolic, and ordered-symbolic attributes. *Continuous* attributes represent continuous intervals in the real domain (e.g. a building height), *numeric* attributes represent finite discrete sets of numeric values (e.g. number of floors in a building), *symbolic* attributes represent finite sets of disordered symbols (e.g. the building style), and *ordered-symbolic* attributes represent finite sets of ordered symbols (e.g. the building phases).

In table 1 we supply a list of domains from the UCI repository [8] which is used to test the different stages of the learning process across the next sections. Together with the domain name the table shows the number of continuous, numeric, symbolic, and ordered-symbolic attributes, as well as, the number of observations for each case.

3   Transforming unsupervised data into supervised data

Unsupervised data integrates observations with none predefined classification. On the contrary, supervised data represents observations as examples of some predefined concept or class. Inductive learning as it is understood here needs the data to be supervised though this representation is not always available, particularly when we are to study new domains, or ill-structured domains, or domains where experts cannot agree on one uniform interpretation. *Clustering*

Table 1. Data set magnitudes.

domain name	No. cont.	No. num.	No. sym.	No. ord.	num
balance scale	0	4	0	0	625
bupa	5	1	0	0	345
glass	9	0	0	0	214
monk1	0	0	6	0	432
monk2	0	0	6	0	432
monk3	0	0	6	0	432
mushroom	0	0	20	2	8124
pima indian	7	1	0	0	768
promoter	0	0	57	0	106
soybean	0	0	35	0	307
tic tac toe	0	0	9	0	958
wine	13	0	0	0	178

is the process that converts those unsupervised domains into supervised. There are many alternative clustering models: *Numerical taxonomy* performs a clustering process in which the set of unsupervised observations is divided into a smaller number of classes in such a way that objects in the same class are similar to one another and dissimilar to objects in other cla sses. Gordon [9] presents four approaches to this kind of clustering: *agglomerative* methods which work by adding observations to classes, *divisive* methods which split classes into subclasses, *constructive* methods which add ob servations to a hierarchical classification of a smaller set of observations, and *direct optimization* methods which see the clustering process as an error minimization problem. At the end of each method, the experts are asked to identify the concept s that the final classes represent.

Conceptual clustering [10,11] proposes another solution to clustering in which a configuration of observations forms a cluster or class if it can be closely circumscribed by a description involving relations on some selected attr ibutes. That is to say, conceptual clustering considers that the interesting classes are not those containing close observations but those containing observations which are similarly described. At the end, the experts have to recognize the concepts that t he final descriptions represent.

Finally, *Bayesian clustering* [12] finds the most probable set of class descriptions given the data and prior expectations. This process is achieved as a trade off between the fitting to the data and the complexity of the class description. At the end, experts have to recognize the concepts that the final classes represent.

Sedàs [6] is a numerical taxonomy clustering system incorporated to the process depicted in figure 1. Sedàs is a highly parametric system which performs two steps. In the first step, the data matrix is used to construct a similarity matrix. Since several similarity functions are implemented, the same data matrix can produce several similarity matrices. Secondly, the similarity matrix is used to construct a dendrogram [9] and the consequent classification. Sedàs can do this step with several sequential, agglomerative, hierarchic, non-overlapping clustering methods.

In spite of the good results obtained with Sedàs [6] and for the sake of being able to compare the results in the next sections with other results in the machine learning bibliography, we will not consider the Sedàs classifications but those supplied in [8].

Our system also incorporates the conceptual clustering system LINNEO+ [13] which is based on a distance function. LINNEO+ represents classes as spheres whose center is the class prototype and the radius is used to know which object s are in the class. The clustering process takes the first observation and place it as a class within the space. The center of this class is the point at which the observation is situated. Then, it takes the second object and places it too in the space. I f it is in the first class, the center is recalculated. Otherwise, a new class is formed. An observation may happen to remain outside the class because the center of the class is displaced. Finally, a set of classes is introduced with all the displaced ob servations.

4   Reducing the supervised data matrix

The data matrix can be seen from two perspectives: horizontal and vertical. The horizontal view presents the matrix as a list of observations, and the vertical view as a list of attributes. Studying the relevance of data from the horizontal and vertical a pproaches has received much attention in the recent research [2] though both lines have not achieved the same degree of maturity.

Selecting relevant features and instances is globally accepted as a suitable process that can benefit the learning task. Being able to separate those features and instances which are important to the learning from those which are not is particularly interesting for handling large data sets. We can separate selection methods into those that embed the selection process within the learning algorithm, those that filter attributes and instances before passing them to the induction process, and those that wrap feature and instance selection around successive calls to the learning technique. Despite this common classification of methods, the field of feature selection has consolidated, on the one hand, a theoretic basis to formalize the study of feature relevance and, on the other hand, a plenty of systems that have been proven to work very efficiently. On the contrary, instance selection has not yet received the same attention [2] and it appears as a new emerging field within data mining.

The filter approach is less common in the machine learning literature than embedded or wrapper methods like *boosting*, *windowing*, or *peepholing* techniques [2]. Nevertheless, as far as this work is concerned, several new filter feature selection algorithms have been integrated in the general system in figure 1. In [5], we propose a subdivision of the filter methods into *exhaustive*, *greedy*, *heuristic*, *iterative*, and *probabilistic* and implement algorithms for each case. In the next paragraphs we will discuss these methods and algorithms.

Exhaustive methods search for the set of relevant features and instances by considering all the possible sets and using some pruning techniques, *greedy* methods make local decisions which are never more reconsidered, *heuristic* methods are a particular case of the greedy methods in which decisions are made according to a heuristic function which represents an approximation to the goodness of the current partial solution, *iterative* methods calculate the relevance of both attributes and instances by means of an iterative process and then take those which are more relevant, *probabilistic* methods apply Las Vegas techniques to obtain the relevant features and instances.

We have implemented the algorithms IFOCUS and IFOCUS2 which perform an exhaustive search of the minimum subset of instances such that it is capable of representing the instances which are not in the subset. *Forward* is a greedy algorithm that incorporates instances in order to obtain a subset which represents the complete data set. ISET is a heuristic algorithm that takes relevant instances according to a function which is an approximation to the relevance function. IRET is an iterative approach to instance selection in which each instance relevance is approximated by means of a repeated process that selects an instance at random and modify the relevances of the instances around that one. Finally, IPRO1 and IPRO2 are probabilistic instance selection methods that take subsets of instances at random, compute their representativity, and give the most representative subset.

All the algorithms are prepared to achieve reductions that guarantee a 100% of accuracy when the instances selected are given to a nearest-neighbor learning procedure. The probabilistic algorithms IPRO1 and IPRO2 are two exceptions in which the percentage of accuracy is an input parameter that permits us to reduce the time required to perform instance selection. Table 2 contains the percentage of instance reduction achieved by any of the above algorithms for the data sets in table 1. The percentage of accuracy is 100% in all the cases except IPRO1 and IPRO2 for which it is at least 80%. IFOCUS1 and IFOCUS2 are not considered because exhaustive methods exhibit a high time cost which we cannot assume.

The main conclusions are: (a) forward and IPRO2 are the algorithms that achieve the largest reductions though forward is more accurate than IPRO2, (b) IRET achieves the poorest reductions, (c) there are many data sets for which more than a 75% of reduction is possible.

5   Transforming the data matrix into a matrix of selectors

In figure 1 we propose three alternatives to generate a rule set from the data matrix. Direct methods like CN2 [3] can learn from the information supplied in the data matrix exclusively. Indirect methods learn an intermediate structure and then they transform that structure into a set of rules. The most used structure is a decision tree [4], though we propose here another called matrix of selectors that furnish some benefits to the learning process that the other approaches do not.

Table 2. Percentage of instance reduction.

domain name	forward	ISET	IRET	IPRO1	IPRO2
balance-scale	56.64%	13.44%	11.36%	55.56%	63.20%
bupa	40.00%	46.37%	16.23%	58.26%	64.05%
glass	50.93%	57.94%	18.22%	59.81%	70.56%
monk1	98.38%	8.33%	10.41%	57.16%	67.22%
monk2	41.90%	19.68%	10.41%	59.06%	62.89%
monk3	96.06%	68.52%	10.41%	51.10%	60.09%
mushroom	99.69%	99.29%	47.15%	63.27%	80.98%
pima indian	50.13%	53.26%	32.29%	57.16%	77.60%
promoter	57.55%	52.83%	13.20%	59.56%	69.78%
soybean	80.46%	75.24%	43.97%	29.77%	72.52%
tic tac toe	71.19%	16.28%	5.11%	55.34%	59.55%
wine	84.27%	83.15%	83.70%	62.92%	98.31%

A selector is defined as a condition on one of the features in the data matrix, for example $age \geq 80$ or $cost \in [100, 150]$. Learning selectors is an interesting process in which, given a data matrix, we obtain a list of selectors such t hat they can describe the data as a set of if-then rules where each rule premise is a conjunction of some of those selectors.

It is important that the list of selectors can describe the data, but it is also important that the final rules can be understood and accepted by human experts. When a list of selectors is accepted, a matrix of selectors is filled with the evaluation of a ll the selectors in the list of selectors for all the data in the data matrix.

Learning with selector-based algorithms presents some benefits if it is compared with the sort of learning of direct or tree-based algorithms. Although a matrix of selectors uses to be larger than the related data matrix and the learning algorithms based on the former use to be slower than the learning algorithms based on the latter, the possibility of accessing the set of selectors increases the control of the knowledge engineer on the learning process. Some of the control actions are: including interest ing selectors, excluding worthless selectors, making some selectors more specific or general, proposing alternative selectors so that we can obtain different descriptions of the same domain, etc. These actions have been qualified as very interesting by th e human experts that use our system.

Here we will only consider the case of learning selectors which are based on continuous attributes. For the sake of completeness, in [5] there is an extended treatment of symbolic, numeric, and ordered-symbolic attributes.

We propose two criteria to classify the learning selector algorithms in figure 1: one which is based on whether the data is considered unsupervised or supervised and other one which is based on whether the algorithm is based on direct, statistical, or information-theory decisions. *Unsupervised* methods produce selectors in such a way that the instance class is not required, *supervised* methods take into account that information. *Direct* methods deal with continuous attributes with regard to their description (i.e. attribute domain) and their measuring (i.e. data matrix attribute values), *statistical* methods are based on the selector frequency which is related to the number of instances that each selector describes, and *information-theory* methods are based on Shanon's entropy function and the quantity of information of the selectors.

Table 3. Learning selector algorithms.

	Unsupervised	Supervised
direct	Exact values Equal-width interval	1R Pure interval Positive exact values
statistical	Equal frequency interval Cuts Smooth	Chimerge Chi2
information-theory	Maximum marginal entropy Even info. intervals quantization	C4.5-based MDLP-based

Table 3 shows some learning selector algorithms sorted according to the above criteria. *Exact values* and *positive exact values* generate a selector for each different value of each attribute in the data matrix. They consider that if an attribute a has a value v in a sample s, the selector $a = v$ can be interesting to describe s. The supervised version does only consider those values which are observed for the positive examples. *1R* and *pure interval* are two algorithms that represent selectors as intervals of values and transform the exact values and positive exact values results by means of extending the selector boundaries so that they include the rounding values if they are not observed in negative examples. 1R is an extension of pure interval that moves the selector boundaries till a predefined number of negative examples have values within the interval. *Equal-width interval* and *equal-frequency interval* partition the attribute domain in a predefined number of intervals such that each interval is as big as any other interval, or contains as many examples as any other interval, respectively. After that, each interval $[x, y]$ of each attribute a is transformed into the selector $a \in [x, y]$. *Cut* and *smooth* are based on the horizontal cut of the value frequency function which has been previously modified to make stand out which are the interesting boundaries. *Chimerge* and *Chi2* are statistical methods that compute χ^2 tests in order to decide whether or not two adjacent selectors must be joined. In Chimerge, the accepting χ^2-threshold is asked, in Chi2 it is computed. *Maximum marginal entropy* is similar to equal-frequency interval but it permits some local disturbances on the boundaries. The *even information intervals quantization* determines the optimal interval boundaries by equalizing the total information gain in each interval. The process can be recursively applied to obtain successive partitions. Finally, the *MDLP-based* algorithm repeatedly applies a binary partition such that it assures the minimal description length principle of the final set of selectors.

In table 4 we show the number of selectors obtained for some of the most representative learning selector algorithms.

Table 4. Number of selectors for exact-value (EV), equal-width interval (EW), equal-frequency interval (EF), smooth (S), pure interval (PI), positive exact value (PE), and MDLP-based (M) algorithms.

database name	EV	EW	EF	S	PI	PE	M
auto mpg	742	50	50	162	363	501	139
bupa	328	57	60	84	314	281	12
cpu	292	57	70	79	243	191	48
glass	939	143	90	231	62	426	25
housing	2836	106	130	366	547	1337	130
hungarian	5162	485	680	1193	3917	1842	109
ionosphere	8148	315	340	227	150	6606	188
iris	123	38	40	33	20	66	17
machine	396	67	80	109	450	107	15
page blocks	9092	97	100	2059	2435	8119	704
pima indian	1254	72	80	305	510	984	280
wine	1276	130	130	352	200	622	83

We can conclude that some of the methods (EV, PI, PE) obtain huge matrices of selectors and, therefore, they will cause the learning process to be slow. The rest of methods obtain matrices whose size is close to the size of the data matrices and, therefor e, the learning process speed will be similar for selector-based algorithms and for direct algorithms. As far as the goodness of the final selectors is concerned, we will study the overall accuracy ratio for cases in the next section.

6 Leaning descriptive rules

In this section, we introduce four new algorithms that learn rules from the information supplied by the matrix of selectors which was obtained in the former section. We will focus our attention in the production of descriptive if-then rules under the gene ral form "*if premise then conclusion*", where *premise* is a conjunction of selectors and *conclusion* is the name of the class that the rule is partially or completely describing.

The four new rule inductive learning algorithms are organized in two groups: instance-based and selector-based. *Instance-based* algorithms incorporate positive instances to the representation of the knowledge base, *selector-based* algorithms inc rease or modify the knowledge base so that more positive instances are accepted and more negative instances are rejected. The new algorithms that we propose are: ALG1, ALG2, ALG3, and ALG4.

ALG1 is an instance-based algorithm that makes rules by means of repeatedly taking an instance which is not yet represented, making a rule that represents that instance and which is the most general rule that does not describe any negative exam ple, and removing the already represented instances.

ALG2 is an instance-based algorithm that represents each instance as a rule and then takes pairs of near rules to be generalized into one.

ALG3 is a selector-based algorithm that takes the most promising selectors to be incorporated to the rule premise which is under construction. When the rule discards all the negative examples and it represents at least one positive example, the rule is closed and a new rule is started.

ALG4 is a selector-based algorithm that constructs rules by adding selectors to an initial empty rule. The difference with ALG3 is that ALG4 considers several premises at the same time while a rule is being made. At each step the mo st promising premise is taken to be improved, and the first one which rejects all the negative examples is incorporated to the knowledge base.

Table 5. Accuracies for the rule learning algorithms.

domain name	selectors	ALG1	ALG2	ALG3	ALG4
bupa	Exact values	85.75	98.48	83.64	100.00
	Equal-frequency interval	80.00	91.81	85.15	100.00
cpu	Exact values	95.00	98.00	92.00	100.00
	Equal-frequency interval	93.50	96.50	94.00	99.50
glass	Exact values	87.45	99.05	92.86	95.24
	Equal-frequency interval	90.48	98.10	90.00	99.52
iris	Exact values	100.00	95.71	96.43	100.00
	Equal-frequency interval	100.00	98.57	99.29	100.00
pid	Exact values	89.87	97.37	85.53	94.99
	Equal-frequency interval	90.97	97.75	83.79	97.31

Table 5 shows the percentage of accuracy achieved by the above algorithms if they are asked to learn from some of the matrices of selectors given in the above section. The main conclusions are: (1) all the algorithms are more accurate for big matrices than for small matrices, (2) ALG1 and ALG3 obtain a 90% of mean accuracy which is less than the accuracy obtained by C4.5 [4], but (3) ALG2 and ALG4 increases the mean accuracy up to a 98%. Further tests have been made on the time cost of the algorithms which show that the instance-based algorithm ALG1 and ALG2 are faster than the selector-based algorithm ALG3 and ALG4. Noisy data has been also considered and the tests [5] show that the selector-based algorithms are more robust than the instance-based algorithms.

7   Reducing the rule set size

We have observed that the set of rules obtained by the algorithms in the above section use to be very large. Large sets present two main drawbacks: one which is the high cost of classifying new cases, and other one which is the difficulty of understanding and validating the set of rules. In order to overcome those difficulties, in figure 1 we propose a last process which is called rule compaction. Here, rule compaction is narrowly related with the idea of learning sub-concepts. That is to say, we propose a mechanism that is capable of discovering new concepts or sub-concepts that, when used, they can simplify the set of rules. After that, a classifier can use the set of rules in order to classify new cases.

In this section we broadly refer to the results in [14]. Rule compaction is achieved after a predefined set of operators are applied to transform the source rules. The operators proposed are those in [15] (inter-construction, intra-construction, absorption, identification, dichotomization, and truncation), and some new ones (intra-construction*, identification*, truncation*) which extend rule compaction to the case of disjunctive rules. See figure 2.

```
Intra-construction*        Identification*              Truncation*

C & (B + D) & E -> X    (A + B) & C & D & E -> X    B & (A + C) & D -> X
A & (B + D) & F -> X    (A + B) & Y          -> X    (A + C) & J & K -> X
---------------------   ------------------------     --------------------
  C & E & Z? -> X         (A + B) & Y -> X            A + C -> X
  A & F & Z? -> X          C & D & E  -> Y
  B + D      -> Z?
```

Fig. 2. New compacting operators.

Intra-construction* introduces a new concept Z? when the same pattern B+D is observed in several rules. Those rules replace the pattern by the new concept. Identification* is an operator that searches for a relation between the different rule selectors (C, D, E, and Y). Finally, truncation* forgets the different selectors of very similar rules.

Rule compaction is an iterative process that, at each step, considers the application of each of the above operators, evaluate the symbol reduction of each case, and applies the one with higher reduction. Truncation and truncation* are special cases which must be applied under some restrictions.

This process has been proved highly time consuming. At the moment, rule compaction has been exclusively tested on the *waste-water treatment plant* problem (wwtp) in which up to a 15% of symbol reduction is achieved. One of the reasons for this reduced test is that we have been more interested in the idea of learning sub-concepts than in the idea of rule reduction. Unlike rule reduction, learning sub-concepts is a process that must be supervised by some human expert which must identify the new concepts. Therefore, since we only work with experts in the wwtp problem [14], results in other domains have not been validated yet.

In the wwtp problem, three of the five concepts introduced by GAR were recognized as *dense-water* (this is water with a great quantity of biomass), *good-extreme performance* (standing for good performance of the plant in extreme situ ations), and *normal-performance* (which is the daily state of the plant). In the next section the wwtp problem is considered in more detail.

8   A case study: the waste-water treatment plant

In this section we introduce the *waste-water treatment plant* problem (wwtp) and use it as an example to study the process depicted in figure 1. Progressively, we will supply a short description of the problem, the data matrix, the classes or plant situations, the feature and instance reductions, the list of selectors and the final rule base before and after compaction.

Figure 3 shows the wwtp problem as a four-stage process in which water is separated from sand, rocks, gravel and other floating elements in the *pre-treatment* stage, then it is calmed in order to permit the first sedimentation in the *primary settler*. After that, the biologic process starts and the organic material which is dissolved in the water demeans. This action is carried out in the *biological reactor* by some micro-organisms that use the water dirt as their food. In a later stage, these organisms that have been growing up must be separated from the water in the *secondary settler*.

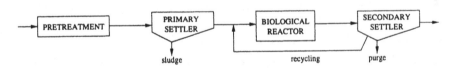

Fig. 3. The waste-water treatment process.

The wwtp problem represents a real world domain that contains the information of a plant in Girona, Spain. This plant has 41 sensors distributed along the treatment process (see figure 3). Sensors measure things like water inflow (Q), pH (PH), biological oxygen demand (DBO), chemical oxygen demand (DQO), suspended solids (SS), volatile suspended solids (SSV), sediments (SED), conductivity (COND), etc. Moreover, these measures are taken at the input of the plant (E), at the output of the em pretreatment (P), at the output of the *primary settler* (D), inside the *biological reactor* (B), at the output of the *secondary settler* (S), or globally (G). So, for instance, DBO-D represents the biological oxygen demand of the water at the output of the primary settler. Notice that some combinations are not useful.

During the *representation* process we attached each sensor to an attribute and observed the 41 attributes during 343 days at the rate of one observation per day between september of 1995 and september of 1996. Figure 4 (a) shows the unsupervi sed data matrix obtained. The first column identifies the day, the rest of columns contain the attribute values for that day. The clustering algorithm LINNEO+ [13] was used to obtain classes that represent wwtp situations. When the clustering radius was set to 3.5, LINNEO+ proposed six classes that the experts recognized as normal, primary low performance, bulking, storm, low performance, and bad influent situations.

day	Q-E	QB-B	QR-G		QUO-D	QUO-S
1/9/95	44077.1	39000.0	39809.3	⋯	0.63	0.14
2/9/95	38669.4	38102.6	39757.2	⋯	?	?
3/9/95	33363.8	32841.2	39712.7	⋯	0.42	0.35
...	...	...	...	⋯	...	...
29/9/96	31504.4	31504.4	41119.0	⋯	0.49	0.11
30/9/96	43412.2	39000.0	43898.8	⋯	0.56	0.50

R0: DBO-S=[22.5,43.0], V30-B=[423.5,596,75] => NORMAL
R1: DBO-S=[2.0,22.5], V30-B=[423.5,596.75] => NORMAL
...
R31: DBO-S=[63.5,84.0] => BULKING
R32: SSV-S=[34.89,68.19], V30-B=[250.25,423.5] => BULKING
R33: DBO-E=[528.0,757.5], PH-S=[7.5,7.75] => STORM
...

(a)   (b)

Fig. 4. The wwtp data matrix and final rule-base.

The next step of the process was to eliminate irrelevant attributes with a feature selection algorithm or, otherwise, indicate the interesting atributes. Experts studied the above classification and they discovered that all the classes could be described with a reduced set of 15 attributes: QA-G, PH-D, SS-D, SSV-D, DQO-D, DBO-D, PH-S, SS-S, SSV-S, DQO-S, DBO-S, V30-B, MLSS-B, MLVSS-B, and MCRT-B.

As far as instance selection is concerned, experts decided to work with all the 343 observations and they asked us not to apply any instance selection algorithm to the data matrix. Then, a supervised data matrix with 15 columns and 343 rows was used to le arn selectors. We applied the *equal-width interval* algorithm and generate selectors to the rate of four selectors per attribute. Some of them are:

Q-E=[20500,28897.1], Q-E=[28897.1,37294.3], Q-E=[37294.3,45691.4], Q-E=[45691.4,54088.6], QB-B=[19883,27973.4], QB-B=[27973.4,36063.8], QB-B=[36063.8,44154.2], QB-B=[44154.2,52244.6], PH-E=[7.2,7.4], PH-E=[7.4,7.6], PH-E=[7.6,7.8], PH-E=[7.8,8], SS-E=[62,210.25], ...

Finally, we used ALG1 to learn the set of rules that figure 4 (b) partially shows. If we study the bulking rules R31 and R32, we observe that R31 describes those days which have a high biological oxygen demand at the output of the plant, and R32 describes those days which have both a high V30 (V30 rates the micro-organism settling) and many volatile suspended solids at the output. Experts agree with these rules and they think that they represent all the bulking situations, which are: there a re many bacterias in the water and therefore the oxygen demand is high, or there are many suspended solids which cannot settle down.

When the compaction process is activated, the size of the rule-set in figure 4 (b) is reduced to a 19.54% of the original size. Many of these reductions affect the rules which conclude about normal days. For example, rules R0 and R1 are replaced by the rule

$$DBO\text{-}S=[2.0,43.0], \; V30\text{-}B=[423.5,596.75] => NORMAL.$$

Moreover, the process discovers that all the rules about normal days can replace the selector $DBO\text{-}S=[22.5,43.0]$ by the selector $DBO\text{-}S=[2.0,22.5]$, the selector $V30\text{-}B=[77.0,250.25]$ by the selector $DBO\text{-}D=[95.5,155.0]$, etc.; and these changes does not modify the knowledge that the rule-base represents.

9   Final remarks and future work

Two main conclusions can be drawn from the work done. On the one hand, we have presented an alternative approach to the classical learning systems. Inductive rule learning is usually seen as a plain problem which is solved by single processes which search a solution through the space of possible solutions. Here, we propose a knowledge engineer approach in which the rule learning problem is decomposed into different subproblems (see figure 1). These subproblems have been identified and solved by using alternative solutions.

On the other hand, we have proposed a general diagram that is able to connect all the above subparts and, therefore, execute the whole process automatically. Moreover, we do not necessarily have to interact with the system at the first step but at any intermediate step.

A first version of the system can be found at http://www.etse.urv.es/~drianyo/software/T6.tar.Z where we supply a tcl/tk interface that integrates the steps of figure 1.

The work is not yet concluded. We center the future improvements in (a) extending the number of algorithms within each step of the learning process, and (b) introducing new steps of the learning process which are not considered now (e.g. learning control rules).

We are also encouraged to realize a more exhaustive test of the whole system. If we have integrated p_1 clustering algorithms, p_2 feature selection algorithms, p_3 instance selection algorithms, p_4 learning selector algorithms, and p_5 learning rule algorithms, the number of combinations is $\Pi_{i=1..5}p_i$. Up to now, we have studied the combined feature and instance selection as well as the combined learning of selectors and rules. In the future, we will compare the alternative complete learning processes in order to know if there is any combination that learns better than the rest in general or under some circumstances as noise or increasing data sizes.

Acknowledgements

I want to thank their always interesting comments to Ulises Cortés and Julian Padget. Thanks to I. R. Roda, M. Poch, and J. Comas the waste-water treatment experts which have contributed with their comments to the section 8. This work has been done with the support of the European Union under the contract VIM:CHRX-CT93-0401 and the CICYT project CIBC-SBC:TIC96-0878.

References

1. P. Langley. Selection of relevant features in machine learning. In *Proceedings of the AAAI Fall Symposium on Relevance*, 1994.
2. A. L. Blum and P. Langley. Selection of relevant features and examples in machine learning. *Artificial Intelligence*, 97:245–271, 1997.
3. P. Clark and T. Niblett. The CN2 induction algorithm. *Machine Learning Journal*, 3:261–283, 1989.
4. J. R. Quinlan. *C4.5: Programs for Machine Learning*. Morgan Kaufmann, San Mateo, California, 1993.
5. D. Riaño. *Automatic construction of descriptive rules*. PhD thesis, Universitat Politècnica de Catalunya, Barcelona, 1997. http://www.etse.urv.es/~drianyo/PhD.ps.Z.
6. A. Valls, D. Riaño, and V. Torra. Sedàs: A semantic-based general classifier system. *Mathware & Soft Computing*, 4:267–279, 1997.
7. F. N. Kerlingen. *Foundations of Behavioural Research*, chapter 25, pages 426–441. William Clowes & Sons Limited, Great Britain, second edition, 1973.
8. P. M. Murphy and D. W. Aha. UCI repository of machine learning databases, ftp address: ftp.ics.uci.edu, directory: /pub/machine_learning_databases/, e-mail address: ml-repository@ics.uci.edu.
9. A. D. Gordon. A review of hierarchical classification. *Journal of the Royal Statistical Society A*, 150(2):119–137, 1987.
10. R. S. Michalski and R. E. Stepp. Learning from observation: conceptual clustering. In R. S. Michalski, J. G. Carbonell, and J. M. Mitchell, editors, *Machine Learning: an Artificial Intelligence Approach, V. 1*, pages 331–360. Morgan Kaufmann, Los Altos, Ca., 1983.
11. D. Fisher. Knowledge acquisition via incremental conceptual clustering. *Machine Learning Journal*, 2:139–172, 1987.
12. P. Cheeseman, J. Kelly, M. Self, J. Stutz, W. Taylor, and D. Freeman. Autoclass: a bayesian classification system. In *In the Fifth international Conference on Machine Learning*, pages 54–64. Morgan Kaufmann Publishers, 1988.
13. M. Sánchez, U. Cortés, J. Béjar, J. Grácia, J. Lafuente, and M. Poch. Concept formation in WWTP by means of classification techniques: A compared study. *Applied Intelligence*, 7:147–165, 1997.
14. D. Riaño and U. Cortés. Rule generation and compactation in the WWTP problem. *Computación y Sistemas*, 1(2):77–89, 1997.
15. S. H. Muggleton. Duce, an oracle-based approach to constructive induction. In *Proceedings of the Tenth International Joint Conference on Artificial Intelligence*, San Mateo, CA, 1987. Milan, Italy, Morgan Kaufmann.

Part III

Coordination and Collaboration

A Service-Oriented Negotiation Model between Autonomous Agents

Carles Sierra*, Peyman Faratin, and Nick R. Jennings

Dept. Electronic Engineering, Queen Mary and Westfield College,
University of London, London E1 4NS, UK.
{C.A.Sierra,P.Faratin,N.R.Jennings}@qmw.ac.uk

Abstract. We present a formal model of negotiation between autonomous agents. The purpose of the negotiation is to reach an agreement about the provision of a service by one agent for another. The model defines a range of strategies and tactics that agents can employ to generate initial offers, evaluate proposals and offer counter proposals. The model is based on computationally tractable assumptions and is demonstrated in the domain of business process management. Initial proofs about the convergence of negotiation are also presented.

1 Introduction

Autonomous agents are being increasingly used in a wide range of industrial and commercial domains [2]. These agents have a high degree of self determination - they decide for themselves what, when and under what conditions their actions should be performed. In most cases, such agents need to interact with other autonomous agents to achieve their objectives (either because they do not have sufficient capabilities or resources to complete their problem solving alone or because there are interdependencies between the agents). The objectives of these interactions are to make other agents undertake a particular course of action (e.g. perform a particular service), modify a planned course of action (e.g. delay or bring forward a particular action so that there is no longer a conflict), or come to an agreement on a common course of action. Since the agents have no direct control over one another, they must persuade their acquaintances to act in particular ways (they cannot simply instruct them). The paradigm case of persuasion is negotiation – *a process by which a joint decision is made by two or more parties. The parties first verbalise contradictory demands and then move towards agreement by a process of concession making or search for new alternatives,* (cf. [3]).

Given its pervasive nature, negotiation comes in many shapes and forms. However in this work we are interested in a particular class of negotiation –

---

* On sabbatical leave from Artificial Intelligence Research Institute –IIIA, Spanish Council for Scientific Research –CSIC. 08193 Bellaterra, Barcelona, Spain. sierra@iiia.csic.es. With the support of the Spanish Ministry of Education grant PR95-313.

J.A. Padget (Ed.): Human and Artificial Societies, LNAI 1624, pp. 201–219, 1999.

namely *service-oriented negotiation.* In this context, one agent (the client) requires a service to be performed on its behalf by some other agent (the server)[1]. Negotiation involves determining a contract under certain terms and conditions. The negotiation may be iterative in that several rounds of offers and counter offers will occur before an agreement is reached or the negotiation is terminated.

When building an autonomous agent which is capable of flexible and sophisticated negotiation, three broad areas need to be considered [7] – what negotiation protocol will be used?, what are the issues over which negotiation takes place?, and what reasoning model will the agents employ? This paper concentrates predominantly on the final point although the protocol and negotiation object are briefly defined. A comprehensive reasoning model for service-oriented negotiation should determine: which potential servers should be contacted, whether negotiation should proceed in parallel with all servers or whether it should run sequentially, what initial offers should be sent out, what is the range of acceptable agreements, what counter offers should be generated, when negotiation should be abandoned, and when an agreement is reached.

This paper presents a formal account of a negotiating agent's reasoning component –in particular it concentrates on the processes of generating an initial offer, of evaluating incoming proposals, and of generating counter proposals. The model specifies the key structures and processes involved in this endeavour and defines their inter-relationships. The model was shaped by practical considerations and insights emanating from the development of a system of negotiating agents for business process management (see [5] and Section 2 for more details). The main contributions of this work are: (i) it allows rich and flexible negotiation schemes to be defined; (ii) it is based on assumptions which are realistic for autonomous computational agents (see Section 3.2 for the set of requirements and Section 7 for a discussion of related approaches); and (iii) it presents some initial results on the convergence of negotiation (see Section 6).

In this paper we concentrate on many-parties, many-issues, single-encounter negotiations with an environment of limited resources (time among them). Section 2 gives details of the type of applications and scenarios we are interested in. Sections 3 to 5 present the proposed model. Finally, some results on negotiation convergence and future avenues of work are outlined.

2   Service-Oriented Negotiation

This section characterises a context in which service oriented negotiation takes place. The scenario is motivated by work in the ADEPT project [5] which has developed negotiating agents for business process management applications. However, we believe that the characteristics emerging from this domain have a wide variety of application. To provide a detailed context for this work, a multi-agent

---

[1] A service is a problem solving activity which has clearly defined start and end points. Examples include diagnosing a fault, buying a group of shares in the stock market, or allocating bandwidth to transmit a video-conference.

system for managing a British Telecom (BT) business process is presented (section 2.1). This scenario is then analysed in terms of its key characteristics and assumptions as they relate to the process of negotiation (section 2.2).

2.1 BT's Provide Customer Quote Business Process

This scenario is based on BT's business process of providing a quotation for designing a network to provide particular services to a customer (figure 1)[2]. The overall process receives a customer service request as its input and generates as its output a quote specifying how much it would cost to build a network to realise that service. It involves up to six agent types: the sales department agent, the customer service division agent, the legal department agent, the design division agent, the surveyor department agent, and the various agents who provide the out-sourced service of vetting customers.

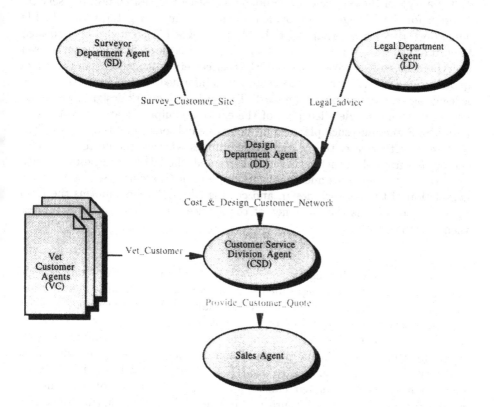

Fig. 1. Agent system for BT's provide customer quote business process.

---

[2] The negotiations between the agents are denoted by arrows (arrow head toward client) and the service involved in the negotiation is juxtaposed to the respective arrow.

The process is initiated by the sales agent which negotiates with the CSD agent (mainly over time, but also over the number of invocations and the form in which the final result should be delivered) for the service of providing a customer quote. The first stages of the *Provide_Customer_Quote* service involve the CSD agent capturing the customer's details and vetting the customer in terms of their credit worthiness. The latter sub-service is actually performed by one of the VC agents. Negotiation is used to determine which VC agent should be selected – the main attributes which are negotiated over are the price of the service, the penalty for contract violation, the desired quality of the service and the time by which the service should be performed. If the customer fails the vetting procedure, then the quote process terminates. Assuming the customer is satisfactory, the CSD agent maps their requirements against a service portfolio. If the requirements can be met by a standard off-the-shelf portfolio item then an immediate quote can be offered based on previous examples. In the case of bespoke services, however, the process is more complex. The CSD agent negotiates with the DD agent (over time and quality) for the service of designing and costing the desired network service. In order for the DD agent to provide this service it must negotiate with the LD agent (over time) and perhaps with the SD agent. The LD agent checks the design to ensure the legality of the proposed service (e.g. it is illegal to send unauthorised encrypted messages across France). If the desired service is illegal, then the entire quote process terminates and the customer is informed. If the requested service is legal then the design phase can start. To prepare a network design it is usually necessary to have a detailed plan of the existing equipment at the customer's premises. Sometimes such plans might not exist and sometimes they may be out of date. In either case, the DD agent determines whether the customer site(s) should be surveyed. If such a survey is warranted, the DD agent negotiates with the SD agent (over price and time) for the *Survey_Customer_Site* service. On completion of the network design and costing, the DD agent informs the CSD agent which informs the customer of the service quote. The business process then terminates.

The structure of the negotiation object is based almost directly on the legal contracts used to regulate agreements in the current manual approach to business process management. This structure is fairly rich and covers both service and meta-service attributes. In more detail, it contains: (i) the service name; (ii) a unique agreement identifier (covering the case where there are multiple agreements for the same service); (iii) the agents involved in the agreement (client and server); (iv) the type of agreement (one off agreement for a single service invocation versus on-going agreements for multiple invocations of the same service); (v) timing information (duration represents the maximum time the server can take to finish the service, and start time and end time represent the time during which the agreement is valid); (vi) the volume of invocations permissible between the start and end times (for on-going agreements only); (vii) the price paid per invocation; (viii) the penalty the server incurs for every violation of the agreement; (ix) the information the client must provide to the server on service invocation; and (x) the policy used for disseminating the service's intermediate and final results to the client.

2.2   Characteristics and Assumptions

The following negotiation characteristics can be noted from the ADEPT business process scenario. Moreover, it is believed that these characteristics are common to a wide range of service oriented negotiations between autonomous agents.

- A given service can be provided by more than one agent (e.g. multiple agents can provide the vet customer service to the CSD agent). The available services may be identical in their characteristics or they may vary along several dimensions (e.g. quality, price, availability, etc.).
- Individual agents can be both clients and servers for different services in different negotiation contexts.
- Negotiations can range over a number of quantitative (e.g. price, duration, and cost) and qualitative (e.g. type of reporting policy, and nature of the contract) issues. Each successful negotiation requires a range of such issues to be resolved to the satisfaction of both parties. Agents may be required to make trade-offs between issues (e.g. faster completion time for lower quality) in order to come to an agreement.
- The social context and inter-relationships of the participants influences the way agents negotiate. Some negotiations involve entities within the same organisation (e.g. between the CSD and DD agents) and hence are generally cooperative in nature. Other negotiations are inter-organisational and purely competitive – involving self interested, utility maximising agents (e.g. between the VC agents and the CSD agent). Some groups of agents often negotiate with one another for the same service (e.g. the CSD and DD agents), whereas other negotiations are more open in nature (for example, the set of VC agents changes frequently and hence the CSD agent often negotiates with unknown agents).
- As the agents are autonomous, the factors which influence their negotiation stance and behaviour are private and not available to their opponents (especially in inter-organisational settings). Thus agents do not know what utilities their opponents place on various outcomes, they do not know what reasoning models they employ, they do not know their opponent's constraints and they do not know whether an agreement is even possible at the outset (i.e. the participants may have non-intersecting ranges of acceptability).
- Since negotiation takes place within a highly intertwined web of activity (the business process) time is a critical factor. Timings are important on two distinct levels: (i) the time it takes to reach an agreement must be reasonable; and (ii) the time by which the negotiated service must be executed is important in most cases and crucial in others. The former means that the agents should not become involved in unnecessarily complex and time consuming negotiations – the time spent negotiating should be reasonable with respect to the value of the service agreement. The latter means that the

agents sometimes have hard deadlines by which agreements must be in place (this occurs mainly when multiple services need to be combined or closely coordinated).

3   The Negotiation Model

The negotiation model for autonomous agents proposed in this Section is based on a variation of the *two parties, many issues* value scoring system presented in [8]. That is, a model for bilateral negotiations about a set of quantitative variables. Our variation transforms that model into a *many parties, many issues* model (that is, multilateral negotiations about a set of variables). Multilateral negotiations are central to the application domains we are interested in. Our model of multilateral negotiations is based on a set of mutually influencing *two parties, many issues* negotiations. We will call the sequence of offers and counter-offers in a two-party negotiation a *negotiation thread*. Offers and counter offers are generated by lineal combinations of simple functions, called *tactics*. Tactics generate an offer, or counter offer, for a single component of the negotiation object using a single criteria (time, resources, etc.). Different weights in the lineal combination allow the varying importance of the criteria to be modelled. For example, when determining values of slots in the negotiation object it may initially be more important to take into account the other agent's behaviour than the remaining time. In which case, the tactics that emphasize the behaviour of other agents will be given greater preference than the tactics which base their value on the amount of time remaining.

To achieve flexibility in the negotiation, the agents may wish to change their ratings of the importance of the different criteria over time. For example, remaining time may become more relevant than the imitation of the other's behaviour as the time by which an agreement must be in place approaches. We use the term *"strategy"* to denote the way in which an agent changes the weights of the different tactics over time. Thus strategies combine tactics depending on the history of negotiations and the mental state of agents, and negotiation threads influence one another by means of strategies (see Section 6).

Before presenting our model, we introduce Raiffa's basic model for bilateral negotiation [8].

3.1   The Bilateral Negotiation Model

Let i ($i \in \{a, b\}$) represent the negotiating agents and j ($j \in \{1, ..., n\}$) the issues under negotiation. Let $x_j \in [min_j, max_j]$ be a value for issue j. Here we consider issues for which negotiation amounts to determining a value between a delimited range. Each agent has a scoring function $V_j^i : [min_j, max_j] \rightarrow [0, 1]$ that gives the score agent i assigns to a value of issue j in the range of its acceptable values. For convenience, scores are kept in the interval $[0, 1]$.

The next element of the model is the relative importance that an agent assigns to each issue under negotiation. w_j^i is the importance of issue j for agent i. We assume the weights of both agents are normalized, i.e. $\sum_{1 \leq j \leq n} w_j^i = 1$, for all i in $\{a, b\}$. With these elements in place, it is now possible to define an agent's scoring function[3] for a *contract* – that is, for a value $x = (x_1, ..., x_n)$ in the multi-dimensional space defined by the issues' value ranges:

$$V^i(x) = \sum_{1 \leq j \leq n} w_j^i V_j^i(x_j)$$

If both negotiators use such an additive scoring function, it is possible to show how to compute the optimum value of x as an element on the efficient frontier of negotiation[4] (see [8], p. 164).

3.2 Service-Oriented Negotiation Requirements

The above mentioned model for bilateral negotiation is valid for some service oriented settings. However, the model contains several implicit assumptions that, although they permit good optimisation results, are inappropriate for our scenarios:

1. *Privacy of information.* To find the optimum value, the scoring functions have to be disclosed. This is, in general, inappropriate for competitive negotiation.
2. *Privacy of models.* Both negotiators have to use the same additive scoring model. However, the models used to evaluate offers and generate counter offers are one of the things that negotiators try to hide from one another.
3. *Value restrictions.* There are pre-defined value regions for discussion (they are necessary to define the limits of the scoring function). However, it is not always possible to find these common regions and in many cases negotiation actually involves determining whether such regions even exist.
4. *Time restrictions.* There is no notion of timing issues in the negotiation. However, time is a major constraint on the agent's behaviour [6]. This is mainly true on the client side; agents often have strict deadlines by when the negotiation must be completed. For instance, a video link has to be provided at 16:00 because at that time a conference should start; negotiation about set up cannot continue after that instant in time.
5. *Resource restrictions.* There is no notion of resource issues in the negotiation. However, the quantity of a particular resource has a strong and direct influence on the behaviour of agents, and, moreover, the correct appreciation of the remaining resources is an essential characteristic of good negotiators. Resources from the client point of view relate directly with the number of servers engaging in negotiations; likewise from the server's point of view. Thus, the quantity of resource has a similar effect on the agents' behaviour as time.

---

[3] Non-linear approaches to modelling utility could be used if necessary without affecting the basic ideas of the model.

[4] Any contract not on this frontier is sub-optimal (i.e. not pareto-optimal) in that possible mutual gains are missed.

Taking the first consideration alone, it is clear that optimal solution cannot be found in our domains: it is not possible to optimize an unknown function. Hence, we shall propose a model for individual agent negotiation that looks for deals acceptable to its acquaintances but which, nevertheless, maximises the agent's own scoring function.

3.3 A Service-Oriented Negotiation Model

In service oriented negotiations, agents exhibit two possible behaviours that are, in principle, in conflict. Hence we shall distinguish (for notational convenience) two subsets of agents[5], $Agents = Clients \cup Servers$. We use roman letters to represent agents; $c, c_1, c_2, \ldots$ will stand for clients, $s, s_1, s_2, \ldots$ for servers and $a, a_1, b, d, e, \ldots$ for unspecific agents.

We adhere to an additive scoring system in which, for simplicity, the function V_j^a is either monotonically increasing or monotonically decreasing.

Clients and service providers may have mutual interest for particular variables. For example, Raiffa cites an example [8, pg. 133–147] in which the Police Officers Union and the City Hall realize, in the course of their negotiations, that they both want the police commissioner fired. Having recognised this mutual interest they quickly agree that this course of action should be selected. However, in general, clients and servers have opposing interests, e.g. a client wants a low price for a service, whereas his potential servers attempt to obtain the highest price. High quality is desired by clients but not by servers, and so on. Therefore, in the space of negotiation values, negotiators represent opposing forces in each one of the dimensions. In consequence, the scoring functions verify that given a client c and a server s negotiating values for issue j, then if $x_j, y_j \in [min_j, max_j]$ and $x_j \geq y_j$ then $(V_j^c(x_j) \geq V_j^c(y_j)$ iff $V_j^s(x_j) \leq V_j^s(y_j))$.

In contrast, where there is a mutual interest, a variable will be assigned one of its extreme values. Hence these variables can be taken out of the negotiation set. For instance, the act of firing the police commisioner can be removed from the set of issues under negotiation and assigned the extreme value "done".

Once the agents have determined the set of variables over which they will negotiate, the negotiation process between two agents $a, b \in Agents$ consists of an alternate succession of offers and counter offers of values for these variables. This continues until an offer or counter offer is accepted by the other side or one of the partners terminates negotiation (e.g. because the time deadline is reached without an agreement being in place). Negotiation can be initiated by clients or servers.

We represent by $x_{a \to b}^t$ the vector of values proposed by agent a to agent b at time t, and by $x_{a \to b}^t[j]$ the value for issue j proposed from a to b at time t. The range of values acceptable to agent a for issue j will be represented as the interval $[min_j^a, max_j^a]$. For convenience, we assume a common global time (the calendar time) represented by a linearly ordered set of instants, namely

---

[5] The subsets are not disjoint since an agent can participate as a client in one negotiation and as a service provider in another.

Time, and a reliable communication medium introducing no delays in message transmission (so we can assume that emission and reception times are identical). The common time assumption is not too strong for our application domains. because time granularity and offer and counter offers frequencies are not too high. Then,

Definition 1. *A* **Negotiation Thread** *between agents* $a, b \in$ *Agents, at time* $t \in$ *Time, noted* $x^t_{a \leftrightarrow b}$ *or* $x^t_{b \leftrightarrow a}$, *is any finite sequence of the form* $\{x^{t_1}_{d_1 \rightarrow e_1}, x^{t_2}_{d_2 \rightarrow e_2}, \dots, x^{t_n}_{d_n \rightarrow e_n}\}$ *where:*

1. $e_i = d_{i+1}$, proposals are alternate between both agents,
2. $t_k \leq t_l$ if $k \leq l$, ordered over time,
3. $d_i, e_i \in \{a, b\}$, the thread contains only proposals between agents a and b,
4. $d_i \neq e_i$, the proposals are between agents, and
5. $x^{t_i}_{d_i \rightarrow e_i}[j] \in [min^{d_i}_j, max^{d_i}_j]$ or is one of the particles $\{accept, reject\}$.

Superindex t_n represents an instant in the set Time such that $t_n \leq t$. We will say that a negotiation thread is **active**[6] *if $x^{t_n}_{d_n \rightarrow e_n} \notin \{accept, reject\}$.*

For simplicity in the notation, we assume in the sequel that t_1 corresponds to the initial time value, that is $t_1 = 0$. In other words, there is a local time for each negotiation thread, that starts with the utterance of the first offer. When agent a receives an offer from agent b at time t, that is $x^t_{b \rightarrow a}$, it has to rate the offer using its scoring function. If the value of $V^a(x^t_{b \rightarrow a})$ is greater than the value of the counter offer agent a is ready to send at the time t' when the evaluation is performed, that is, $x^{t'}_{a \rightarrow b}$ with $t' > t$, then agent a accepts. Otherwise, the counter offer is submitted. The interpretation function I^a expresses this concept more formally:

Definition 2. *Given an agent a and its associated scoring function V^a, the* **interpretation** *by agent a at time t' of an offer $x^t_{b \rightarrow a}$ sent at time $t < t'$, is defined as:*

$$I^a(t', x^t_{b \rightarrow a}) = \begin{cases} accept & \text{If } V^a(x^t_{b \rightarrow a}) \geq V^a(x^{t'}_{a \rightarrow b}) \\ x^{t'}_{a \rightarrow b} & otherwise \end{cases}$$

where $x^{t'}_{a \rightarrow b}$ is the contract that agent a would offer to b at the time of the interpretation.

The result of $I^a(t', x^t_{b \rightarrow a})$ is used to extend the current negotiation thread between the agents. This interpretation also models the fact that a contract unacceptable today can be accepted tomorrow merely by the fact that time has passed.

In order to prepare a counter offer, $x^{t'}_{a \rightarrow b}$, agent a uses a set of tactics that generate new values for each variable in the negotiation set. Based on the needs of our business process applications (Section 2), we developed the following families of tactics:

---

[6] We assume that any offer is valid (that is, the agent that uttered it is commited) until a counter offer is received. If the response time is relevant it can be included in the set of issues under negotiation.

1. **Time-dependent**. If an agent has a time deadline by which an agreement must be in place, these tactics model the fact that the agent is likely to concede more rapidly as the deadline approaches. The shape of the curve of concession, a function depending on time, is what differentiates tactics in this set.
2. **Resource-dependent**. These tactics model the pressure in reaching an agreement that (i) the limited resources —e.g. remaining bandwidth to be allocated, money, or any other— and (2) the environment —number of clients, number of servers or economic parameters— impose upon the agent's behaviour. The functions in this set are similar to the time dependent functions except that the domain of the function is the quantity of resources available instead of the remaining time.
3. **Imitative**. In situations in which the agent is not under a great deal of pressure to reach an agreement, it may choose to use imitative tactics that protect it from being exploited by other agents. In this case, the counter offer depends on the behaviour of the negotiation opponent. The tactics in this family differ in which aspect of their opponent's behaviour they imitate, and to what degree the opponent's behaviour is imitated.

We do not claim that these family types are complete, nor that we have enumerated all possible instances of tactics within a given family. These are merely the types of tactics we found useful in our applications.

4   Negotiation Tactics

Tactics are the set of functions that determine how to compute the value of a quantitative issue (price, volume, duration, ...), by considering a *single* criteria (time, resources, ...). The set of values for the negotiation issue are then the range of the function, and the single criteria is its domain. The criteria we have chosen for the application domain, as explained in the previous section, are time, resources and previous offers and counter offers.

Given that agents may want to consider more than one criterion to compute the value for a single issue, we model the generation of counter proposals as a weighted combination of different tactics covering the set of criteria. The values so computed for the different issues[7] will be the elements of the counter proposal. For instance, if an agent wants to counter propose taking into account two criteria: the remaining time and the previous behaviour of the opponent, it can select two tactics: *boulware* (sec. 4.1, based on the remaining time, and *Tit-For-Tat* (sec. 4.3) to imitate the behaviour of the oponent. Each of the so selected tactics will suggest a value to counter propose for the issue under negotiation. The actual value which is counter proposed will be the weighted combination of the two suggested values.

Given an issue j, for which a value is under negotiation, an agent a's initial offer corresponds to a value in the issue's acceptable region, that is, a value in

---

[7] values for issues may be computed by different weighted combinations of tactics.

$[min_j^a, max_j^a]$. For instance, a client with a range $[\pounds0, \pounds20]$ for the price p to pay for a good may start the negotiation process by offering the server $\pounds10$ –what initial offer should be chosen is something the agent can learn by experience. The server, with range $[\pounds17, \pounds35]$ may then make an initial counter-offer of $\pounds25$. With these two initial values, the strategy of the first agent may consist of using a time-dependent tactic giving $\pounds12$ –e.g. if it has a short time to reach an agreement, it will start conceding. And then if the strategy of the latter agent is to use an imitative tactic, it could generate a counter-proposal of $\pounds23$ (imitating the $\pounds2$ shift of its opponent). And so on.

4.1   Time-Dependent Tactics

In these tactics, the predominant factor used to decide which value to offer next is time, t. Thus these tactics consist of varying the acceptance value for the issue depending on the remaining negotiation time (an important requirement in our domain –Section 2.2). This requires a constant t_{max}^a in agent a that represents an instant in the future by when the negotiation must be completed. We model the initial offer as being a point in the interval of values of the issue under negotiation. Hence, agents define a constant κ_j^a that multiplied by the size of the interval determines the value of issue j to be offered in the first proposal by agent a.

We model the value to be uttered by agent a to agent b for issue j as the offer at time t, with $0 \leq t \leq t_{max}^a$, by a function α_j^a depending on time as the following expression shows:

$$x_{a \to b}^t[j] = \begin{cases} min_j^a + \alpha_j^a(t)(max_j^a - min_j^a) & \text{If } V_j^a \text{ is decreasing} \\ min_j^a + (1 - \alpha_j^a(t))(max_j^a - min_j^a) & \text{If } V_j^a \text{ is increasing} \end{cases}$$

A wide range of time-dependent functions can be defined simply by varying the way in which $\alpha_j^a(t)$ is computed. Functions must ensure that $0 \leq \alpha_j^a(t) \leq 1$, $\alpha_j^a(0) = \kappa_j^a$ and $\alpha_j^a(t_{max}^a) = 1$. That is, the offer will always be between the value range, at the beginning it will give the initial constant and when the time deadline is reached the tactic will suggest to offer the reservation value[8]. We distinguish two families of functions with this intended behaviour, polynomial and exponential. Both families are parameterised by a value $\beta \in \Re^+$ that determines the convexity degree (see Figure 8) of the curve. We have chosen these two families of functions because of the very different way they model concession. For the same big value of β the polynomial function concedes faster at the beginning than the exponential one, then they behave similarly. For a small value of β, the exponential function waits longer to start conceding than the polynomial one. Many other functions could eventually be defined.

---

[8] The reservation value for issue j of agent a represents the value that gives the smallest score for function V_j^a. The reservation value for agent a and issue j depends on the function V_j^a and the range $[min_j^a, max_j^a]$. If V_j^a is monotonically increasing, then the reservation value is min_j^a; if it is decreasing the reservation value is max_j^a.

- **Polynomial.** $\alpha_j^a(t) = \kappa_j^a + (1 - \kappa_j^a)(\frac{min(t,t_{max})}{t_{max}})^{\frac{1}{\beta}}$
- **Exponential.** $\alpha_j^a(t) = e^{(1 - \frac{min(t,t_{max})}{t_{max}})^{\beta} \ln \kappa_j^a}$

These families of functions represent an infinite number of possible tactics, one for each value of β. However to better understand their behaviour we have classified them, depending on the value of β, into two extreme sets showing clearly different patterns of behaviour. Other sets in between these two could be defined:

1. **Boulware tactics [[8], pg. 48].** Either exponential or polynomial functions with $\beta < 1$. This tactic maintains the offered value until the time is almost exhausted, whereupon it concedes up to the reservation value[9]. The behaviour of this family of tactics with respect to β is easily understood taking into account that $\lim_{\beta \to 0+} e^{(1 - \frac{min(t,t_{max})}{t_{max}})^{\beta} \ln \kappa_j^a} = \kappa_j^a$ or $\lim_{\beta \to 0+} \kappa_j^a + (1 - \kappa_j^a)(\frac{min(t,t_{max})}{t_{max}})^{\frac{1}{\beta}} = \kappa_j^a$.

2. **Conceder [[3], pg. 20].** Either exponential or polynomial functions with $\beta > 1$. The agent goes to its reservation value very quickly. For similar reasons as before, we have $\lim_{\beta \to +\infty} e^{(1 - \frac{min(t,t_{max})}{t_{max}})^{\beta} \ln \kappa_j^a} = 1$ or $\lim_{\beta \to +\infty} \kappa_j^a + (1 - \kappa_j^a)(\frac{min(t,t_{max})}{t_{max}})^{\frac{1}{\beta}} = 1$.

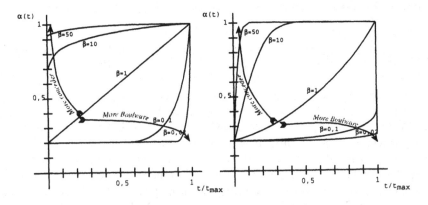

Fig. 2. Polynomial (left) and Exponential (right) functions for the computation of $\alpha(t)$. Time is presented as relative to t_{max}^a.

---

[9] Besides the pattern of concession that these functions model, Boulware negotiation tactics presume that the interval of values for negotiation is very narrow. Hence, when the deadline is reached and $\alpha(t_{max}) = 1$ the offer generated is not substantially different from the initial one.

4.2   Resource-Dependent Tactics

These tactics are similar to the time-dependent ones. Indeed time-dependent tactics can be seen as a type of resource-dependent tactic in which the sole resource considered is time. Whereas time vanishes constantly up to its end, other resources may have different patterns of usage. We model resource-dependent tactics in the same way as time-dependent ones, that is, by using the same functions, but by making the value t^a_{max} dynamic. Its value represents a heuristic about how many resources are in the environment. The scarcer the resource the more urgent the need for an agreement to be reached. In our application domains the most important resource to model is the number of agents negotiating with a given agent and how keen they are to reach agreements. On one hand, the greater the number of agents who are negotiating with agent a for a particular service s, the lower the pressure on agent a to reach an agreement with any specific individual. While on the other hand, the longer the negotiation thread, the greater the pressure on a to come to an agreement. Hence, representing the set of agents negotiating with agent a at time t as: $N^a(t) = \{i|x^t_{i\leftrightarrow a}\text{is active}\}$, we define the dynamic time deadline for agent a as:

$$t^a_{max} = t_c + \mu^a \frac{|N^a(t_c)|^2}{\sum_i |x^{t_c}_{i\leftrightarrow a}|}$$

where μ^a represents the time agent a considers reasonable to negotiate with a single agent, t_c is the current time and $|x^{t_c}_{i\leftrightarrow a}|$ represents the length of the current thread between i and a. Notice that the number of agents is in the numerator – so quantity of time is directly proportional to it, and averaged length of negotiation thread is in the denominator – so quantity of time is inversely proportional to it.

4.3   Imitative Tactics

This family of tactics compute the next offer based on the previous attitude of the negotiation opponent. These tactics have proved important in co-operative problem-solving negotiation settings [1], and so are useful in a subset of our contexts (see Section 2.2). The main difference between the tactics in this family is in the type of imitation they perform. One family imitates proportionally, another in absolute terms, and the last one computes the average of the proportions in a number of previous offers. Hence, given a negotiation thread $\{\ldots, x^{t_{n-2\delta}}_{b\rightarrow a}, x^{t_{n-2\delta+1}}_{a\rightarrow b}, x^{t_{n-2\delta+2}}_{b\rightarrow a}, \ldots, x^{t_{n-2}}_{b\rightarrow a}, x^{t_{n-1}}_{a\rightarrow b}, x^{t_n}_{b\rightarrow a}\}$, with $\delta \geq 1$, we distinguish the following families of tactics:

1. **Relative Tit-For-Tat**
   The agent reproduces, in percentage terms, the behaviour that its opponent performed $\delta \geq 1$ steps ago.

$$x_{a \rightarrow b}^{t_{n+1}}[j] = \begin{cases} min(max(\frac{x_{b \rightarrow a}^{t_{n-2\delta}}[j]}{x_{b \rightarrow a}^{t_{n-2\delta+2}}[j]} x_{a \rightarrow b}^{t_{n-1}}[j], min_j^a), max_j^a) & n > 2\delta \\ min_j^a + \kappa_j^a(max_j^a - min_j^a) & n \leq 2\delta, V_j^a \text{ decr.} \\ min_j^a + (1 - \kappa_j^a)(max_j^a - min_j^a) & n \leq 2\delta, V_j^a \text{ incr.} \end{cases}$$

Depending on the value of the quotient between two consecutive counter offers, the agent exhibits a range of different behaviours: **mirror** if the quotient is greater than 1, **retaliatory** if it is lower than 1, and a type of time independent **boulware** if it is exactly 1.

2. **Random Absolute Tit-For-Tat**

   The same as before but in absolute terms. It means that if the other agent decreases its offer by £2, then the next response should be increased by the same £2. Moreover, we add a component that modifies that behaviour by increasing or decreasing (depending on the value of parameter s) the value of the answer by a random amount. (This is introduced as it can enable the agents to escape from local minima.) M is the maximum amount by which an agent can change its imitative behaviour.

$$x_{a \rightarrow b}^{t_{n+1}}[j] = \begin{cases} min(max(x_{a \rightarrow b}^{t_{n-1}}[j] + (x_{b \rightarrow a}^{t_{n-2\delta}}[j] - x_{b \rightarrow a}^{t_{n-2\delta+2}}[j]) + \\ \qquad +(-1)^s R(M), min_j^a), max_j^a) & n > 2\delta \\ min_j^a + \kappa_j^a(max_j^a - min_j^a) & n \leq 2\delta, V_j^a \text{ decr.} \\ min_j^a + (1 - \kappa_j^a)(max_j^a - min_j^a) & n \leq 2\delta, V_j^a \text{ incr.} \end{cases}$$

   Where $s \in \{0, 1\}$ and $R(M)$ is a function that generates a random integer in the interval $[0, M]$.

3. **Averaged Tit-For-Tat** The agent computes the average of percentages of changes in a window of size $\gamma \geq 1$ of its opponents history when determining its new offer. When $\gamma = 1$ we have the relative Tit-For-Tat tactic with $\delta = 1$.

$$x_{a \rightarrow b}^{t_{n+1}}[j] = \begin{cases} min(max(\frac{x_{b \rightarrow a}^{t_{n-2}}[j]}{x_{b \rightarrow a}^{t_{n-2\gamma+2}}[j]} x_{a \rightarrow b}^{t_{n-1}}[j], min_j^a), max_j^a) & n > 2\gamma \\ min_j^a + \kappa_j^a(max_j^a - min_j^a) & n \leq 2\gamma, V_j^a \text{ decr.} \\ min_j^a + (1 - \kappa_j^a)(max_j^a - min_j^a) & n \leq 2\gamma, V_j^a \text{ incr.} \end{cases}$$

5   Negotiation Strategies

The aim of agent a's negotiation strategy is to determine the best course of action which will result in an agreement on a contract x that maximises its scoring function V^a. In practical terms, this equates to how to prepare a new counter offer.

In our model we consider that the agent has a representation of its mental state containing information about its beliefs, its knowledge of the environment (time, resources, etc.), and any other attitudes (desires, goals, obligations, intentions, etc.) the agent designer considers appropriate. The mental state of agent a at time t is noted as MS_a^t. We denote the set of all possible mental states for agent a as MS_a.

When agent a receives an offer from agent b it becomes the last element in the current negotiation thread between both agents. If the offer is unsatisfactory, agent a generates a counter offer. As discussed earlier, different combinations of tactics can be used to generate counter offers for particular issues. An agent's strategy determines which combination of tactics should be used at any one instant. Hence, the following definition:

Definition 3. *Given a negotiation thread between agents a and b at time t_n over domain $X = X_1 \times \ldots \times X_p$, with $x_{a \leftrightarrow b}^{t_n} = \{\ldots, x_{b \to a}^{t_n}\}$, and a finite set of m tactics[10] $T^a = \{\tau_i | \tau_i : MS_a \to X\}_{i \in [1,m]}$, a **weighted counter proposal** is any lineal combination of the tactics that generates the value at time t_{n+1} in the thread. That is, for issue j*

$$x_{a \to b}^{t_{n+1}}[j] = \gamma_{j1}\tau_1(MS_a^{t_{n+1}})[j] + \gamma_{j2}\tau_2(MS_a^{t_{n+1}})[j] + \ldots + \gamma_{jm}\tau_m(MS_a^{t_{n+1}})[j]$$

such that for all issues j, $\sum_{i \in [1,m]} \gamma_{ji} = 1$ and $x_{a \leftrightarrow b}^{t_{n+1}} = \{\ldots, x_{b \to a}^{t_n}, x_{a \to b}^{t_{n+1}}\}$

Given a set of tactics, different types of negotiation behaviour can be obtained by weighting the tactics in a different way. That is, by changing the matrix Γ – particular to each negotiation thread:

$$\Gamma_{a \to b}^t = \begin{pmatrix} \gamma_{11} & \gamma_{12} & \cdots & \gamma_{1m} \\ \gamma_{21} & \gamma_{22} & \cdots & \gamma_{2m} \\ \vdots & \vdots & \vdots & \vdots \\ \gamma_{p1} & \gamma_{p2} & \cdots & \gamma_{pm} \end{pmatrix}$$

An example of when this weighted combination may be useful is when modelling a *smooth* transition from a behaviour based on a single tactic (e.g. Boulware, because the agent has plenty ot time to reach an agreement) to another one (e.g. Conceder, because the time is running out). Smoothness is obtained by changing the weight affecting the tactics progressively (e.g. from 1 to 0 and from 0 to 1 in the example).

We model many-parties negotiations by means of a set of interacting negotiation threads. The way this is done is by making a negotiation thread influence the selection of which matrix Γ is to be used in other negotiation threads. Thus,

Definition 4. *Given $a, b \in Agents$, $t \in Time$, a's mental state MS_a^t, and $\Gamma_{a \to b}^t$, a **Negotiation Strategy**, is any function f of the following type:*

$$\Gamma_{a \to b}^{t+1} = f(\Gamma_{a \to b}^t, MS_a^t)$$

---

[10] This definition uses the natural extension of tactics to the multi-dimensional space of issues' values.

A simplistic example of the application of our model would be to have a matrix Γ built up of 0s and 1s and having $\Gamma_{a\to b}^{t+1} = \Gamma_{a\to b}^t$ for all t. This would correspond to using a fixed single tactic for each issue at every instant in the negotiation.

6 Convergence Results

Convergence in negotiation is achieved when the scoring value of the received offer is greater than the scoring value of the counter offer the agent intended to respond with. That is,

Definition 5. *A Negotiation thread* $x_{a\leftrightarrow b}^{t_n} = \{\ldots, x_{b\to a}^{t_n}\}$ *converges at time* t_{n+1} *iff* $V^a(x_{b\to a}^{t_n}) \geq V^a(x_{a\to b}^{t_{n+1}})$

With this definition in mind, we have obtained some preliminary results on convergence for a single variable, single tactic, bilateral negotiation. Wider convergence criteria will be forthcoming as future work. The second proposition (1.2) is particularly interesting because it allows an agent using a time-dependent tactic to know if the negotiation will converge with an agent playing relative Tit-For-Tat. Knowing if an opponent is playing Tit-For-Tat can easily be guessed by using a strategy that makes some initial random offers and then examines the responses.

Notice, however, that convergence cannot be guaranteed in general. For example, two agents using a Tit-For-Tat tactic might stay negotiating forever if no limitation on time is established.

Proposition 1. *If two agents a and b negotiate values for an issue j over the value regions* $[min_j^a, max_j^a]$, $[min_j^b, max_j^b]$, *satisfying* $[min_j^a, max_j^a] \cap [min_j^b, max_j^b]$ $\neq \emptyset$, *then the following properties hold:*

1. *If a and b follow a time-dependent tactic with V_j^a decreasing (resp. increasing), V_j^b increasing (resp. decreasing) and $t_{max}^a = t_{max}^b$ then the negotiation for issue j converges.*
2. *If a uses a time-dependent tactic with V_j^a increasing (resp. decreasing) and b uses a relative Tit-For-Tat tactic with V_j^b decreasing (resp. increasing), and a starts the negotiation thread, then the negotiation converges if $x_{a\to b}^{t_1}[j] x_{b\to a}^{t_2}[j]$ $< (min_j^a)^2$ (resp. if $x_{a\to b}^{t_1}[j] x_{b\to a}^{t_2}[j] > (max_j^a)^2$).*

Proof. (1) *We prove it for V_j^a decreasing, the other case is similar. We have* $[min_j^a, max_j^a] \cap [min_j^b, max_j^b] \neq \emptyset$, *then* $max_j^a > min_j^b$. *When time runs out the $\alpha(t)$ functions of both agents become 1, that is* $\alpha_j^a(t_{max}^a) = \alpha_j^b(t_{max}^b) = 1$ *and then their acceptance values will become* $min_j^a + \alpha_j^a(t)(max_j^a - min_j^a) =$ max_j^a *and* $min_j^b + (1 - \alpha_j^b(t))(max_j^b - min_j^b) = min_j^b$. *So, b will make the offer* $x_{b\to a}^{t_{max}^b}[j] = min_j^b$ *at the deadline. But given that a uses a monotonically decreasing function and $max_j^a > min_j^b$ we have $V_j^a(max_j^a) > V_j^a(min_j^b)$. In other words, by* using the assumption $t^a_{max} = t^b_{max}$ we have $V^a_j(x^{t^a_{max}}_{b \to a}[j]) > V^a_j(x^{t^a_{max}}_{a \to b}[j])$. So the negotiation converges.

(2) Again we prove it for V^b_j increasing, the other case is similar. Without loss of generality assume that the thread is:

$$x^{t_{n-1}}_{a \leftrightarrow b} = \{x^{t_1}_{a \to b}, x^{t_2}_{b \to a}, \dots, x^{t_{n-1}}_{a \to b}\}$$

and that $\delta = 1$. By using the definition of relative Tit-For-Tat, it can be seen that:

$$x^{t_n}_{b \to a}[j] = \frac{x^{t_{n-3}}_{a \to b}[j]}{x^{t_{n-1}}_{a \to b}[j]} x^{t_{n-2}}_{b \to a}[j] = \frac{x^{t_{n-3}}_{a \to b}[j]}{x^{t_{n-1}}_{a \to b}[j]} \frac{x^{t_{n-5}}_{a \to b}[j]}{x^{t_{n-3}}_{a \to b}[j]} x^{t_{n-4}}_{b \to a}[j] =$$

$$= \frac{x^{t_{n-3}}_{a \to b}[j]}{x^{t_{n-1}}_{a \to b}[j]} \frac{x^{t_{n-5}}_{a \to b}[j]}{x^{t_{n-3}}_{a \to b}[j]} \cdots \frac{x^{t_1}_{a \to b}[j]}{x^{t_3}_{a \to b}[j]} x^{t_2}_{b \to a}[j] = \frac{x^{t_1}_{a \to b}[j]}{x^{t_{n-1}}_{a \to b}[j]} x^{t_2}_{b \to a}[j]$$

The thread converges if $V^b_j(x^{t_{n-1}}_{a \to b}[j]) \geq V^b_j(x^{t_n}_{b \to a}[j])$, but given that V^b_j is monotonically decreasing, this happens only if $x^{t_n}_{b \to a}[j] < x^{t_{n-1}}_{a \to b}[j]$. Then, by substituting we get $\frac{x^{t_1}_{a \to b}[j]}{x^{t_{n-1}}_{a \to b}[j]} x^{t_2}_{b \to a}[j] < x^{t_{n-1}}_{a \to b}[j]$, that is $x^{t_1}_{a \to b}[j] x^{t_2}_{b \to a}[j] < (x^{t_{n-1}}_{a \to b}[j])^2$. But when time approaches t^a_{max} we have $\lim_{t \to t^a_{max}} x^t_{a \to b}[j] = min^a_j$ (by V^a_j being increasing). So, at the limit, if $x^{t_1}_{a \to b}[j] x^{t_2}_{b \to a}[j] < (min^a_j)^2$ the negotiation converges.

7 Related Work

Research in negotiation models has been pursued in different fields of knowledge: game theory, social sciences and artificial intelligence. Each field has concentrated on different aspects of negotiation, making the assumptions that were pertinent for the goal of their study. In game theory, researchers have been interested in mechanism design: the definition of protocols that limit the possible tactics (or strategies) that can be used by players. For instance they are interested in defining protocols that give no benefit to agents that mis-represent or hide information [9]. In this work disclosure of information is acceptable, because by doing so it will benefit the agent in finding an optimal solution for itself. Contrary to our model, and as we discussed in Section 2, this is an inappropriate assumption from the point of view of real applications. As has been argued elsewhere [10], these and other assumptions limit the applicability of game theory models to solve real problems.

Our interests lie in invertigating the process of negotiation among agents and not only on the outcome. Hence, our study, and those forthcoming, are much more in the experimental line of [4]. Although we do not concentrate on learning, some similarities can be found with the formalism by Zeng and Sycara [10]. We have not concentrated however on the description of negotiation protocols that has been an important focus of attention for the community of distributed artificial intelligence (see [7] for extensive references).

8   Discussion and Future Work

The next stage in the development of our model is to undertake an experimental evaluation of the tactics and strategies described herein. We believe adequate strategies have to be developed in accordance with the desired properties and characteristics of the domain at hand. These strategies then need to be tested in repeated games over a range of typical scenarios to determine which are the most successful. Some initial modeling of concrete strategies has been made considering several variables in the mental state of an agent: (i) an approximation of the first and second derivatives of the other agent's behaviour, (ii) the relation between both negotiating agents (e.g. members of the same company, boss/employee, ...), and (iii) the time remaining to reach an agreement (in this case time is playing a role at both strategic and tactic levels). This model is being used in the real modeling of the domain presented in Section 2. Currently there are two versions of the model implemented in CLIPS and PROLOG.

The initial results on convergence, although simple, encourage us to make a more complete analysis of the types of negotiation situations that are likely to occur.

We have identified many research opportunities in extending the model. For instance, fuzzy control techniques could be used to relate a qualitative estimate of the first and second derivatives of the opponent and a qualitative value for the β to be used in a tactic; we imagine a rule like: *If the agent concedes* quite a lot *(first derivative) and the agent concession ratio (second derivative)* increases *then Beta is* Medium. Genetic algorithms could also be used to determine experimentally which weighted combinations of tactics survive better in the line of [4]. Moreover, genetic algorithms may help to determine which negotiating agents show the desired behaviour by using the strategies as the genetic code. Finally, case-based reasoning could be used to model strategies. The case memory could be used by the agent to determine which past combinations of tactics worked best in similar circumstances.

9   Acknowledgements

This project has received the support of the Spanish Research projects DISCOR and SMASH SMASH (CICYT numbers, TIC94-0847-C 02-01 and TIC96-1038-C04001) and the DTI/EPSRC Intelligent Systems Integration Programme (ISIP) project ADEPT.

References

1. R. Axelrod. *The Evolution of Cooperation.* Basic Books, Inc., Publishers, New York, USA., 1984.
2. B. Crabtree and N.Jennings (eds.). *The Practical Application of Intelligent Agents and Multi-Agent Technology.* London, UK., 1996.
3. D. G.Pruitt. *Negotiation Behavior.* Academic Press, 1981.

4. A. Ito and H. Yano. The emergence of cooperation in a society of autonomous agents - the prisoner's dilemma gamme under the disclosure of contract histories. In Victor Lesser, editor, *Proceedings of the First International Conference on Multi-Agent Systems*, pages 201–208, San Francisco, USA, 1995. AAAI Press/The MIT Press.

5. N. R. Jennings, P. Faratin, M. J. Johnson, T. J. Norman, P. O'Brien, and M. E. Wiegand. Agent-based business process management. *Int Journal of Cooperative Information Systems*, 5(2–3):105–130, 1996.

6. S. Kraus, J. Wilkenfeld, and G. Zlotkin. Multiagent negotiation under time constraints. *Artificial Intelligence Journal*, 75(2):297–345, 1995.

7. H.J. Mueller. Negotiation principles. In G. M. P. O'Hare and N. R. Jennings, editors, *Foundations of Distributed Artificial Intelligence*, Sixth-Generation Computer Technology Series, pages 211–229, New York, 1996. John Wiley.

8. H. Raiffa. *The Art and Science of Negotiation*. Harvard University Press, Cambridge, USA, 1982.

9. J. S.Rosenschein and G. Zlotkin. *Rules of Encounter*. The MIT Press, Cambridge, USA, 1994.

10. D. Zeng and K. Sycara. How can an agent learn to negotiate. In J. Mueller, M. Wooldridge, and N. Jennings, editors, *Intelligent Agents III. Agent Theories, Architectures, and Languages*, number 1193 in LNAI, pages 233–244. Springer Verlag, 1997.

Competing Software Agents Support Human Agents

Sabine Geldof[1] and Walter Van de Velde[2]

[1] Vrije Universiteit Brussel
Artificial Intelligence Laboratory
Pleinlaan 2, B-1050 Brussels, Belgium
sabine@arti.vub.ac.be
http://arti.vub.ac.be
[2] StarLab
Riverland Next Generation
Excelsiorlaan 42, B-1930 Zaventem, Belgium
wvdv@starlab.net
http://www.starlab.net

Abstract. A community of interacting software agents can support an activity of human agents. We describe an experiment based on an existing information server showing how software agents compete for the attention of the user with the intention to support her in an information-rich task through providing her some useful comment. To be successful in the competition, agents have to capture contextual parameters about the current activity of the user and render them in a context-sensitive annotation to information. The outcome of the competition for attention consists of a weighted topic structure, annotated with text templates. The annotated topic structure is the basis for generating a context-sensitive navigation node by a process of template expansion and aggregation.

1 Introduction

1.1 Problem Statement: Context for Information

With the rapid increase of information available through networks the users of this information face the critical problem of getting the right information at the right time in the right form. A variety of tools are being developed to alleviate some of these problems, e.g. AltaVista, Yahoo! and their likes – allow for users to locate relevant information rapidly. The impressive exploratory power of such engines, however, does not compensate for the lack of precision in the retrieval. Clearly the Net knows too little of its user to perfectly serve its needs. Recent advances in human-computer interaction are promising serious enhancements in that respect, in particular through humanized interfaces and intelligent agents that act as personalised and adaptive assistants to the user. The underlying assumption is that contextual parameters must influence information provision. Context includes static models and highly dynamic parameters.

J.A. Padget (Ed.): Human and Artificial Societies, LNAI 1624, pp. 220–233, 1999.

Our research fits in a broader picture of what will be the future Net. We think of it as turning the network inside-out: rather than having users looking for information, a huge collection of agents (encapsulating information and services) looking for users. In a nutshell we emphasize that the user's attention is limited and that agents must compete for this attention, based on how they judge themselves relevant and competent to interact with that user in the context that this one finds herself in [1].

This paper proposes a scalable approach to realising the future Net by creating a virtual society where software agents compete for the attention of the user. In the experiment described here, the bridge between the artificial society and the human society takes the form of a context-sensitive comment on webpages viewed by the user.

1.2   Solution: Co-habited Mixed Reality

A co-habited mixed reality [2] consists of a pair of a real and a virtual space that are loosely coupled-there is a minimal awareness of one space within the other. The real world is inhabited by humans, whereas the virtual one is inhabited by software agents. The originality of this concept relies on the type of relationship between both realities, which also gives it its strength. Contrary to augmented-reality models, we are relieved from the task of establishing a mapping between both realities, or of trying any kind of perceptual integration. Instead, the processes in the two spaces must only serve each other, without the real participants having a feeling of virtual presence or the other way around. We only provide a personal link between both spaces, that ensures some form of " synchronization" so that the activities in one space further the ones in the other.

In the full blown version of a co-habited mixed reality, as aimed at in the COMRIS research project [1] the link is an electronic badge and earphone device which each participant wears as her personal assistant (e.g. while visiting a conference). It establishes a bidirectional link between both realities. It perceives what is going on around its host (conte xt perception) and points her to relevant information (information push). At the same time, a similar event is going on in the virtual space. The purpose of each agent is to represent, defend and further a particular interest or objective of the real part icipant, including those she is not explicitly attending to. The experiment described here explores a reduced version of a mixed reality by way of feasibility study. Here the link consists of automatically generated comments on webpages the user is actual ly looking at, adapted to the context of the user. Section 2 elaborates on the process of context perception. Section 3 treats the technical details of information push: generation of the comments. Section 4 situates our approach with respect to other ong oing research. The remainder of this section introduces the application and the agents active in the virtual space.

---

[1] Project COMRIS (Esprit LTR 25500, 97-2000) funded by the EU within the Long-Term Research initiative Intelligent Information Interfaces (I3 www.i3net.org). The views in this paper are not necessarily those of the COMRIS consortium.

1.3   Approach: Agents Competing for Attention

The experiment concerns an interactive information server for Brussels' summer movie festival, Ecran Total [3]. The user can find information about the movies on show in the festival, both regarding the contents and the practical issues. A typic al movie page of the existing information server is integrated in Fig. 1. The various page types are connected via hyperlinks. Figure 2 gives an overview of the navigation structure.

Our goal is to provide a user with an indication of why certain elements of information in the Ecran programme are considered useful in her current context. We propose to add a contextual frame to the existing information server. It provides the user wit h a context-sensitive navigation point, i.e., a hypertext node in which the relevance of hyperlinks is justified w.r.t. the context of the interaction. For example when the user intends to choose a movie to see that very evening, the list of movies showin g that day is obviously relevant. An advice agent may infer from that user's profile that she may particularly like one specific movie because her favorite actor plays in it. When the user does not live nearby the cinema, some information on how to get th ere may also be useful. This context might be reflected in a navigation node as "Several movies are showing today, but you may be particularly interested in Enfants Perdus, featuring Gérard Depardieu (you may check this opinion here). It shows at 8.30 in Arenberg Galeries (see map and public transportation)." The hyperlinks point to the actual information pages, while the text justifies the usefulness of the information or service with respec t to the context.

The extended interface of the Ecran Total information server (see Fig. 1) consists of 3 panes, one for the context-sensitive navigation point (context pane, top right), one for the existing information server (text pane, bottom right) and one for the topic structure (topic pane, left). The topic pane refers explicitly to the different aspects of the information. When clicking on items of the topic structure (cf. infra 2.1), the user gets in the context pane the context- sensitive navigation po int for that particular topic. The hyperlinks embedded in the context pane link to the various pages provided by the information service, and displayed in the text pane.

We will now explain how this comment generation results from agent inter- action in the virtual space. The basic idea in our approach to interfacing large scale networks to its users is to view it as a large collection of software agents competing for the users' attention. In general 'an agent is an electronic represen- tative of a particular interest' [4]. The agent has the purpose to serve (or defend) that interest, on behalf of its owner (not necessarily the user). Whereas a passive information system can not be said to have a goal of its own, in this view both user and system have their goals. Every software agent therefore needs to eval- uate its relevance for interacting with a particular user in a particular context. Moreover, every software a gent must consider its competence for doing so. For example, an agent may find it relevant to make a better offer on a product to a user, but if the price is already too low it can not.

Fig. 1. Three-pane window for a typical Ecran Total movie page. The context-pane supposes a user who is primarily interested in the contents of movies:*'La Fille Seule' tells the story of Valérie, on her first work day in a big hotel. Earlier tha t morning, she had a discussion with her boyfriend about the fact that she is pregnant...(for more details see the complete movie page).Some shots.It is part of category Inédits. The movie was produced by Benoît Jâcquot and will be shown on Wednesday, August 14th, 4.30pm at Arenberg Galeries.*

Consider the Ecran Total application as a collection of agents competing for the attention of the user. More precisely, there are six software agents: three information agents, and three task agents. Each of the three information agents is specialized in a particular aspect of the provided information (i.c. programmation, production or contents). These agents serve the interest of the information provider and compete to provide as much information as possible. For an information agent, the relevance is r elated to the expected usefulness of its topic in the context of the user. Competence is related to availability of the information (and therefore mostly constant in this application).

Task agents constitute a second class of agents providing a value-added service to the user (although they really serve the festival organizer's interest). The advice agent recommends from the programme those movies that a user may particularly like. The agenda agent maintains a user's movie-going agenda, and sends reminders for sessions that the user has indicated she wants to attend. The advertising agent, finally, throws teasers to the user about upcoming movies. All these agents compete for the atten tion of the user and will accordingly be able to contribute more or less to the comment to be generated.

Since agents have to evaluate their relevance and competence w.r.t. the context of the user, this context is a key issue, as well as the way in which elements of the user's context are captured. This is explained in the next section. Central to these pro cesses is the topic structure (cfr. 2.1) which is, first, weighted by observing the user's browsing behavior (2.2), and then accordingly annotated by the various agents (2.3) with the text templates that they want to communicate to the user.

2   Agent Competition Creates an Annotated Topic Structure

2.1   Topic Structure

The topic structure of an information server expresses what the information is all about. It is, in our demonstration, a hierarchical structure of topics and subtopics. The notion of topic structure is related to that of ontology, which has been proposed as an important modeling principle in the effort to reuse and share information or knowledge [5,6] and is also becoming a basic instrument in state of the art text generation systems [7]. The topic structure shows the objects of the d iscourse as the leaves of a tree hierarchy relating them through higher level concepts. Figure 2 shows how the topic structure for the Ecran application relates to the navigation structure of the server. Note that a single topic can be touched upon in multiple pages in the navigation structure. Similarly a single page does not necessarily correspond to a single topic.

For the Ecran festival, there are 3 main information topics about movies: programmation, production, contents. For instance, the information about when and where a particular movie will be shown belongs to the programmation aspect (particular to this fes tival), on the other hand, the plot of the movie or the

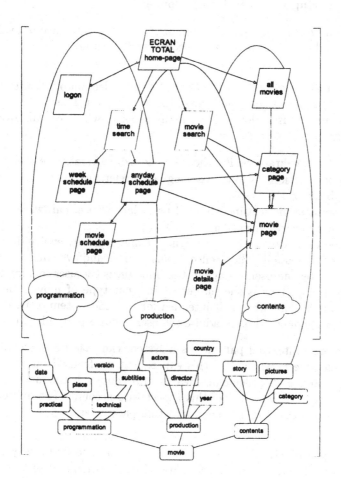

Fig. 2. Mapping of the navigation structure (top) on the topic structure (bottom) in the Ecran Total application.

category to which it belongs pertains to the contents of the movie, what can be told about the movie in a more general way. Details about the director, the year and place in which the movie has been realized constitute the production aspects.

2.2   Capturing and Rendering Context

In their competition for the attention of the user, agents have to evaluate their relevance and competence w.r.t. the context of the user.

Definition of 'context'. We call context the collection of features that determine the desirable content and form of the information. This context is obviously broader than the user alone. It has many aspects, which we can group along 3 dimensions:

- general user characteristics: those are more or less static, i.e. stable across different interaction sessions, like language preference, user acquaintance with the subject or the system;
- situation specific features: time of use, place of use, hardware and software used, weather conditions, and so on;
- teleological features: these are dynamic and typically evolve during a single interaction session. They reflect goals of user and system, i.e., what is the desired - by the user - usage of the info (eg. is the user looking for a movie to see tonigh t or is she interested in what type of movies the festival is providing?), and what is it intended for - by the system or its designer (eg. a system goal could be to advise the user about a particular movie to see) [2].

The more contextual parameters a system can take into account, the more context-sensitive it will be. In this experiment we focused on the user's topic preferences and goals (teleological features) because it is the most innovative for an information ser ver to take this aspect into account. The approach is such that it can be extended to other contextual parameters.

Capturing and Rendering 'Context'. We need to find a way of capturing the contextual parameters, to select useful information and services, and to tie them together in a coherent context-sensitive hypertext node. This node should reflect the proper balance between potentially relevant el ements.

The context is represented as a tri-dimensional space of which essential characteristics need to be captured through 'sensors'. In our experiment they are captured by observing the user's browsing behaviour in the catalog. Our setup allows for 2 ways to monitor the user's behaviour. Every click of the user in the topic pane increases the weight on the corresponding node in the topic structure. We thus assume that the nodes she clicks on are the topics she is most interested

---

[2] The idea of competing user and system goals appears also in [8] where the system goals need to be pursued opportunistically wrt user goals.

in. After some time of interac tion in that way, the profile of the user is expressed as weights on the branches of the topic structure. The second way to capture context parameters occurs while the user freely navigates through the catalog: her clicks on particular pages can also be r elated to the main topics, as the mapping in Fig. 2 (navigation- topic structure) suggests. Note that we defined for every page type in the catalog which topics are represented on it. The user's monitored behavior is used as an indication of t opic preferences and user goals, and reflects as weights on the topic structure.

Context representation creates the framework for a competition amongst agents. In principle the collection of agents is an open one. In this experiment 6 agents come into play, competing for 'doing their thing' to the user. The outcome of the competition is an annotated topic structure: each topic node is linked to text templates and schemata, contributed by the various agents. These are the basis for putting the information in context, for example by expressing what features of the user's context deem a particular page interesting or useful to the user. Finally, the annotated topic structure is expanded into a full-blown hyper-text by the aggregation of the templates. The recursive depth of the aggregation is, in turn, determined by the weights on the to pic structure. In this way, the user feedback drives the dynamics of the whole system.

The following figure summarizes our approach:

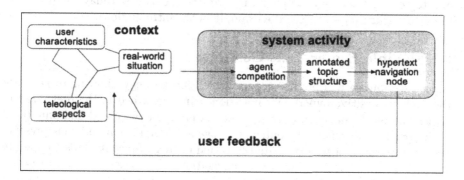

Fig. 3. Overview of our approach to generate context-sensitive navigation points.

2.3   From Weighted to Annotated Topic Structure

The weighted topic structure reflects, at each moment, the user's preferred topics and, indirectly, her objectives. These weights can be used in a straightforward manner by the agents to evaluate their relevance scores. For example, when a topic has received a high weight, the corresponding information agent will be obviously relevant. When a user goal relates to a particular information agent, this agent will also have a high relevance score. The story is slightly more complicated for the task agents. Topic weights capture topic preferences of the user during a session. These do not, however, indicate directly what this user is up to. We assume that, whenever the information needs of a task agent overlap significantly with the topics that the user seems interested in, the agent and user have similar objectives. This will increase the relevance of the corresponding task agent.

Competence values are usually more agent-specific. For the information agents it depends on availability of information. Since they all have a similar amount of information about all the movies of the festival, their competence score is stable. Since the advice agent works by comparing user profiles its competence depends on the size of the present user's profile. In other words, if the agent knows little about a user it can not give good advice, although doing so may be relevant. Similar analyses can be made for the other task agents.

Based on competence and relevance values agents decide what they want to say about a particular topic. In this way, the topic structure is annotated with various text templates, contributed by the different agents. For example, if the production agent finds it particularly relevant for this user to say something about the producer it will annotate the 'production' topic with the template 'Note that' to complete the standard text template 'the movie was produced by (director) in (year) in (country)' (cfr. infra). Task agents will contribute their own topic structure, for example for referring to the 'best of today's movies' and the actors featuring in it (see the example in the introduction).

3 Flexible Hyper-Text Generation

In this section we will propose a text generation strategy allowing to generate the context-sensitive hypertext navigation-points described in the previous sections. The text generation strategy takes as input the weighted and annotated topic structure to reflect the outcome of agents' competition and thus presents the information in a way that fits the actual context. Since it needs to operate in the (real-time) application area of navigation and browsing, the strategy has to satisfy one major requirement: efficiency. Given the state of the art in text generation technology, it is not advisable to use full text generation, neither at sentence nor at discourse level. It has been argued in several places [9,10] that using templates in combination with text generation techniques is a promising approach. This hypothesis has been confirmed in practise by well-known hypertext generation systems [8,11] a.o. Also at the discourse level, the pay-off of performing text planning versus using text schemata would be negative, at least in the application we envisage, the text structuring task is stereotypical and can be captured in a schema as exemplified below.

3.1 Templates and Schema for Ecran

Thus at sentence level, we will define templates to present information about the ontology concepts. These will be combined (at discourse level) according to a (text) schema based on the topic structure. The topic structure annotated with templates for ou r application is shown in Fig. 4.

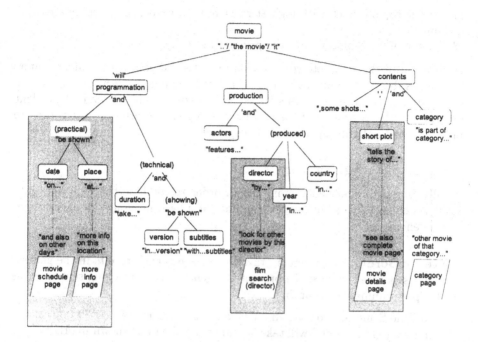

Fig. 4. Topic structure with text templates for the Ecran Total application.

It is a schema, as defined in [12], i.e. a "frozen text plan" in which every growth point (node) is optional. In this application, most nodes correspond to the ontology concepts, but this is not necessarily the case. The schema could be more exten sive than the topic structure or it could be that not all the nodes of the topic structure correspond to an expansion node. In our application some leaf nodes point further to additional information pages, which are also introduced by a text template.

The schema contains the maximum text plan, i.e. the text that would be realised if all agents were allowed to maximally contribute to the text. The agent competition determines how this schema is pruned. The weights allocated by the agents to each of the topic branches (as a result of their relevance and competence score), determine first their relative importance and ranking, and secondly, the degree of expansion of each topic branch. By these mechanisms a balanced text will be produced. Text templates are accumulated as the branches of the tree are traversed in a depth-first way. The order of the branches is free in principle. However, as stated in [12], an additional control mechanism is required for ordering components of a text plan. What Hov y defines as the focus, 'the locus of the principal inferential effort needed to understand the text' corresponds to our information agents' competition score.

Concretely, the algorithm for pruning the topic structure goes as follows:

1. for the topic branch with highest relevance score: realize the complete topic sub-tree
2. for the other topics: realize the primary leaf only.

Realization of the complete subtree also includes the pointers to further information, as shown on some leaf nodes of the topic-template structure (Fig. 4). To make the algorithm more sophisticated, this feature could be made dependent on a pa rticular threshold of the score of the topic. The primary leaf nodes are indicated on the figure by a dotted background.

3.2   Template Aggregation

Finally, linguistic knowledge is needed in order to combine the templates into valid sentences. This brings us to a number of interesting issues in natural language generation.

Sentence Border. In principle, traversal of each branch results in the generation of a separate sentence. To prevent the generation of too long sentences, as in the 'programmation' branch:

> 'La Fille Seule' will be shown on Wednesday, August 14th, 4.30 p.m. at Arenberg Galeries and will take 90 minutes and will be shown in original version with Dutch subtitles.

principles for additional sentence borders (e.g. no second 'and' in one sentence) need to be introduced in the traversal procedure.

Conjunction, Ellipsis. Some annotations [3] of non-leaf nodes are related to conjunction and ellipsis. The topic tree of our example illustrates several types of conjunction, either without coordination mark, with a comma, or with a conjunction (e.g. 'and'). Coordination marks are encoded as annota tions of a coordinating arch, to be realised, just as the templates, when the node is traversed. A special type of annotation occurs on top of a node, as with the 'programmation' node. This template fragment ('will') needs to be realised whenever a subord inate 'and' is realised. Consider the example:

> 'La Fille Seule' will take 90 minutes and *will* be shown in original version with Dutch subtitles.

This corresponds to an aspect of the linguistic phenomenon called ellipsis, that we rather regard as an exception to the aggregation rule (stating which parts of sentences can be omitted when sentences are combined): *will* is not considered as a redu ndant text element in the second sentence and can thus not be 'eliminated'.

---

[3] In Fig. 4 surrounded by single quotes ('..')

Nominalization. Another mechanism that characterizes naturally produced text is the usage of referring expressions. People tend to use different expressions to refer to the same object. Computer programs are not designed to cope with this. The phenomenon has been object of extensive research (e.g. see [13]). At present, our system can do with a basic strategy by introducing the possibility to define alternative templates. For instance, a principle of decreasing specificity is applied: after using the concrete movi e title ("La Fille Seule"), the nominal ("the movie") and pronominal realization ("it") create a natural chain of referring expressions. Applying this principle results in the following text:

'La Fille Seule' will be shown on Wednesday, August 14th, 4.30 p.m. at Arenberg Galeries and will take 90 minutes. The movie will be shown in original version with Dutch subtitles. It was produced by Benoît Jâcquot.

Referring expressions become a real issue when more than one object needs to be referred to. For being able to cope with such cases we will have to extend our strategy. Obviously alternative templates allow also for a greater stylistic variation, e.g. 'b e projected' could be an alternative for 'be shown' without imposing too much burden on the generation process.

4   Related Work

The different aspects of our work relate it to as many other approaches in various fields. Context-sensitivity is an important concern in natural language generation (NLG) systems, but the focus is often very much on the linguistic context: the need for coherence with the preceding discourse. A good overview is provided in [14]. The emergence of wearable technologies both requires and supports the need for extra-linguistic context capturing, e.g. for a wearable museum guide [15]. NLG systems have also recognized very early the importance of the user model [16], focusing mainly on the user's level of expertise. More recent work takes into account a more dynamic model of the user's expertise by tracing her browsing behaviour and adapti ng object descriptions to earlier visited hypertext nodes [17]. Our approach aims at capturing the extra-linguistic context of the user, including its most dynamic aspects, i.e. her minute-to-minute evolving intentions. The mechanism of competition for attention constitues an innovative way of treating the user's context. It can be compared with opportunistic NLG in [18], where system goals compete with user goals in order to generate at each moment the most effective museum object descripti on. The set-up of a virtual (agent) society allows us to scale this competition to large numbers of competing interests and to introduce the notion of community-ware: virtual societies supporting humans in social processes [19]. In that sense our a pproach also differs from agent systems focusing on rational and belief-based agent modeling [20].

5   Conclusion

In this paper we have outlined an approach toward context-sensitive navigation in large information spaces. It claims that natural language is ideally suited to express in a compact and balanced way why a collection of information pages are relevant to th e user in the context that she is using the system in. We have illustrated this idea with an example application, based on an existing information service. The key to our approach is a model of competition for attention between software agents, the outcom e of which is reflected in a weighted topic structure, annotated with text templates. The annotated topic structure is the basis for generating a context-sensitive navigation node.

Several issues remain to be further investigated. First, all the elements of the current system (pages, topic structure, agents) have been properly designed to work together. However, to realize the full vision of the future network, our mechanisms shoul d be able to cope with open-ended and larger collections of pages, topics and agents. This will require additional mechanisms (from natural language research and others) to dynamically generate the relations between topic structures, navigation structure and agents.

A second direction is to exploit the notion of ontology to a fuller extent. It is clear that, the more a system knows about the universe of discourse, the more accurate it can render the context to the user. Ontologies typically reflect such elements as r elations between concepts, constraints on them, all of which can be (and are) exploited for better text production.

Related to the previous is the challenge of using more advanced text generation techniques. Extensive use of aggregation, for example, must be combined with co-referencing techniques to avoid repetitions and overly explicit sentences. A deeper understandi ng of the user's goals, and the relations with the agent goals, must allow to offer added-value services in pertinent ways. Future work will also emphasize the historical nature of the context pane: it should not only reflect the short-term context relate d to a single click, but capture the rationale of a longer series of interactions during a session.

Acknowledgments. This work is supported by the MAGICA and COMRIS projects, funded by the European Union program Telematics Engineering (IE2069, LTR25500). Additional funding is provided by the NMS project, funded by IWT, and the project SACEA funded by the Belgian Office of Scientific, Technical and Cultural Affairs. Walter Van de Velde holds an honorary position as senior researcher for the Flemish Science Foundation (FWO).

References

1. Van de Velde, W., Geldof, S., Schrooten, R.: Competition for Attention. In: Singh, M.P., Rao, A.S., Wooldridge, M.J.(eds.): Proceedings of the 4th ATAL. Lecture Notes in Artificial Intelligence, Springer-Verlag, Heidelberg, Germany (1998) 282–296
2. Van de Velde, W.: Co-Habited Mixed Realities. Proc. of IJCAI'97, Nagoya, Japan (1997) 00–00
3. Geldof, S.: Hyper-text generation from databases on the Internet. In Proceedings of the 2nd International Workshop on applications of Natural Language to Information Systems- NLDB, IOS Press, Amsterdam (1996) 102–114

4. Van de Velde, W.: Mediation Agents in Multi-Party Decision Making: An Experiment. In Proceedings of the First International Conference on the practical application of intelligent agents and multi-agent technology (PAAM'96) PAP, Blackpool, UK. (1996) 629– 654
5. Gruber, T.: A Translation Approach to Portable Ontology Specifications. Knowledge Acquisition, 1993(5) 199–220
6. Benjamin, J., Borst, P., Akkermans, J.M., Wielinga, B. J.: Ontology Construction for Technical Domains. In: Shadbolt, N.R., O'Hara, K., Schreiber, A.Th. (eds.): Advances in Knowledge Acquisition; Proceedings of the Ninth European Knowledge A cquisition Workshop EKAW '96. Springer-Verlag Berlin Heidelberg New York (1996) 98–114
7. Sheremetyeva, S., Nirenburg, S.: Knowledge elicitation for authoring patent claims. Computer, **29(7)** (1996) 57–64
8. Knott, A., Mellish, C., Oberlander, J., O'Donnel, M.: Sources of Flexibility in Dynamic Hypertext Generation. In proceedings of the 8th Int. Workshop on Natural Language Generation, Herstmonceux, East-Sussex (1996) 151-160
9. Reiter, E.: NLG vs. Templates. In Proceedings of the 5th European Workshop on Natural Language Generation (EWNLG'95) Leiden, The Netherlands (1995) 95-106
10. Busemann, S., Horacek, H.: A Flexible Shallow Approach to Text Generation. In Proceedings of the 9th Int. Workshop on Natural Language Generation, Niagara-on-the-Lake, Canada (1998) 238-247
11. Cawsey, A.: Personalised Explanations for Patient Education. In Proceedings of the Fifth European Workshop on Natural Language Generation, Leiden, The Netherlands (1995) 59-74
12. Hovy, E.: Automated Discourse Generation Using Discourse Structure Relations. Artificial Intelligence **63** (1993) 341-385.
13. Dale, R.: Generating referring expressions. MIT Press, Cambridge, MA (1992)
14. van Deemter, K., O'Dijk, J.: Context Modeling for Language and Speech Generation. In Proceedings of the International and Interdisciplinary Conference on Modeling and Using Context, Univ. Fed. do Rio de Janeiro. Brazil. (1997) 75-86
15. Not, E., Zancanaro, M.: Content Adaptation for Audio-based Hypertext in Physical Environments. In Proceedings of the 2nd Workshop on Adaptive Hypertext and Hypermedia, Pittsburgh, USA (1998)
16. Paris, C.: Tailoring Object Descriptions to a user's level of expertise. Computational Linguistics, **Vol. 14, 3** (Sept. 1988)
17. Milosavljevic, M., Tulloch, A., Dale, R.: Text Generation in a Dynamic Hypertext Environment. In Proceedings of the 19th Australasian Computer Science Conference, Melbourne, Australia (1996)
18. Mellish, C., O'Donnell, M., Oberlander, J., Knott, A.: An Architecture for Opportunistic Text Generation. In Proceedings of the 9th Int. Workshop on Natural Language Generation, Niagara-on-the-Lake, Canada (1998) 28-37
19. Ishida, T.(ed): Community Computing - Collaboration over Global Information Networks. John Wiley & Sons (1998)
20. Rao, A.S., Georgeff, M.P.: BDI Agents: From Theory to Practice. In: Lesser, V. (ed.) Proceedings of the First International Conference on Multi-Agent Systems (ICMAS-95). AAI Press/The MIT Press. Menlo Park-Cambridge-London (1995) 312 – 319.

Coordination Developed by Learning from Evaluations

Edwin D. de Jong

Artificial Intelligence Laboratory
Vrije Universiteit Brussel
Pleinlaan 2, B-1050 Brussels, Belgium
tel: +32 2 629 37 00
fax: +32 2 629 37 29
edwin@arti.vub.ac.be

Abstract. This paper reports on research into the origins of communication and coordination. Several problems with defining communication and coordination are noted. A research methodology is described that circumvents these problems. The methodology is used in an experiment concerning the development of coordination. The aim of the experiment is to see whether a learning agent can use *coordination signals*, which represent evaluations of its behavior, to learn to coordinate its actions in an unknown environment. The task is a pursuit problem where four agents are needed to capture a randomly moving prey. One of these agents adapts its behavior based on the coordination signals it receives from the three other agents. The development of coordination increased the capture rate in this pursuit problem from an initial 5% to 93%. Thus, in combination with a general learning mechanism, coordination signals may be sufficient for the development of coordination.

1 Introduction

The work reported in this paper is part of Luc Steels' programme of research into the origins of language, in which principles are investigated that may explain how languages develop, see e.g. [16,18,5]. From an evolutionary point of view, the development of communication may be explained by the increased potential for coordinated action that comes with it. Since these two phenomena are interrelated, we study them in combination.

en applied to an experiment where an agent adapts its behavior such that the coordination between its actions and the actions of the other agents improves considerably.

Ultimately, our aim is to let agents autonomously develop communication which improves the coordination they may develop between their actions. In the experiments reported here, communication does not develop, but is fixed by the experimenter. A risk with designing a fixed system of communication is that it constrains the response patterns of agents, thus limiting their ability to adapt. To avoid this, the signals agents send are as basic as possible. They are real values

J.A. Padget (Ed.): Human and Artificial Societies, LNAI 1624, pp. 234–245, 1999.
© Springer-Verlag Berlin Heidelberg 1999

between zero and one representing the quality of the coordination between the sender and the receiver of the signal. These *coordination signals*, which were proposed in [4], are sent by some of the agents to a subset of the agents. An agent that receives these signals may interpret them as evaluations of its own actions. Using this information, it can learn to select actions that, given the situation, yield high evaluations. The aim of this research is to determine whether these basic coordination signals are sufficient for developing co ordination. The experiments reported in this paper concern the development of coordination in the Pursuit Problem described in [1].

The structure of the paper is as follows. First, several difficulties with defining communication are noted. Following these considerations, a research methodology is described that despite of these problems enables the investigation of communication, and analogously of coordination. In section 3, the pursuit problem and the learning agent are described. Section 4 contains the results of the experiments, and the final section contains conclusions and future work.

2 Methodology

2.1 Defining Communication

In this subsection, several possibilities are considered on which definitions of communication might be based.

Advantage When one attempts to define communication, an idea that might spring to mind is that communication allows one agent to influence the behavior of another agent, causing some benefit. It can easily be seen though that this is problematic. As an example, consider two people who are dining in a restaurant. After a while, the waiter asks if they have been able to make a choice, upon which both of them inform the waiter of their selection. The waiter hears and understands both answers. When he brings in the food, he puts down one of the plates, but just before serving the other guest, he stumbles and thereby drops the food right over the clothes of the second guest. If communication depends on advantage to the signaler, only one of the guests has communicated in this scenario. In our view however, both guests have communicated with the waiter. Although I assume that communication has evolved by virtue of its selective advantage, this does not imply that *all* communication has some advantage to the signaler or his group.

Probability of Advantage These considerations may lead one to a more refined definition by relaxing the condition of advantage to its statistical probability. The result of this would be a definition similar to that from [2] used in [11]:

> Communication is the phenomenon of one organism producing a signal that, when responded to by another organism, confers some advantage (or the statistical probability of it) to the signaler or his group.

Although this definition is more precise than our first attempt, the central concept of advantage does not clarify the *nature* of communication. This can be appreciated more readily by considering the analogy of using the criterion of evolutionary ad vantage for defining communication, given by Ezequiel Di Paolo in [6]: 'We do not *define* "wings" in terms of their selective advantages even if we may *explain* their presence in those terms.'

Information Several definitions of communication use "information", see e.g. [7], p.7. In [15], a sound and generally accepted definition of information has been given. Although this definition does provide a formalization of information, it does not directly lead to a solid definition of communication since part of the information in messages can be implicit, i.e. can only be interpreted successfully in the light of the context. The context is here taken to include the history of interaction between the sender and the receiver as well as the knowledge they have in common. Shannon defines information as a decrease in uncertainty. With this definition, the presence of inf ormation in a message implies that the uncertainty in the knowledge of the receiver decreases. A problem with (human) communication is, that often, part of the information in a message is implicit. Therefore, the presence or the amount of information in a message cannot be determined by an outside observer. We will illustrate this using another example.

A couple is sitting in a room with a clock on the wall that is visible to both of them. They have an appointment, and need to leave around nine o'clock. The woman now says "It's nine o'clock." to remind the man of their appointment. If this message is i nterpreted literally, it contains no information, since the receiver of the message had already seen the time at the clock. The real message was that the man should not forget their appointment, and prepare to leave. The information conveyed by this message was implicit and might not have been recognized by an outside observer, since outside observers can generally not be assu med to have complete knowledge of the context in which communication has taken place. Determining the decrease of uncertainty caused by an implicit message is difficult when the context that determines this implicit meaning is unknown to the observer. Apa rt from the problem of implicit meaning, even determining the informational content of the explicit meaning of a message is seldom susceptible to mathematical analysis.

Meaning In contrast with [12], which deals with the relationship between meaning and words, we do not exclude asymbolic expressions, such as the dance of a bee, or the pheromone trail of ants indicating the presence of food. These signals can also be s een as having a meaning, since they reveal information to the receiver that is able to understand them.

In the above, it has become clear that the meaning of a message can sometimes refer to implicit information, and at other times to explicit information. Thus, one might say that communication is the successful transfer of *meaning* from one agent to one or more other agents. On second thought, the notion of meaning only complicates matters. An obvious problem is that it raises the question of how meaning should be defined. However, this is overshadowed by a more fundamental issue. The definition requires that both agents attribute the same meaning to (the constituent parts of) a message. But, at least for human communication, the meaning of words differs among persons. This is because people learn the meaning of most words by encountering them in several contexts. The contexts in which two people have encountered a word are never exactly equal. Even a relatively clear concept, such as "wood", evokes different associations for a lumberjack and a carpenter.

2.2   Description of the Methodology

In the literature, many different definitions of communication have been proposed. One reason may be that each researcher's concept of communication is shaped by experience in a particular field of research. This affects the definitions that are proposed, and thus we end up with definitions that do not capture a generally accepted conception of communication. Furthermore, as we have seen above, even a nonoperational, descriptive definition that truly captures the nature of communication is not obvious.

Instead of looking for a single general and operational definition that determines the presence of communication or coordination in all its appearances, one might well ask whether such a definition is necessary in order to investigate these phenomena. For scientific experiments, what is important is to have objective, testable criteria. The fact that a general operational definition is not available does not imply that we cannot use such criteria. The solution we adopt is to focus on finding operationa l criteria specific to experimental conditions. In many situations, an outside observer can observe indications that communication or coordination takes place. We use the term *measures* for such observable indications. Measures are defined quantitatively and can thus be determined exactly. Using these measures, researchers can investigate communication in many different types of experiments, even though a general definition of communication is not available. Within the origins of language programme, measures are used extensively, see e.g. [17], [8]; furthermore, see [11].

Another way to test whether agents communicate is to replicate the supposedly communicative behavior. If this induces the predicted effect, it indicates that the behavior under consideration was indeed used for communication. This method has been demonstrated convincingly in an investigation of communication among vervet monkeys [14]. Alarm calls produced by the monkeys on seeing different classes of predators were recorded. When replayed, these sound caused the monkeys to respectively look down for snake alarms, run into trees for leopard alarms, and look up for eagle alarms.

2.3   Defining Coordination

With coordination, a similar definition problem as with communication arises. It is intuitively clear that coordination involves agents that adjust their actions according to their expectations of the behavior of other agents. But whether two (or more) agents coordinate their actions cannot be determined with certainty by an external observer. Analogous to our solution for the aforementioned definition, I propose to look for observable criteria specific to the experimental conditions that indicate to what extent coordination takes place.

It is important to notice that the detection of coordination is no guarantee for the outside observer that some form of communication must have taken place. In other words, coordination without communication is also possible. Good examples of coordination without communication, based on bias towards of *focal points* (points that draw more attention than other points), are given in [9] and [10].

3   Learning to Coordinate

In the experiments, agents have to solve the *pursuit problem* as defined in [19], which was introduced in [1]. Two types of agents are distinguished. Agents of the first type have knowledge about their environment. The other type of agent does not have this knowledge, but should develop appropriate behavior by learning from coordination signals. In this particular environment, agents need to capture a random moving prey. Agents of the first type know that:

- they need to capture a prey
- to capture a prey, they have to coordinate their actions with both of their neighbors. This coordination consists of striving for a low average distance to the prey and an appropriate spreading angle between themselves and their neighbors.

They choose their actions by maximizing the coordination with both of their neighbors. In [4], it has been shown that if four agents with this coordination knowledge would be present, they would nearly always be able to catch the prey. However, only three of these hunting agents are present. Since three agents cannot capture a prey (all its neighbors in the four-connected sense need to be occupied), a fourth agent is needed. This fourth agent is of the second type, and is put into the environment without any knowledge about the hunting task. It is a learning agent, and it receives the same information as the hunting agents, but doesn't know its meaning. It only knows that the coordination signals it receives are to be treated as evaluations, and that it should adapt its behavior in order to maximize these evaluations.

In accordance with the methodology described in the first part of this paper, we define a problem specific measure that indicates whether coordination takes place or not. This measure is the capture rate, i.e. the fraction of the games that ends in a capt ure. It allows us to investigate whether coordination is learned by monitoring its development over time and by comparing the capture rate of the learning agent with that of a random moving agent.

Coordination signals are sent by the hunting agents to both of their neighbors. An agent's neighbor is the agent that is first encountered when the environment

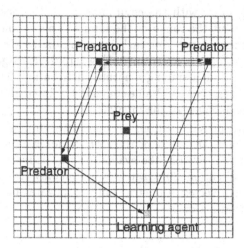

Fig. 1. The Pursuit Problem. Predators send coordination signals to both of their radial neighbors, and so the learning agent receives two signals

is scanned along lines starting from the prey and crossing a point that moves away from the agent at a constant distance to the prey in one of the two poss ible directions (i.e. clockwise or counterclockwise). This implies that the learning agent will nearly always receive two signals, one representing the coordination with its left neighbor and one representing the coordination with its right neig- bor. The only exception to this occurs when a hunter and the learning agent are in line with the prey, in which case the other two hunting agents might both choose the hunter as their neighbor instead of the learning agent, which will in that case not receive a coordination signal.

We will now describe the technical details of the learning experiments. At each timestep, the learning agent receives as input the cartesian coordinates of all agents (including its own). Thus, it receives ten numbers. The agent does not know the domain of the inputs in advance (i.e. the inputs are not scaled). It can select one out of 5 possible actions: moving one posistion up, down, to the left or to the right, or staying. After selecting an action, it receives coordination signals from its neighbors. These signals, usually two in number, are values between 0 and 1 and the difference between two subsequent values is used for learning. The task of the agent can thus be described as a reinforcement learning problem; it needs to learn the value of actions depen ding on the situation, and it has to select actions based on this knowledge. We now describe these two aspects in more detail.

3.1 Learning

The agent uses a standard backpropagation neural network [13] to learn. Each input is represented by a corresponding input neuron. As was mentioned above, the agent is not familiar with the environment, and is therefore not provided with kn owledge about the range of the inputs. This problem is addressed by adaptively scaling each input. For each input, statistics are maintained. Using these statistics, each input is scaled to [0..1], where the average value of the input is mapped onto 0.5 a nd, assuming a normal distribution, 0.0 and 1.0 represent $\mu - 2\sigma$ and $\mu + 2\sigma$ respectively. Values outside the interval $[\mu - 2\sigma..\mu + 2\sigma]$ are clipped to the closest bound of the interval.

Each of the five possible actions is represented by an output neuron. An output neuron predicts the value of the corresponding action. The value of an action is the difference between the evaluation that is received after the action and the previous evalu ation. Since action selection only yields information about the action that was selected, the error only propagates back from the neuron corresponding to that action.

3.2   Action Selection

This function selects the action the agent takes, based on the value of each action according to the learning function. Merely choosing the action with the highest estimated value at each timestep results in poor performance. Using that policy, actions wh ich as a result of the random initial weights of the network have low initial predicitions would never be selected. If this lowest action corresponds for example to 'moving left', then the agent will never, except by side effects due to generalization, be able to go to the left. Therefore, this will not lead to an optimal solution. The solution is to use exploration. In [3], a new algorithm for finding a balance between exploration and exploitation has been introduced. This algorithm, called t he *Exploration Buckets algorithm*, fills a bucket for each action with a value proportional to the error in the prediction of the value of the action (i.e. the evaluation it will yield) when it was last selected. Additionally, the increment of the bu cket is influenced by the average prediction error of all actions. This ensures that changes in the environment also stimulate exploration of actions with a low predicted value and consequently a low probability of being selected. The increase of the bucket is multiplied by a factor that determines the general influence of exploration. When the agent has to select an action, it chooses the one with the highest sum of predicted value and bucket. The bucket of this selected action is emptied. Furthermore, the difference between the prediction of the value for the action is compared to the real evaluation the agent receives; this difference consitutes the prediction error, which is stored now and used in subsequent timesteps to fill the action's bucket. This algorithm combines recency-based and error-based properties [20], and h as the advantage that it can be used for online learning. Many other exploration methods lack this last property since they depend on a decreasing influence of randomness over time.

4 Results

An experiment lasting 2,000 pursuit games was carried out. Initially, before the learning agent has learned anything, a capture occurs in 5% of the games. This has been determined by setting the learning factor α of the learning agent's neural net work to zero, and averaging the number of captures over a hundred games. The reason for this poor performance is, that the agent initially has a random prediction of the value of each action, since the weights of its neural network are randomly initialize d. The action with the highest initial prediction is thus selected far more often than the other actions (these are still selected sometimes because the buckets algorithm explores other actions too). Likewise, the second highest is selected more often tha n the remaining actions. As a result of this, the agent has a preference for a certain corner of the grid. This decreases the chance of a capture considerably. For comparison, we also replaced the agent by a random agent. Now, on average 29% of the games resulted in a capture. The reason for this surprisingly high score, is that the 3 predators with coordination knowledge 'drive' the prey into the arms of the random agent because they surround it and thus constrain the directions in which the prey can move. This is because the prey randomly selects between moving to one of the empty positions surrounding it (and staying).

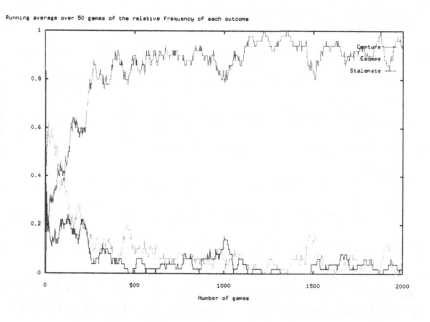

Fig. 2. The relative number of captures increases over time as the agent learns to coordinate its actions based on the coordination signals it receives from its neighbors

The neural network of the learning agent has 1 hidden layer with 15 neurons. The learning rate is 0.15, and no momentum is used. The influence of exploration, called exploration factor, is 0.5. During learning, the performance of the agents steadily incre ases. Figure 2 shows the running average over 50 games of the relative number of games that end in Capture, Escape and Stalemate. For definitions of these concepts, see [19]. After about a hundred games, the agents more often capture the pre y than letting it escape. In figure 3, the total number of games that has ended in a capture is shown. After about 120 games, the number of captures exceeds both the number of escapes and the number of stalemates. After 150 games, the agents capture the p rey in the majority of the games. Still, the learning agent keeps increasing its coordination by learning the results of its actions ever more accurately. After 500 games, the agents averagely capture the prey in 90% of the cases. From that moment on, th e coordination the agent has learned is stable. Between the 1000th and 2000th game, 925 games result in a capture, i.e. 93% of the games. This is considerably higher than the 29% that was achieved by the random moving agent, and thus we may conclude tha t the agent has learned to coordinate its behavior with that of the other agents.

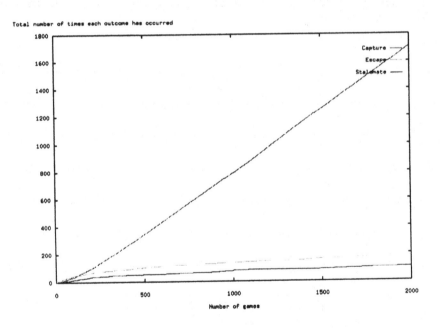

Fig. 3. The total number of captures steadily increases over time. After 125 games, the total number of captures exceeds the total number of escapes

5   Conclusions and Future Work

A methodology for investigating communication and coordination has been described that circumvents the difficulties with defining these concepts. It comprises defining operational criteria specific to a domain, called measures, that allow experimental inv estigation of the phenomena.

Using this methodology, the development of coordination has been studied in a pursuit problem. The purpose was to investigate whether coordination signals are sufficient for the development of coordination. In this domain, the capture rate is a good measu re of whether coordination takes place or not. We have presented the results of experiments where a single learning agent has to adapt its behavior based on evaluations of its coordination with the other three agents that are present. Initially, the learn ing agent, together with the other agents, captures the prey in only 5% of the cases, even less than a random agent; in the other cases, the prey either escapes or encounters a stalemate. Then, it learns to accurately predict the evaluations it receives. After sufficient experience, the learning agent has adjusted its behavior successfully, causing a substantial increase in coordination. Eventually, after several hundreds of games, this results in stable coordination where the agents capture the prey in 93% of the cases. Thus, coordination signals, although very basic in nature, have been demonstrated to be sufficient in this domain to allow an agent to learn to coordinate its behavior with that of other agents.

In these experiments, communication was determined by the investigator and consisted of numerical evaluations of coordination, called coordination signals. Current and future work does not assume the prior existence of communication, but instead investiga tes how communication and coordination may develop simultaneously.

6   Acknowledgements

The author wants to thank Luc Steels for invaluable discussions about the ideas that are fundamental to this work, Bart de Boer for comments on an earlier version, and Paul Vogt and Frederic Kaplan for useful discussions and suggestions. This research was partially funded by EU Telematics Information Engineering projects MAGICA and GEOMED. GEOMED (IE 2037) stands for 'Geographical mediation systems'. MAGICA (IE 2069) stands for 'Multi-Media Agent-based Interactive Catalogs'. Additional funding has been pr ovided by an OZR contract for research on *models for coordination and competition in multi agent systems*.

References

1. M. Benda, V. Jagannathan, and R. Dodhiawalla. On optimal cooperation of knowledge sources. Technical Report BCS-G2010-28, Boeing AI Center, 1988.
2. G. M. Burghardt. Defining 'communication'. In J. Johnston, D. Moulton, and A. Turk, editors, *Communication by Chemical Signals*, pages 5–18, New York, 1970. NY: Appleton-Century-Crofts.

3. E. D. de Jong. An accumulative exploration method for reinforcement learning. In *Proceedings of the AAAI'97 Workshop on Multiagent Learning, available as AAAI Technical Report WS-97-03*, July 1997.

4. E. D. de Jong. Multi-agent coordination by communication of evaluations. In M. Boman and W. V. de Velde, editors, *Proceedings of the 8th European Workshop on Modelling Autonomous Agents in a Multi-Agent World MAAMAW'97*, Berlin, 1997. Springer Verlag.

5. E. D. de Jong and P. Vogt. How Should a Robot Discriminate Between Objects? A comparison between two methods. In *Proceedings of the Fifth International Conference of The Society for Adaptive Behavior SAB'98*, volume 5, Cambridge, MA, 1998. The MIT Press.

6. E. A. Di Paolo. Social coordination and spatial organization: Steps towards the evolution of communication. In P. Husbands and I. Harvey, editors, *Proceedings of the 4th European Conference on Artificial Life ECAL'97*, Cambridge, MA, 1997. The MIT Press/Bradford Books.

7. M. D. Hauser. *The evolution of communication*. The MIT Press, Cambridge, MA, 1997.

8. F. Kaplan. A new approach to class formation in multi-agent simulations of language evolution. In *Proceedings of the Third International Conference on Multi Agent Systems ICMAS'98*. IEEE Computer Society Press, 1998.

9. S. Kraus and J. Rosenschein. The role of representation in interaction: Discovering focal points among alternative solutions. *Decentralized Artificial Intelligence III*, 1992.

10. S. K. M. Fenster and J. Rosenschein. Coordination without communication: Experimental validation of focal point techniques. In V. Lesser, editor, *Proceedings of the First International Conference on Multi-Agent Systems ICMAS'95*, San Francisco, California, USA, 12–14 June 1995. AAAI Press/The MIT Press.

11. B. MacLennan. Synthetic ethology: An approach to the study of communication. In C. G. Langton, C. Taylor, J. Farmer, and S. Rasmussen, editors, *Artificial Life II, SFI Studies in the Sciences of Complexity*, volume X. Addison-Wesley, 1991.

12. C. Ogden and I. Richards. *The Meaning of Meaning: a study of the influence of language upon thougth and of the science of symbolism*. Routledge & Kegan Paul Ltd., London, 1923.

13. D. Rumelhart, J. McClelland, and et. al. *Parallel distributed processing; explorations in the microstructure of cognition*, volume 1-2. The MIT Press, Cambridge, MA, 1987.

14. R. Seyfarth, D. Cheney, and P. Marler. Monkey responses to three different alarm calls: Evidence of predator classification and semantic communication. *Science*, 210:801–803, 1980.

15. C. Shannon and W. Weaver. *The mathematical theory of communication*. University of Illinois, Urbana, 1949.

16. L. Steels. The spontaneous self-organization of an adaptive language. In S. Muggleton, editor, *Machine Intelligence 15*. Oxford University Press, Oxford, UK, 1996.

17. L. Steels. Language learning and language contact. In W. Daelemans, A. van den Bosch, and A. Weijters, editors, *Workshop Notes of the ECML/MLnet Familiarization Workshop on Empirical Learning of Natural Language Processing Tasks*, pages 11–24, 1997.

18. L. Steels and P. Vogt. Grounding adaptive language games in robotic agents. In C. Husbands and I. Harvey, editors, *Proceedings of the Fourth European Conference on Artificial Life*, Cambridge MA and London, 1997. The MIT Press.

19. L. M. Stephens and M. B. Merx. The effect of agent control strategy on the performance of a dai pursuit problem. In *Proceedings of the 1990 Distributed AI Workshop*, 1990.

20. S. Thrun. *Handbook of Intelligent Control: Neural, Fuzzy and Adaptive Approaches*, chapter The role of exploration in learning control. Van Nostrand Reinhold, Florence, Kentucky, 1992.

Rules of Order for Electronic Group Decision Making – A Formalization Methodology

Henry Prakken[1] and Thomas F. Gordon[2]

[1] Department of Computer Science
Utrecht University, The Netherlands
henry@cs.uu.nl
http://www.cs.uu.nl/staff/henry.html
[2] GMD – German National Research Center for Information Technology
Sankt Augustin, Germany
thomas.gordon@gmd.de
http://nathan.gmd.de/persons/thomas.gordon.html

Abstract. This paper reports on an ongoing research project, consisting of formalizing rules of order for group decision making, and implementing them as a procedural component of automated mediation systems for group decision making. The component should ultimately assist a human mediator in maintaining order at electronic meetings, and in giving advice to the participants on their options, rights and obligations in the decision making process. A main requirement for the system is that order can be maintained in a flexible way, allowing to set the rules aside when needed. This paper presents the first research result of the project: a way of formalizing rules of order that makes it possible to maintain order in such a flexible way.

1 Introduction

1.1 Background

Electronic meetings are an important object of research in Computer-Supported Cooperative Work (CSCW). One aspect of ordinary meetings is that they are usually governed by rules of order, which should ensure that the group involved in a meeting can conduct their business in a way that is both fair and effective. A natural research goal is how these benefits can also be made to hold for electronic meetings. This is an important research topic, since the participants in meetings are, unlike in many other CSCW applications, not always cooperative but often have conflicting goals and interests. In such circumstances it becomes important that a decision is made according to a procedure accepted by all those involved.

In this respect, electronic meetings provide both problems and prospects. A problem is how rules of order can be enforced given that the participants are not all physically present in one room. A prospect is that the setting of computer systems might enable different ways of maintaining order than in a traditional seting. This paper focuses on these issues with respect to a particular kind of

J.A. Padget (Ed.): Human and Artificial Societies, LNAI 1624, pp. 246–263, 1999.

electronic meeting, viz. one which should result in collective decisions of the group that meets.

In particular, we shall report on research done in the context of the ZENO computer system, developed at the GMD Bonn [3]. This system serves as an automated assistance tool for human mediators of discussions and group decision processes. It is currently applied to urban planning procedures, in the context of the GeoMed project [5], funded by the European Union. One component of the ZENO system is a discussion forum that is accessible via the World Wide Web, and where participants can raise issues, state positions with respect to these issues, put forward arguments for or against a position, and collectively decide an issue. The system, which is fully implemented, provides automated tools for maintaining and inspecting the resulting argumentation structure, and for recording the decisions. It combines elements of Horst Rittel's issue-based information system (see e.g. [9]) with insights from logic and argumentation theory.

At present the use of ZENO's discussion forum is completely unregulated. However, one research goal of the ZENO project is to study how the benefits of rules of order can also be made available for electronic meetings. More specifically, the aim is to extend ZENO's discussion forum with rules of order, and with a corresponding module (ROBERT) that assists the human mediator in maintaining order at the forum, and in giving advice to the users of the forum on their options, rights and obligations in the discussion and decision making process.

As for the rules of order, in this project a choice has been made for Robert's Rules of Order (RRO), which is the standard procedure for deliberative societies of all kinds in the USA. This choice requires some explanation, since the applicability of RRO to electronic discussion is not obvious. In particular, they are meant for synchronous discussion, i.e. discussion in meetings where all participants are present in the same place, at the same time, and where each participant can immediately observe and respond to all procedural events that are taking place. By contrast, in electronic discussion forums participants often have no full knowledge of who else is taking part in a discussion, and communication can be delayed: messages that are sent before another message can arrive later, and so on. Therefore it is still an open question which rules of order are suitable for electronic meetings. Moreover, the answer might very well be different for different types of electronic meetings, depending, for instance, on the size of the meeting, and on the degree of cooperativeness of the participants.

Nevertheless, RRO have still been chosen for this project, for two reasons. Firstly, RRO are well-known, precisely formulated, and well-tested in practice, and it is therefore expected that, even if they are not directly suitable for electronic applications, their formalization will still give useful insights into the problems and prospects of adding a procedural component to automated mediation systems. Second, as far as we know, suitable rules of order for electronic and asynchronous discussion do not yet exist. In fact, developing such rules is one of the goals of the ZENO research project, and we think that a good way to develop such rules is to first formalize and implement existing rules of order, and to then use the result to experiment with alternative adaptations of the rules.

It might also be asked what the value is of formalizing particular rules of order, when different kinds of meetings might require different kinds of rules of order, at diferent levels of detail. Our answer is that the ultimate aim of the ROBERT and ZENO project is not just to find a particular body of suitable rules of order for electronic meetings, but to arrive at an general 'ontology' of the world of meetings, and at a general methodology for extending mediation systems with rules of order. Such an ontology and methodology can be derived from 'first principles', but it can also be induced from a well-known, well-tested and elaborate example. We think that both research strategies are equally valid, but the latter strategy is the one we are following. And the results so far indicate that it is a good strategy.

To summarize the research context of this paper, it is part of a project that aims to develop a formalization methodology for rules of order for electronic discussions, to apply this methodology to an example, to implement the formalization as a module of ZENO's discussion forum, and then to test how the rules must be adapted to electronic discussions of various kinds. The underlying research goal is to provide an ontology of the world of meetings and a method for maintaining order at electronic discussion forums. The present paper focuses on the formalization of a particular set of rules of order, viz. RRO, and on an aspect of its implementation in ZENO.

1.2 Problem Statement

The problem discussed in this paper is the following: given that we want an automated mediation system that maintains order in electronic meetings in a flexible way, how can rules of order can be formalized in a way that enables such a flexible enforcement? With 'flexible' enforcement we mean two things. Firstly, the system should make violation of the rules of order by the participants physically possible, instead of being designed in such a way that only correct acts can be performed. And, secondly, it should be possible for the chair to set the rules aside when needed to conduct a meeting efficiently. The underlying assumption here is that a system which strictly enforces a certain procedure will not be attractive for the users. Similar concerns have been expressed with respect to workflow management systems, e.g. by Suchman [13], calling for research on more flexible workflow management systems.

The results reported in this paper are twofold: a methodology for formalizing rules of order that enables their flexible enforcement at electronic meetings, and an application of this methodology to an example, viz. Robert's Rules of Order.

1.3 Related Research

As for RRO, in the literature at least one earlier suggestion for using them for similar tasks can be found, viz. Page [7], who suggests their use for controlling communication between intelligent artificial agents. However, we have not found whether Page has carried out his suggestion. Vreeswijk [15] also refers to Stary [12], who would have made a similar suggestion, but we have not been able to trace that publication. Formal and computational aspects of legal procedures have been studied by Vreeswijk, e.g. in [15], who has attempted to formalize aspects of Peter Suber's [14] NOMIC game, a game of which the purpose is to modify the rules of the game. Vreeswijk's insights are directly relevant for the ROBERT project, since many rules of order contain provisions for changing them (although this issue is not discussed in the present paper). Finally, Gordon [2] has formalized and implemented his normative model of procedural justice in civil pleading, which became a source of inspiration of the ZENO project.

1.4   Structure of this Paper

Following a brief overview of RRO in Section 2, in Section 3 a high-level design is proposed for maintaining order at electronic meetings in a flexible way. That section includes a discussion of the various types of order violation that are possible. Then in Section 4 our methodology for formalizing rules of order is presented, and illustrated by applying it to RRO. Finally, in Section 5 the main results of this paper are summarized, and the current state of the ROBERT project is briefly sketched.

2   Overview of Robert's Rules of Order

This section briefly outlines the example rules of order chosen in our project, Robert's Rules of Order. These rules are based on parliamentary procedure in the USA. They were described by general H.M. Robert in 1876, and perfected by him for 35 years, in communication with many users of the rules. Over the years, Robert's rules have turned from a description into a definition of parliamentary procedure (cf. [7, p. 360]), and have become the standard rules of order for meetings of all kinds in the USA. Although both several watered-down and several extended versions have appeared over the years, the ROBERT project is based on the original text. The references in this paper are to a 1986 paperback publication of this text [10].

The 'world' of RRO is the world of meetings (more accurately, of sessions: each session is a series of meetings separated by adjournments). The main objects of this world are an *assembly*, consisting of *members*, which can have several *roles* (ordinary member, chair, secretary, ...), and finally, *issues*, or *questions* which are to be decided by the assembly.

RRO defines an extensive repertoire of procedural speech acts with which those present at a meeting can communicate. The primary topic treated by RRO is how to bring business before the assembly, and how to have this business dealt with. The main 'loop' of RRO is that a member has to act to obtain the floor, after which s/he should state a proposal (for which RRO uses the technical term 'motion'), which must be seconded by another member before the chair can open the motion to debate by stating it. Debate is followed by a vote, after which new business can be introduced.

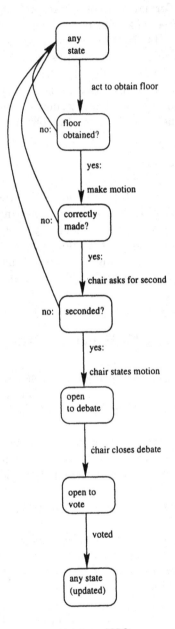

Main loop of RRO

This main loop has many exceptional cases, while also many complications can arise. As for the exceptions, some motions can be made while not having the floor, some do not need to be seconded, some are not debatable, and some motions are not decided by vote but by the chair. (A motion that satisfies all these exceptions is a point of order). Virtually all of these exceptions are motions that, when adopted, have a certain procedural effect, like a point of order, an amendment, an appeal, an objection to the consideration of a question, a motion to adjourn, and so on. These procedural effects are one source of complications. Another source of complications is that certain motions can be made when another motion is pending and, when seconded, must be dealt with before the pending motion. This is captured by an order of precedence among motions, determining which motions can be made while another motion is pending.

The main precedence ordering is not defined on individual motions but on four categories of motions, which, in descending order of precedence are:

- *Privileged motions* (fix time of adjournment, adjourn, questions of privilege, orders of the day);
- *Incidental motions* (appeal/questions of order, objection to the consideration of a question, reading papers, withdrawal of a motion, suspension of the rules);
- *Subsidiary motions* (lay on the table, previous question[1], postpone to a certain day, commit, amend, postpone indefinetely);
- *Principal motions* (any other motion, usually motions related to the purposes for which the meeting is held).

The largest part of RRO is devoted to a discussion of all these types of motions. Their further order of precedence is defined, special conditions for when they are in order are given (e.g. an objection to a consideration of a question must be made immediately after the question has been introduced), the required majority for acceptance is defined, it is stated whether they can be made without having the floor, whether they require a second, whether they are debatable, renewable, amendable, reconsiderable, etc . . . , and their procedural effects when made and when adopted are defined.

In addition to motions, RRO regulates the way debate and vote are conducted, the rights and duties of the officers of an assembly, the minutes, the functioning of committees, and some other things, like the quorum, and orders of business.

A main feature of RRO is that they acknowledge that sometimes it is better to temporarily put them aside (e.g. RRO 1 and RRO 3, p. 34). For instance, many questions of routine are not formulated as a motion and then seconded and stated; instead, the chair often announces after informal discussion that if no one objects, such an such is the action of the assembly. The general rule is that anything goes until any member objects, after which RRO must be strictly applied.

---

[1] This is a technical name for a motion to immediately put the pending question to vote.

3   How to Maintain Order at Electronic Meetings in a Flexible Way

As stated in the introduction, the formalization and implementation of RRO, or other rules of order, (called ROBERT) should ultimately be integrated with ZENO's discussion forum. This section discusses the functions that ROBERT can have within ZENO, and the corresponding tasks that it should be able to perform. On the basis of this discussion we propose how ROBERT can deal in a flexible way with violations of the rules of order by the users of ZENO's discussion forum (including the human mediator).

In the following, it should be kept in mind that ZENO's discussion forum is monitored by a human mediator, who not only acts as the chair but also processes the messages into a format that is readable for the ROBERT component.

3.1   Functions and Tasks of ROBERT within ZENO

As a component of ZENO, ROBERT can be made to perform two different functions.

1. As an autonomous expert system, giving advice to users of ZENO's discussion forum and to the human mediator, on procedural possibilities, rights, obligations. Here the human mediator independently maintains order at the forum, and ROBERT fulfills much the same role as a book copy of the rules of order at the chair's or a participant's table in an ordinary meeting.
2. Connected with the discussion forum, as a tool for maintaining order at the forum. Here ROBERT performs certain actions on behalf of the chair (or the secretary), like warning participants that they are out of order, and maintaining a list of decisions.

The aim of the ROBERT project is that the same core system can perform both functions (although for each of the functions probably some specific additional components are needed). Accordingly, the formalization of any rules of order should be such that it can be used for implementing both of these functions.

To fulfill these functions, ROBERT should be able to perform the following two tasks:

1. Update the current state of the procedure;
2. Determine of any procedural act whether it conforms to the rules.

The formalization of rules of order (in our case RRO) has to take these tasks into account. In Section 4 we shall explain how our current formalization does so.

3.2   How ROBERT Should Deal with Violations of the Rules of Order

Like any set of norms for human behaviour, rules of order can be violated. How should ROBERT deal with these violations? At first sight, one might think that the implementation of ROBERT as a computer system yields an opportunity that human chairs of ordinary meetings rarely have: ZENO's discussion forum could be set up in such a way that violation becomes physically impossible. For instance, if in a meeting governed by RRO a participant wants to push a button 'Make motion' just after another participant has moved a motion that requires a second, the system might, instead of returning a window for typing the motion, return a window saying "You are out of order, change your input". Such an implementation of rules of order would be what Jones & Sergot [4] call 'regimentation' of norm-governed behaviour: the system is implemented in such a way that all meetings will as a matter of fact conform to the rules of order.

However, as Jones & Sergot remark, regimentation is not always a good idea (see also [13], as mentioned above). ZENO's discussion forum is a good example of a system that should not be regimented. It seems that to be workable in practice, the system must not be too rigid: there is a real danger that if the system strictly enforces a certain procedure on the participants of a discussion, they will be discouraged from using the discusion forum. This is even acknowledged by many existing rules of order, such as RRO, which, as noted above, at various places formulates the principle that its formalities can be dispensed with as long as no member objects. Therefore, in our example we want that the system, instead of the above window, returns a window "You are out of order, do you want to sustain your input?"

Accordingly, a basic idea of the current project is that as an implemented system, ROBERT should satisfy the following constraints.

1. It must be physically possible for the users (including the chair) to violate the rules of order;
2. It must be possible for the chair to set the rules of order aside when needed.

We shall now look in more detail at the various ways in which rules of order might be violated, how ROBERT should deal with them, and what this means for a formalization of rules of order. Although we shall do so for our example rules of order, RRO, our observations apply to rules of order in general.

Violations by Ordinary Participants Ordinary participants can violate rules of order in only two ways, which are structurally similar, viz. by performing an act that is not in order (not at the right moment) or improper (not of the right kind).[2] ROBERT can deal with such violations as follows. As for knowledge representation, it suffices to specify under which conditions an act has the property of being out of order, or improper. Then every time ROBERT derives that an act is out of order or improper, it notifies all participants of the violation, possibly with advice on an action that is possible (for instance, a point of order). This message should not only be sent to the chair (i.e., the human mediator),

---

[2] RRO do not explicitly distinguish these two notions; the distinction has been introduced into the formalization to make it more structured. We expect this to be useful for other rules of order as well.

but to all participants, since usually all participants have the right to rise to a point of order (see in RRO section 14). Furthermore, the 'sanction' for these kinds of violation is simply that the intended procedural effect does not occur. For instance, according to RRO an incorrectly moved motion does not become open for seconding. And, of course, the chair can call the participant to order, and any other participant can rise to a point of order.

Violations by the Chair The mediator can, in its role of the chair, violate the rules of order in several different ways, which are not easy to deal with in a uniform manner. Firstly, it is possible that the chair does not perform an act that s/he must perform: for instance, in meetings governed by RRO, not stating a seconded and debatable motion, or not putting a motion to vote after debate has been closed. A variant of this kind of violation is when the chair incorrectly performs such an act: for instance, when stating a motion, the chair uses substantially different words than the person who made the motion.

A completely different kind of violation is when the chair incorrectly applies a rule of order: for instance, the chair incorrectly rules a proposal out of order, or declares a proposal adopted that needs a 2/3 vote but received only 56 % of the votes. Why is this a different kind of violation?

With the first two kinds it is easy to make a simple syntactic difference between the obligatory act and the act as it actually takes place. For instance, a formalized rule can say then when a proposal to end debate has been adopted, the next act of the chair must be putting the proposal to vote. Whether the chair indeed performs the obligatory action is then a matter of factual input to the system, just as with the behaviour of ordinary participants. In RRO and many other rules of order the sanctions for this kind of violation that ordinary participants can rise to a point of order, and that the obligation to perform the act stays in effect as long as it is not performed. Since the difference between actual and required behaviour is made with syntactic means, it is easy for ROBERT to detect such violations.

However, with the last kind of situation, erroneous application of a rule of order by the chair, things are different. Here it does not make much sense to formalize the rules of order in such a way that if, for instance, a participant starts debating a proposal before it has been opened to debate, the chair *ought to* rule the participant out of order. Instead, we want that ROBERT *infers* that the participant is out of order, and informs the chair about this fact, who can then accordingly rule the participant out of order. If otherwise, then virtually no rule application can be made automatically by the system; nearly every logical inference step that a reader of the rules of order would make will have to be replaced by factual input concerning the chair's actual behaviour. Clearly, such a system would not be very useful. On the other hand, we have just stated that ROBERT should make violations of the rules of order possible, so we must have at least some way of modelling erroneous application of a rule of order.

We have chosen for a design in terms of consistency checking and belief revision. The idea is that such violations are added as factual input by the chair, after which the system detects and reports that the chair's input contradicts ROBERT's conclusions. For example, suppose that in a meeting governed by RRO that the chair mistakenly opens a motion to debate that has not yet been seconded. The system then asks the chair: note that according to my information the motion is not open to debate, so are you sure? Then the chair might ask: why is it not open to debate?, after which the system exlains why, viz. because the motion needs a second but has not yet been seconded. Then the chair might decide whether to follow the system and withdraw his/her input (i.e. to acknowledge violation of a rule of order), or whether to sustain the input (i.e. to set the rule aside), in which case the system revises its state.

Note that this interaction procedure might be very useful: it makes the chair (or other users) aware of which conclusions have to be changed if the user's input is to be sustained. And this might make the user aware of the mistakes s/he has made.

3.3 Formalization Requirements

Our design proposal is still general, and its implementation involves several non-trivial technicalities, such as the belief revision procedure and matters of user-interface design. Nevertheless, for present purposes it is specific enough to check a formalization of rules of order on adequacy. In particular, on the basis of our analysis we can state the following formalization requirements.

- The formalization must cope with the changing world of meetings, so that the system can update the state of the procedure each time something relevant happens.
- For violations by ordinary participants, and for certain types of violations by the chair, a syntactic distinction must be made between required and actual behaviour, so that the system can detect and report such violations.
- By contrast, a special type of violation by the chair, viz. erroneous application of a rule of order, should be detected as a contradiction between procedural conclusions drawn by the system and those typed in by the chair.
- Our aim of flexible enforcement of rules of order requires that when the chair sustains erroneous input, then in this 'subideal' state all other rules of order still apply. For instance, when a chair opens debate on an undebatable proposal, and no participant objects, the rules on how to conduct débate and on which proposal can be made while another one is pending, should still apply.

4 Formalizing Rules of Order

In the present section we shall present a formalization methodology that respects the requirements of the previous section, and illustrate it with our formalization of RRO. Our methodology uses the language and semantics of standard first-order predicate logic (FOL), and assumes that reasoning with a formalization is valid first-order reasoning. It should be noted that the methodology is not meant to result in a directly exectutable logic program, but rather in a formal specification for a designer of an expert system; further decisions on implementation are still necessary.

As for our choice for standard first-order logic (which leaves open the possibility of a more structured format using description or terminological logics), at several points computer science and Artificial Intelligence provide alternative formalisms (such as nonmonotonic logics for formalizing change, and deontic logics for formalizing normative concepts). We shall briefly discuss them when relevant. However, the pragmatic constraints of the ZENO project have led us not to use them. FOL is well-understood and sufficiently expressive, and many ways to implement it exist. Moreover, FOL enables a style of formalization that can be easily implemented in standard expert system tools. Nevertheless, even when other formalisms are chosen, our formalization has its use, since it is much easier to change one formalization into another than to formalize a natural language text.

We next explain some details on notation. As for the logical symbols, $\neg$ stands for logical 'not', $\wedge$ for 'and', $\Rightarrow$ for 'if ... then', and $\Leftrightarrow$ for 'if and only if'. When relevant, first-order predicates have an argument for a state term. A discretely and linearly ordered set of states is asssumed. State variables are written as possibly indexed or primed s, while person variables are written as y, y', ..., and variables for acts as x, x', ... or z, z', ... Type `writer` strings are predicate symbols when they begin with a capital, otherwise they are function symbols. If an argument of a predicate symbol has more than one letter, like $chair$, it is an object constant. Finally, formulas with free variables are implicitly assumed to be universally quantified, as in logic programming.

In the present paper we use, for purpose of presentation, a quasi-natural-language notation, which is inspired by [6]. For instance, we write

x `Is stated by` $chair$ `at` s

instead of the more standard FOL notation

`Is stated by`$(x, chair, s)$

which we have used in [8], or even

`Is_stated_by`$(x, chair, s)$

Note that in the expression

$\neg\, x$ `Is stated by` $chair$ `at` s

the negation symbol $\neg$ does not apply to the term x (which would not be well-formed in FOL) but to the entire expression; in standard notation:

$\neg$ `Is_stated_by`$(x, chair, s)$

The choice between these styles of formalizing is not something which is essential for our methodology. We note that [6] defines a systematic way to convert standard FOL notation into the above quasi-natural-language form.

4.1   Procedural Speech Acts

Among other things, rules of order define the possible procedural speech acts, usually as a taxonomy of types and subtypes. We first discuss the representation of such a taxonomy. This is specified as an inheritance hierarchy with exceptions, where each class has at most one superclass. Each class of speech acts has certain attributes with specified values. Some attribute values are given directly, others by way of rules. When attribute values are not explicitly specified for a certain class, it inherits the values of its immediate superclass. In [8] it is specified how this hierarchy can be translated into predicate logic formulas.

We now illustrate our speech act representation with the specification of a motion according to RRO.

Type: x **Is a motion**
Superclass: x **Is an act**
Attributes:
- x **Is debatable** (motions are debatable)
- $\neg\, x$ **Is in order when another has floor** at s (motions are not in order when another has the floor. This attribute has a second argument for the state because sometimes its value depends on the situation)
- x **Requires second** (motions require a second)
- **Required majority for** x **is** *simple* (The required vote for motions is a simple majority)
- **Decision mode of** x **is** *vote* (motions are decided by vote (alternative: by chair's decision))
- z **Is applicable to** x? See rules. (all subsidiary motions except postpone indefinitely)
- x **Is renewable at** s? See rules.
- x **Is reconsiderable** (motions are reconsiderable)
- $\neg\, x$ **Is to be entered on the record when made** (motions need not be entered on the record when made (only exception: reconsider))

The attribute **Is applicable to** captures the subsidiary motions that are applicable to a motion.

Some attribute values are defined by logical rules. For instance, the attribute **Is renewable at** receives its value by rules that say that motions are renewable after the introduction of any motion that alters the state of affairs).

What is also specified by rules is the special order conditions for a speech act, and the procedural effects of performing a motion and of adopting it. For instance, according to RRO an objection to the consideration of a motion is only in order when made immediately after that motion has been introduced, making such an objection has the procedural effect that the pending question is changed to the objection, and adopting it has the effect that the objected motion is removed from before the assembly.

To illustrate inheritance and exceptions, consider the specification of RRO's class of incidental motions.

Type: x Is an incidental motion
Superclass: x Is a motion
Attributes:
- ¬ *x* Is debatable
- *z* Is applicable to *x*? See rules (all subsidiary motions except amendment and motion to postpone indefinetely)

Thus the class of incidental motions inherits all its attribute values from the class of motions, except the values for Is debatable and Is applicable to. In the latter case this is since the rules for which subsidiaries are applicable are different than those for motions in general, and thus override these rules.

4.2   Coping with the Changing World of Meetings

The world of meetings is a constantly changing world. Speakers obtain or yield the floor, and motions are introduced, debated and decided. Accordingly, different *states* of a meeting can be distinguished, with different speakers, different pending questions, and several other differences. States are *changed* by procedural speech acts (moving, seconding, acting to obtain the floor, voting, etc . . .), according to their procedural effects as defined by the rules of order.

In computer science and Artificial Intelligence (AI) formalizing changing worlds is a heavily studied topic. In AI a debate has been going on between those who 'want to do it all in logic', e.g. [11], and those who admit procedural elements in their specification. We have chosen for a method of the latter kind, essentially based on the so-called STRIPS approach to planning [1].

The logical component of our method is as follows. In the knowledge base, procedural facts are not just true or false, but true or false relative to a state of a meeting. Accordingly, a state is conceived as a first-order object, and aspects (attributes) of a state are expressed with predicates having the state as an argument. For instance, the pending question of a state *s* is expressed as *x* Is the pending question at *s*, and the speaker (who has the floor) at state *s* is expressed as *y* Has the floor at *s*. Events occurring in a state are expressed likewise. For instance, that a motion *m* is seconded at *s* by person *p* can be expressed as *m* Is a motion ∧ *m* Is seconded by *p* at *s*.

State changes are formalized as follows. For any state *s*, we denote its immediate successor with *s'*.[3] Then a state change is defined by rules that have a term *s* in their antecedent predicates, and a term *s'* in their consequent predicates. For instance, RRO's rule that a debatable motion becomes open to debate after it is stated by the chair can be written as

x Is stated by *chair* at *s* ∧ *x* Is debatable ⇒
x Is open to debate at *s'*

---

[3] A full formalization should contain axioms that justify this intended reading.

The procedural element of our method (adapted from STRIPS) comes in to solve the following problem, which in AI is called the 'frame problem'. Assume that we have derived that a certain motion m is open to debate at s, and assume also that a participant p becomes the new speaker at the next moment s'. Then we want to conclude that m is still open to debate at s'. However, in standard first-order logic this can only be derived if the knowledge base also contains the following rule, a so-called 'frame axiom':

x Is open to debate at s $\wedge$ *'nothing relevant happens'* $\Rightarrow$
x Is open to debate at s'

where *'nothing relevant happens'* is the negated disjunction of all ways in which a motion ceases being open to debate at s'. For various reasons this way of formalizing the effects of actions, where for each state not only what has changed must be specified, but also what has not changed, is widely considered to be unattractive. In logic, so-called nonmonotonic logics have been developed, in which it can be *assumed* that things do not change unless an explicit reason for change becomes known.

However, for the pragmatic reasons sketched above, we shall not use one of those logics, but instead add an extralogical component to our method. The idea is that any state of affairs that persists until it is changed by some event, is an attribute of a data structure called the *record*. The record is not made relative to a state, but exists 'globally'. So it says m Is the pending question instead of m Is the pending question at s_1. Its attribute values are updated when needed: each time the knowledge base derives a change in the value of some attribute, its value on the record is changed. For instance, when a conclusion n Is the pending question at s_2 is derived from the knowledge base, then at the record the value of Is the pending question is changed from m to n. And each time the logical reasoning process needs the value of a record attribute, a look-up at the record is performed.

An intuitive way to understand this method is to think of a meeting where behind the chair stands a blackboard, at which the values of the record are written. Each time an event triggers a change in, say, the pending question, the chair erases the old value and writes down the new one. And each time the chair wants to know what is the pending question, s/he looks at the blackboard.

As for the content of the record, the general rule is that any procedural property of which we want to assume that it persists until it is explicitly changed, is an attribute of the record. In addition, the record keeps track of the procedural acts that have been made during a session, as well as the decisions on the motions made. This component is useful when information is needed about the past, for example, when of a motion that cannot be renewed it must be known whether it has already been made.

In our formalization of RRO (and probably of any rules of order), some important record attributes are the following:

- *The speaker.* This says who is the speaker, i.e., who has the floor, if any.
- *The question stack.* This lists the motions that at any state are before the assembly (debated or decided), being brought before the assembly (the phase from being correctly moved to being stated), or temporarily set aside by another motion with higher precedence. The top of the question stack is:
- *The pending question.* This is the question that is currently before the assembly. It is the motion that is either being brought before the assembly, or being debated, or being decided.
- *What is open to debate.* This says which motion is currently debated, if any.
- *The session history.* This records the procedural acts made during a session, as well as the decisions on the motions made.

This completes our discussion of how the first formalization requirement of Section 3.3 can be met, viz. how the dynamic aspect of meetings can be formalized. We now turn to the other three requirements, which are about violation and flexible enforcement of rules of order.

4.3   Distinguishing Actual and Required Behaviour

The second requirement on formalizations of rules of order is that for several types of behaviour they make a syntactic distinction between actual and required behaviour. How can this be done? Various ways are possible, including the use of a full-fledged deontic logic. Deontic logic is a branch of modal logic, which adds to standard logic the logical operators O for 'obligatory', P for 'permitted', and F for 'forbidden'. Thus it becomes possible, for instance, to say O chair Puts the affirmative of $motion_1$ at s_1, which says that the chair must put the affirmative vote on a particular motion at state s_1. However, as explained above, the present formalization stays within first-order logic. The normative character of rules of order is captured by three special 'quasi-deontic' predicates, Is proper at, Is in order at, Correctly makes at and a surrogate deontic predicate Is obliged to make at, which can be used to define more special versions Is obliged to ... at. The quasi-deontic predicates are used in the following 'top level' rules.

x Is an act $\wedge$ y Makes x at s $\wedge$ x Is in order at s $\wedge$ x Is proper at s
$\Leftrightarrow$ y Correctly makes x at s

This rule says that a procedural act is correctly made if and only if it is in order and proper. In our formalization of RRO, the latter predicates are defined in further rules. For motions, the 'top level' definition of Is in order at is as follows.

x Is a motion $\wedge$ y Makes x at s $\wedge$
y Fulfills floor condition of x at s $\wedge$
y Fulfills precedence condition of x at s $\wedge$
Renewal condition of x is fulfilled at s $\wedge$

Mode condition of x is fulfilled at s $\wedge$
Special order conditions of x are fulfilled at s
$\Leftrightarrow x$ Is in order at s

The atomic expressions in the conditions of these rules have the following intuitive reading (the page numbers refer to [10]).

- y Fulfills floor condition of x at s (pp. 27–32) means that the rules concerning having the floor do not prevent making the motion (either one has the floor, or having the floor is not required).
- y Fulfills precedence condition of x at s (p. 12) means that no pending question prevents making the motion (either there is no pending question, or the pending question yields to the moved motion).
- Renewal condition of x is fulfilled at s (pp. 178/9) means that the rules on renewing motions do not prevent making the motion (either it can be renewed, or it is moved for the first time).
- Mode condition of x is fulfilled at s says that the rules requiring special acts at certain moments (e.g. seconding when a motion that requires second has been made) do not prevent making the motion.
- Special order conditions of x are fulfilled at s means that any special conditions for the relevant type of motion are fulfilled.

The quasi-deontic predicates are convenient for formalizing prohibitions (Is in order at) and obligations to make an act, if it is made, in a certain way (Is proper at). However, they are less suitable for obligations to perform a certain act, like in RRO the obligation for the chair to state a motion after it has been seconded. For such obligations the surrogate deontic predicate, Is obliged to make at (or special versions) will be used, as in, for instance, the following rule of RRO's voting procedure:

x Is open to vote at s $\wedge$ $\neg$ Ballot is ordered for x at s $\wedge$ $\neg$ Roll call is ordered for x at s $\Rightarrow$
$chair$ Is obliged to put the affirmative of x at s

This rule says that when a motion is open to vote (e.g. since debate has closed) and no ballot or roll call has been ordered, the chair is obliged to put the affirmative.

The use of quasi-deontic predicates is not so strange, since the law also often uses such predicates, like 'tort' and 'criminal offence' instead of the deontic term 'forbidden'. For example, the Dutch criminal code hardly contains any deontic expression: it mainly defines the notion of criminal offence and its subcategories, and specifies the penalties for when actual behaviour satisfies these categories. It is left to the citizens to pragmatically infer from these penalties that they had better not commit criminal offences.

Our third formalization requirement is that erroneous application of a rule of order by the chair is detected in terms of a contradiction check. Our formalization method also meets this requirement. When, for instance, the chair incorrectly rules a motion in order, s/he inputs a fact $Motion_1$ Is in order at s_1. Since this is incorrect, the system will derive ¬ $Motion_1$ Is in order at s_1 and then recognize the contradiction with the chair's input.

Finally, as for the last formalization requirement, here is how the chair can set the rules of order aside on one point without ignoring them completely. In our example, s/he can do so by sustaining the erroneous input $Motion_1$ Is in order at s_1. The belief revision component of the system then withdraws its own contradictory conclusion and the system then further reasons with the chair's input. Note that thus setting the rules of order aside on a certain point does not render the rules inapplicable on other points. For instance, the system can (if the other relevant conditions are also fulfilled) derive (for the maker p of the motion) p Correctly makes $Motion_1$ at s_1, after which other rules apply as usual, for instance, a rule saying that when a motion that needs a second is correctly moved, the motion is open for being seconded.

5   Conclusion

In this paper we first presented a (high level) design for how order can be maintained at electronic meetings in a flexible way. The main features of the design are

- The system keeps track of the changing state of a meeting;
- The system recognizes and reports violations of the rules of order;
- The system does not physically enforce the rules of order;
- The system allows the chair to set the rules of order aside when needed.

Then we stated some requirements for any formalization of rules of order that is to be used in such a design, after which we presented a formalization methodology that meets these requirements.

The current state of the ROBERT project is as follows. The ZENO discussion forum is fully implemented, but as yet it contains nothing of the above design. However, the formalization of RRO with the above-sketched methodology is reaching its completion. The main formalization problems have been solved, RRO's top level structure is formalized, and most of the details are filled in. The state of the formalization at the moment of the writing of this paper is reported in [8]. That report also contains further discussions of some of the alternative formalisms that were briefly mentioned in this paper.

References

1. Fikes, R.E. & Nilsson, N.J. STRIPS: a new approach to the application of theorem proving to problem solving. *Artificial Intelligence* 2 (1971), 189–208.
2. Gordon, T.F. *The Pleadings Game. An Artificial Intelligence Model of Procedural Justice.* Kluwer Academic Publishers, Dordrecht (1995).
3. Gordon, T.F., & Karacapilidis, N. The Zeno argumentation framework. In *Proceedings of the Sixth International Conference on Artificial Intelligence and Law*, ACM Press, New York (1997) 10–18.
4. Jones, A.J.I. & Sergot, M.J. On the characterisation of law and computer systems: the normative systems perspective. In J.-J.Ch. Meyer & R.J. Wieringa (eds.): *Deontic Logic in Computer Science: Normative System Specification.* John Wiley and Sons, Chicester (1993) 275–307.
5. Karacapilidis, N.I., Papadias, D., Gordon, T.F & Voss, H. Collaborative environmental planning with GeoMed. *European Journal of Operational Research*, Special Issue on Environmental Planning, Vol. 102, No. 2 (1997) 335–346.
6. Kowalski, R.A. Legislation as logic programs. In Z. Bankowski, I. White & U. Hahn (eds.): *Informatics and the Foundations of Legal Reasoning.* Law and Philosophy Library, Kluwer Academic Publishers, Dordrecht etc. (1995) 325–356.
7. Page, C.V. Principles for democratic control of bounded-rational, distributed, knowledge agents. *Proceedings of the European Simulation Conference*, ed. E. Mosekilde, (1991) 359–361.
8. Prakken, H. Formalizing Robert's Rules of Order. An Experiment in Automating Mediation of Group Decision Making. GMD Report 12 (1998), GMD – German National Research Center for Information Technology, Sankt Augustin, Germany. Electronically available at http://nathan.gmd.de/projects/zeno/publications.html
9. Rittel, H.W.J. & Webber, M.M. Dilemmas in a general theory of planning. *Policy Sciences* (1973), 155–169.
10. Robert, H.M. *Robert's Rules of Order. The Standard Guide to Parliamentary Procedure.* Bantam Books, New York etc. (1986).
11. Shanahan, M.P. *Solving the Frame Problem.* MIT Press, Cambridge, MA (1997).
12. Stary, C. Modelling decision support for rational agents. *Proceedings of the European Simulation Conference*, ed. E. Mosekilde (1991) 351–356.
13. Suchman, L. Do categories have politics? The language/action perspective reconsidered. *Computer-Supported Cooperative Work* 2 (1994) 177–190.
14. Suber, P. *The Paradox of Self-amendment: a Study of Logic, Law, Omnipotence, and Change.* Peter Lang, New York (1990).
15. Vreeswijk, G.A.W. Formalizing Nomic: working on a theory of communication with modifiable rules of procedure. Technical report CS 95-02, Dept. of Computer Science, University of Limburg, Maastricht, The Netherlands (1995).

Broadway: A Case-Based System for Cooperative Information Browsing on the World-Wide-Web[1]

Michel Jaczynski and Brigitte Trousse

INRIA Sophia Antipolis - Action AID
2004 route des Lucioles - BP 93
06902 Sophia Antipolis Cedex, France
Tel: +33 (0) 4 93 65 77 45 Fax: +33 (0) 4 93 65 77 83
E-mail: {Michel.Jaczynski, Brigitte.Trousse}@sophia.inria.fr

Abstract. The World Wide Web is a huge hypermedia where finding relevant documents is not an easy task. In this paper, we present our case-based system for cooperative information browsing, called BROADWAY. BROADWAY follows a group of users during their navigations on the WWW (proxy-based architecture) and advises them by displaying a list of potentially relevant documents to visit next. BROADWAY uses case-based reasoning to reuse precise experiences derived from past navigations with a time-extended situation assessment: the advice are based mainly on similarity of ordered sequence of past accessed documents. In addition, the dynamic nature of the WWW is addressed in the reuse step and with a specific method for case forgetting.

1 Introduction

The World Wide Web (WWW) [15] is an hypermedia of heterogeneous and dynamic documents. This virtual space is growing more and more every day, offering to the user a huge amount of data [3]. Two kinds of methods can be used to locate a relevant document through this space: *querying* and *browsing*. Querying is appropriate when the user has a clear goal which should usually be expressed through a list of keywords. Different servers on the WWW (such as Yahoo, Lycos, Altavista) can be then used to retrieve matching documents based on their indexing capability. Browsing is well suited when the user cannot express his goal explicitly or when query formulation by keywords is not adequate. Then, the user must navigate through this space, moving from one node to another, looking for a relevant document. These two approaches can be mixed so that querying gives a list of reasonable starting points for browsing [13]. However, the huge size and the structure of this space make difficult the indexing of the documents required by querying access methods and could disorient the user during a browsing session. This article focuses on the assistance given to the user during a browsing session, and more precisely on the

---

[1] This article is an extended version of the work presented in [11].

J.A. Padget (Ed.): Human and Artificial Societies, LNAI 1624, pp.264 -283, 1999.

design of a *browsing advisor*. A browsing advisor is able to follow the user during a browsing session to infer his goal, and then must advise him of potentially relevant documents to visit next.

Our approach of the advice computation is based on the user behaviours during their browsing sessions as others existing advisors [6,20,29]. But we want to address this problem by taking the *time-extended browsing situation* into account. A time-extended situation represents not only the current state of the observed navigation but also its past sequence of events. We claim indeed that a particular state of the navigation (current document and/or an *instantaneous* description) is not sufficient to compute relevant advice. In order to better describe the user's implicit intent during browsing, we want to consider past visited documents and their access order. More, in order to improve the relevance of advised documents and to enable a wide use of the system, we add three other requirements:

- the browsing advisor must *learn from a group of users* how to improve the advice computation,
- the browsing advisor must be *designed for the WWW*: its use must not be restricted to a localised site, and it must take the dynamic aspect of WWW documents,
- the browsing advisor must be *independent* of the user's browser software.

Other works have proposed browsing advisors [6,19,7,16,2,20,28] but they do not satisfy our four requirements (cf. Table 2). Thus, we propose a browsing advisor, named BROADWAY[2][11], based on the Case-Based Reasoning (CBR) paradigm [1]. In CBR, a case basically represents a problem situation and the solution that has been applied. The first step of the reasoning is the retrieval through indexes of relevant cases which are somehow similar, or partially match the current problem situation. The goals of others steps are mainly the reuse of the past solutions by adaptation and the learning of the new experience in the memory for future reuse. BROADWAY uses CBR to learn from users' navigations the set of relevant cases, which can be reused to improve and to keep updated the advising process. The use of CBR is based on the following hypothesis: if two users went through a similar sequence of documents, they might have similar browsing intent, so that we can advise one user of the documents evaluated as relevant by the other one (cf. Fig. 1).

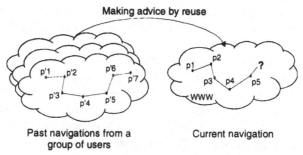

Fig. 1. Reusing past navigations to advise users

---

[2] BROADWAY : a BROwsing ADvisor reusing pathWAYs.

This paper describes BROADWAY, our case-based system for cooperative[3] information browsing for the WWW. In section 2, we first introduce the architecture of BROADWAY that is appropriate to follow and advise a group of users independently of their browsers. Then, in section 3, we propose a representation of navigational cases that integrates time-extended situation. In section 4, we describe the steps of the case-based reasoner embedded in BROADWAY, and used to compute the list of advised pages which are displayed to users during their navigations. We describe briefly in section 5 the related works according to our requirements. Finally, section 6 gives the results of the experiment made with real users in order to evaluate the assistance given by the current version of BROADWAY.

2   BROADWAY Architecture

Before describing the Broadway detailed architecture, we present the user interface and introduce the type of the architecture chosen for our application.

2.1   User Interface

The user is able to communicate with BROADWAY by two means: the manager and the toolbars. The BROADWAY manager is displayed in a separate small window and is used to configure the system, to control the navigation (a navigation can be started or stopped) and to display the advice. The toolbars are inserted in each page when a navigation has been started. Toolbars provide a set of actions related to the page where the toolbar is actually displayed: evaluation of the page with four levels, consultation of the current navigation, management of textual annotations of the page. This interface allows the browsing with multiple windows and different toolbars are then displayed. The evaluation of each page is not a feedback of advice given by BROADWAY, but a comment the user gives on its own navigation as if he was advising another user. We allow users to write and read annotations related to each page so that textual explanation of the evaluation can be attached and even discussions on a document may start. Pages with annotations will be preferred by BROADWAY in the advice computation. A typical layout of the browsing windows is presented in the Fig. 2 and Fig. 3.

The advice is presented through a list of URLs with a percentage representing an estimated relevance; the user can select one page to display it directly. For each user, BROADWAY operates in one of the two following modes: *advice upon request* or *continuous advice*. In the first mode, the user may ask for help and the reasoning will start to update the advice list. If the user selects to be advised continuously, the list of advised pages in the manager will be updated automatically after each navigation move.

---

[3] In our context, the cooperation is indirect i.e. based on shared navigations and evaluations given by users.

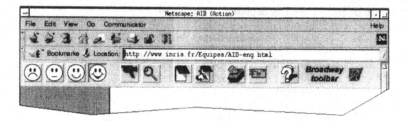

Fig. 2. The toolbar is inserted at the top of each page and can be hidden or displayed

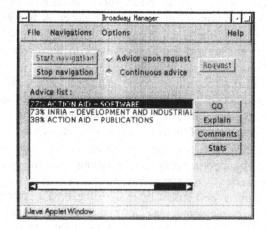

Fig. 3. The manager is used to control the recommendation process (navigation, modes). The user can also select one of the advised pages and click on the *go* button to display it

2.2 Watching User's Navigations behind the Scene

Based on the analysis given in [18], two kinds of architecture can be used to design a *browsing assistant* on the WWW: *stream transducers* and *browsing associates*. Transducers are inserted into the HTTP (HyperText Transport Protocol) communications between a client and the rest of the Web, in order to analyse and possibly alter the stream of requests and responses from the Web. Browsing associates are small and autonomous applications accessing the WWW independently to achieve a specific task. Our goal is to follow each user in its navigation through the WWW and the activity of this kind of browsing assistant is highly coupled with the streams of requests and responses. Thus, we have designed BROADWAY as a stream transducer to watch all navigation moves of a group of users. BROADWAY also manages an internal information space that can be accessed by users through a graphical interface mainly to get the advised pages and submit their evaluation. Based on this global architecture, BROADWAY integrates a case-based reasoner that computes advised pages asynchronously from the user's navigation. The overall architecture of BROADWAY is depicted in the Fig. 4.

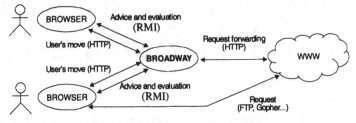

Fig. 4. BROADWAY global architecture

BROADWAY integrates a Jigsaw[4] proxy server developed by the W3C (WWW Consortium), in order to implement a stream transducer. A WWW proxy is a special HTTP server that waits for client requests, forwards them when needed to the appropriate server, and returns the answers back to the clients. At the beginning proxies were only used to do security filtering or document caching [17]. In the first case, the proxy, called a firewall, intercepts and checks every HTTP communication between the secured network and the external network. In the latter case, the proxy manages an internal cache of documents, and will retrieve the up-to-date document from an external server only if its local copy is obsolete. These uses of proxy servers are usual inside the WWW: any well known browser (Internet Explorer, Netscape Navigator, Hotjava) supports proxy configurations, and the request forwarding is transparent to the users.

Proxy architecture is well suited to analyse the HTTP communications and the document content in a transparent way, and can also be used to change the content of a reply dynamically before sending it back to the client. These properties have been studied in many works [17,4] and lead to the development of high level applications such as a WWW document annotation server [24] to support a group of users. The global architecture of BROADWAY is in the straight line of these works. Other browsing advisors have also chosen a proxy-based architecture [20]. BROADWAY accepts multiple simultaneous connections allowing a group of users to share their navigation experiences on the Web. Each user is identified by a user name and a password based on the standard proxy authentication mechanism defined in the HTTP protocol. When a user opens its browser, a pop-up window is automatically displayed, asking for its Id and password. Once provided, these data will not be asked again until the end of the browser process, and the browser will transmit them with every move of the user. This authentication is important because: it guarantees private access to the proxy which may manage private navigational data and user profiles, and it is used to follow a user through its different moves through the WWW. BROADWAY intercepts all HTTP replies containing an HTML (HyperText Markup Language) document: all the HTTP headers and the contents of the documents are available for further processing. In addition, BROADWAY provides caching by itself (by using

---

4 http://www.w3.org/Jigsaw/

Jigsaw caching) which is more effective than browser caching because the cache is shared by several users.

2.2 Detailed Architecture

BROADWAY is composed of different processes (cf. Fig. 5): the Jigsaw proxy, the event server, the page information server, the user server, the annotation server and the advice server. All these modules are written in the object-oriented Java programming language and use ObjectStore PSE[5] for persistency. Shaded modules are part of Broadway*Tools[6], a core set of tools designed to be reused in other assistance applications.

The proxy forwards the requests and alters the replies by inserting dynamically a piece of code (Java applet). The applet will notify BROADWAY when the pages are displayed even when pages are loaded from personal cache memory [25]. This applet is also used to display the toolbars. The manager is also an applet loaded from the proxy at starting time. At the process communication level between the applets and the servers, we use standard Java Remote Method Invocation (RMI).The event server collects browsing events from users: page loading and errors, page content, display duration, navigation start and stop, page evaluation... These events are then transmitted to the other appropriate modules. The page information server analyses the content of pages to extract mainly the titles, the headers and the keywords. The user information server stores the user Ids and their profiles. The annotation server is used to retain textual annotations linked to Web pages. Finally, the advice server computes the advice using case-based reasoning. This distributed architecture allows a better performance and is easily extendible by adding new modules.

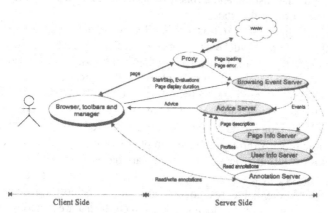

Fig. 5. BROADWAY detailed architecture

---

[5] http ://www.odi.com/products/pse/psej.html

[6] Broadway*Tools [28] is a project starting at 1997 with the ambitious goal is to provide an object oriented framework that facilitates the design and the implementation of various concrete Java-based Collaborative Information System (CIS) applications

The advice server communicates with the other modules and summarises the browsing activity of each user according to four variables that evolve over time:

1. URL of the document,
2. document content description (keywords of the title and the headers),
3. user's evaluation of the document,
4. display time ratio: time spent displaying a document relatively to its size (number of characters).

The following sections will explain the reasoning process of the advice server.

3   Representation of Navigational Cases

Our goal is to make a time-extended situation assessment during the reasoning. We have previously led an analysis of the management of time-extended situations in case-based reasoning [10] and we have designed a model for case representation and indexing with time-extended situations [9]. We first summarise the main features of our model supported by our object-oriented framework called CBR*Tools. Then we apply our model to the representation of navigations and navigational cases.

3.1   Cases Indexed by a Time-Extended Situation

In case-based reasoning, the situation of a case defines when its knowledge is relevant, and we make in our work a clear distinction between case indexing techniques based on an *instantaneous situation*, a set of indices giving the state of the world at a particular instant, and a *time-extended situation*, a set of indices describing mainly the evolution of this state.

Few existing applications in Case-Based Reasoning have tried to represent and use behavioural situations inside cases (robot control [21], plant nutrition control [9], WWW navigation [6,7], cf. [10] for a detailed analysis). To cope with this kind of situations, we have designed and implemented a generic model for case-based reasoning where cases are indexed by a time-extended situation [9,12]. In our model, we propose the separation of observation data stored in *records* from the cases which reference relevant data inside a record. Records are used to store the observation data of the dynamic process through a fixed number of variables and during a defined time interval. The evolution over time of each variable is represented as a time series. Above the concept of a record, we have defined two types of cases: *concrete* and *potential* cases. Potential cases do not have any concrete representation, and the knowledge they represent is hidden inside the records that are stored in memory. They can be identified by a direct search inside the records according to a *potential case template* defining typical situation constraints. These cases cannot be used directly, but due to some new problems, potential cases could become explicit as concrete cases.

This model has been implemented in CBR*Tools, our object-oriented framework written in Java for case-based applications. This framework provides abstract and concrete classes to represent and manage cases with time-extended situations. BROADWAY is developed using this framework: the records are specialised into the concept of *navigation* and the *navigational cases* reference precise experiences inside a navigation. BROADWAY uses the two proposed types of cases: concrete cases to represent explicit experiences acquired from a navigation, and potential cases which are hidden in the navigations.

3.2 Representation of a WWW Navigation

The WWW is composed of a set of resources which are identified by an address, the URL[7]. Each resource may contain other resources or references to other resources so that the WWW appears to be an hypermedia. Many protocols and data types are used in the WWW, and it is important for a browsing advisor such as BROADWAY to define the part of the web it aims to support. In our current version of BROADWAY, the WWW is represented as a directed graph of HTML *pages* identified through a HTTP URL. This means that other types of documents (images and videos for instance) and other types of URL (such as Gopher, Wais, FTP and files[8]) are not taken into account by BROADWAY but can be still accessed by the user. An HTTP URL is a string composed of different parts[9] :

HTTP_URL = "http://" host [":" port] ["/" path ["?" query] ["#" fragment]]

Based on the requirements about URL comparison[9], we have defined our concept of page address with specific equality constraints. In BROADWAY, two page addresses are *equal* if: they have the same host and port, the same path and the same query. The fragment is ignored because it references a part of the same document. The port 80 is assumed by default. The comparison of the host is case-insensitive, and if two host names are different, their IP addresses are then checked.

Table 1. Example of different Urls for a page

Urls for the same page A	Urls for the same page B
http://www.inria.fr	http://www.inria.fr/index.html
http://www.inria.fr :80	http://WWW.inria.fr/index.html
http://www.inria.fr/	http://www.inria.fr/index.html#theme

Using this representation of the WWW, the *current location* of a user is the last accessed page and a browsing *move* is a transition from a page address to a different one. A *browsing session* also called a *navigation* is mainly a sequence of pages representing the moves of one user over time. A navigation is assumed to be *coherent* in such a way that the user do not mix different browsing intent during a single navigation.

---

[7] Universal Resource Locator.
[8] See RFC1738 for information about URL types.
[9] See RFC2068:§3.2.2 and RFC 1738.

In BROADWAY, the navigations are recorded based on the evolution of the four variables coming from the analysis of the HTTP request/reply stream: page address, page content description, user's evaluation, display time ratio. The evolution of each variable is represented by a time series. These time series are *sampled* since the unit of the chosen model of time is a change of pages. We associate to each navigation a *context* containing a synthetic description of the pages accessed during the navigation (most used keywords in page contents, and hosts accessed). The Fig. 6 gives an example of a navigation where the user intent was to find more information about BROADWAY; so the user navigated through the INRIA server, found the research team AID and finally found one relevant page about this software.

Navigation #16 from mjaczyn

start date: Wed Nov 26 19:28:20 GMT+03:30 1997

end date: Wed Nov 26 19:30:51 GMT+03:30 1997

keywords (stems): PEOPLE, REPORT, INRIA, PUBLIC, CONFER, ACTIV, STAGE, MICHEL, THEME, SITE, SOFTWAR, DEADLIN, JACZYNSKI, ACTION, RESEARCH, PREFER

hosts: www.inria.fr

#	Page address	Content (stems)	Display	Evaluation
0	http://www.inria.fr/Recherche/activites-eng.html	INRIA, ACTIV, RESEARCH	1.0	0
1	http://www.inria.fr/Themes/Theme3-eng.html	INRIA, THEME	1.0	0
2	http://www.inria.fr/Equipes/AID-eng.html	ACTION	3.0	0
3	http://www.inria.fr/aid/aid-eng.html	ACTION	6.0	😊
4	http://www.inria.fr/aid/people.html	PEOPLE, ACTION	8.0	0
5	http://www.inria.fr/aid/personnel/Michel.Jaczynski/michel-eng.html	MICHEL, SITE, JACZYNSKI, PREFER	38.0	0
6	http://www.inria.fr/aid/personnel/Michel.Jaczynski/pub-eng.html	REPORT, PUBLIC, MICHEL, JACZYNSKI	10.0	0
7	http://www.inria.fr/aid/personnel/Michel.Jaczynski/michel-eng.html	MICHEL, SITE, JACZYNSKI, PREFER	1.0	0
8	http://www.inria.fr/aid/people.html	PEOPLE, ACTION	4.0	0
9	http://www.inria.fr/aid/aid-eng.html	ACTION	8.0	0
10	http://www.inria.fr/aid/confs.html	CONFER, DEADLIN, ACTION	0.0	0
11	http://www.inria.fr/aid/aid-eng.html	ACTION	2.0	0
12	http://www.inria.fr/aid/training.html	STAGE, ACTION	1.0	0
13	http://www.inria.fr/aid/software.html	SOFTWAR, ACTION	2.0	😊

Fig. 6. Extract of a navigation recorded by BROADWAY that can be displayed to the user.

3.3 Navigational Cases

In BROADWAY, potential cases (based on a situation template) and concrete cases are composed of:

- a time-extended situation from a navigation,
- a list of pages which can be advised in that situation,
- a set of data used to manage the case such as the date of creation.

The time-extended situation has an instantaneous part and a behavioural part. The instantaneous part contains the navigation context which is shared by all the cases based on the same navigation. The behavioural part defines which pages or sequence of pages are relevant in the description of this situation.

We have defined a situation template that can be applied at a precise instant of the navigation to build the situation. The rules described in this template create a behavioural description composed of (cf. Fig. 7):

- The last three pages and their keywords. This selection is used to describe a precise step in the user's navigation and is called the *case position* ;
- A set of past relevant pages (with their content description, user's evaluation and display time ratio). For this selection, relevant pages are pages evaluated by a user (positively or negatively) and/or pages with a high display time ratio. We use explicit (user's evaluation) and implicit (display time ratio) features to select relevant pages to improve the selection accuracy [23] ;
- A set of *before* constraints which are used to relate selected pages.

This template is used to create concrete cases. A concrete case references a navigation at a specific instant (*time reference*), making the separation between the past and the future. The list of advised pages represents the future pages of the case, which have been evaluated relevant or highly relevant by the user. The Fig. 7 shows an example of the association of a behavioural description with advised pages inside a concrete case. This example is based on the navigation of the Fig. 6. The page #3 is selected because of its evaluation, and the page #5 is selected because of its high display time ratio (above 20). The page #13 is advised by this case because it has been evaluated as relevant by the user.

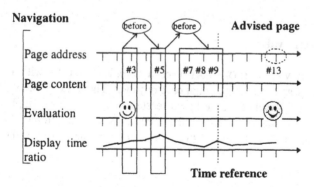

Fig. 7. Example of a concrete case

4   Reusing Past Navigations

BROADWAY is accessed by multiple users, and when an advice must be given to a user, the advice server starts a new reasoning. The user's current navigation represents the indices of the current problem to solve. The reasoner uses four steps (cf. Fig. 8): 1/ it retrieves cases with similar time-extended situations, 2/ it reuses the past navigational cases to give appropriate advice, 3/ it revises cases based on the user evaluation during his browsing session and   4/ finally it retains this current experience. In this section, we describe the retrieval and reuse steps of the case-based reasoner of BROADWAY and we propose a case forgetting method required to cope with dynamic changes of the WWW documents.

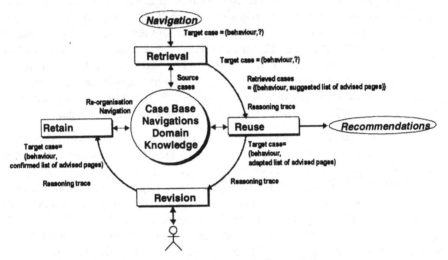

Fig. 8. Reasoning of the Broadway advice server

4.1 Case Retrieval

The case retrieval in BROADWAY uses a complex strategy with two alternatives: concrete case retrieval and potential case retrieval. The retrieval step is built using our framework CBR*Tools for case-based reasoning that provides simple index structure which can be composed to define composite indexes. In addition to these alternatives, we want to emphasise the use of three similarity measures used in the comparison of situations.

4.1.1 Retrieval Alternatives
The first alternative only considers concrete cases. If no concrete cases with enough similarity are found, the second alternative will be executed to retrieve matching potential cases. This strategy encourages the reuse of existing concrete cases rather than identifying potential cases. In addition, this strategy leads to a better efficiency of the retrieval step because the first alternative requires less computations.

The first alternative is composed of two steps:
1. *concrete case position filtering*: inside its behavioural situation, each case defines its position. Each case position has the same structure and defines a

vector of values. BROADWAY uses a K-Nearest Neighbour (KNN) approach to filter the cases which are above a similarity threshold. The aims of this step are to ensure a minimal relevance of retrieved cases and to speed up the retrieval process.

2. *concrete case selection*: for a fine grained selection, additional selected pages with their evaluation and temporal constraints are used to select best cases through another KNN search.

The second alternative requires three steps :

1. *navigation filtering*: a crisp comparison is made between the current context and the past navigation contexts. The goal of this step is to discard navigations that have totally different contexts from the retrieval step in an efficient way. BROADWAY uses hashtables to get navigations that have at least one host or one keyword in common with the current context.

2. *potential case position filtering*: the identified navigations are scanned through a sequential search to find positions that are above a similarity threshold. For these positions, the situation template is instanciated and a potential case is created.

3. *potential case selection:* as in the concrete case selection, a fine grained KNN search is done on the potential cases. Selected potential cases will be then stored in the case base as concrete cases by the retain step of the reasoner.

4.1.2 Similarity Measures

BROADWAY defines local similarity measures for each variable and for the temporal constraints comparison. Then a standard global similarity measure (weighted average) is used to aggregate local similarities. We describe the three main local similarity measures used to compare: page addresses, page contents and temporal constraints.

The similarity measure of page addresses uses the underlying hierarchical structure of addresses (cf. Fig. 9). Pages are indeed grouped into directories. Each directory has an implicit meaning and contains pages that are somehow related. In addition, deeper directories contain more precise information. We must take these features into account in the similarity measure.

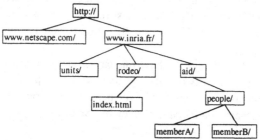

Fig. 9. Hierarchical structure of page addresses

A page address is then identified by its last node and we use the following similarity measures [5], if p and q are two addresses of pages:

$$S_{ad}(p,q) = 1 - \frac{h(p, MSCA(p,q)) + h(q, MSCA(p,q))}{h(p, root) + h(q, root)}$$

where h() gives the number of links between two nodes and MSCA() gives the most specific common abstraction of two nodes.

For instance:

S_{ad}(http://www.inria.fr/aid/people/memberA, http://www.inria.fr/aid/people/memberB) = 0.75

S_{ad}(http://www.inria.fr/aid/people/memberA, http://www.inria.fr/rodeo/index.html) = 0.28

S_{ad}(http://www.inria.fr/rodeo, http //www.inria.fr/aid) = 0.5

Each page content is summarised by a list of keywords. A similarity measure based on the number of common words is computed (cf. [26]), if v and w are two sets of words:

$$S_c(v,w) = \frac{Card(v \cap w)}{Card(v \cup w)}$$

Finally, we use a similarity measure based on the number of satisfied constraints in the current navigation according to the constraints defined in each case. If v is the set of constraints in a case and w is the set of constraints satisfied in the current situation:

$$S_{tc}(v,w) = \frac{Card(w)}{Card(v)}$$

4.2 Case Reuse

The retrieval step has identified a list of relevant cases and each case gives a list of advised pages. In the reuse step, the k-most reusable pages are selected and ordered according to their *reusability*. The reusability of each page is computed by a weighted average of features based on:

- the number of cases that advise this page,
- the average similarity of the cases that advise this page,
- the average user's evaluation of the page in the retrieved cases,
- the attachment of annotations given by users,
- the average loading time of the page.

Thus, BROADWAY selects the pages not only for their relevance but also for their access features. The WWW is a dynamic hypermedia where pages are deleted, moved or modified. In addition, depending on the location of the user and the page server, different loading time may be observed. BROADWAY keeps track of access to pages and these data are taken into account in the reuse step for better advice.

4.3 Case Revision

The goal of this revision step is to revise the solution i.e. the suggested list of advised pages issued from the previous step - the reuse step -. In our application, the revision step is done by the user evaluation when he navigates by following the advice given by Broadway or the links proposed by the displayed pages.

4.3 Case Forgetting

The WWW is a dynamic space and some past experiences may become obsolete. For this reason, we have designed a module which runs on a regular basis in order to delete from the memory obsolete cases and navigations (*case forgetting*). A concrete case is obsolete when the advised pages are all obsolete or when more than 25% of the pages selected in its time-extended situation are obsolete. A page is considered as obsolete when it is no more accessible (after multiple retry) or when the similarity of the page content stored in the case and its current content is under a threshold. Navigations are also checked in the same way, and if the navigation is obsolete then all its cases and the navigation itself are forgotten. Thus, potential cases will not be retrieved again in this navigation.

5 Related Works

We first compare the different hypermedia browsing advisors according to our goals, separating the case-base approaches from others. Then we summarise in Table 2. the comparison between BROADWAY and these advisors.

5.1 Case-Based Browsing Advisors

Radix [6] is based on a deeper description of the browsing session than BROADWAY. The observation of users' actions, such as bookmark selection, page address edition, back or forward link selection, are required to represent a session and its components. A case is an entire information retrieval session whereas in BROADWAY a case represents a specific experience in a navigation. A time-extended situation is taken into account with an event-driven similarity during the retrieval step. It is not clear how Radix could manage a group of users even if it uses an object-oriented database to store cases. Radix uses a specific browser with customised functions to watch user's actions, so its use is restricted to a specific platform.

Hypercase [19] is a browsing advisor designed to help a user on a delimited hypermedia. The definition of each node is required and this approach is not appropriate to address WWW navigation assistance. In addition, Hypercase cannot learn from real navigations of a group of users because its reasoning is only based on pre-stored cases built by experts.

The goal of Hospitext [7] is to assist different types of users during the browsing of medical records of patients. It learns from past navigation and a hierarchy of navigation behaviour is built. Hospitext uses domain knowledge mainly in the definition of a taxonomy of documents used in the case matching. This approach is not appropriate from WWW browsing since a taxonomy of documents seems hard to define.

5.2 Non Case-Based Browsing Advisors

Letizia [16] is an agent that assists a user by browsing concurrently and autonomously from the current page. Letizia uses the time spend by the user reading the current document to explore the neighbourhood and anticipate user's browsing. However, Letizia does not learn from its experiences and it builds only a description of the user's interest for the current session by recording its actions.

WebWatcher [2] follows the user along its navigation and highlights the hyperlinks of the current page that are of interest. WebWatcher learns from previous navigation of different users based on several machine learning algorithms. However, the situation assessment does not take the past sequence of events into account, but only an instantaneous summary through vector of keywords. WebWatcher is based on a HTTP stream transducer not implemented by a proxy, and the all HTML pages must be analysed and altered to redirect hyperlinks to itself. Personal WebWatcher (PWW) [20] is similar to WebWatcher but it aims to assist only one user a proxy-based architecture.

Yan et al. [28] propose a modified WWW server that logs all documents access for a user session. The browsing sessions are then analysed off-line to build clusters of access patterns. Then when the user gets connected to this specific site, his document access is analysed, a set of matching clusters are identified and the documents not yet accessed are advised to the user. However, the order of the accessed pages is not taken into account and inaccuracy may be caused by caching mechanisms from proxies and browsers.

5.3 Synthesis

We can summarise the comparison of related works according to the type of advice computation and our four requirements introduced in the section 1. As the Table 2. shows us, the main originality of the BROADWAY approach compared to the user behaviour-based advisors lies in the observation of a sequence of ordered visited pages (time-extended situation). Compared to Radix, we propose the observation of user's behaviours at the variable level (4 observation variables in the current version of BROADWAY) and we propose a generic model in order to take new variables into account [9]. In addition, this model is supported by our object-oriented framework for

CBR, called CBR*Tools [12], so that we allow the designer to modify easily the set of observation variables.

Table 2. Comparison of related works according to our goals

	Behaviour based Advice	time-extended situation	learn from a group of users	Designed for the WWW	browser independent
Hospitext [7]	no	-	yes (CBR)	no	-
Letizia [16]	no	-	no	yes	no
WebWatcher[2]	no	-	yes	yes	yes
PWW [0]	no	-	no	yes	yes
Hypercase [19]	yes	no	no	no	-
Yan et al [8]	yes	no	yes	No	yes
Radix [6]	yes	yes	yes (CBR)	Yes	no
Broadway [11]	yes	yes	yes (CBR)	Yes	yes

6 Experimental Evaluation

An experimentation with real users has been lead by ergonomists to evaluate whether BROADWAY effectively assists users during the information searching so that the time spent and the number of visited pages are reduced [8]. For this experimentation, 10 students in Cognitive Psychology were chosen to play the role of users looking for information on the Web. Two groups with equal skills in Web browsing were constituted: the first one had access to recommendations of BROADWAY unlike the second one. All the users were given the same goal : « find information about the biography of Patrick Sommier, a contemporary artist that works probably in the dramatic art ». The starting page was constituted by the first five links given by the Altavista search engine. This subject was carefully selected: none of the students had previously heard about Patrick Sommier and his biography was not directly accessible from the starting page. A preliminary test was made to ensure that the information was reasonably accessible within 30 minutes without assistance so that the searching task was considered as a failure after this delay. An initial case base was created and the goal of the experimentation was to compare behaviors of these two groups using different criteria (cf. Table 1): number of success, duration and length of navigations.

Table 3. Main results of the experimentation

	With BROADWAY (4 people)	Without BROADWAY (6 people)
Number of success (percentage)	75%	33%
Duration of successful navigations (average)	18 min	24 min
Length of successful navigations (average)	19 pages	39 pages

Thus, in the context of this experimentation, the use of BROADWAY has facilitated the information retrieval: there are more successful retrievals, the duration of navigations is reduced and their lengths too. This test shows the first evaluation with real users who were not linked to the development of BROADWAY. Of course we need more experimentations with larger sets of users to generalize the results but the basis of our approach is confirmed.

However, during this experimentation, the users were told to evaluate systematically every visited pages (this is not required by BROADWAY), and the expectations were that evaluations would be homogeneous. In fact, some users seemed to evaluate pages based on the theme and others based on the precise request. However, there was a consensus on the most positive evaluation level. Thus, in order to improve the results we are currently studying different alternatives: reduction of the evaluation levels, explicit definition of the semantic of each level, and modification of the evaluations at the end of the navigation by taking the most positively evaluated pages into account.

7   Conclusion

In this paper we have presented BROADWAY, our cooperative browsing advisor for the World Wide Web, which uses case-based reasoning to advise pages by reusing past navigations of a group of users. BROADWAY is based on a proxy architecture so that it is able to follow a group of users on any sites of the Web. As it communicates with the user through standard protocols, BROADWAY is independent of the browser which enables its use on different platforms, with an up-to-date browser chosen by each user.

BROADWAY integrates, for the advice computation, a case-based reasoner with concrete and potential cases. Concrete cases represent specific experiences in a navigation which can be retrieved efficiently. When concrete case cannot be used, potential cases are searched in the past navigations for knowledge discovery. BROADWAY takes time-extended situations into account: its advice is based on similarity of past navigational behaviours. We have defined a similarity for each page using mainly its address and its content. The similarity of the page ordering is computed using temporal constraints between pages. We take into account that WWW pages can be altered or deleted in the reuse step and we have defined a specific method for case forgetting.

The relevance of advice given by BROADWAY has been evaluated in our research team and also in the context of an experimentation designed by students in Cognitive Psychology: positive results have been drawn based on some interesting shortcut observed in navigations. We also plan to apply our system in a restricted domain such as electronic business where the user satisfaction can be implicit (for example, the payment of a good). The use of our object-oriented frameworks CBR*Tools and BROADWAY*Tools will facilitate the specialisation of BROADWAY to such a context [12]: key concepts such as similarities, observation variables, retrieval and adaptation steps can be modified. We also plan to improve some parts of the design: integration of user and session profiles in the navigation context, and use of expert knowledge about navigations.

More generally, our current and future work for Collaborative Information Systems (CIS) concerns mainly two axes : 1/ the relevance of our original behaviour-based advisor approach (based on our model for case representation and indexing with time-extended situations), in particular for recommendation systems on the Web (such as Broadway). Further evaluations of our approach are in progress with two new applications for information retrieval on the Web (supported by France Telecom and Xerox); 2/ the integration of direct collaboration oriented tools in BROADWAY*tools [27]: for example, an argumentation server will be soon proposed issued from our work on HERMES, an argumentation computer aided system [14] in order to allow an annotation as a argumentation graph attached to a specific document.

Acknowledgments

We would like to thank N. Bonnardel and her students from the University of Provence for the experimental evaluation of BROADWAY, and Rushed Kanawati who is involved in our Xerox CIS application for his helpful remarks.

References

1. A. Aamodt and E. Plaza. Case-based reasoning: foundational issues, methodological variations, and system. *AI Communications*, 7(1) :36–59, March 1994.

2. R. Amstrong, D. Freitag, T. Joachims and T. Mitchell. WebWatcher: A learning Apprentice for the World Wide Web. In *AAAI Spring Symposium on Information Gathering from Heterogeneous, Distributed Environments*, March 1995.

3. T. Bray. Measuring the Web. In *Proc. of the 5th International World Wide Web Conference*, Computer Network and ISDN Systems, 28 :993–1005, 1996.

4. C. Brooks, M. S. Mazer, S. Meeks and J. Miller. Application-specific proxy servers as HTTP stream transducers. In. *Proc. of the 4th International World Wide Web Conference*, pages 539–548, Boston, 1995.

5. Cognitive System. Remind: developer's reference manual. 200-230, Commercial St., Boston MA 02109, 1992.

6. F. Corvaisier, A. Mille, J.M. Pinon. Information retrieval on the World Wide Web using a decison making system. In *Proceedings of RIAO'97*, June 97.

7. S. Elkassar and J. Charlet. Représentation de connaissances et aide à la navigation hypertextuelle à partir de cas : application au dossier médical. In *Journée Ingénierie des connaissances et apprentissage automatique (JICAA'97)*, pages 387–401, Mai 1997. In French.

8. C. Hébraud, M. Rech and A. Thébault. Test of the Usefulness of the Browsing Assistant BROADWAY. Internal Report, University of Provence, Aix en Provence, 19 pages, 1998. In French.

9. M. Jaczynski. A Framework for the Management of Past Experiences with Time-Extended Situations. In *Proceedings of the 6th International Conference on Information and Knowledge Management (CIKM'97)*, ACM Press, pages 32–39, Las Vegas, 1997.

10. M. Jaczynski and B. Trousse CBR*Tools: an object-oriented library for indexing cases with behavioural situation. Research Report n°3215, INRIA, July 1997. In French.

11. M. Jaczynski and B. Trousse. WWW Assisted Browsing by Reusing Past Navigations from a Group of Users. In *Proceedings of 4th European Workshop on Case-Based Reasoning (EWCBR98)*, volume 1488 of Lecture Notes in Artificial Intelligence, Springer Verlag, pages 160–171, Dublin, 1998.

12. M. Jaczynski and B. Trousse. An object-oriented framework for the design and the implementation of case-based reasoners. In *Proceedings of 6th German Workshop on Case-Based Reasoning (GWCBR'98)*. Berlin, March 1998. To appear.

13. K-H. Jerke, P. Szabo, A Lesh and H. Rossler. Combining hypermedia browsing with formal queries. In D. Diaper et al., editors, *Human-Computer Interaction - Interact'90*, pages 593–598, 1990.

14. N.I. Karacapilidis, B. Trousse and D. Papadias. Using Case-Based Reasoning for Argumentation with Multiple Viewpoints. In *Case-Based Reasoning Research and Development, Proceedings of the 2nd International Conference on Case-Based Reasoning (ICCBR'97)*, volume 1266 of *Lecture Notes in Artificial Intelligence*, pages 541–552, Springer, 1997.

15. T.B.Lee *et al.* The World Wide Web. *Communication of the ACM*, 37(8) :76–82, 1994.

16. H. Lieberman. Letizia: an agent that assists Web browsing. In *Proceedings of International Joint Conference on Artificial Intelligence*, Montreal, August 1995.

17. A. Luotonen and K. Altis. World-Wide Web Proxies. In *1st International World Wide Web Conference*, Geneva, 1994.

18. W. S Meeks, C. Brooks and M. S. Mazer. Transducers and associates: circumventing limitations on the World Wide Web. In *Proceedings of etaCOM'96*, Portland, Oregon, May 1996.

19. A. Micarelli and F. Sciarrone. A case-based system for adaptive hypermedia navigation. In I. Smith and B. Faltings, editors, *Advances in Case-Based Reasoning*, volume 1168 of *Lecture Notes in Artificial Intelligence*, pages 266–279. Springer, 1996.

20. D. Mladenic. Personal WebWatcher: design and implementation. Technical report IJS-DP-7472, School of Computer Science, Carnegie Mellon University, October 1996.

21. A. Ram and J.C. Santamaria. Continuous case-based reasoning. In *AAAI Case-Based Reasoning Worksop*, pages 86–93, 1993.

23. H. Sakagami and T. Kamba. Learning personal preferences on line newspaper articles from user behaviors. In *Proc. of the 6th International World Wide Web Conference*. 1997.

24. M. A. Schicker, M. S Mazer and C. Brooks. Pan-browser support for annotations and other meta-information on the World Wide Web. In *Proc. of the 5th International World Wide Web Conference*, Computer Network and ISDN Systems, 28:1063–1074, May 1996.

25. C. Shahabi, A. M. Zarkesh, J. Adibi and V. Shah. Knowledge discovery from users Web-page navigation. *In Proceeding of 7th International Workshop on Research Issue in Data Engineering, High Performance Database Management for Large-Scale Applications*, pages 20–29. IEEE Comput. Soc. Press, 1997.

26. A. Tversky. Features of similarity. *Psychological Review*, 84(4): 327–352, 1977.

27. B. Trousse, M. Jaczynski and R. Kanawati. Towards a framework for building collaborative information searching systems. In *Proceedings of Digital Libraries 98 (poster)*, *Lecture Notes in Artificial Intelligence*, Springer, 1998. To appear.

28. T.W. Yan, M. Jacobsen, H.Garcia-Molina and U. Dayal. From user access patterns to dynamic hypertext linking. In *Proc. of the 5th International World Wide Web Conference*, Computer Network and ISDN Systems, 28:1007–1014, 1996.

Towards a Formal Specification of Complex Social Structures in Multi-agent Systems

Juan A. Rodríguez-Aguilar, Francisco J. Martín, Pere Garcia, Pablo Noriega, and Carles Sierra

Artificial Intelligence Research Institute, IIIA
Spanish Council for Scientific Research, CSIC
08193 Bellaterra, Barcelona, Spain.
{jar,martin,pere,pablo,sierra}@iiia.csic.es
http://www.iiia.csic.es

Abstract. In this paper we summarize the results obtained so far in the course of the Fishmarket project concerning the study of the formalization, design and construction of agent-mediated electronic institutions (AMIs). We argue that AMIs are the most appropriate social structure for a large variety of multi-agent systems. Here we present the realization of an actual AMI, FM, inspired on the traditional fish market that we employ as a case study in our proposal for the formalization of electronic institutions.

1 Introduction

The notion of interaction between agents makes up the core of all multi-agent systems. Interactions are the observable part of these systems' behaviour: cooperation, coordination, collaboration and negotiation.

Our aim is to build agents that help humans negotiate. Eventually, humans can rely on autonomous agents for their negotiation tasks. However, these must be able to cooperate, not only with other autonomous agents, but also with humans. Consequently, we ar e interested in the interaction models that take into account the special features of human negotiation. Particularly, as a basic feature, the notion of dialogue, since we consider negotiation, and interaction in general, as a dialogic activity: humans an d agents reach agreements through conversations. Because of the interaction between agents and humans no notion of omniscience or perfect rationality can be assumed in the counterparts to our agents.

Dialogic exchanges assume that agents are entities capable of establishing commitments. In negotiation terms, the dialogue participants are in relation with social conventions and institutions that enforce the acomplishment of these commitments. For instan ce, a separation agreement is established trough a contract which is mediated and validated by a judge; heritage transfers require a registry office and the concurrence of a notary; shares are exchanged at stock markets.

J.A. Padget (Ed.): Human and Artificial Societies, LNAI 1624, pp. 284–300, 1999.

Also note that even though human negotiation can profit from the elucidatory and explanatory resources of conversations, the mediated negotiations in
the aforementioned institutions exclude this necessity imposing a strict interpretation of the language u sed in the dialogue through the conventions established
by such institutions. This is the case of price calls in an auction house, or number
sequences in a stock market. Similarly, in agent-mediated interactions meaning
has to be made explicit. Even thoug h one can imagine that dialogic interactions have an elucidatory content, restricting negotiation —and interactions in
general— to those which use perfectly defined languages is a much more practical option. In this work, we consider institutions as the most appropriate social
structure for handling the interactions among agents in a large variety of multi-
agent systems.

The notion of institution is founded on three pillars which contain the elements already mentioned:

1. *A dialogic framework.* Some aspects of an institution are fixed, constituting
   the context or framework of interaction amongst agents. In an institution,
   agents interact trough illocutions. Institutions define which are the acceptable illocutions, which is the ontology —including roles, place and time—,
   the common language to refer to the "world", a common language for communication, and a common metalanguage. An institution can often consider
   social relationships between participating agents as relevant —in terms of
   authority, for instance— or some "personality" feature which can affect the
   interactions. All of these contextual features are what we call dialogic framework.
2. *A performative structure.* Interactions between agents are articulated
   through agent group meetings, which we call scenes, with a well-defined
   communication protocol. We consider the protocol of a scene to be the possible dialogues agents may hold. Furthermore, a performative structure also
   includes the specification of the transitions between scenes.
3. *Rules of Behaviour.* Agent actions in the context of an institution —as far
   as we are concerned, dialogic actions or utterances[1]— have consequences;
   usually commitments which either impose or relax restrictions on dialogic
   actions of agents in the scenes wherein they will act in the future. Behaviour rules affect the behaviour of agents, or more generally the performative
   structure.

As a starting point for the study of electronic institutions in the framework of the Fishmarket project, we chose auction houses as a paradigm of traditional human institutions. Auctions are an attractive domain of interest for
AI researchers in at least two areas of activity. On the one hand, we observe
that the proliferation of on-line auctions in the Internet —such as Auction-
line(www.auctionline.com), Onsale(www.onsale.com), eBay(www.eBay.com) In-
terAUCTION(www.interauction.com), and many others— has established auc-

---

[1] "utterance suggests human speech or some analog to speech, in which the message
between sender and addressee conveys information about the sender"[15]

tioning as a main-stream form of electronic commerce. Thus, agent-mediated auctions appear as a convenient mechanism for automated trading, due mainly to the simplicity of their conventions for interaction when multi-party negotiations are involved, but also to the fact that on-line auctions may successfully reduce storage, delivery or clearing house costs in many markets. This popularity has spawned AI research and development in computational auction markets [24,19] as well as in trading agents and heuristics [5,8]. On the other hand, auctions are not only employed in web-based trading, but also as one of the most prevalent coordination mechanisms for agent-mediated resource allocation problems (f.i. energy management [26,25], climate control [6], flow problems [22]).

The rest of the paper is organized as follows. In Section 2, we describe a traditional trading institution, the fish market, along with the essential notions of how its electronic counterpart (FM) works. Then a proposal for a formalization of electronic institutions follows in Section 3. Next Section 4 introduces the first attempts towards the realization of such a formal specification based on the usage of interagents. Finally, Section 5 presents some conclusions and outlines some challenging issues to be faced as future work.

2   The Fish Market: A Case Study of Human Institutions

Traditional trading institutions[2] such as auction houses —and the fish market in particular— have successfully dealt with the issues of diversity (of goods, trading conventions, participants, interests) and dispersal (of consumers and producers, and also of resources and opportunities). For instance, by defining strict trading conventions where goods of specified kinds (e.g. fish of certain quality) are traded under explicit time/location restrictions (e.g. twice a day at fixed times at the fish market building) under strict negotiation protocols (e.g. downward bidding[3]). Participating agents are subject to terms and conditions —involving identity, credit and payment, guarantees, etc.— whereby the soundness of transactions becomes a responsibility of the institution itself, who in turn enforces those terms and conditions on its own behalf.

From our view, the fish market can be described and modelled as a place where several *scenes* run simultaneously, at different places, but with some causal continuity[19,12]. The principal scene is the auction itself, in which buyers bid for boxes of fish that are presented by an auctioneer who calls prices in descending order —the *downward bidding protocol*. However, before those boxes of fish may be sold, fishermen have to deliver the fish to the fish market, at the

---

[2] We use the term *institution* in the sense proposed by [14] as a "set of artificial constraints that articulate agent interactions".

[3] The Spanish fish market still uses the traditional *downward bidding* protocol in which boxes of fish are adjudicated to the buyer who *stops* a descending sequence of prices that is called by an auctioneer in front of all registered buyers. This protocol is also called a *Dutch auction* because it is the way flowers have been traditionally traded in Holland. For historical references and the classical economic-theoretical outlook on auctions, cf., [9,10].

sellers' registration scene, and buyers need to register for the market, at the *buyers' registration scene.* Likewise, once a box of fish is sold, the buyer should take it away by passing through a *buyers' settlements scene,* while sellers may collect their payments at the *sellers' settlements scene* once their lot has been sold. Each scene is supervised by one of the market intermediaries (auctioneer, buyer admitter, buyer manager, seller admitter, seller manager, and boss) which represent and work for the institution.

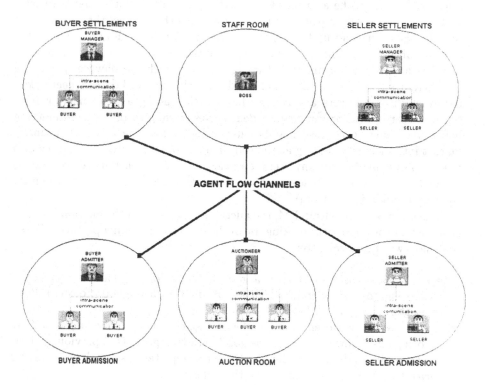

Fig. 1. FM Multi-scene Structure

In practice, the fish market upholds the fairness of the negotiation process and the accountability of transactions by defining and enforcing stable conditions on:

- the eligibility requirements for participating buyers and sellers;
- the availability, presentation and delivery of goods;
- acceptable behaviour of participants within the site; and
- the satisfaction of public commitments made by participants.

We believe that similar functions may advantageously be instituted for multi-agent systems. This mimetic strategy lead to a *proof of concept*-level electronic auction house presented in [11], and subsequently refined in order to produce FM96.5 [19], a rather complete implementation of the actual fish market. Later on FM96.5 was extended in order to obtain a test-bed for trading agents, FM (see [17] and [18] for a more thorough discussion)[4].

In a highly mimetic way, the workings of FM also involve the concurrency of several scenes governed by the market intermediaries identified in the fish market. Therefore, seller agents register their goods with a seller admitter agent, and can get their earnings (from a seller manager agent) once the auctioneer agent has sold these goods in the auction room. Buyer agents, on the other hand, register with a buyer admitter agent, and bid for goods which they pay through a credit line that is set up and updated by a buyer manager agent. Figure 1 shows the conceptual model of FM as a multi-scene multi-agent scenario. We regard each scene as a virtual scene inhabited by agents that might be physically running at different sites. Observe also that we draw a distinction between *agent flow*, corresponding to buyers and sellers (henceforth trading agents) moving from scene to scene, and *communication flow*, corresponding to both the interaction between trading agents and market intermediaries and the interaction among market intermediaries aiming at the coordination of their activities. Notice also that agents cannot enter any scene because the institution imposes constrains on the transitions between scenes (f.i. a buyer cannot leave the auction room for entering the admission room).

The main activity within FM, the auctioning of goods in the auction room, is governed by the auctioneer making use of the downward bidding protocol (DBP) that next we state explicitly:

[**Step 1**] The auctioneer chooses a good out of a lot of goods that is sorted according to the order in which sellers deliver their goods to the sellers' admitter.

[**Step 2**] With a chosen good g, the auctioneer opens a *bidding round* by quoting offers downward from the good's starting price, (p_α) previously fixed by the sellers' admitter, as long as these price quotations are above a *reserve price* (p_{rsv}) previously defined by the seller.

[**Step 3**] For each price called by the auctioneer, several situations might arise during the open round:

Multiple bids Several buyers submit their bids at the current price. In this case, a collision comes about, the good is not sold to any buyer, and the auctioneer restarts the round at a higher price. Nevertheless, the auctioneer tracks whether a given number of successive collisions (Σ_{coll}) is reached, in order to avoid an infinite collision loop. This loop is broken by randomly selecting one buyer out of the set of colliding bidders.

One bid Only one buyer submits a bid at the current price. The good is sold to this buyer whenever his credit can support his bid. Whenever there is an unsupported bid the round is restarted by the auctioneer at

---

[4] The current version of FM [16] is now available and can be downloaded from the Fishmarket project web page [27]

a higher price, the unsuccessful bidder is punished with a fine, and he is expelled out from the auction room unless such fine is paid off.

No bids No buyer submits a bid at the current price. If the reserve price has not been reached yet, the auctioneer quotes a new price which is obtained by decreasing the current price according to the price step. If the reserve price is reached, the auctioneer declares the good *withdrawn* and closes the round.

[**Step 4**] The first three steps repeat until there are no more goods left.

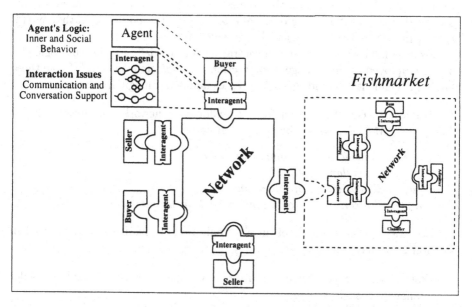

Fig. 2. *Fishmarket*: A multi-agent system using interagents

Analogously to the actual fish market, FM must be regarded as an *electronic institution* wherein heterogeneous (human and software) agents of arbitrary complexity can trade goods as long as they comply with the *fish market institutional* conventions. Those conventions that affect buyers and sellers are enforced by a special type of software agents owned by the institution, the so-called *interagents*, that establish what utterances can be said by whom and when. They constitute the unique mean through which trading agents interact within the market scenario (see Figure 2). Thus, as a rule, agents' external behaviour is managed and mandated by interagents, while their individual logic, knowledge, reasoning, learning, or other capabilities are internal to agents. A thorough description of interagents appears in Section 4.

3 A Formal View of Agent-mediated Electronic Institutions

Throughout this section we elaborate a proposal for formalizing electronic institutions taking inspiration on the example of electronic institution presented above. Thus we must first remember that we based our notion of electronic institution on three pillars (dialogic framework, performative structure, rules of behaviour) that we formally define in what follows.

First, we observe that each agent participating in an institution takes on a role. Consequently, the notion of *role* is a core concept for our model of institution. Henceforth we denote the role set of an institution as *Role*. From this we can define a partial order over *Role* to capture the notion of authority (f.i. $r_i \geq r_j$ means that role r_i has authority over role r_j).

From [13,20] we take that the central notion for defining the ontologic elements employed during an agent interaction is a *dialogic framework*. Since these ontologic elements depend on each role, we define a dialogic framework as:

Definition 1. *Given a role set Role, a* Dialogic Framework *is a family of tuples* $DF_r = (L_r, ML_r, \iota_r, Time)$ *for each* $r \in Role$ *where*

- L_r *is a language for the domain of role r;*
- ML_r *is a metalanguage on* L_r;
- ι_r *is the illocution set of role r; and*
- *Time is a discrete and totally ordered set of instants.*

Considering the example of an electronic auction institution introduced in Section 2, we have that:

- *Role* = {auctioneer, buyer admitter, buyer manager, seller admitter, seller manager, boss, buyer, seller}
- *boss* $\geq r$ for all $r \in Role$
- $r \geq buyer$ and $r' \geq seller$ if $r \in Role - \{seller\}$ and $r' \in Role - \{buyer\}$
- $L_{auctioneer} = \{good(id, type, weight), lot(id), sold(buyer\_id, price), offer(price), \dots\}$
- $L_{buyer} = \{good(id, type, weight), bid, offer(price), admission(scene), \dots\}$
- $\iota_{auctioneer} = \{question, request, inform, commit, refuse\}$
- *Time* = $\mathbb{R}$

We assume in this work that each agent keeps its role regardless of the scene in which it participates.

Be now *Ag* a finite agent variable set, and *As* : *Ag* $\longrightarrow$ *Role* the function which assigns to an agent variable an agent role. Then, we build the communication language as the set of all legal (allowed) illocutions between agents:

$CL = \{\iota_{As(x)}(x, y, \varphi_{As(x)}, t)\}$ where $x, y \in Ag$, $\varphi_{As(x)} \in L_{As(x)}$ and $t \in Time\}$

Then the institution's language L_I is formed in the usual way from CL and the $\wedge, \vee$ and $\neg$ connectives —which stand for the conjunction, disjunction and negation respectively. Given R a subset of roles, the L_I sublanguage wi th respect to R, denoted as L_R, is composed of the formulae with agent variables whose roles belong to R.

Next we provide an example of illocutions within the communication language and the institution's language for FM corresponding to a price called by the auctioneer during a bidding round:

- $inform(auctioneer, buyer_i, offer(1300), 17:00) \in CL$
- $\bigwedge_{k=0...n} inform(auctioneer, buyer_k, offer(1300), 17:00) \in L_I$

The notion of performative structure is the most complex and interesting of this formalism, since it models the whole dialogic activity within an institution. The definition is based on the notion of scene that we present next. Conceptually, a scene is th e specification of a conversation involving a group of agents. And formally,

Definition 2. *A scene is a tuple* $s = (R, G_e, W_i, W_f)$ *where*

- R *is a multi-set[5] formed by elements of Role;*
- $G_e = (W, A, Es)$ *stands for a directed and labelled graph, where* W *is the set of states,* $A \subseteq W \times W$ *is the set of directed edges, and* $Es : A \longrightarrow L_R$ *is the labelling function;*
- $W_i \in W$ *is the non-empty scene state, and*
- $W_f \subseteq W$ *the final states of the scene.*

Thus a scene is a directed graph labelled by language statements of L_I whose vertices stand for the states of the conversation and whose edges stand for transitions between such states. Given a particular state of the scene w and a transition(labelled edge) to an adjacent state w', we say that the transition occurs when the formula f labelling the edge is satisfied (the labelling function Es outputs the formula to be satisfied in order to go from one state to the the other, so $Es((w, w')) = f$). At every non-final state of the scene there is at least one transition to another state. A scene is considered to be finished when it reaches one of its final states. Note that the transition and state sets determine the scene's protocol, i.e. the possible dialogic interactions.

If we want a scene to be deterministic the following restriction must be imposed: given a state, the same formula cannot lead to different states, therefore Es must satisfy: $Es((w, w')) \not\equiv Es((w, w''))$ where $\not\equiv$ means that the formul ae are not equivalent.

Observe also that the definition of scene does not depend on agents, but on their roles. Then a scene can start whenever there is a role assignment, i.e. there is a group of agents capable of assuming the roles specified by the scene. Note that an institution may allow for the simultaneous execution of more than one scene with different groups of agents.

---

[5] A multi-set is a set where elements may be repeated.

A complex social structure, as is the case of an institution, is formed by multiple interrelated scenes which are executed either concurrently or sequentially. Establishing the interrelations among scenes amounts to specifying how and when agents leave and enter scenes. Restrictions imposed on this agent flow determine the flexibility of the formalism. For this purpose we define the notion of transition between scenes as the specification of the conditions that an agent must verify to leave a scene and enter another.

Definition 3. *A transition tr is an ordered pair of statements of the metalanguage ML, i.e., $tr = (Pr, Po)$ where Pr and Po are the precondition and postcondition sets (written in the metalanguage)*

We define the metalanguage ML as the set of all metalanguages ML_r, and T denote the set of all transitions. Both preconditions and postconditions refer to the state of the scenes, the role of the agents, etc.

Now it is time to define the fundamental notion of performative structure.

Definition 4. *Given a dialogic framework $(DF_r)_{r \in Role}$, a performative structure is a directed graph labelled by transitions with scenes as vertices. Formally, $PS = (S, A, Et)$ where*

- S is a finite and non-empty set of scenes.
- A is a set of edges, i. e., $A \subseteq S \times S$.
- Et is a labelling function,i.e., $Et : A \longrightarrow T$.

Back to our example based on FM, we may define the following examples of performative structure:

- $S = \{$buyer admission, buyer settlement, auction room, seller admitter, seller settlement, out of market$\}$
- $A = \{$(buyer admission,auction room),(auction room,buyer settlement),...$\}$
- $Et(($ buyer admission,auction room$)) = (\{As(x) =$ buyer, admitted(x) $=$ true$\}, \{$scene_state(auction_room) $=$ init$\})$
- $PS_1 = (S, A, Et)$
- $PS_2 = (S' = S - \{$buyer admission,seller admission$\}, A_{|S'}, Et_{|S'})$

The transition above indicates how an agent can leave the buyer admission scene to enter the auction room scene. In general, we shall consider that an agent can leave a scene:

- when requesting for leaving, it fulfils the transition conditions between scenes;
- if an agent with superior authority orders so; and
- if the scene reaches a final state.

There remains the matter of defining where the agent is incorporated into another scene once a transition occurs. There are essentially two options:

- in the current state of the scene; and
- in a predetermined entrance state of the scene —in this case the agent must wait until the scene reaches such state.

More concretely, let x be an agent in scene s, if x wants to move from s to s', and we assume that $(s, s') \in A$ and $Et((s, s')) = tr$, then the following procedure must be followed:

- if x does not satisfy the tr preconditions then the entrance to s' is denied;
- if x satisfies the tr preconditions then:
  - if s' satisfies the postconditions the entrance is permitted; and
  - if s' does not satisfy the postconditions the entrance is denied until these are satisfied.

We understand that the agent's speech acts introduce subsequent acting commitments that have to be interpreted as acting obligations in a certain direction, and, consequently, as a limitation or enlargement in the acting possibilities. In particular, this implies imposing or removing restrictions on the inter-scene transitions of the agent acquiring the commitments or, in a more general sense, producing changes in the performative structure. In this approach we formalize such commitments with the so-called *behaviour rules* that we define as:

Definition 5. *Given a dialogic framework* $(DF_r)_{r \in Role}$ *and a set of performative structures* $\mathcal{PS}$, *a behaviour rule* RB *is a function of the form:* $RB : L_I \times \mathcal{PS} \longrightarrow \mathcal{PS}$

Following the example above, the rule of behaviour below makes explicit the change in the performative structure (closing both the buyer and seller admission scenes) when the boss declares that the market is closed.

$$RB(inform(boss, sellermanager, close\_market(now), 17 : 30), PS_1) = PS_2$$

Finally, we can define an electronic institution by grouping together all the elements introduced so far:

Definition 6. *An electronic institution is a triplet* $EI = ((DF_r)_{r \in Role}, \mathcal{PS}, \mathcal{RB})$, *where* $(DF_r)_{r \in Role}$ *is a dialogic framework,* $\mathcal{PS}$ *is a set performative structures and* $\mathcal{RB}$ *is a set of behaviour rules.*

Only left to remind that the execution of an institution consists on the generation of scene instances, the allocation of specific agents to the agent variables to roles of a scene, and the movement of agents through scenes respecting the transitions given in the performative structure, and the evolution of the performative structure specified by the rules of behaviour.

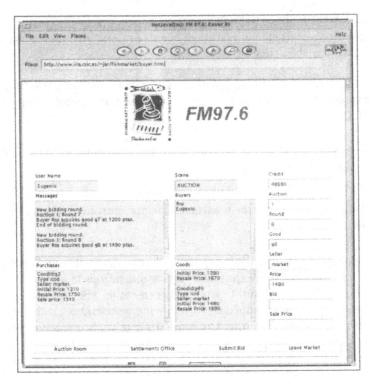

Fig. 3. *GUI offered by an interagent to a human buyer*

4   On the Implementation of AMIs: An Interagent Approach

In [7] we introduced interagents as autonomous software agents that mediate the interaction between an agent and the agent society wherein this is situated. In this section we sketch out their functionality and we discuss how they have been employed for realizing the particular formal specification of the fish market.

The management of *conversation protocols*(CPs) was identified in [7] as the main task of interagents. We view conversations as the means of representing the conventions adopted by agents when interacting through the exchange of utterances [23,3]. More precisely, such conventions define the *legal* sequence of utterances that can be exchanged among the agents engaged in conversation: what can be said, to whom and when. Therefore, CPs are coordination patterns that constrain the sequencing of utterances during a conversation held between two agents.

We differentiated two roles for the agents interacting with an interagent: *customer*, played by the agent exploiting and benefiting from the services offered by the interagent; and *owner*, played by the agent endowed with the capability of dynamically establishing the policies that determine the interagent's behaviour.

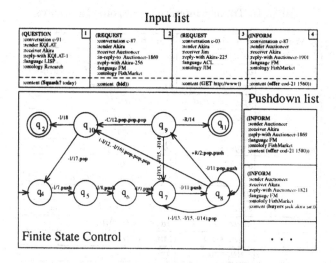

Fig. 4. View of the CP used by buyers' trading interagents in the auction room.

Needless to say that an agent can possibly play both roles at the same time. An interagent is responsible for posting utterances of its customer to the corresponding addressee and for collecting the utterances that other agents address to its customer. This *utterance management* abstracts customers from the details concerning the agent communication language and the network protocol. Each interagent owns a collection of relevant CPs used for managing its customer conversations. When its customer intends to start a new conversation with another agent the interagent instantiates the corresponding conversation protocol. Once the conversation starts, the interagent becomes responsible for ensuring that the exchange of utterances conforms to the CP specification.

Table 1. Trading Interagent Incoming Predicates

#Message	Predicate	Parameters
1	admission	buyerlogin password
2	bid	[price]
3	exit	

We shall differentiate two types of interagents in FM: *trading interagents*, owned by the institution but used by trading agents, and *institutional interagents*, both owned and used by those agents functioning as market intermediaries. Therefore, all interagents are owned by the institution, but we identify two types of customers: the trading agents and the institution itself.

Trading interagents constitute the sole and exclusive means through which trading agents interact with the market intermediaries representing the insti-

Table 2. Trading Interagent Outgoing Predicates

#Message	Predicate	Parameters
4	deny	deny_code
5	accept	open|closed auction_number
6	open_auction	auction_number
7	open_round	round_number
8	good	good_id good_type starting_price resale_price
9	buyers	{buyerlogin}*
10	goods	{good_id good_type starting_price resale_price}*
11	offer	price
12	sold	good_id buyerlogin price
13	sanction	buyerlogin fine
14	expulsion	buyerlogin
15	collision	price
16	withdrawn	good_id price
17	end_round	round_number
18	end_auction	auction_number
19	going	{single|multiple} + {1, 2}
20	gone	
21	tie_break	buyerlogin
22	closed_market	

tution. Within each scene, a trading interagent must employ a different CP to allow its customer to talk to the market intermediary in charge of it. Therefore, trading interagents are responsible for enforcing the protocols that guarantee that every trading agent behaves according to the rules of the market.

As to market intermediaries, they must hold several conversations at the same time with the agents in the scene that they govern. For this purpose, the institutional interagents that they employ must exploit their capability for supporting multiple conversations by building collections of simultaneous CP instances (one per trading agent). Thus, for example, the auctioneer's interagent maintains an instance of the CP corresponding to the DBP for each buyer agent in the auction room. Moreover, not only are institutional interagents used to support conversations with trading agents, but also to allow those agents working as market intermediaries to coordinate their activities.

Anyhow, notice that an interagent does not handle the whole graph encoding all the interactions permitted within a scene, but a CP obtained as a projection of the graph corresponding to the role of its user.

The finite state control of the CP employed by the interagent for allowing its customer (a buyer agent) to participate in a bidding round in the auction room is depicted in Figure 4. For the sake of simplicity, the arcs of the finite state control are labelled with the predicates in Tables 4 and 2, corresponding to the propositional content of the utterances permitted by the CP. The diagram displays the interaction between a buyer agent and his interagent from the agent's view. Therefore, message numbers followed by / stand for messages sent by a buyer agent, while message numbers preceded by / stand for messages received by a buyer agent. For instance, 2/ means that the buyer submits a bid at the price called by the auctioneer within /11. Note that that trading interagents handle differently their interaction with human customers. In such a case, they offer a GUI for the human traders to interact (see Figure 3).

There still remains the matter of capturing the central notion of performative structure, i.e. the transitions of agents between scenes. Trading interagents in FM allow their users to jump from one scene to another by connecting each final state in a CP with the initial state of the CP corresponding to the destination scene. However the actual peformative structure required by FM is hard-wired into interagents, which are not capable yet of handling specifications of performative structures.

Interagents have been endowed with further capabilities. On the one hand, they are in charge of conveying monitoring information to the auditing agent (also called monitoring agent), so that market sessions can be monitored, and analyzed step-by-step. On the other hand, interagents provide support for agent failure handling. For example, when a trading agent either goes down or simply fails to consume the utterances conveyed by its interagent (say that the trading agent lapses into an extremely demanding deliberative process for elaborating its strategies), this interagent pro-actively unplugs its customer from the market and leaves the market on its behalf.

Finally, the interagents in FM can dynamically (at run-time) reconfigure CPs in order to guarantee the verification of the liveness, termination, and the deadlock and race condition free properties in order to ensure protocol compatibility.

Summarizing, the successful incorporation of interagents into FM has proven their usefulness by coping with several tasks: i) to handle the interplay between trading agents and the market institution; ii) to handle the coordination between market intermediaries' tasks; iii) to provide support for the monitoring of market sessions; iv) to handle agents' failures; v) to reconfigure CPs so as to ensure protocol compatibility. Ideally further, gradual extensions of interagents' capabilities will permit coping with the required functionalities of an AMI.

5   Conclusions and Future Work

Up to date not much work has attempted to employ organizational approaches for the specification and design of multi-agent systems [4]. We argue that the use of organizational concepts (such as roles, groups or institutions) can prove to be valuable for the deployment of complex social structures in multi-agent systems. In this work we summarize the contributions in this direction made in the course of the Fishmarket project concerning the study of the formal specification, design, and construction of a special type of multi-agent systems: agent-mediated electronic institutions (AMIs). We exemplify our current conceptualization of electronic institution by means of an actual implementation, FM, an electronic auction house inspired on the traditional fish market. Such an example also serves to identify the fundamental components of an electronic institution that are subsequently employed for elaborating a proposal for formalizing electronic institutions, along the lines of [21] that provides solid foundations for the design of a specification language. There are still several open issues concerning our formal view:

- how to allow that agents play different roles within different scenes;
- how to allow that agents participate in different scenes at the same time; and
- how to allow for the multiple instantiation of the same scene.

These features will surely lead to a much more flexible formalization of electronic institutions so that a wider range of practical institutions can be covered.

Therefore our future work is to concentrate on the completion of a stable formalization that leads to the design of a (both graphical and textual) specification language for electronic institutions ([2] accounts for the first attempts in this direction). Ideally such a language shall support the automatic generation of electronic institutions as well as some of their participating agents. For instance, such a language would permit to specify an auction house in order to obtain the infrastructure (conversation protocols and interagents in the sense proposed in [7]) required for ensuring a sound multi-agent trading interaction. For this purpose, the specification language must address a fundamental issue: the generation of the CPs to be managed by interagents from the specification provided by the institution designer.

Acknowledgements

This work has been partially supported by the European TMR number PL93-0186 VIM, CEC/HCM VIM project, contract CHRX-CT93-0401 (cf. [1]); the Spanish CICYT project SMASH, TIC96-1038-C04001, and the Mexican CONACYT grant [69068-7245]. J. A. Rodríguez-Aguilar and F. J. Martín enjoy the CIRIT doctoral scholarships FI-PG/96-8.490 and FI-DT/96-8.472 respectively.

References

1. VIM. European Comission TMR project VIM. http://www.maths.bath.ac.uk/-jap/VIM.
2. Tere Alsinet, R. Béjar, C. Ansótegui, C. Fernández, and F. Manyà. Jafdis, a java framework for dialogical institution specification. In *Proceedings of the Primer Congrès Català d'Intel.ligència Artificial*, pages 172–176, 1998.
3. Mihai Barbuceanu and Mark S. Fox. Cool: A language for describing coordination in multi-agent systems. In *Proceedings of the First International Conference in Multi-Agent Systems (ICMAS-95)*, pages 17–24. AAAI Press, June 1995.

4. Jacques Ferber and Olivier Gutknetch. A meta-model for the analysis of organizations in multi-agent systems. In *Proceedings of the Third International Conference on Multi-Agent Systems (ICMAS-98)*, pages 128–135, 1998.

5. Pere Garcia, Eduard Giménez, Lluís Godo, and Juan A. Rodríguez-Aguilar. Possibilistic-based design of bidding strategies in electronic auctions. In *The 13th biennial European Conference on Artificial Intelligence (ECAI-98)*, 1998.

6. B. A. Huberman and S. Clearwater. A multi-agent system for controlling builging environments. In *Proceedings of the First International Conference on Multi-Agent Systems (ICMAS-95)*, pages 171–176. AAAI Press, June 1995.

7. Francisco J. Martín, Enric Plaza, and Juan Antonio Rodríguez-Aguilar. An infrastructure for agent-based systems: An interagent approach. *International Journal of Intelligent Systems*, 1998.

8. Noyda Matos, Carles Sierra, and Nick R. Jennings. Determining successful negotiation strategies: An evolutionary approach. In *Proceedings of the Third International Conference on Multi-Agent Systems (ICMAS-98)*, 1998.

9. R. P. McAfee and J. McMillan. Auctions and bidding. *J. Ec Lit.*, XXV:699–738, jun 1987.

10. P. R. Milgrom and R. J. Webber. A theory of auctions and competitive bidding. *Econometrica*, 50(5):1089–1122, sep 1982.

11. Claudia Napoli, Maurizio Giordano, Mario Furnari, Carles Sierra, and Pablo Noriega. A pvm implementation of the fishmarket. In *IX International Symposioum on Artificial Intelligence, Cancun, Mexico*, 1996.

12. Pablo Noriega. *Agent-Mediated Auctions: The Fishmarket Metaphor*. PhD thesis, Universitat Autonoma de Barcelona, 1997. Also to appear in IIIA mongraphy series.

13. Pablo Noriega and Carles Sierra. Towards layered dialogical agents. In *Third International Workshop on Agent Theories, Architectures, and Languages, ATAL-96*, 1996.

14. D. North. *Institutions, Institutional Change and Economics Perfomance*. Cambridge U. P., 1990.

15. H. Van Dyke Parunak. Visualizing agent conversations: Using enhanced dooley graph for agent design and analysis. In *Proceedings of the Second International Conference on Multi-Agent Systems*, 1996.

16. Juan A. Rodríguez-Aguilar, Francisco J. Martín, Francisco J. Giménez, and David Gutiérrez. Fm0.9beta users guide. Technical report, Institut d'Investigació en Intel.ligència Artificial. Technical Report, IIIA-RR98-32, 1998.

17. Juan A. Rodríguez-Aguilar, Francisco J. Martín, Pablo Noriega, Pere Garcia, and Carles Sierra. Competitive scenarios for heterogeneous trading agents. In *Proceedings of the Second International Conference on Autonomous Agents (AGENTS'98)*, pages 293–300, 1998.

18. Juan A. Rodríguez-Aguilar, Francisco J. Martín, Pablo Noriega, Pere Garcia, and Carles Sierra. Towards a test-bed for trading agents in electronic auction markets. *AI Communications*, 11(1):5–19, 1998.

19. Juan A. Rodríguez-Aguilar, Pablo Noriega, Carles Sierra, and Julian Padget. Fm96.5 a java-based electronic auction house. In *Second International Conference on The Practical Application of Intelligent Agents and Multi-Agent Technology(PAAM'97)*, pages 207–224, 1997.

20. Carles Sierra, N. R. Jennings, Pablo Noriega, and Simon Parson. A framework for argumentation-based negotiation. In *Proceedings of the 4th International Workshop on Agent Theories, Architectures and Languages (ATAL-97)*, 1997.

21. Carles Sierra and Pablo Noriega. Institucions electròniques. In *Proceedings of the Primer Congrès Català d'Intel.ligència Artificial*, 1998.
22. Michael P. Wellman. A market-oriented programming environment and its application to distributed multicommodity flow problems. *Journal of Artificial Intelligence Research*, (1):1–23, 1993.
23. T. Winograd and F. Flores. *Understanding Computers and Cognition*. Addison Wesley, 1988.
24. Peter R. Wurman, , Michael P. Wellman, and William E. Walsh. The Michigan Internet AuctionBot: A Configurable Auction Server for Human and Software Agents. In *Second International Conference on Autonomous Agents (AGENTS'98)*, 1998.
25. Fredrik Ygge and Hans Akkermans. Power load management as a computational market. In *Proceedings of the Second International Conference on Multi-Agent Systems (ICMAS-96)*, 1996.
26. Fredrik Ygge and Hans Akkermans. Making a case for multi-agent systems. In Magnus Boman and Walter Van de Velde, editors, *Advances in Case-Based Reasoning*, number 1237 in Lecture Notes in Artificial Intelligence, pages 156–176. Springer-Verlag, 1997.
27. The FishMarket Project. http://www.iiia.csic.es/Projects/fishmarket.

Author Index

Lecture Notes in Artificial Intelligence (LNAI)

Vol. 1611: I. Imam, Y. Kodratoff, A. El-Dessouki, M. Ali (Eds.), Multiple Approaches to Intelligent Systems. Proceedings, 1999. XIX, 899 pages. 1999.

Vol. 1612: R. Bergmann, S. Breen, M. Göker, M. Manago, S. Wess, Developing Industrial Case-Based Reasoning Applications. XX, 188 pages. 1999.

Vol. 1617: N.V. Murray (Ed.), Automated Reasoning with Analytic Tableaux and Related Methods. Proceedings, 1999. X, 325 pages. 1999.

Vol. 1620: W. Horn, Y. Shahar, G. Lindberg, S. Andreassen, J. Wyatt (Eds.), Artificial Intelligence in Medicine. Proceedings, 1999. XIII, 454 pages. 1999.

Vol. 1621: D. Fensel, R. Studer (Eds.), Knowledge Acquisition Modeling and Management. Proceedings, 1999. XI, 404 pages. 1999.

Vol. 1623: T. Reinartz, Focusing Solutions for Data Mining. XV, 309 pages. 1999.

Vol. 1624: J. A. Padget (Ed.), Collaboration between Human and Artificial Societies. XIV, 301 pages. 1999.

Vol. 1630: M. M. Huntbach, G. A. Ringwood, Agent-Oriented Programming. XIV, 386 pages. 1999.

Vol. 1632: H. Ganzinger (Ed.), Automated Deduction – CADE-16. Proceedings, 1999. XIV, 429 pages. 1999.

Vol. 1634: S. Džeroski, P. Flach (Eds.), Inductive Logic Programming. Proceedings, 1999. VIII, 303 pages. 1999.

Vol. 1637: J.P. Walser, Integer Optimization by Local Search. XIX, 137 pages. 1999.

Vol. 1638: A. Hunter, S. Parsons (Eds.), Symbolic and Quantitative Approaches to Reasoning and Uncertainty. Proceedings, 1999. IX, 397 pages. 1999.

Vol. 1640: W. Tepfenhart, W. Cyre (Eds.), Conceptual Structures: Standards and Practices. Proceedings, 1999. XII, 515 pages. 1999.

Vol. 1647: F.J. Garijo, M. Boman (Eds.), Multi-Agent System Engineering. Proceedings, 1999. X, 233 pages. 1999.

Vol. 1650: K.-D. Althoff, R. Bergmann, L.K. Branting (Eds.), Case-Based Reasoning Research and Development. Proceedings, 1999. XII, 598 pages. 1999.

Vol. 1652: M. Klusch, O.M. Shehory, G. Weiss (Eds.), Cooperative Information Agents III. Proceedings, 1999. XI, 404 pages. 1999.

Vol. 1669: X.-S. Gao, D. Wang, L. Yang (Eds.), Automated Deduction in Geometry. Proceedings, 1998. VII, 287 pages. 1999.

Vol. 1674: D. Floreano, J.-D. Nicoud, F. Mondada (Eds.), Advances in Artificial Life. Proceedings, 1999. XVI, 737 pages. 1999.

Vol. 1688: P. Bouquet, L. Serafini, P. Brézillon, M. Benerecetti, F. Castellani (Eds.), Modeling and Using Context. Proceedings, 1999. XII, 528 pages. 1999.

Vol. 1692: V. Matoušek, P. Mautner, J. Ocelíková, P. Sojka (Eds.), Text, Speech, and Dialogue. Proceedings, 1999. XI, 396 pages. 1999.

Vol. 1695: P. Barahona, J.J. Alferes (Eds.), Progress in Artificial Intelligence. Proceedings, 1999. XI, 385 pages. 1999.

Vol. 1699: S. Albayrak (Ed.), Intelligent Agents for Telecommunication Applications. Proceedings, 1999. IX, 191 pages. 1999.

Vol. 1701: W. Burgard, T. Christaller, A.B. Cremers (Eds.), KI-99: Advances in Artificial Intelligence. Proceedings, 1999. XI, 311 pages. 1999.

Vol. 1704: Jan M. Żytkow, J. Rauch (Eds.), Principles of Data Mining and Knowledge Discovery. Proceedings, 1999. XIV, 593 pages. 1999.

Vol. 1705: H. Ganzinger, D. McAllester, A. Voronkov (Eds.), Logic for Programming and Automated Reasoning. Proceedings, 1999. XII, 397 pages. 1999.

Vol. 1711: N. Zhong, A. Skowron, S. Ohsuga (Eds.), New Directions in Rough Sets, Data Mining, and Granular-Soft Computing. Proceedings, 1999. XIV, 558 pages. 1999.

Vol. 1712: H. Boley, A Tight, Practical Integration of Relations and Functions. XI, 169 pages. 1999.

Vol. 1714: M.T. Pazienza (Eds.), Information Extraction. IX, 165 pages. 1999.

Vol. 1715: P. Perner, M. Petrou (Eds.), Machine Learning and Data Mining in Pattern Recognition. Proceedings, 1999. VIII, 217 pages. 1999.

Vol. 1720: O. Watanabe, T. Yokomori (Eds.), Algorithmic Learning Theory. Proceedings, 1999. XI, 365 pages. 1999.

Vol. 1721: S. Arikawa, K. Furukawa (Eds.), Discovery Science. Proceedings, 1999. XI, 374 pages. 1999.

Vol. 1730: M. Gelfond, N. Leone, G. Pfeifer (Eds.), Logic Programming and Nonmonotonic Reasoning. Proceedings, 1999. XI, 391 pages. 1999.

Vol. 1733: H. Nakashima, C. Zhang (Eds.), Approaches to Intelligent Agents. Proceedings, 1999. XII, 241 pages. 1999.

Vol. 1735: J.W. Amtrup, Incremental Speech Translation. XV, 200 pages. 1999.

Vol. 1747: N. Foo (Ed.), Adavanced Topics in Artificial Intelligence. Proceedings, 1999. XV, 500 pages. 1999.

Lecture Notes in Computer Science